HISTORY OF THE OLD TESTAMENT

V

VOL. V

HISTORY OF THE
CLAUS SCHEDL

OLD TESTAMENT
THE FULLNESS OF TIME

alba house
A DIVISION OF THE SOCIETY OF ST. PAUL
STATEN ISLAND, NEW YORK 10314

First published under the title: **Geschichte des Alten Testaments** by Tyrolia-Verlag, Innsbruck, Austria

Library of Congress Cataloging in Publication Data

Schedl, Claus.
    History of the Old Testament.

    Translation of Geschichte des Alten Testaments.
    Includes bibliographical references.
    CONTENTS: v. 1. The ancient Orient and ancient Biblical history.—
v. 2. God's people of the covenant.—v. 3. The golden age of David. [etc.]
    1. Bible.   O. T.—History of Biblical events.
I. Title.
BS1197.S3213   221.9   70-38990
ISBN 0-8189-0231-0 (set)
ISBN 0-8189-0230-2 (v. 5)

THE THEOLOGIAN AND
THE OLD TESTAMENT

BY theologian we understand not merely the professional theologian who studies the Bible in connection with his vocation in order to qualify himself for the exercise of his office, but every believer for whom the Bible is an interesting and venerable document of the history of the ancient Eastern mind and religion. The Bible is not the private literature of a specially elect band of devotees, but the life book of God's people. It is in this book that the Word of God, binding on all men, has become flesh.

Just as the person of Christ "who, though he was in the form of God, did not count equality with God a thing to be grasped, but emptied himself, taking the form of a servant, being born in the likeness of men" (*Phil.* 2, 6-7) is the key to all theology, it is also the only approach to the Bible. Just as the God-man Jesus spans a mighty dichotomy in his person, by uniting what appear to be strictly disparate elements in one divine-human unity, so the word of the Bible is filled with a dynamism which surpasses human measurement. Are we now about to do away with this involvement in the sphere of human affairs by advancing a theology of the word of the Bible that concentrates too heavily on the overpowering splendor of that Word which was in the beginning with God and which is incapable of being incorporated into "the shards of letters"? [1]

Not at all. Just as the man who repudiates Christ's bodily

---

1. Origen, *Commentary on St. John*, Migne, PG 13, 29B-32B.

existence and ascribes only a phantom human existence to the Incarnate Word is guilty of seriously misinterpreting Christ, so the man who refuses to recognize the fact of the Incarnation entirely misses the mystery of Scripture. Just as Christ was a true man of his times, speaking the Galilean dialect and wearing the dress of his century, so every word in the Bible is spoken in a concrete, unique, and historical setting. This very fact determined its fate. The dust of centuries has grown heavy upon it. The Word has made its way into history, as every other, earlier or later, profane document of history.

If we mean to approach this word, we must face the difficult task of entering into all the stipulations of historical development and not rest comfortably in our secure position by pointing to the fact of inspiration. Whoever wishes to approach the Bible in a scientific manner necessarily takes on the total load of a profane exegesis. The Old Testament is a written document of the Ancient Near East, and it has undergone a development over the course of more than a thousand years before reaching its present form. For the most part it is written in the Hebrew language. A scientific examination of the Old Testament, therefore, becomes impossible without the study and knowledge of this language. The man who bases his approach only on translations is always something of a stranger to the concrete call of the revealed word; for every translation is, in some respects, a betrayal. Only the original text is inspired, and not the translations, no matter how venerable they might be.

The Old Testament is also a literary document. Thus we are also obliged (and it would be a serious error to omit this task) to approach the text in terms of the principles of philology and literary criticism in order to critically test every passage. But a literary criticism always runs the danger of being too removed from life and reality, unless it constantly keeps in sight the *Sitz im Leben* — its position in actuality.

The written document thus appeals to the mute witnesses of ancient history, which are made articulate by archaeological excavation. Philology, literary criticism, archaeology, and the history of the Ancient Near East are the guideposts for this pro-

fane exegesis; without them we are irrevocably lost in the realm
of unreality, and we miss the full "incarnation of the Word."
The personal religious conviction of the investigator plays no
role in this. In fact, we might go so far as to claim that if there
were one ideal technique for carrying out this methodology of
examination, then the results of a study by an atheistic philologist
and a believing theologian would be completely in agreement.
And, in practice, to a large extent, this is exactly what happens.

But if we mean to rest content with this *profane exegesis,*
we fail to recognize the inexhaustible reality of the Bible word.
Profane exegesis must be enlarged upon, not only as a mere
supplement, but as an ultimate fulfillment, by "pneumatic" exegesis. The primary source of Scripture is at once both human
and divine. If one of the pillars is missing here, the whole construction collapses in ruin.

This is not the place to fully treat on the nature of inspiration,[2]
although the study of Scripture wanders about blindly without
a clear idea of it. Both Church and synagogue have always
attested to the fact that the Bible contains God's word. Disagree-
ments were only on questions concerning how the authorship of
Scripture was to be ascribed to God, and how it was possible
to speak of human authorship. The Patristic age [3] was fond of
parables: the Holy Spirit, it was claimed, used the human author
like a musical instrument (organ, flute, lyre, etc.). Though it is
an attractive metaphor, it runs the risk of considering human
cooperation too exclusively in terms of a dead "instrument,"
without any proper activity of its own. When God overshadows
a human author, he does not extinguish human existence; he
elevates it into greater light, into a freedom untrammeled by sin.
Inspiration is the elevation of the human faculties. If God calls
upon man to compose a book, he directs this call to a concrete,
historically qualified man, who, under the divine impulse, takes up
the historical source material available and forms it into a unity
that has been revealed to him. In this process, it is only too easy

---

2. A. Merk, *De Inspiratione S. Scripturae,* Biblical Institute, Rome 1951.
3. Cf. J. Schildenberger, *Vom Geheimnis des Gotteswortes,* 1950, p. 17.

to recognize the awkward hand of the human author, who was obviously not always an accomplished literary artist. But it is from this very defect that God's power sounds its clearest note. Thus the word formed by man becomes the true "bounty of the divine Word." [4] We can then speak of personal literary style, power of poetic expression, artistic or faulty composition without thereby calling into question the divine reality of inspiration.

Once the divine origin of Scripture is properly grasped, there are some ponderable conclusions. The basic concept of this book is divine and grandiose. It lays bare the deepest abysses of sin and judgment; but it also discloses the glories of forgiveness and grace. There is nothing superficial or monotonous about this book. It sounds depths of such great dimensions that they shine like lightning "from the beginning to the end of days." This book was not composed without a plan; it storms along towards its goal. The "shards of the individual words" announce the irresistible and passionate arrival of the Eternal Word. The words are all oriented towards *the* Word. The Old Testament is the "educator towards Christ." Thus, if you tell how you look at Christ, I will tell you how you read the Old Testament. The ultimate understanding of Scripture comes only from faith and Spirit. Once a man has tasted the "sweetness of the word" (*Ps.* 34, 8), he is awake to the "passion of the divine." Since the Spirit who has inspired this book is passion and love, the man who has once experienced this "divine taste" can never again turn away. Even the mighty waters of boredom, which every study necessarily involves, will not be able to destroy this love. The final object of theological instruction does not consist in the imparting of knowledge, but in the development of the "theological eros." If this succeeds, the small spark becomes a conflagration which can inflame the entire world.

Thus we raise our voice in a complaint which is perhaps also an accusation: Why is there so much weakness and fragility in Christianity? Obviously, because the word has been dulled. We are taken up with New Testament exegesis and frequently

---

4. Origen, *Commentary on Jeremiah*, Migne, PG 13, 544C.

lose ourselves in spiritualistic conclusions. The bread of the Old Testament is not broken enough. And still the Catholic Church is, much more than we dare to realize, *the* Church of the Bible. The liturgical missal is almost exclusively Old Testament in its sung texts. If we would remove the Old Testament from our liturgy the Church would be without song. Take away the powerful readings from Law and Prophets from the liturgical year, and Christianity is made incomplete. The Old Testament is neither old nor ancient; it is a living reality in our midst. But how many of us recognize the power coming from this book? Today, more than ever, we must call upon the tidings of the Old Testament, in order to recognize the hand of Yahweh in a world on the verge of collapse. Yahweh is a God of history, and he directs the chaos of human history towards a goal and purpose he has set.

The concluding words of this introduction are taken from Origen, one of the greatest Scripture scholars and interpreters of the Greek Church, and for that matter, the whole Church: "If we have once admitted that these writings owe their origin to the creator of the world, we must be convinced that whatever is encountered by those who examine into the fundamental meaning of the world will also be met with in the study of Scripture. The further we progress in reading, the higher the mountain of mysteries towers above us. And just as a man who sets out upon the sea in a tiny ship is unafraid so long as he is close to the land but, when he gradually approaches the high seas and the waves begin to swell and he begins to be lifted high upon their crests or, when they gape open and he begins to be swarmed under into the abyss, it is then that his spirit is seized by a monstrous fear and anxiety for having entrusted such a tiny ship to such monstrous floods — this is the experience we seem to have when, from the smallness of our merit and the narrowness of our spirit we dare to approach so wide a sea of mysteries." [5]

---

5. Origen, *Homily on Genesis.*

CONTENTS

SECTION THREE
THE JEWISH RELIGION IN THE PERSIAN DIASPORA

SECTION FOUR
PROPHETS AND REFORMERS IN JERUSALEM

SECTION FIVE
THE HELLENISTIC ERA

ABBREVIATIONS

AASOR	Annual of the American School of Oriental Research
ABEL	F. M. Abel, *Géographie de la Palestine* (Études Bibliques), Paris, vol. I, 1933, vol. II, 1938
AfO	E. Weidner, *Archiv für Orientforschung*, Graz
AJA	American Journal of Archaeology
ANEP	J. P. Pritchard, *The Ancient Near East in Pictures relating to the Old Testament*, Princeton Univ. Press, 1954
ANET	J. P. Pritchard, *Ancient Near Eastern Texts relating to the Old Testament*, Princeton Univ. Press, 1955
AnglTR	Anglican Theological Review
Ann. PEF	Annual of the Palestine Exploration Fund, London
AnOr	Anacleta Orientalia, Rome
Ant.	Flavius Josephus, *Antiquitates Judaicae, Jüdische Altertümer*
AO	Alter Orient
AOB	H. Gressmann, *Altorientalische Bilder zum Alten Testament*, Berlin/Leipzig, 1927
AOT	H. Gressmann, *Altorientalische Texte zum Alten Testament*, 1926
APAW	Abhandlungen der Preussischen Akademie der Wissenschaften, Berlin
ARM	Archives Royales de Mari, Paris
Arch	Archaeology
ArOr	Archiv Orientální
AT	Altes Testament
ATD	Hentrich and Weiser, *Das Alte Testament Deutsch*, Göttingen
BA	The Biblical Archaeologist
BASOR	Bulletin of the American Schools of Oriental Research

BB	Bonner Bibelkommentar
Bibl	Biblica
BiblArch	The Biblical Archaeologist
BibLex	H. Haag, *Bibellexicon*
BibLit	Bibel und Liturgie
BHK	R. Kittel, *Biblica Hebraica*, adapted by Stuttgart, 1954
BJRL	K. Galling, The Bulletin of the John Rylands Library
BK	M. Noth, *Biblischer Kommentar, Altes Testament,* Neukirchen
BRL	Biblisches Reallexicon
BZ	Biblische Zeitschrift, Neue Folge, Paderborn
BZAW	Beihefte zur ZAW
CalwK	Calwer Kommentar: Die Botschaft des Alten Testaments, Stuttgart
CBQ	The Catholic Biblical Quarterly
ClamB	Pirot-Clamer, *La Sainte Bible*, Latin and French text with both exegetical and theological comment, Paris
DB	Vigouroux, *Dictionaire de la Bible*, Paris, 1861-1912
DBS	Supplément au Dictionaire de la Bible, Paris, 1926
DOT	Winton-Thomas, *Documents to the Old Testament*
EB	Echter Bibel, Würzburg
EinlAT	O. Eissfeldt, Einleitung in das Alte Testament unter Einschluss der Apokryphen und pseudepigraphen sowie der apokryphen und pseudepigraphenartigen Qumrān-Schriften. Entstehungsgeschichte des Alten Testaments, Tubingen, 1956
EnchBibl	Enchiridion Biblicum. Documenta ecclesiastica Sacram Scripturam spectantia, Rome, 1956
EncMikr	Encyklopaedia Mikra'it. Encyclopaedia Biblica. Thesaurus rerum biblicarum, Hebrew University, Jerusalem, 1950
EphThLov (ETL)	Ephemerides Theologicae Lovanienses
ET	The Expository Times
EvT	Evangelische Theologie
FF	Forschungen und Fortschritte, Berlin
Fs	Festschrift
GAV	H. Schmökel, *Geschichte des Alten Vorderasien*, Leiden, 1957

GTT	J. Simons, *The Geographical and Topographical Texts of the Old Testament*, Leiden, 1959
GVA	A. Moortgat, *Geschichte Vorderasien bis zum Hellenismus*, Munchen, 1950
HAT	Handbuch zum Alten Testament
HistM (HM)	Fritz Kern, *Historia Mundi*, 1952
HUCA	Hebrew Union College Annual, Cincinnati
IEJ	Israel Exploration Journal, Jerusalem
IntBib	The Interpreters Bible. A Commentary in twelve volumes, New York
JAOS	The Journal of the American Oriental Society
JBL	The Journal of Biblical Literature
JEArch	Journal of Egyptian Archaeology
JerB	Jerusalem Bible
JNES	The Journal of Near Eastern Studies
JSS	The Journal of Semitic Studies
KAT	E. Sellin, *Kommentar zum Alten Testament*, Leipzig
KB	Keilschriftliche Bibliothek
LexVT	L. Koehler — W. Baumgartner, *Lexicon in Veteris Testamenti Libros*, Leiden, 1953
LXX	Septuaginta
Migne, PG	Migne, *Patres Greci*
Migne, PL	Migne, *Patres Latini*
MiscBibl	Mischellania Biblica
MT	R. Kittel, *Masoretischer Text nach der Biblica Hebraica*, 1954
NouvRevThéol	Nouvelle Revue Théologique
OLZ	Orientalische Literaturzeitung, Leipzig
Or	Orientalia, Rome
PEQ	Palestine Exploration Quarterly, London
PG	Migne, *Patres Greci*
PL	Migne, *Patres Latini*
RA	E. Eberling and Br. Meisnner, *Reallexicon der Assyriologie*
RB	Revue Biblique, École Biblique, Jerusalem
RCB	Rivista di Cultura Biblica
REHM	Die Bücher der Könige, Echter Bibel, Würzburg, 1949
RSR	Recherches de Science Religieuse

Rev HistRel	Revue de l'Histoire des Religions, Paris
SAT	Gunkel — Gressmann, *Die Schriften des Alten Testaments,* Göttingen
ST	Studia Theologica
TGI	K. Galling, *Textbuch zur Geschichte Israels,* Tubingen, 1950
ThLZ	Theologische Literaturzeitung, Leipzig
ThZ	Theologische Zeitschrift, Basel
TTZ	Trierer Theologische Zeitschrift
UM	C. H. Gordon, *Ugaritic Manual,* Rome, 1955
VD	Verbum Domini
VT	Vetus Testamentum
WTJ	Westminster Theological Journal
ZAW	Zeitschrift für Alttestamentliche Wissenschaft
ZDMG	Zeitschrift der Deutschen Morgenländischen Gesellschaft
ZDPV	Zeitschrift des Deutschen Palästinavereines
ZKT	Zeitschrift für Katholische Theologie, Innsbruck
ZTK	Zeitschrift für Theologie und Kirche

CYRUS, SHEPHERD OF YAHWEH AND THE LIBERATION OF ISRAEL

Thus says the Lord to his anointed, to Cyrus: "He is my shepherd, and he shall fulfill all my purpose"; saying of Jerusalem, "She shall be built," and of the temple, "Your foundation shall be laid" (Is 45, 1; 44, 28).

THE last public statement by the prophet Ezekiel dates from the 27th year of Exile (570/69). The new Jerusalem which he proclaimed existed only in the world of faith. The daily life of the people was harsh and bitter. Nothing seemed to point to the realization of the gospel of redemption. Only a sorry remnant of the ancient glory had survived.

Nebuchadnezzar's soldiers had done a thorough job. Not only had Jerusalem fallen into ruins, according to the testimony of modern excavation,[1] but at the same time all the Judaean fortresses in the low country (*šephelah*) and in the mountains. Only in the southern territory of the Negeb, which was probably already independent of Judah during Nebuchadnezzar's first campaign (597), and in the territory north of Jerusalem which probably already belonged to the Assyrian province of Samaria, did a few individual

---

1. G. E. Wright, *Biblical Archaeology*, (1958), 199.

fortresses remain. The population of Judah in the eighth century is set at 250,000 inhabitants, and after the first return from Exile, the number is only 20,000; in the interval there must have been a considerable drop in population.[2] The Assyrians had repopulated the Northern Kingdom with new settlers from the east; the Babylonians did not do the same in Judah. In the years after the destruction of Jerusalem Judah must have presented a dismal and solitary picture, without a single dweller. After the murder of Gedaliah Judah simply ceased to function as a political concept. The territory north of Beth-sur (near Hebron) was annexed to the province of Syria, while the Edomites made their way into the southern territories under pressure from the Arabs who drove them from their hereditary tribal seats. All that survived was the impoverished population of the countryside, who eked a harsh and scanty existence from the land. Judah itself gave no promise of the restoration of the chosen people. The nation's strength was broken.

The number of the expatriates deported to Babylon is not a fantastically high figure. Jeremiah 52, 28-30 records the number 4600 as the total for the three deportations (597, 586, 581). This number probably refers only to adult males. The full number of expatriates, including women and children, would be three or four times as high, and this is certainly a credible figure.[3] If Nebuchadnezzar had scattered the Judaeans to the four corners of the earth, as the Assyrians treated the tribes of the Northern Kingdom, the expatriate Judaeans would certainly have perished as a nation and as a religion. As it was, however, they were able to live in closed settlements in Babylonia, and the practical order of daily life was soon established. It was here that the intellectual and political leaders of the people were interned. This tiny community, however, was but a fraction of the great Babylonian world empire (Is 40, 15).

The people dispersed into Egypt could no longer be relied

2. Bright, HistIsr 324.
3. Kittel, GVI III, 60-62, reaches somewhat higher numbers, between 50,000 and 70,000.

upon for any help. The group that Jeremiah had brought with him settled along the Egyptian frontier in Taphanhes (Daphne) (Jer 43, 7); a second group sought refuge in the cities of the Delta, where they apparently lived in closed quarters and thus laid the groundwork for the Jewish colonies which later flourished throughout Egypt. A third group made their way as far as the southern frontier of Egypt, where they were installed on an island in the Nile River, Elephantine (Jeb),[4] as a military border guard. Since their documents refer to them expressly as Judaeans, they could hardly have come from the territory of the former Northern Kingdom of Israel; they must actually have come from Judah. It is not clear precisely when they hired themselves out as mercenaries; but probably it was in the last years before the destruction of Jerusalem, since this era witnessed a cordial and friendly relationship between Judah and Egypt. In Elephantine they even managed to erect a temple to Yahweh and develop a syncretistic cult. For the history of salvation, the Jewish religion in Egypt takes on significance only in the Hellenistic Era, since it was in Egypt that the Scriptures were first translated into Greek, thereby making them available to the world at large. During the time of exile, the Judaeans in Egypt form only a tiny remnant of their people; they remained without effect upon the nation as a whole. Equally unimportant for the history of salvation are the Jewish settlements in Arabia, which might well date back to the time of the ten-years' residence of Nabonidus in the oasis of Thema. Nabonidus got his mercenaries from the "land of Hatti and Akkad." Since Palestine belonged to Hatti, there is some grounds for assuming that Jewish mercenaries served in Nabonidus' army, and later settled in Arabian cities.[5]

At all events, Nebuchadnezzar had a firm hold upon the

---

4. EncMikr III, 425-444; E. G. Kraeling, *New Light on the Elephantine Colony*, BA 15 (1952), 50-67. Describes the precise location of the Nile island, its significance for Egyptian history, the schismatic temple and its cult, the discovery of the papyri. He assigns the founding of the military colony to 588-570 B.C.

5. E. Vogt, Bibl 40 (1959), 101: *Coloni judaici Nabonidi.*

reins of world empire. In the year 568 he undertook a campaign against Egypt, the results of which remain a mystery.[6] The campaign could not have been aimed at conquest, but only a demonstration of power, an attempt to exclude further Egyptian intrigues in foreign policies. Thus the world lay quietly at mighty Nebuchadnezzar's feet, and Israel was at rest in the grave of the nations. Was this quiet destined to result in death or resurrection? In this pivotal moment of history, when all hope seemed to be abandoned, the spirit of the great prophet Isaiah, whose lifetime had witnessed a similar threat to the existence of the chosen people, awakened to new power. An unnamed prophet raised his voice as a herald in the wilderness, pointing the way from the contemporary crisis of the national faith to the great future of promised salvation. Soon the Babylonian world empire fell apart at the seams, and the hour of return from exile was about to dawn.

---

6. L. Delaporte, *Les Peuples de l'Orient Méditerranéen*, I. *Le Proche-Orient Asiatique*, (1948), 283.

CHAPTER I

THE FALL OF THE BABYLONIAN KINGDOM AND THE RISE OF PERSIA

AFTER the destruction of Nineveh, Asia Minor was divided by the victors into two spheres of influence, to maintain a balance of power. In the north the Iranian kingdom of the Medes was gathering strength; in Mesopotamia and in the western countries, the Neo-Babylonians claimed the heritage of the Assyrians. The future, however, belonged to the stronger Iranian stock.

1) NABONIDUS' POLITICAL AND RELIGIOUS ADVENTURES (556-539)

In early October of the year 562 Nebuchadnezzar died. He was followed by Awil-Marduk (Evil Merodak), who hardly had an opportunity to initiate his rule over the country before he was murdered between August 7 and 13 of the year 560. For the expatriate Jews this short reign involved considerable changes. For "the year of his kingship,[1] the 37th year of the

---

1. Chronology: On the basis of the chronology established in Volume IV, the year 37 of the captivity is equivalent to the second year of King Amel Marduk. According to the Babylonian calendar usage, the second year bore the name of the new king (Limu tables) and was regarded

captivity," that is, early in 560, he pardoned the captive king Jehoiachin. He released him from custody and maintained friendly relations with him. Such an event must have considerably alleviated the condition of the expatriate population.

Under Nergal-shar-usur (Nergal-šar-ussur 560-556) there was already some indication that the balance of power among the world rulers was facing a severe threat. In northern Asia Minor the Medes had made their way as far as the Halys River. For the year 557/56 the Babylonian chronicle [2] speaks of a campaign in Cilicia which was calculated primarily to secure Babylonian interests in Asia Minor. Nergal-shar-usur left behind him his minor son, Labashi-Marduk, who was no sooner raised to the throne than he was put aside by Nabonidus between May 3 and 22 of the year 556.

"The riddles surrounding this last Babylonian king Nabonidus (Nabuna'id) are not completely solved; recent investigation, however, puts us in a position to correct the traditional picture in some essential points. Thus, Nabonidus, when he acceded to the throne, was well advanced in years, but he was certainly not a recluse, or an archaeologically oriented dreamer full of strange and impossible fancies. He was a sober politician who made every effort to control the confusion of the day by vigorous and energetic activity. The crises which he opposed and to which he was finally forced to yield would have been a match for much

---

simply as the "king's year." Awil Marduk's "king's year" began with the New Year festival on 1 Nisan, March 26, 560. Three days earlier, on the 27th day of the 12th month, March 23, 560, he released the Judaean King Jehoiachin from prison (2 K 25, 27; according to Jer 52, 31, this occurred already on the 25th day of the 12th month). What was involved here was a general amnesty on the occasion of the beginning of the "king's year" of Awil Marduk, which is the second year of his reign, the 37th year of the captivity. Cf. also my article: "Nochmals das Datum der Zerstorung Jerusalems," ZAW 74 (1962), 209-213, which requires some amplification, since I was not then aware of the true character of the new year's amnesty.

2. Wiseman, Chronicle, 37-42, 75-77.

stronger and more able men." [3] His mother was a priestess of the moon god in Harran, as we learn from recently discovered inscriptions.[4] It was in Harran, in the year 610, that the last remnants of the Assyrian resistance had entrenched themselves; there is, accordingly, some possibility that Nabonidus was somehow descended from Assurbanipal. This would certainly explain much of his religious and political undertakings. As a worshiper of the moon god Sin, he was little interested in the Marduk cult in Babel, a form of worship which he neglected in the most provocative manner. For the cult drama on the occasion of the new year festival the presence of the king was absolutely mandatory. But the chronicle of Nabonidus makes this lament:[5] "Seventh year: the King did not come to Babel; the god Nabu did not come to Babel; the god Bel did not make his way from Babel; the new year festival was not observed." It is understandable that the resistance of the priests of Marduk in Babel grew in strength. In one defamatory poem,[6] Nabonidus is mocked as a godless person. Nabonidus was a very pious king in his own light, rebuilding destroyed temples and beautifying ancient houses of worship. In a dream vision [7] he received a mandate to rebuild the "house

---

3. Schmoekel, GAV 317.
4. On an excavation in 1956 S. D. Rice found, in the ruins of ancient Moshee in Harran, three large stone inscriptions, which had been placed, with the writing facing down, as foundation stones at the gates of Moshee. At the Eastern and Western gate there were two inscriptions of Nabonidus, while at the Northern gate there was an inscription of his mother Adad-guppi. Nabonidus' mother was 104 years old when she died. Her account embraces the time from Assurbanipal to Nabonidus, and thus forms one of the most important sources for the history of this shadowy era. Published in Bibl 49 (1959), 89-106.
5. W. Thomas, DOT 90.
6. ANET 317.
7. "I am Nabonidus .... I was just a nobody who did not enjoy kingly power; but the gods and goddesses intervened in my behalf; the god Sin called me to royal dignity. During the hours of the night he showed me a dream and said to me: 'Ehulhul, the temple of the god Sin, build it up quickly; for all countries shall in truth be given over to your hand." Bibl 40 (1959), 53.

of joy" (E-hulhul) of the moon god in Harran and not to let
this work be interrupted by the threat of danger from the Medes.
He built the temples in Sippar and Larsa. He invested his own
daughter as "bride of god" in the temple of the moon at Ur. In
his own way, Nabonidus was a religious man, but not in the tradition of the priests of Marduk in Babel. This circumstance
contributed to his demise.

In the political sphere Nabonidus was far from inactive, although his undertakings appear most questionable in the judgment of history. During his rule, new revolutions were in the
making throughout the territory of Iran. As a counter-balance
to the beginnings of the Persian world empire in the north he
attempted to hew a wilderness empire for himself based on
the oasis of Tema [8] where he spent a ten year's residence.[9] Tema
lies along the crossroads of the caravan routes between Damascus
and Mecca on the one hand and the Persian Gulf and Egypt on
the other hand. Nabonidus seized this vital communications point,
killed the city's prince, and made Tema his base of operations
for the further campaign. Even Jatrib, modern Mecca, belonged
to his wilderness empire. The control of the home government
had been handed over to his son, the crown prince Bel-šar-ussur
(Belsazar). It was, all in all, an ingenious distribution of power
between an aging father and his certainly mature son. Belsazar
held a position of power in Babylonia, while his father, by laying
the foundation of a mighty caravan empire, increased his kingdom.
His policies brought the entire trade of the Orient under his
power. Ingenious as the plan appears in its inception, in the
years that followed it proved to be an unworkable political ad-
venture. The three columns upon which Nabonidus supported
his power, Babel, Harran and Tema, lay too far apart from
each other: the first serious shock was destined to collapse them.

---

8. B. Segall, *The Arts and King Nabonidus*, AJA 60 (1956), 165-170.
   Strategically important position of the oasis of Tema, Nabonidus' building activity there, investigation of the contemporary art, especially
   the theme of the fighting of lions.
9. "The God Sin had me withdraw from my city Babel; on an expedition
   I made my way through the cities of Tema, Dedana, etc., for ten
   years." Bibl 40 (1959), 93, 100.

2) CYRUS II, FOUNDER OF THE PERSIAN EMPIRE ([559] 550-530)

In the course of the great Iranian migrations, the Persians under the rule of Cyrus I (640-600) had emigrated from western Iran into southern Iran. They settled in the territory of ancient Elam, which had been wrested away from Assyria in 640. This contact with the Ancient Near Eastern heritage of Elam assured the Persian tribes of a powerful advantage in the years that followed, superior even to the position of the Medes. To the west, Elam borders on the territory of Babylonia, whose control was the basis of every workable and lasting attempt at empire in western Asia.[10] The kingdom of the Medes was a loosely federated feudal state which flourished only as long as a powerful ruling personality, such as Cyaxares (*huwahšatara*), stood at its head. His successor Astyages (*Ištuwegu*, 585-550) was not made of the same stuff. The dissatisfaction he provoked among the Median nobility created a splendid opportunity for Cyrus (*Kuraš*). His first move was to shake off the Median sovereignty in his own tribal territory of Anshan (559). In the year 550 the time was ripe for Cyrus. He marched against the Median capital of Ecbatana. The army dispatched to meet him, under Harpagos, defected to his side. Thus was the fate of the great king decided. With the full backing of the Median and Persian nobility, Cyrus declared himself king of Media and Persia.

The other powers, threatened by Cyrus' rise to power, were forced to reevaluate the situation. Nabonidus of Babylonia, Amasis of Egypt (569-525), and Croesus of Lydia (560-546) joined forces in a triple alliance. Opposed to them, Cyrus enjoyed one clear advantage. Since the allies were so widely scattered, he was able to fight them one after the other. His first attack was aimed at the weakest opponent, Lydia. Confident of Babylonian support in his rear, Croesus advanced beyond the Halys (547), the traditional boundary of the Median kingdom, and invaded Cappadocia. The Persian counter-offensive forced the Lydians to quickly abandon their newly acquired territory and withdraw westward across the Halys. It was winter, and no one counted

---

10. E. Kornemann, *Weltgeschichte des Mittelmeerraumes*, I (1948), 18.

on a further Persian offensive. But with his youthful daring Cyrus pushed on to the Lydian capital of Sardes where he won a decisive victory. It is reported that the battle's turning point was the confusion that his camel troops created among the hostile ranks. Croesus became Cyrus' prisoner; he was treated with mercy and given a city in Media. The whole eastern Mediterranean, and especially the Greeks, were powerfully impressed by the Persian victory.[11] A new era of history was unfolding in this part of the world.

Babylonia, the second member of the anti-Persian triple alliance, was granted a momentary reprieve before the final onslaught. Turning from the extreme west, Cyrus threw his military strength against the distant east. The gateway to the steppes of inner Asia, from which a steady succession of mounted invaders had always issued, must be closed and sealed. The territories of Bactria as far as the Jaxartes, Magdiana and Sogdiana were all incorporated into the empire. The territory that lay beyond, the kingdom of Saka in the east, was at least neutralized by diplomacy, in a treaty that involved the obligation to send auxiliaries in the event of war. The treaty was secured by the erection of the powerful frontier fortress of Kyrešata on the Jaxartes.[12]

Cyrus was now free to take up the battle against Babylon. Under the pressure of imminent war, Nabonidus himself had withdrawn into Babel, for the decisive confrontation. In this crisis he turned to the gods for help. He finally celebrated the long neglected new year festival in Babylon (April, 539). What is more, he had the statues of the gods transferred from the provincial cities into the capital. But the eventual collapse could no longer be put off. For years the priests of Marduk had been

---

11. H. Bengtson, *Griechische Geschichte. Handbuch der Altertumswissenschaften*, 3, 4 (1950), 118ff.

12. Kornemann, *loc. cit.*, 19 — The border against the Steppe of Turkestan was protected by a series of fortified camps, some of which have been rediscovered and investigated once again in recent years. The interior of these walled camps contained smaller buildings; there was a rather large parade grounds. The soldiers were quartered in barracks which had been built into the larger wall. H. H. v. d. Osten, *Die Welt der Perser, Grosse Kulturen der Fruhzeit*, (1956), 64.

his enemies. And now Gobryas (*Gubaru*) Nabonidus' administrator in the territory east of the Tigris, along the ancient buffer province of Gutium, defected to Cyrus. In summer of 539 the Persian troops stood before the Babylonian frontier. The decisive battle occurred at Opis on the Tigris. The fate of the Babylonian empire was sealed. On October 12, 539, Gobryas marched into Babylon without resistance. On October 29 Cyrus followed his general and was jubilantly greeted as liberator. The transfer of power was accomplished in perfect order and tranquillity. Plundering was forbidden. Nabonidus managed to escape but was later taken prisoner. How he met his end is unknown.

The breath-taking sequence of events is fully recorded in the Cyrus-cylinder.[13] Cyrus came as liberator. The gods which had been brought into the capital were sent back to their home cities. The Marduk cult was once again celebrated in all its glory. It is only one small episode in this great drama of world history that the expatriate Judaeans were also granted freedom to return to their native land and rebuild the ruined temple of the god of heaven.

The world empire which Cyrus had thus founded had four capitals: three of them lay within Persia: Ecbatana, Susa, and Paragada, and the fourth was Babylon. Cyrus accordingly assumed the title "king of Babylon, king of the lands." Here in Babylon he received homage and tribute from governors and kings of every land that had previously been subjected to the yoke of Babel, including the tribes of the wilderness. Whether the western countries were subject to his rule before the fall of Babylon or only after its collapse is unknown. At all events, they were not long without a master.

During this unsettled era, where kingdoms were collapsing and new powers rising, where unheard of horizons opened to the future, there arose among the expatriates a prophet, strong in the spirit like a second Isaiah, to show his uprooted people the way into their new home. But before we examine the career of Deutero-Isaiah, we must briefly outline the religious world

---

13. Galling, TGI 70-72; W. Thomas, DOT 92-94 with illustrations of the cylinder.

of the Persians which now furnishes the background and foil for the religion of the Old Testament.

3) AHURA-MAZDA AND ZARATHUSTRA

The rise of Persia brought her religion into intimate contact with the faith of the Old Testament. Assyrian and Babylonian influences, which had frequently occasioned a crisis in Israel's allegiance to Yahweh, will serve as constant points of reference. The profound change in world politics makes it only logical that the influence of the Iranian religion should be felt upon the Bible. Thus, if similarities can be pointed up between Iran and the Bible, this is not surprising. It would only cast more light upon the way in which the biblical thinkers react to this new confrontation. What is decisive in the study of biblical theology is not so much the similarities as rather the dissimilarities with the religions of the world around Judah. It is what is distinct and different that represents her abiding contribution.

It is customary to distinguish three forms of religion in the Persian empire:[14] the religion of the royal family, that of the magi, and that of the common people. Herodotus [15] has this to say about the popular religion: "The Persians are not accustomed to raise statues, temples, or altars; in fact those who want to do so are considered foolish . . . . Originally they sacrificed to the sky-god Zeus on high mountains, to the sun, the moon, fire, water, and the winds; from the Egyptians (i.e., the Babylonians) and the Arabs they have learned to sacrifice also to Aphrodite, daughter of Uranus . . . . For their sacrifices they erect no altars, and they kindle no fires; they have no food or drink sacrifices, and

---

14. H. H. von der Osten, *Die Welt der Perser*, 82-83. — H. Lommel, *Die Religion Zarathuštras nach dem Awesta dargestellt*, (Tubingen 1930). — H. S. Nyberg, *Die Religionen des alten Iran*, (Leipzig 1938).

15. For a critique of the Greek and Latin authors who have written on the subject of the Persian religion, cf. G. Messina, *Der Ursprung der Magier und die zarathustrische Religion*, (Rome 1930), 13-48. It is clear that Herodotus is describing only the religion of the people; he had no real acquaintance with the mysteries of the Magi.

no cakes or music . . . ." [16] It is clear that the Persian people worshiped divine beings who had no image, the elementary divinities of nature, and that the cult took place in the open air. In addition to this cult there are two divinities which enjoyed the greatest popularity and devotion, the god of light and preserver of justice, Mithra, and the equally ancient Aryan mother divinity Anahita, a figure which gradually came to be identified with the goddess of war, fertility, and love, Ištar. Witness the numerous small terra cotta and alabaster figurines which represent Anahita in the same manner as the ashera, generally unclad and holding her breasts.[17]

The Achaemenid princes revered Ahura-mazda as the supreme god. He is the luminous god of the sky who watches over truth and honesty. It is his favor that grants power and dominion to the Persian kings. Thus, for example, Darius begins his funerary inscription: "When Ahura-mazda saw that the earth was in the throes of battle, he gave the earth to me, making me king . . . . Everything that has been done I have done according to the will of Ahura-mazda. Ahura-mazda gave me his aid until my work was accomplished." [18] From the testimony of inscriptions we actually get the impression that Ahura-mazda was the god of the royal house, just as the Assyrian rulers boasted the personal protection of the god Assur and the Babylonian kings claimed to be chosen by Marduk. Ahura-mazda, however, is not the only god to whom the Persian rulers paid worship; the royal inscriptions also refer to many other gods, some of them of ancient Aryan origin, others taken over from the subjected peoples. Darius, upon his triumphal entry into Babel, took the hand of the god Bel and gave homage to Marduk. In individual detail, the position of the various Persian rulers might have been a matter of some variance; Xerxes was intolerant; he condemned the cult of the non-Indo-Aryan gods and had the statues of Marduk in Babylon melted down. Artaxerxes, on the other hand, paid particular homage to Mithra and Anahita. The only obvious conclusion is

16. Osten, l. c. 82.
17. *Ibid.*, 13, 83, 87.
18. *Ibid.*, 80.

that the Persian kings were certainly not exclusive worshipers of Ahura-mazda. They sacrificed to Ahura-mazda before an altar with a burning flame; there were also sacrifices of animals, and perhaps even human sacrifice.

The so-called third religion, that of the magi, cannot be precisely described, simply because the personality of the great Iranian "prophet" Zarathustra, as well as the date of his appearance and the content of his message, are all contested. Nietzsche's work has nothing in common with the Iranian Zarathustra excepting for the name. When did he live? The Greek author Xanthos [19] suggests a date 6000 years before the campaigns of Xerxes, but this is an impossible conjecture. Messina [20] reduces the number to 600 years, and thus Zarathustra would have made his first appearance in eastern Iran sometime around the beginning of the first millennium before Christ. The frequent migrations of the nomad tribes would have carried his religious ideas far and wide from their original circle of disciples. The prophet's name is most easily interpreted as belonging to an era of transition from nomadic to settled existence. *Zarat-uštra* means "the lean camel" or "the old camel," a title which is not meant to be derogatory. At the head of the caravan it was customary to place not a young and inexperienced beast, but an old and wise camel who was familiar with the trails and thus in a position to lead. There is only a slight extension of meaning when the name Zarathustra is applied to the religious leader.[21] This early dating puts the Iranian prophet on a contemporary basis with Moses. Other scholars, however, following the lead of Plutarch, date Zarathustra's career between the years 570 and 500, when the kingdom was being founded.[22] If the problem can be solved at all it can only be solved on the basis of the writings left by Zarathustra himself. Scholarship is unanimous in attributing the 17 Gathas, or "songs," to his pen;

---

19. Xanthos quoted in Diogenes Laertios, Prooemion 2.
20. G. Messina, *Der Ursprung der Magier und die zarathustrische Religion*, (Rome 1930), 102.
21. Oral statement by Prof. Brandenstein, University of Graz. The names of other animals were also common, e.g., those formed with the suffix -*aspa*, "horse."
22. Fr. König, *Christus und die Religionen der Erde*, II (1951), 620.

these form the most ancient part of the Avesta, the "Bible" of the Persians.[23]

On the basis of some very precise calculation, Hinz has suggested March 22, 630 B.C. as Zarathustra's date of birth. The prophet lived, he claims, for 77 years, and thus his career would extend from 630 to 550. "Thus the ancient Iranian prophet suddenly bursts from the cloud of historical uncertainty into the clear light of history even though — and this is to be expected — the reckoning of his career in terms of month and day is subject to some uncertainty. At all events we are no longer groping about in the uncertainty of 'a thousand years before Christ' — a long cherished hypothesis which has radically falsified our picture of Zarathustra since it transplants the prophet's career into a primeval and almost pre-historical situation.

"On the other hand, the sixth century B.C., the time in which Zarathustra's activity certainly falls, is an era relatively informed by history. It begins with the conquest of the Holy Land by the Babylonians. It reaches a climax in the collapse of the Median kingdom by Cyrus the Great, who allowed the Jews to return to Jerusalem from their Babylonian captivity. Its end is marked by the gigantic enterprise of Darius, the newly established world empire of the Persians. This sixth century is also the age of the Jewish prophets Jeremiah, Ezekiel, Daniel, and the second Isaiah; the Chinese sage Confucius and perhaps also Lao-tse; and the great Indian religious teacher Gautama Buddha. The teaching of the Iranian prophet is not simply a distant reflection in this prolific century." [24]

Zarathustra belongs among the extra-biblical prophets. Just like Mohammed, he begins his activity with a powerful experience of enlightenment and vocation. He became aware of the one god who is to be worshiped not by the sacrifice of animals but in

---

23. For a more detailed account, cf. H. Humbach, *Die Gathas Zarathustras*, vol. I: Einleitung Text, Paraphrase; vol. II: *Kommentar. Indogermanische Bibliothek, Erste reihe, Lehrund Handbücher*, (Heidelberg 1959). (skeptical on the history.) — Ferner W. Hinz, *Zarathustra*, (Stuttgart 1961). (optimistic on the history.)
24. Hinz, l. c. 25.

the symbol of fire. This insight involved a fierce battle with the Mithra cult and its bull sacrifice, a rite which was firmly established among the people. "It was with this very ancient god of the Iranians and Indians and with the entire circle of divinities surrounding the figure of Mithra that Zarathustra was forced to wage war from the time of his first call. His battle was aimed not only at dethroning the ancient Iranian pantheon, but also at putting a stop to the evils and injustice suffered by the shepherds and peasants of Bactria from the constant slaughter of their cattle, a practice which had admittedly grown beyond all bounds of reason." [25] Such a position was clearly not destined to find favor with those in power. The situation had reached such a point that the only solution lay in flight. Zarathustra left Bactria for Chorasmia, where King Vištaspa granted asylum to the exiled prophet. In the year 588 Vištaspa and his entire court went over to the new faith and there was no further obstacle to its spread. The more detailed history of its spread is still surrounded by shadow. But the fact remains that the Persian ruling house of the Achaemenids remain loyal to Ahura-mazda the god of Zarathustra.

Zarathustra called the creator of all things not "god" (*baga*), but simply "master" (*ahura*).[26] To make the name more precise he adds the epithet *mazda*, derived from *manas-dah*, "he who outlines thought"; generally translated as "wise." The content of the word is, however, much more dynamic. Ahura-mazda is the god who thinks, who, as such, brings the world into existence. The experience that not all men were willing to accept this new knowledge of the divinity forced Zarathustra to refine his concept of the principle of evil, so that actually the result of his theological speculation involves a sharp dualism between light and darkness, the good and evil principles. In Zarathustra's teaching, it is important to make a clear distinction between the religious side, which is more a philosophico-theological system of doctrine than a religion and was incapable of being generally understood by reason of its abstract formulation which was difficult to grasp — and its social side. The former

---

25. *Ibid.*, 75.
26. There seems to be a parallel in the development of the Canaanite religion. The earlier supreme god El gradually yields to the figure of the "master" (*ba'al*). Zarathustra, however, has succeeded in completely demythologizing the cosmogenic system.

was for a select circle of initiates, the magi, while the latter left a deep impression upon the life of the nation, demanding both social reform and the giving up of their nomadic existence. It was precisely his demands for social justice that brought him most into opposition with the ruling circles, resulting in persecution and flight. Under these pressures it is only to be expected that the disciples of this new teaching banded together and gradually formed a social class or caste, not, however, as Herodotus believed, an ethnic unity. It was these magi who, as Zarathustra's spiritual heirs, did indeed propagate his thinking; but by their acceptance of essentially different elements they gradually drew away from the original thought of Zarathustra. At all events it is clear that both in the Median and in the Persian court they achieved considerable influence and were retained as the educators of the royal family. When, accordingly, the Persian kings give allegiance to Ahura-mazda in their inscriptions, their faith is the same as that of the magi, which is to say that it is the religion of a small circle of initiates, but certainly not the popular and national religion of the Persian empire.[27] Owing to the fragmentary nature of our sources, it is impossible to describe a more accurate history of the magi in this era.[28] As a result, any thorough-going conclusions as to the Bible's dependence upon Iran must remain questionable. The figure of the great prophet Zarathustra remains a monolith standing out sharply from the paganism that surrounds him.

The possibility of Deutero-Isaiah and Daniel being somehow influenced by the Iranian dualism cannot be excluded. The teaching of the prophets always takes place within a definite historical situation. But two points must be borne in mind. Israel's conception of God was bound up with fire from the most ancient times; fire was the form in which God chose to appear upon Sinai, and to the prophet Elijah, etc. We must also remember that light and darkness are, as it were, natural symbols for good and evil and, as such, were frequently used in the prophetic vocabulary long before Israel's confrontation with Iran. At all

---

27. G. Messina, *Der Ursprung der Magier und die zarathustrische Religion*, 93.
28. The name Magi comes from *maga*, "gift, present, grace, i.e., religion." The derivation is *maga-van*, "he who has a share in the favor." The "gift" of Zarathustra, which came from heaven, was his new knowledge of God and the world. Zarathustra was thus, as a called prophet, *the* Magi, *the* receiver of revelation *par excellence*. Messina, *loc. cit.*, 74.

events, it could certainly be probable that these theological ideas were given fresh emphasis by the influence of Iranian thinking, and thought through to their final conclusions. Nowhere in the Bible, however, do we encounter even the symbolical representation of two original principles. Yahweh is always the one God, who judges over good and evil. Thus, if some so-called Iranian elements make their appearance in the later prophets, this is only evidence of the fact that they understood the signs of their times. One thing is clear: Iran had nothing to contribute to Israel's monotheism. Zarathustra's original monotheistic doctrine quickly yielded to the need for compromise. Israel, on the other hand, had an ancient heritage to preserve; it was hers to give but not to receive.

CHAPTER II

THE BOOK OF CONSOLATION
OF THE PROPHET ISAIAH
(DEUTERO-ISAIAH)

"NEXT to the Pentateuch, no other book of the Old Testament
has been so fragmented and outraged by criticism as the second
half of the Book of Isaiah" (ch. 40-66). This is the view of
Dennefeld in his commentary on Isaiah.[1] A reference to the
decree of the Pontifical Biblical Commission of June 28, 1908,
is sufficient, in his opinion, to cut the Gordian knot; the Book of
Isaiah, he maintains, is, in its totality, the work of the prophet
of that name from the eighth century. It is true that the Biblical
Commission declared, some 50 years ago, that the arguments
advanced prior to that time were insufficient to warrant the
ascription of the second half of this book to another author
and another era. "Since 1908, however, there have been many
scholarly investigations into the matter of Isaiah 40-66, and
they have adduced sufficient proof that the second half of
the book cannot possibly have been written by the prophet

---

1. L. Dennefeld, *Les Grands Prophètes*, ClamB VII (1952), 19.
2. *Ibid.*, 148. — Cf. Ench. Biblicum, (Rome 1963), Nos. 291-295.

Isaiah in the eighth century. The authors of ch. 40-66 wrote these sections as his disciples and made them a part of the prophet's own book so that even the most recent texts bear the name of Isaiah, since they have been written wholly in accord with his spirit." [3] This interpretation can be considered today as the *sententia communis* of Catholic scholarship. The names of the individual authors are unknown; they did not mean to preach any new or different message; they simply took up the words of the great Isaiah and made them live for their own age. There are rules for interpreting the process in which the words of an earlier prophet are taken up later by his school; this is the surest key to interpreting the problem of Isaiah. Isaiah's words were living words, and they had the power to come back to life in a new era, with renewed strength, and in a different dress.[4]

A) THE NAMELESS DISCIPLE OF ISAIAH

1) THE LITERARY GENRE OF ISAIAH 40-66

The complicated history of interpretation of these chapters cannot be adequately treated here. We can simply list the more explicit commentaries which are available.[5] The essentials are easily outlined. The problem was first posed by Doderlein (1775) and Eichhorn (1792). They distinguished three blocs in the Book of Isaiah: chs. 1-39 belonged to the prophet of the eighth century; chs. 40-55 are the work of an unknown prophet from the time of the Exile, referred to as Deutero-Isaiah; chs. 56-66 are also the work of a nameless writer dating from post-Exilic days, and called Trito-Isaiah. This position is essentially unaltered today. The individual sections were examined and rearranged according to different principles of criticism in the time that followed. Thus, Duhm in his commentary on Isaiah

---

3. J. Ziegler, vol. III, 15.
4. D. R. Griffiths, Dt. – *Jesaiah and the Fourth Gospel; Some Points of Comparison,* ET 65 (1954), 357-360, compares it with the Gospels; Jesus speaks differently in the Synoptics than he does in St. John, and yet John's Gospel presents the same message in a newly worked form.
5. Cf. Robert-Feuillet, EinlAT 543-554, which contains a good bibliography.

(1892) isolated the poems 42, 1-4 (7), 49, 1-6; 50, 4-9; 52, 13—
53, 12 as independent units, referring to them as the "songs
of the servant of Yahweh." The rest of the text was further dis-
sected into minute elements — the number ranges from 40 to
70 — and assigned to several authors and a wide variety of
dating.[6]

As a reaction against this extreme fragmentation of the text,
modern scholarship is more inclined to see Deutero-Isaiah as
one definite individual, and perhaps the greatest of the prophets.[7]
If we subscribe to the final results of investigation on the subject
of the "servant of Yahweh songs," according to which Deutero-
Isaiah has at least the first and best claim to authorship,[8] then
we must indeed realize that we are in the presence of a compact
body of writing produced by a nameless prophet, and that his
message can be properly understood only if we interpret it in
terms of its historical situation, which is not the age of the great
Isaiah, but the time of Exile. The traditional opinion, namely
that the entire Book of Isaiah is the work of the prophet of
that name, can still be maintained insofar as Deutero-Isaiah is
clearly a spiritual descendant of the great prophet; a clear distinction must be made, however, insofar as the unity of faith and
spirit does not imply a similar unity in the literary product. Surrendering the claim to literary unity does nothing to weaken the
continuity of faith and spirit; quite the contrary.[9] The work
gains considerably in power and conviction, since it is powerful

---

6. Eissfeldt, EinlAT 406.
7. Bright, HistIsr 336 — IntB 5 (1956), 382. "Is 40-55 is the most
   magnificent piece of literature that has come down to us from semitic
   antiquity."
8. Eissfeldt, EinlAT 411: A qualitative distinction between the songs of
   the servant and their immediate context cannot be established, only
   a quantitative one, insofar as more individualized traits are here
   described than in the surrounding text. In these circumstances, the
   claim that the Ebed Yahweh songs were written by Deutero-Isaiah
   clearly has the right of prior claim on its side.
9. Robert-Feuillet, IntrAT 550: La question est en effet d'ordre critique:
   elle n'interesse pas directement la foi. He also collects the arguments
   for deciding the issue, in terms of the following points of departure:
   historical, doctrinal, literary.

evidence of the fact that the word has been made flesh, that is, that the word has entered bodily into the manifold of historical development. We shall thus treat Isaiah 40-55 as a unified literary work dating from the era of the great upheaval which began with the rise of Cyrus, King of Persia, and reached its climax in the conquest of Babylon. Deutero-Isaiah is the prophetic answer to the history of the years before and after 538 B.C. Chapters 56-66, on the other hand, form a new prophetic reincarnation of the great prophet's original words; they are aimed at the crisis of faith that Judah suffered between the time of her return to the Holy Land and the rebuilding of the Temple.

2) THE PERSONALITY OF THE DISCIPLE OF ISAIAH

"Two men served as instruments for the liberation and return home of the exiled Jews, Cyrus who created the political situation, and the man whom, unawares even of his name, we refer to simply as 'Deutero-Isaiah.' At approximately the very time that the walls of the city of Jerusalem fell and the Jewish people lost forever their independence as a state, thus between the years 590 and 580, Deutero-Isaiah was born, probably in exile, in a family of Jewish expatriates, and in the person of this man the Jewish community was given a powerful leader, a man destined to re-build their national character and give them a new spiritual heritage. We do not know his name; he does not tell us where he grew up and where he worked; only occasionally does he make a reference to the political, social, cultural, and religious events of his milieu; in his message there is nothing of his vocation, nothing of his personal career; he is entirely impersonal, the most impersonal of all the great prophets." [10] And thus the work stands for the man. World history was at a turning point, standing between two eras,[11] kingdoms were collapsing and new powers were arising — the situation called for a new interpreter of the way of God. As he had in every other crisis of

---

10. P. Volz, *Jesaia* II, KAT (1932), XV.
11. H. Frey, *Das Buch der Weltpolitik Gottes*, CalwK (1954), 10.

his people's history, Yahweh sent a herald into this pivotal era.

3) THE POET

a. *Lyric style*: Deutero-Isaiah has been called "the singer of Paradise Regained." [12] The herald of good tidings to Zion is to lift his voice with strength (40, 9); his is a voice of jubilation (48, 20), like the sound of a trumpet (58, 1): the whole nation is ordered to listen to the sound of the new melody (51, 3). Again and again his lips pour forth inspired song (45, 8). He calls to heaven and earth to sing with him (44, 23; 49, 13): "Sing to Yahweh a new song!" (42, 10-13). Even abandoned Zion is to raise her voice in song (52, 7-12; 54, 1-10). The basic tone of chs. 40-55 is one of exuberant enthusiasm, triumphant joy. This enthusiasm imparts a dithyrambic character to the entire work.

b. *Rhapsody*: The dilemma of criticism in its attempt to decide whether the work was produced in a single burst of poetic inspiration or whether it represents a series of poems dating from different stages of the poet's career, is really meaningless. In the powerfully sweeping flood of his words, in the outbursts of holy passion, we catch a glimpse of the same great ideas and hopes, always new and always the same, without any apparent logical order — just as we see the stars shining through the clouds whenever the wind opens a window for our view. Isaiah 40-55 is neither a literary unity with a progression in theme and construction, as for example the Book of Job, nor is it a collection of songs like the Book of Lamentations or Psalms: it is rather a passionate and sweeping rhapsody. In ever renewed outpourings of the spirit, the poet strives to come to grips with his central concept: but the form always dissolves in favor of yet a new and grander insight that makes its stormy way into his poetic view.[13]

---

12. Pfeiffer, IntrOT 463 compares Deutero-Isaiah with Milton, the poet of Paradise Lost; Job is compared with Shakespeare.
13. *Ibid.*, 465.

c. *Dramatic theology*: Despite the rhapsodic character — or perhaps because of it — Deutero-Isaiah is like an eschatological drama. Creation of the world, history, redemption — these are the central themes of the drama. Each of the three themes is developed in a dramatic manner. God is the principal actor from beginning to end. Israel's life and fate are dynamically woven into the history of human events, and in this history God himself is revealed. The climaxes of ancient history: the deluge in the days of Noah, the call of Abraham, the Exodus from Egypt, the wandering in the desert, the covenant with David — all these are called into review and fitted into the divine plan of the drama. God's will and God's direction is the whole point and key of the great play. The Persian King Cyrus has an important role to play; the focus is not so much upon his accomplishments in the sphere of world history, but rather upon the role he was destined to fulfill in Israel, God's people in their time of crisis. Israel's call and election, her mission into the world as bringer of salvation and servant of God, her blinding and her stubbornness, the sentence passed upon her and the even greater favor shown to her — all this is developed not in a logically abstract manner, but with such a burst of dynamism that Deutero-Isaiah has been called a "dramatic theology." [14]

B)   THE MESSAGE OF THE DISCIPLE

1) YAHWEH, THE ONE GOD AND MASTER OF HISTORY [15]

The primary mission of this "disciple" of the great Isaiah was the consolation of his broken people; that is how he first begins his message: "Comfort, comfort my people!" (40, 1). But it is no cheap reference to the imminent reversal of his nation's fortunes in terms of merely human history that serves as the basis for his consolation. His consolation wells up from the depths of faith. Yahweh, the One, is God and Master of history. It is God who bids him announce: "Her time of service

14. J. Muilenberg, IntB 5 (1956), 388.
15. Bright, HistIsr 336-338.

is ended, and her iniquity is pardoned" (40, 2). His message is in the service of his faith that God himself will come to set his people free and be their redeemer. It was not the meteoric rise of Cyrus and the foreseeable fall of Babylon that prompted him to this message. It was his knowledge of Israel's God that pointed out his way in this time of upheaval. Yahweh is the creator of all things, and no one has resisted him; he is master of the powers of the heavens and the laws of nature; no power can resist him and no thing can represent him (40, 12-26). The pagan gods are dismissed with biting mockery (44, 12-20); they are only wood or metal (40, 19ff.; 46, 5-7); they have no power to affect human history because they are nothing (41, 21-24). Yahweh, however, is the first and last, the One God, and there is none beside him (44, 6; 45, 18; 46, 9).

The preaching of such a faith in God must have certainly announced to the people in their time of crisis that the whole course of human history stands under the absolute control of Yahweh. By way of contrast, the "disciple" of Isaiah presents a powerful scene, a council of the gods of nations. Let them show if they have power to form history, to call kings into being, to cause kingdoms to collapse and come back to life (41, 1-4; 43, 9). They cannot; they tremble in the presence of Cyrus whose rise they could neither predict nor effect (41, 5-7; 46, 1ff.). Their impotence shows that they are no gods at all (41, 21-24). Yahweh, however, is the Creator of the universe, the Lord of all that lives and breathes (45, 11-13; 48, 12-16). He has outlined his plan of history from of old; it was he who called Abraham and Jacob to be his servants (41, 8-10; 51, 1-3). His chosen people too can testify that Yahweh has carried out his plans and is thus truly God (43, 8-13; 44, 6-8). Like the other prophets, Deutero-Isaiah interprets the Exile as just punishment for the sins of his people (42, 24ff.; 48, 17-19). But not even Israel's many sins — it would be a blasphemy to think so — could affect Yahweh's plan of salvation (48, 9-11). Cyrus himself must play the part of an unconscious tool in the hands of God, accomplishing Yahweh's own plans for the rebuilding of Zion (44, 24-45, 7; 41, 25f.; 24, 8-11). This was the answer of the "disciple" and prophet to the most burning issue of his day. The upheaval in world politics not only lies in God's hand; it is deliberately occasioned by God's will as the beginning of redemption. Truly this is a faith from which his people might draw constant strength in their time of adversity (40, 27-31; 51, 1-16).

2) THE NEW DAWN

Although the prophet looked to Cyrus for liberation from captivity, his hopes for the future go far beyond the common expectations of the expatriates who were more or less counting on the restoration of the state of Judah. "What he looked forward to was nothing less than the return of the miracles of the Exodus from Egypt, the restoration of Israel and the establishment of God's dominion over the whole world. This is the message he hammers in again and again: something new is going to dawn (42, 9; 43, 19; 48, 3, 6-8). Yahweh is full of impatience until the new order is "born" (42, 14ff.). The labor pains of this new era have already begun. The birth of the new order is immediately imminent. The decisive experience is frequently compared with the trek through the wilderness: the wilderness begins to bloom, fountains of water spring up (40, 3-5; 41, 8; 42, 16; 49, 9-11; 55, 12; ch. 35). The images are from the traditional account of the Exodus from Egypt. Like other prophets before him (Hos 2, 14-20; Is 10, 24-27; Jer 31, 2-6; Ez 20, 33-38), Deutero-Isaiah interprets the Babylonian Exile as a second sojourn in Egypt. The new order that is destined to come must, accordingly, be called a new Exodus (43, 16-21; 48, 20; 52, 11). An actual event of ancient history, in which God's will for salvation was made manifest to his people, thus takes on a new actuality and a meaning beyond what was ever expected. It is not history that is the important element, but rather God's revelation in the course of history. What Yahweh began of old he now, as creator and redeemer, brings to its climax. There is more at stake than a simple restoration: there is a whole new creation (51, 9-11).

This new order involved a new view of the covenant. It is

not as though the people had ever been deserving of their divine vocation; just as God had called an undeserving people out of Egypt, even now, he calls to a people who is blind and deaf and even leprous (42, 18-21; 48, 1-11), to make them the partners of a new and everlasting covenant of peace (54, 9f.). Deutero-Isaiah did not refer to this as a new covenant as Jeremiah had done (Jer 31, 31); he was convinced that Yahweh's covenant had, in the last analysis, never really ceased (50, 1); the Exile was not a divorce; it was only a transitory separation. But now Yahweh leads the errant Israel back home (54, 1-10); he holds to the covenant which he has made with Abraham (49, 20; 54, 1-3). Although this new covenant to come is destined to fulfill the messianic hopes associated with the house of David in an unexpected and glorious way, our prophet's whole view of the future accords the ruler from David's line only an intermediate role (55, 3-5). Yahweh himself is the king; his earthly "messiah" is the pagan king Cyrus (45, 1), who is an unwitting instrument in his hand. Yahweh will in person lead his flock through the wilderness back to Zion (40, 1-11), where he will establish his kingdom (51, 17 — 52, 12) and, through the outpouring of his spirit, create a new Israel that will recognize and worship him as God (44, 1-5).

A still grander horizon is opening: God's dominion and kingdom embraces even the pagans. Deutero-Isaiah does not for a moment doubt Israel's favored position in the divine plan of salvation; but he looks beyond the frontiers of his own age into an era in which all the nations will recognize Yahweh as God (49, 6). He hoped that the peoples of the world would interpret the upheaval of his day as the revelation of Yahweh's power, that they would turn aside from their pagan deities as an idle superstition and be converted to the one God of Israel (45, 14-25). Cyrus himself would then take Yahweh's hand in triumph and do him homage (45, 1-7). This universal horizon had been seen before in Scripture (Gn 12, 1-3; Amos 9, 7), but never with such a full degree of light. Yahweh takes the rule of the whole world upon himself; the people of the world are called to submit to his dominion. Thus the monotheism of

Israel has abandoned the national restrictions of the past and embarked upon a path which was to find its realization in the fullness of time. Volz refers to Deutero-Isaiah as the first missionary of the pagans.[16]

3) THE SONGS OF THE SERVANT OF GOD — 'EBED-YAHWEH [17]

In Yahweh's plan of world history which he means to realize in the immediate future, the "servant" (*'ebed*) has a particularly important role to play, as described in greater detail in the four songs. Whether the servant is a definite historical or eschatological person, or merely the personification of the people of Israel, or perhaps both at once, is a subject for later discussion. First we must examine the evidence of the four songs themselves in the more important points:

a. The spirit-judge (first *'ebed* song, 42, 1-4): with the exclamation "behold" the attention of the reader is directed to something new that God means to accomplish in the future. The perplexity of the pagan gods (42, 24, 29) is opposed by the will of Yahweh which directs human history. His will of history is concentrated on the figure of the "servant." His introduction (42, 1) recalls the vocation of the judges. He is seized upon by Yahweh and endowed with "spirit," that is, with the power of God (*rûaḥ*). For what purpose? So that he will accomplish judgment (*mišpat*) upon the nations (*gôyîm*). What we could be led to look for next, following the pattern of the Book of Judges, would be the description of the military campaign in the course of which the enemy would be driven from the heritage of God and freedom once again established. But there is no

---

16. Iesajah II, (1932), XVIII.
17. Cf. also: Ch. R. North, *The Suffering Servant in Deutero-Isaiah*, (1948). — H. H. Rowley, *The Suffering Servant and the Messiah*, Stud. 8 (1950), 100ff. — W. Zimmerli, ThWNT V, 655ff. — H. Kruse, *De Carminum servi dei nova quadam interpretatione*, VD 30 (1952), 341-348. — C. Lindhagen, *The Servant of the Lord*, ET 67 (1956), 279-283, 300-302. — O. Cullmann, *Die Christologie des NT*, (1958), 50-81.

battlecry, and no sound of war. The servant, as a judge endowed with the spirit, makes a quite different appearance. The broken reed he will not break, and the glowing wick he will not extinguish. How can he be a saving judge? Simply because he will not fail or be discouraged until he has established justice upon this earth; even the coastlands await the wise decisions of his law (*tôrah*). The servant is destined for judgment,[18] that is, for the establishment of God's dominion. The horizon is world-wide. The nations and the coastlands await his appearance. Cyrus, who made his entry into the world of the nations like a mighty storm wind, is followed by the quiet calm of the servant of God, whose appearance can hardly be noticed. Yet it is he who is destined to accomplish the great changes in history.[19]

b. God's sword and arrow (2nd *'ebed* song, 49, 1-6): The horizon of the song is once again universal. The coastlands and the nations of the far distance are called to listen. Just as in the first song, there is a combination here of seemingly ir-reconcilable traits in the person of the servant. He is truly *'ebed,* servant, standing under the will of Yahweh. It is not he who chooses his mission; the mission is given to him. His is the obligation of strict obedience. God will use him like a sword and an arrow. "He made my mouth like a sharp sword, . . . [20] and he made me a polished arrow" (49, 2). Once again there is no talk of war, simply the weapon of God's word. God's word is ir-resistible, inescapable, smooth and sharp like an arrow which holds fast to its target. But the comparison is not finished: for the servant himself is the word of God, and as such he accomplishes judgment. Despite his call from heaven, there is some lack of sense and mean-ing to his life. He must confess: "I have labored in vain, I have spent my strength for nothing and vanity" (49, 4). There is

---

18. "Judgment" always has the positive meaning of "redemption."
19. H. Frey, *Das Buch der Weltpolitik Gottes,* Chs. 40-55 in *Buches Jesaja,* CalwK (1954), 58ff.
20. Cf. Jer 1, 10: kings are cut down with the sword of the word, Jer 23; the word of God shatters rock: Heb 4, 12: the word of God is keener than a two-edged sword.

one powerful qualification to the meaningless efforts of his life (49, 4b). The power of this powerless man is in God; it is through him that God will gather Israel and effect the conversion of Jacob (49, 5, 6). From his toil and hardship he becomes the light of the nations. In him the salvation ($y^e \check{s} \hat{u}\,'ah$) of God will be manifest to the very ends of the earth. He is truly a "servant," an instrument in the hands of Yahweh who means to accomplish mighty things through him.

c. The song of the disciple (3rd 'ebed song, 50, 4-8): The 'ebed is eager to hear the word of God, just like the young Samuel. He does not deviate from the word of God, even when it causes him hostility. He is beaten, spat upon, mocked, and his beard is pulled. The song portrays a tragic scene. The servant of God is condemned as godless. But he stands unbroken in the midst of judgment, his face like a flint; for God is his helper. God will do him justice and dissolve the human judgment passed upon him. All human glory is only an aging garment eaten by moths; but God's glory abides forever. It is not a philosopher who is sung of in these lines, a wise man who has learned to suffer in patience; nor is it the hero who knows how to endure hardship; it is rather the servant who is simply obedient to his call to be God's disciple and accomplish his work.

d. Expiatory death and redemption (4th 'ebed song, 52, 13 — 53, 12): This song is written in retrospect; the singer asks, "My God, what has happened!" In the figure of this suffering servant of God, God himself was in our midst and we did not recognize him. The section 52, 13-15 describes the unexpected miracle of the servant's rise to glory; this is counterbalanced in 53, 1-3 by an *Ecce-homo* picture. There is no beauty in him, no comeliness, for he is a man of sorrows. All this came upon him not of himself: mankind must recognize the fact: the burden that he bears is their burden; the sin that weighs him down is their guilt. He was transfixed, led like a lamb to the slaughter (53, 4-9). His death is the redemption of many. "The life and death of the servant is inextricably bound up with the life and salvation

of the many. How this can be possible can never be explained
in a comprehensible manner. It is a powerful exchange of fates
between the servant and us." [21] God's plan of history arrives
at its goal through the suffering of the servant. God gives him
the many for his heritage (53, 10-11).

e. Who is the *'ebed?* When the songs are read without the light
shed by the New Testament, there are many possible answers.
The question of the chamberlain of Candace (Acts 8, 34) puts
the matter in a compact form: "Of whom is the prophet speaking?
Does he say this of himself or of another man?" The chamberlain
was thinking of an historical person; the songs would thus be the
precipitate of the bitter sufferings of the nameless prophet. Opposed to this personal interpretation are serious grounds for
consideration. It is one of the commonplaces of prophetical diction
to personify peoples and cities in such a way that their fates and
activities are felt to be those of real persons.[22] The name *'ebed,*
servant, is, in Isaiah, not reserved for the *'ebed-Yahweh,* the
servant of God, alone. Israel as a whole is called the servant
of Yahweh. Does this mean that the songs are a portrayal of
the fate of Israel? Must the *'ebed* be understood collectively as
a symbol for the community of the chosen people?

Closer examination of the prophetic usage reveals a distinction between *'ebed-Yahweh* and *'ebed-Yisrael.*[23] The servant Israel is obstinate,
hard-hearted; he refuses God's call and must be warned that conversion is
necessary (40, 27; 41, 8; 44, 1-2, etc.); the servant of God, on the
other hand, is completely receptive to God's call (49, 4; 50, 7-9). The
servant of Israel is sinful from his birth on (48, 4; 43, 27); the servant of
God is an expiatory sacrifice for the sins of others (53, 4-6, 9, 11-12).
The servant Israel suffers against his will because of his own transgressions
(42, 18-25; 43, 22-28; 47, 6; 50, 1; 54, 7); the servant of God freely
bears his sufferings (53, 7). Moreover, the servant of God has a mission
to fulfill in Israel and is thus distinct from Israel (52, 12 − 53, 12).
The two magnitudes cannot simply be equivalated. Is it possible that the
servant of God is to stand for the ideal and faithful Israel who would

---

21. Frey, l. c. 265.
22. Cf. the personification of Jerusalem and Samaria, Ezek 16, 23ff.
23. For fuller treatment, cf. J. Muilenberg, IntB 5 (1956), 408ff.

redeem sinful Israel by her sufferings? [24] Such a solution is unlikely in view of the personal characteristics in the picture of the servant of God. Some scholars have thought that Moses or Jeremiah was the original type for this servant. But there has as yet been no satisfactory attempt [25] to equivalate the servant of God with any historical personality or to fit him into the myth of the dying and resurgent divinities of the vegetation cycle.[26] "The reality which shines through these songs is immeasurably grander than any historical personality could ever represent." [27]

It follows that the servant of God is a messianic figure, and can be only understood in view of the passion and resurrection of Jesus. The Old Testament text demands a New Testament realization. Still, one aspect must be clearly separated from the others. Despite the personal interpretation, the 'ebed-Yahweh always stands in reference to the community. He is king, prophet, or expiatory victim. But without the reference to his people, his mission is meaningless. He is the principal character in the divine-human tragedy and his fate must be shared by the chorus of Israel and humanity, whether it is in tones of lamentation or jubilation.[28] He is, accordingly, both identical with Israel and still not identical. This essential oscillation between two fates and two identities has recently been expressed by the term "corporate personality." [29] This idea is a genuine Old Testament concept, although it is not common to the semitic mind. It is a necessary result of a strong genealogical awareness. The present gene-

24. H. G. May, *The Righteous Servant in Second Isaiah's Songs*, ZAW 66 (1954), 236-244.
25. Robert-Feuillet, IntrAT 557 and 559.
26. The incorporation of pagan ideas is, in itself, quite possible. IntB V, 412. On the subject of derivation from the Babylonian New Year ritual, cf. S. H. Hooke, *The Theory and Practice of Substitution*, VT 2 (1952), 2-17. There is a good study of the difference between the 'Ebed songs and the Tammuz liturgy, the "suffering" of the King in the Babylonian New Year ritual, and the concept of representation in the *šar-puhi* texts, in J. Scharbert, *Stellvertretendes Sühneleiden in den 'Ebed-Jahwe-Liederb und in altorientalischen Ritualtexten*, BZ, NF 2 (1958), 190-213.
27. IntB V, 409.
28. J. Morgenstern, *The Suffering Servant — a new Solution* (1), VT 11 (1961), 292-320, considers the 'Ebed songs as a poetic unity in the manner of a Greek tragedy. He thus divides the text among the

ration forms a unity with the ancestors and with the posterity to come, a unity which goes back to the original tribal father as its fountainhead.[30] The servant of Yahweh stands at the beginning of a new Israel. The dual reference and partially interchangeable character of his name is an inescapable result of his essence and his mission. He alone is at one and the same time the climax, the high point, and the summing up of the entire people. Delitzch [31] has compared his figure to that of the pyramid. Israel as a whole is the base of the pyramid; the middle stages of the pyramid correspond to Israel in the spirit; but the apex of the pyramid is the servant of God, the king of the new Zion and its redeemer. The apex cannot exist for itself alone; it is the end and goal of the entire edifice and still it is not identical with the other sections. From the New Testament point of view this comparison suggests the *Corpus Christi mysticum,* an idea that Paul took, not from the Gnosis, but as a new development of the thought of the disciple of Isaiah.[32] The relationship between Christ and Church has a clear and precise type in the relationship between the servant of God and Israel.

In an era in which a new world war was gathering like a storm on the horizon and the collapse of the Babylonian empire and the rise of the Persians were clearly visible signs, the ex-

---

dramatis personae: God, King, Chorus, etc. This would make the poems an Israelite drama of salvation. This royal interpretation is also represented by V. de Leeuw, *Die königliche Auslegung der Ebed-Jahwe-Lieder,* EphThLov 28 (1954), 449-471. — Cf. G. Pidoux, *Le serviteur souffrant d'Essaic,* RThPh 1 (1956), 36-46: "L'ebed est le roi de la nouvelle Sion."

29. The problem is thoroughly discussed in J. de Fraine, *Adam und seine Nachkommen. Der Begriff der "Korporativen Personlichkeit" in der Heiligen Schrift,* (Cologne 1962). — Also: R. J. Tournay, *Les chants du Serviteur dans la Seconde partie d'Isaie,* RB 59 (1952), 335-384; 481-512.

---

30. The underlying concept is thoroughly examined by J. Scharbert, *Solidarität in Fluch und Segen im AT und in seiner Umwelt,* I (1958).
31. Fr. Delitzsch, *Kommentar uber den Propheten Jesaja,* (1889), 432.
32. E. Schweizer, cf. article *SOMA* in ThWNT. — Also in ThLZ 86 (1961), 161-174; 241-256.

patriate Jews were buffeted back and forth between their dreams of hope and the depths of their despair. It was at this moment of history that the nameless prophet arose, the disciple of the great Isaiah, to be the consoler of his generation and the generations to come. His book, which begins with the call: "Comfort, comfort, my people," is truly a book of consolation. He announces not only the resurrection of the tiny Jewish nation from death and exile, but the grander prospect of the servant of God, condemned to death but triumphant in his resurrection to establish the new Israel in the spirit. History and eschatology are more than ever commingled. "The temporal is everywhere radiant with eternal glory." [33] The marvelous experience of liberation from the bondage of Babylon is radiant with the dawn of a new dominion of God; the servant Cyrus is a type [34] for the redeemer; the temporal upheaval in human history is pregnant with eternity.

33. Frey, *Das Buch der Weltpolitik Gottes*, 11.
34. U. Simon, *König Kyros und die Typologie*, Judaica 11 (1955), 83-88.

CHAPTER III

RETURN AND RECONSTRUCTION

THE return home had been prepared historically by the rise of the Persian King Cyrus and in the religious sphere by the preaching of the disciple of Isaiah. The historical and supra-historical are closely intertwined. There was considerable danger that the promised dawn of God's dominion would be seen, in the shortness of human vision, simply as the dawn of a new world empire. Truly the temporal is everywhere radiant with eternal glory,[1] so much so that the disciple, in fixing his vision upon the eternal, appears to lose the very ground he stands on. His preaching was like a triumphal march to usher in the world dominion of God. The hopes were placed too high; disillusion was the consequence. This crisis in the religious faith called for new prophets to interpret the signs of their time.

1) CYRUS' EDICT OF LIBERATION

In the first year of his reign, Cyrus published the following edict from Babylon: The expatriate Judaeans are released from captivity; they are free to return home and rebuild the ruined temple of the God of heaven. There are two accounts of this, one

---

1. Frey, l. c. 11.

in Hebrew and one in Aramaic. Ezra 6, 3-5 belongs to the Aramaic documents which by reason of their importance were probably preserved in the Temple archives at Jerusalem and incorporated by the historian into his work. Their genuinity can hardly be doubted.[2] The document bears the date of the first year of Cyrus (spring 538).[3] It represents a sort of record protocol (*dikrōna* — record, Ezr 6, 2) which was put down in writing in terms of the oral decision of the great king and then deposited in the archives. It authorized the reconstruction of the temple and made provision for defraying the expense from the royal treasury; the gold and silver vessels which Nebuchadnezzar had stolen from the Temple in Jerusalem were also to be restored.

The second account (Ezr 1, 2-4) is composed in Hebrew, and is probably a free rendering of the Aramaic document. In the form of a royal proclamation, Cyrus declares that the God of heaven (*'elohê-haśśāmayim*) has given him all the kingdoms of the world and charged him with the building of a temple in Jerusalem. The people are to go back home and accomplish this work. Those who choose to remain in Babylon are to help with contributions of money and material. Even the vessels of the Temple are to be returned (Ezr 1, 7-11).

Seen in the light of Cyrus' policies, such a decree is nothing strange. Cyrus had already given orders that the gods carried off by Nabonidus in his last-ditch resistance should be returned to their home cities; he had also reestablished the Marduk cult in Babylon in all its ancient glory. The Persian policy was diametrically opposed to that of the Assyrians and Babylonians. Whereas the latter deliberately destroyed all evidence of ethnic and religious individuality, the Persians allowed their subject nations the greatest possible degree of political and religious autonomy. The Jewish edict of liberation is, accordingly, only one among many, certainly the best known to our scholarship

---

2. R. de Vaux, *Les decrets de Cyrus et de Darius sur la reconstruction du temple*, RB 46 (1937), 29-57.
3. Since Cyrus took the hands of Bel in Babylon, Oct. 29, 539, and thereby became king, the time from then to Nisan of 538 counted as his year of accession. His first year ran from spring 538 to spring 537.

since it is of the utmost significance in determining the further development of revealed religion.

2) THE FIRST RETURN UNDER SHESH-BAZZAR

After the proclamation of the edict, the heads of the families from Judah and Benjamin all assembled (rā'šê hā'ābôt, Ezr 1, 5), as well as the priests and Levites, in order to organize the return home. Despite their common joy at the restoration of their freedom, this was no mass exodus. Josephus [4] records that many did not want to abandon their property, and remained behind in Babel. The previously mentioned archives of the firm "Murasu and Sons" in Nippur show that after the edict of liberation many Jews must have remained in Babylon and achieved a considerable influence in the economy of the country. Those who returned to Judah were primarily the religious enthusiasts whom the spirit (rû^ah) had stirred up to return home and rebuild the house of Yahweh (Ezr 1, 5). The execution of the plans for return was, in keeping with the liberal Persian policy, entrusted to a descendant of David, Shesh-bazzar,[5] a son of the captive king Jehoiachin (Ezr 5, 14). He was given the title of peḥāh (Ezr 5, 14), which is probably not to be understood in the strictest sense of "governor of Judah," but in the more general meaning of "special plenipotentiary for the solution of the Jewish question." Politically, Judah was still under considerable control from the governor of the province of Samaria, who, in the time that followed, made his power unpleasantly evident in Jerusalem. Although Shesh-bazzar's successor Zerubbabel [6] is explicitly called "governor of Judah" (pāḥat yᵉhûdah, Hag 1, 1, 14), the political status of Judah, as must be expected

---

4. Ant. XI, I, 3.
5. šešbassar is probably to be identified with šen'assar (1 Ch 3, 16); both forms of the name are derived from a Babylonian original, perhaps sin-ab-ussur, "May the moon-god Sin protect the father" (Bright, HistIsr 343) or šamaš-apla-ussur, "May the sun-god protect the son" (Noth, GeschI 279); Noth, however, denies that the two names are equivalent.

in this stage of reconstruction, was very much in flux.

Of the fate of the first returned prisoners we know practically nothing. The activity of Shesh-bazzar and that of Zerubbabel seem to have been confused with each other. It is probable that Shesh-bazzar set to work immediately upon arriving in Judah and laid the cornerstone for the new Temple (Ezr 5, 16); other documents attribute the honor of the laying of the cornerstone to Zerubbabel (Ezr 3, 6-11; Zc 4, 9). The answer might well be that one began the work and the other continued his efforts. It is impossible to ask for a more precise answer. At all events, the beginning was made. The cult could be resumed on the desecrated site, although not in its full glory.

3) SECOND RETURN HOME UNDER ZERUBBABEL AND JESHUA

Upon their return home, the exiles were not greeted by the paradise that their religious enthusiasm might well have led them to expect; they met with crisis and had to fight for their existence. A series of poor harvests made the situation worse (Hag 1, 9-11; 2, 15-17). Their Samaritan neighbors regarded the repatriates with suspicion, while the remnant of the earlier population that had remained in the land of Judah saw them as a possible threat to their peaceful existence. The fact that the returnees from exile regarded themselves as the true Israel only aggravated the situation. The tensions mounted into deeds of violence, and public security was threatened (Zc 8, 10). It is no wonder that the work begun on the temple had to be abandoned. The repatriates themselves had insufficient means to continue the construction; the promised support from the royal treasury was not immediately forthcoming. The work on the temple took second place to the fight for daily existence.

The precise date of the aged Shesh-bazzar's death remains unknown.[7] The claim that he was deposed and forced to return

---

6. On the political activity of Zerubbabel, cf. EncMikr II, 938-941. His name is not Hebrew, but Babylonian, probably *zêr-babili*, "Man from Babel."

7. Since he was Jehoiachin's fourth son (1 Ch 3, 17ff.), he may have

to Babylonia is purest conjecture. His work was, at all events, continued by his nephew Zerubbabel, the son of Shealtiel, the elder son of Jehoiachin. In the interval between 538 and 520 he came to Jerusalem at the head of the second caravan returning from exile. The religious power lay this time in the hands of the high priest Jeshua the son of Jozadak (Ezr 3, 2). The seventh month — the year is not given — they erected the altar of holocausts and celebrated the feast of huts. Then they collected funds and began to build the temple with renewed vigor (Ezr 3, 7). But here the Samaritans enter the picture. By false representation at the royal court they managed to have the building program stopped (Ezr 3, 1 — 4, 5). Eighteen years after the first return, around the year 520, the construction had still not got beyond the foundations, a severe disillusion after the religious enthusiasm of the liberation from captivity.

4) THE PREACHING OF TRITO-ISAIAH

In this hour of crisis to the national faith there once again echoes the voice of a nameless consoler, a prophet whose gift was to look beyond the ruins of this first beginning and sing the glory of the Zion that was to be. He is called Trito-Isaiah, or third Isaiah. His message is contained in chs. 56-66 of the Book of Isaiah. Actually he draws upon the heritage of the ancient prophet Isaiah and makes it live anew for his own time.[8]

a. *The literary problem of Trito-Isaiah*: Duhm's commentary on Isaiah (1892) first prompted modern scholarship to regard chs. 56-66 as an independent literary unit. They must be regarded as the work of an individual author whom, for want

---

been born before 592. This follows from the Jehoiakim tablets, ANET 308.

---

8. W. Kessler, *Studie zur religiösen Situation im 1, nachexilischen Jahrhundert und die Auslegung von Jes 56-66*, WZ Halle 5 (1956/57), 41-73. — J. Morgenstern, *Two Prophecies from 520-516 B.C.*, HUCA 22 (1949), 365-431, dates Is 55, 1-5 in the year 520. Is 60, 1-3, 5-7 on New Year's Day of 516.

of his real name, scholars have called "Trito-Isaiah." Since that time, most literary critics have abandoned the concept of a literary unity for these chapters, dividing the various songs transmitted in this section among some dozen authors, dating from over a wide span of years, from the eighth to the third centuries. Eissfeldt thinks that it is impossible to achieve more than probability in this question; at all events, Isaiah 40-66 must be the work of some prophetic circles who felt themselves called to be disciples of the spirit of Isaiah, guardians and propagators of his heritage.[9]

Pfeiffer [10] is opposed to this radical dismemberment of the chapters among so many authors and times of composition. He feels that the interior arguments advanced for this type of treatment are insufficient. The poet of the Ancient Near East did not construct his literary work after the pattern of modern European logic; he cast his ideas intuitively into figurative images, quite unconcerned at any seeming inconsistencies. Scholarship can certainly not rule out the possibility that Isaiah 56-66 is the work of one individual poet. If literary criticism can no longer determine precisely whether it is one or several authors who are responsible for these 11 chapters,[11] it can at least claim with certainty that the chapters were composed in the time after the return from Exile and before the completion of the Temple. Interpreted within this historical frame of reference, they take on a power of illumination that transcends the purely temporal.

b. *Faith in Zion*: Trito-Isaiah can be called the singer of the new Zion: "Arise, shine; for your light has come, and the glory of Yahweh has risen upon you" (60, 1 — 62, 12). Zion is the focal point of existence. All the nations come to her, for Jerusalem is the "City of Yahweh," the "Zion of the Holy One of Israel" (60, 14). The Zion of which the prophet sings transcends

---

9. Eissfeldt, EinlAT 413-419.
10. Pfeiffer, IntrOT 480-481; W. Kessler, TLZ 81 (1956), 335-338 also decides in favor of unity.
11. Robert-Feuillet, IntrAT 567-569 argues for a "collection of various poems."

the bounds of earth: "The sun shall be no more your light by day, nor for brightness shall the moon give light to you by night; but the Lord will be your everlasting light, and your God will be your glory" (60, 19-20). His prophetic eye is fixed already upon the time of final fulfillment. This he can announce with confidence only because the spirit of the Lord rests upon him. He feels himself called like one of the earlier prophets to proclaim God's great plan for the future as a message of salvation to the poor (61, 1ff.). In the synagogue at Nazareth Christ took up a statement from this chapter: "The spirit of the Lord is upon me," and gave it new meaning by referring it to his own mission (Lk 4, 18ff.). The faith in the new and everlasting covenant (61, 8), the faith in a new espousal (62, 4), the faith in a new promised land streaming with every blessing (62, 8ff.) — this is what gives the songs such a triumphant cadence. They must surely have made the hesitant take heart, they must surely have shaken the slothful from their slumber. The difficulties encountered by the repatriates that made their return home and the reconstruction of the temple so impossible a task, must not appear as any reason to despair of God's promise. The songs call for action; the ancient ruins must be rebuilt, the desolate cities must be raised again (60, 4), for in these very ruins there lives the glory of the hidden God who has now chosen Zion for his own and means to stand revealed here. Trito-Isaiah makes Zion a symbol of faith. Zion refers primarily to the temple of Yahweh in Jerusalem, but the concept expands to embrace the unspeakable wonder of a God who condescends to dwell unveiled in the midst of his creation, man. What results is a *complexio oppositorum,* a complex of absolutely irreducible opposites, a situation which continues to prevail in the basic structure of the Church. St. John, in his Book of Revelations, renews this symbolism of the new Zion coming down out of heaven, and it is this description that marks the climax and finale of his prophetic vision (Rev 21, 9ff.).

IN THE SHADOW OF AHURA-MAZDA

Thus speaks King Darius: All these things which I did, I performed under the "shadow" of Ahura-mazda, and Ahura-mazda gave me his support until I had accomplished everything.

From the funeral inscription of Darius in Nakš-i-Rustam (ANET 316).

EIGHTEEN years after the return home the temple had still not been built. The religious enthusiasm engendered by the songs of Zion might indeed strengthen the faith in the future, but there was little they could do to advance the reconstruction of the temple. The times were opposed to such an undertaking. It would require a political as well as a prophetic impulse to get beyond the sorry beginnings.

The great Cyrus was mortally wounded in a border skirmish against the mounted invaders from the north-Iranian steppe. His corpse was carried back to his residence at Pasargada,[1] where it was embalmed, contrary to Iranian practice prior to this time, and interred in the "grave of Cyrus,"[2] which is still preserved. His eldest son and successor Cambyses II (530-522) had already been residing as crown prince in Babylon for eight years. The conquest of Egypt which had been planned by his father had meantime become a political necessity, for the many Greek states along the coast of Asia Minor were absolutely not prepared to regard Persian sovereignty as an unalterable situation,

---

1. The residence of Pasargada is, in its general outlines, characteristic of Cyrus. He was an equestrian leader, and he liked to have wide open territories at his disposal. In Pasargada he had enough room to set up a huge camp for himself and his retinue. His palatial residence lay in the midst of a wild preserve, called Paradise. Outside the park he could devote his time to a series of war games with his knights. Pasargada was his personal royal seat, the holy place of the Achaemenid royal house. Every king had to come here to be legitimately crowned. Echatana, Susa, and Babylon remained the administrative centers of the kingdom. H. H. von der Osten, *Die Welt der Perser*, (1956), 72.
2. *Ibid.*, Illustration 40.

and they found in Egypt a ready ally for their future plans. Moreover, the Phoenician cities were not unwilling to make common
cause with Egypt against the Persian enemies.[3]

Cambyses first forced the Phoenicians to join ranks with him
and thus acquired a powerful fleet. He next set out against Egypt
in a well organized campaign. Under Amasis II (569-525)
Egypt had experienced a long period of peace. Herodotus characterizes him simply as a friend of the Greeks and tells the charming
story of his friendship with Polycrates, tyrant of Samos. Herodotus
also recounts considerable building activity in his capital city
of Sais. But the rise of Persia threatened the very existence of
Egypt. Amasis hoped, with the help of Greek mercenaries and
the support of the Phoenician fleet, to become master of the
situation. He died, however, shortly before the final confrontation.
His son Psammetich III was barely six months in his rule when
the final battle was fought at Pelusium at the very gate to Egypt,
in the year 525. The Persian victory meant the end of Egypt's
history as an independent nation. Cambyses made his way as far
as Memphis, where he put the crown of the Pharaohs on his
head. Psammetich was, at first, well treated as a prisoner; when,
however, he fomented a revolution he was quickly dispatched.[4]
The incompetence and deeds of terror which Herodotus ascribes
to Cambyses have, thanks to the discovery of Egyptian inscriptions, been unmasked as slanderous propaganda. He was,
like Cyrus, a man full of gigantic plans. He even entertained the
ambition of subjugating Kush. His next objective, an attack upon
Carthage, was unsuccessful. In the year 522 he was forced to
march back to Persia, but before he reached Mesopotamia he
met his end in circumstances that have not been adequately explained. The revolution of "Gaumata the Magi" cast its shadow
in advance.

In the famous rock inscription in Behistun (Bagistana)[5] on

---

3. H. Bengtson, *Griechische Geschichte. Handbuch der Altertumswissenschaften*, (1950), 120.
4. A. Scharff, *Geschichte Ägyptens*, 184.
5. Osten, l. c. Illustrations 45, 46.

the "gateway to Asia," [6] Darius describes the turbulent events
of the year 522 B.C. Cambyses, upon his accession to the throne,
had attempted to kill his brother Bardiya, whom he feared as
a rival. "When Cambyses had departed for Egypt, the people
grew hostile towards him, and lies spread throughout the land . . . .
There was a certain man, a magi, whose name was Gaumata . . . .
He told this lie to the people: I am Bardiya, son of Cyrus, brother
of Cambyses. Then all the peoples arose in revolt, and from
Cambyses they went over to him, from Persia, Media, and the other
provinces. He seized the royal power. Afterwards, Cambyses died
by his own hand." — The inscription goes on to say that Gaumata
introduced a reign of terror: "No one dared to say no until I
came . . . . Ahura-mazda gave me his help." Darius undertook
a war with this "counterfeit brother," called Smerdes by the Greeks,
conquered the fortress of Sikauvatish, and killed his opponent.
There then arose a series of nine counterfeit kings, who had to be
met and defeated in a series of 19 campaigns. Eight of these
kings are represented on the relief inscription, all of them in
chains, doing homage to Darius. Above them hovers the victorious
sign of Ahura-mazda, who is proffering Darius the ring of world
dominion.

So much for the official Persian version of Darius' rise to
power. There are some well-justified doubts as to its accuracy.[7]
Gaumata might have been the true Bardiya, really the brother
of Cambyses. Since Cambyses died without issue, Bardiya would
then have been the legitimate successor to the throne. Darius the
son of Hystaspes, a descendant of the older line of the Achaemenids
who traced their origin from Cyrus, took advantage of the opportunity to seize the throne for himself. His public recognition as
legitimate ruler did not take place in the feudal assembly as was

---

6. The cliffs of Behistun lay within the "Gate to Asia," whose occupation
   guaranteed sovereignty over the Fertile Crescent and the highlands of
   Iran. Year in and year out the great caravans made their way along this
   route, carrying the report of Darius' exploits to the most distant countries. *Ibid.*, 76.
7. H. S. Nyberg, *Das Reich der Achämeniden*, HistM III, 74ff.

the custom; it was a divine portent that marked him out as king: of all the horses of his fellow conspirators, his was the first to neigh.[8]

Though it is impossible to have absolute certainty on the actual course of events, one thing is clear: the death of Cambyses marked the collapse of the tightly knit Persian empire. In this turbulent era, when the world was coming apart at the seams, the prophetic word was not wanting. In Babylon, the inevitable center of much of the controversy of this period, the prophet Daniel arises to interpret the events of his time. A faithful witness to the struggle for power might also be reflected in the Book of Judith. And hardly had the fury of war abated when, in Jerusalem, the prophets Haggai and Zechariah called their faltering countrymen to the reconstruction of the temple.

---

8. Osten, l. c. 70.

CHAPTER IV

THE PROPHET DANIEL

THE simplest solution to the difficulties surrounding the Book of Daniel is to regard Daniel as a literary pseudonym for the anonymous writer from the period of the Maccabees. In order to achieve credibility, the writer from the Maccabean era felt the need of some prophetic authority; accordingly, he veils his message in the cloak of the prophet Daniel, who is supposed to have lived during the Exile. The name Daniel has a proper ring to it and a certain literary attractiveness, so to speak, as witness, for example, the discovery of the Daniel epic in Ugarit.[1] Daniel, as a protector of justice and defender of widows and orphans, was a celebrated king of Phoenician legendary antiquity. It might also be that the prophet Ezekiel is referring to this Daniel (Ez 14, 14, 20), since he could obviously not be quoting the prophet Daniel who lived after his own time. "Daniel," like Job and Noah, is one of the great men of God from times of old; he would share nothing with the Book of Daniel excepting for its literary name. Whether the present Book of Daniel is the work of one hand or several hands is a question that cannot be adequately determined.[2] Proving that Daniel is actually a pseudepigraph does nothing to destroy the foundations of our faith.

---

1. A. Jirku, *Kanaanäische Mythen und Epen aus Ras-Schamra-Ugarit*, (1962), 115-137: "Das Epos von Dani-il und seinem Sohne Aqhat."
2. H. L. Ginzberg, *The Composition of the Book of Daniel*, VT 4 (1954),

Why should not this literary genre be capable of divine inspiration, just as it can be in the case of the "wisdom of Solomon"? But it is by no means definitely proven that Daniel is simply the pseudonym of a Maccabean writer. Taking a position against the critical and skeptical solutions to the problem, Eissfeldt eventually reaches the conclusion that we must not exclude the possibility that the book has points of reference with a Daniel who lived in the eastern diaspora in the sixth or fifth century.[3] All the doubts which have been expressed on the subject of the existence of the prophet Daniel have been based primarily upon the historical inaccuracies of the book. Anyone knowledgeable in history could hardly have created such an utter historical confusion as this book represents. "The writer appears to be poorly informed on the course of Babylonian history; Belsazar (5, 2) becomes the son of Nebuchadnezzar, whereas he is actually the son of Nabonidus. Gubaru is replaced by a certain Darius the Mede (6 and 9), a person otherwise unknown to history."[4] It is a tragedy that such annihilating verdicts have been passed on the Book of Daniel. As we shall soon demonstrate, Daniel was well informed on the course of Babylonian history, not only in its general outlines, but down to the least detail, fine points of distinction which, by reason of their very singularity, soon passed from common knowledge, thereby creating the so-called historical chaos in the book. In my opinion, accordingly, it is no longer admissible to characterize Daniel as a pseudepigraph. In this book we have a genuine prophetic writing from the stormy period 522 — 520 B.C., an account which was revived and reinterpreted in the age of the Maccabees.

246-275, distributes the book among five different authors working between the years 292 and 165 B.C. — H. H. Rowley, *The Unity of the Book of Daniel*, HUCA 23 (1952), 233-273, argues for the literary and intellectual unity of the book (Maccabean era). Likewise Pfeiffer, IntrOT 760ff. Robert-Feuillet, IntrAT 700 considers the possibility of a pseudepigraph.

---

3. Eissfeldt, EinlAT 647.
4. Robert-Feuillet, IntAT 698.

A) DANIEL'S INAUGURAL VISION

In the prophets Jeremiah and Ezekiel, the inaugural vision is placed at the beginning of the book; in Isaiah it occurs only in ch. 6; in Daniel, however, it is placed at the end of the book (chs. 10-12). This makes it clear that the book has had a history. Even in the Maccabean reworking of the text, the inaugural vision of the original book is clearly recognizable.

The three chs., 10-12, form a compact unity.[5] They can be compared to the three acts of the great drama of world history, with ch. 11, in the middle, representing the principal act in terms of human judgment, since it is here that the political drama of our world history is unfolded. Heroes and kings, godless men, criminals, liars, captains, political women and children walk across the stage, making so much commotion that one might be tempted to regard this as the entire history. What this chapter presents — and no exegete doubts this fact —is a retrospective analysis of history from the era of the Maccabees, and we shall accordingly treat it in a later section. But this ch. 11 is preceded by ch. 10, which penetrates the veil of mystery surrounding our world and makes it clear that history is made not only by the human agent; angelic powers are at work. The battle must first be decided in the realm of the spiritual before the warring spirits make their way into human affairs, stirring up hostilities among mankind. Chapter 10 acts as a prologue in the world of the supernatural; it presents a concrete picture of the angelic princes. The triumphal conclusion in ch. 12 is also played beyond the limitations of earth. Death has already been passed, and the deceased are arising to their eternal reward or to their eternal shame. This would be the decisive moment in the drama of world history. But between time (ch. 11) and end-time (ch. 12) there remains one inevitable question: "What will be the end of all these dread things?" (12, 6). There is no answer to this question;

---

5. W. Kessler, *Zwischen Gott und Weltmacht. Das Buch Daniel,* CalwK 22 (1956), 155.

it is sealed.[6] As in the Revelations of John, the seals must first be opened, and this can be done only by God. For everything has been written down in the "Book of Truth," [7] which is safe with God in heaven. At a definite moment in history, however, the "word" [8] is revealed to Daniel (10, 1).

The vision that opens is a fearsome one. The introductory words of 10, 1 are abruptly cast into the third person. The first vision of the history of the world is at once a vision of marching columns and endless hosts of warriors. In verse two the narrative suddenly switches to the first person and it has a reference to the temporal setting: "In those days." Those days were days of extreme crisis. Daniel was looking for a religious explanation. For three weeks he had been fasting and praying. On the 24th day of the first month he went to the river, the customary place of prayer during the Exile. His fasting coincided with the Easter season. How could he celebrate a festival in such a tragic time? Then the "word" fell upon his soul with such violent power that it almost overwhelmed him.

1) THE NAMELESS HERALD

Then he saw a "man" (10, 5). He does not give his name. His appearance was not like that of any earthly creature. "He was clothed in linen, and his loins were girded with gold of Uphaz. His body was like beryl, his face like the appearance of lightning, his eyes like flaming torches, his arms and legs like the gleam of burnished bronze, and the sound of his words like the noise of a multitude" (10, 5-6). Daniel alone saw the figure; those with him saw nothing. But such a look of shock emanated from his face that his companions were terrified; they fled away and hid. Daniel was left alone to his overpowering experience. He too fell

---

6. The root ršm (determine, set up, establish) carries the connotative force of irrevocability (Dn 6; 9, 10, 11, 13).
7. Dn 10, 21: the expression "Book of truth" (ketab 'emet) occurs only here.
8. Hebrew dabar can mean either "thing, happening, history," or the "word" in its proper sense of the term. Theodotion translates: logos.

to the ground, forced to his knees by the power of what he beheld, powerless and close to death.[9] A terrible shuddering, not unlike the agony of death, not unlike the pangs of birth, carried him to the very limit of what a man can bear. The state of visionary rapture is very like that of mystic death. Daniel can still hear the voice which is speaking to him; suddenly he feels a hand touching him; he rises from the ground, to his hands and knees. This man has not come to destroy him. Otherwise he could never begin his message with the words: "O Daniel, man greatly beloved" (10, 11, 19).[10] These are the very words that a man who has been prostrated by the terrible power of the vision needs to hear first. The apparition was not destined to be his death, but evidence of a special privilege; hence the greeting: "Peace be with you" (10, 19): "Do not be afraid" (10, 12). From his hands and knees he rises to his feet, to speak face to face with this nameless messenger. But there can be no dialogue between this fiery creature and the prophet, earthling and mortal. A creature like a man (10, 16) touches Daniel's lips, and then the unequal dialogue is free to begin.

This is not the first description of the appearance of a supraterrestrial being. Whenever a creature from the hereafter makes his presence felt in this world, the human agent always experiences it as an invasion from without (*tremendum mysterium*). Moses was afraid to look upon the face of God (Ex 3, 6); Joshua threw himself upon the ground when the prince of the hosts of Yahweh came to meet him (Josh 5, 14); the parents of Samson were seized with dread when the angel of Yahweh made his way towards heaven from the sacrificial flames before their very eyes (Jg 13, 20); they were all afraid that they would have to die. A similar fear of death came upon the prophet Gideon (Jg 6, 23); Isaiah

---

9. The text speaks of losing the senses four times (8a, 8b, 15, 17): the breath of life escapes him (17).

10. In MT: *'iš hᵃmudôt;* LXX ἄνθρωπος ἐλεεινός; i.e., "you are a man to be sympathized with": Theodotion: ἀνὴρ ἐπιθυμιῶν "man of desiring"; Vulgate: *vir desideriorum,* "man of desirings." The Hebrew root *hamad* means "to desire, to find pleasure in something"; *hᵃmudôt* is the passive participle, feminine plural with the meaning of the neuter; hence, "something in which pleasure has been found"; literally "man of favor"; equivalent in meaning to "you favored man." Cf. the Angel's salutation to the Blessed Virgin (Lk 1, 28).

crys: "Woe to me, I am lost" (Is 6, 3). The closest parallel to Daniel is to be found in the case of Ezekiel; in his vision of the chariot and the cherubim he fell to the earth as if struck dead; he was made to realize the full misery and impoverishment of the human condition, what it means to be a "son of man," a creature made from clay and earth. It takes an express command from God before the dialogue can begin: "Son of man, stand upon your feet; I want to speak with you" (Ez 2, 1). The nameless messenger in the Book of Daniel is another in this series of divine apparitions. In the course of Old Testament history it is, accordingly, not surprising for a supernatural being to approach a human person.[11] What is new is the explicit detail of description and the nature of his mission.

2)   THE "PRINCES OF THE KINGDOMS"

The most difficult verses to analyze are Dn 10, 13, 20, 21; 11, 1b. The nameless messenger whose appearance has brought Daniel to the very portals of death, explains why he makes his appearance only on the 21st day, that is, at the end of a three-weeks' prayer and fasting, and not at its beginning. The "prince of the kingdom of Persia" (*sar malkût pāras,* 10, 13) had been trying to hinder him. It would follow that this "prince of the Persians" must have been a being equal in power to the messenger himself. A similar "prince" (*sar*) was placed in charge of the kingdom of the Greeks. Both these princes are hostile towards the nameless herald. He is, however, assisted by Michael, one of the first "princes" (10, 13). Does this mean to say that the political situation on earth is represented by a similar balance among the spiritual princes in the world beyond?[12] This faith in "princes of the nations, supraterrestrial beings who determine the fates of their nations, is nothing new in the Book of Daniel. The roots of this faith go back into the pre-Exilic era. In war, according to the concepts of the Ancient Near East, it is not only kings and peoples, but also their gods who are conquered. Isaiah

---

11. The account of the Annunciation in Luke exhibits the same characteristics, quite void of any humiliation. Mary, too, must have been deeply shaken by the apparition of the angel: hence the words, "Do not be afraid, highly favored one."
12. The conception of "angels of the nations" occurs elsewhere as well:

asks whether the gods of the nations have been able to deliver them from the hand of the Assyrians (Is 34, 10ff.). What is new in the case of Daniel is the fact that, unlike the ancient prophets, he does not call the pagan gods by name; he refers to them in general terms as "prince," person of power.

Thus, corresponding to the map of earth, upon which the various political powers are clearly delineated, there is also a map in the spiritual world. Scripture does not deal lightly with these creatures; the Bible reckons with their real power. Such a "prince" has been placed in charge of the kingdom of Persia (and a second over the kingdom of the Greeks); but Israel's "prince" is Michael.

The commentaries on this passage like to speak of "guardian angels for the nations." This interpretation, however, does not strike at the essence of the question. The "princes" are not serving spirits,[13] they are the real figures of authority (*imperatores*) of the people who are their subjects. In much the same manner, the ancient rulers of countries never thought of themselves as the servants of their people. Moreover, guardian angels, by reason of their nature and their mission, would have to be good spirits. But in the present text, both the "prince" of Persia and the "prince" of Greece are united in hostile opposition to the nameless messenger of revelation as well as "prince" Michael. This would probably mean that demonic powers are manifest in these "princes." [14] In itself, the belief in angelic princes is im-

---

"When the most high gave to the nations their inheritance, when he separated the sons of men, he fixed the bounds of the peoples according to the number of the sons of God" (Dt 32, 8). Instead of "sons of God," MT reads "sons of Israel," which is already a diminution of the original thought. Also in the apocalypse of Isaiah: "On that day the Lord will punish the host of heaven, in heaven, and the kings of the earth, on the earth" (Is 24, 21). Even more clearly in Jesus Sirach: "He appointed a ruler for every nation, but Israel is the Lord's own portion." The same interpretation applies to the 70 shepherds of the nations in the Book of Henoch (89, 59ff.) — probably a development of the list of nations in Genesis.

---

13. Only in Heb 1, 14, does the serving character of the Christian angels come to the fore.

14. This interpretation is confirmed by the Gospel of John. Jesus has

mediately derivable from the nature of the Old Testament concept of God. Yahweh is never represented as a lonely God; he is always surrounded by a heavenly court of angels. That these angels represent not simply a disorganized throng, but rather a disciplined army is evident from the divine title "Lord God of Hosts" (*Yahweh s^ebaôt*).

Since, however, the faith in angels received its fullest expression only during the Exile or in the post-Exilic era, it has often been maintained that it develops from a confrontation with the religion of the Persian Empire, if indeed it is not entirely derived from that source. But such an over-simplified formula cannot solve the problem. The only Iranian sources for this era are, once again, the Gathas of Zarathustra.[15] In reading these songs we are struck by the fact that the prophetic singer refers to the divinity sometimes in the singular and sometimes in the plural. This fact has given some weight to the opinion that Zarathustra is not a monotheist. This argument found further support from those two passages in the Gathas where the prophet addresses not only Ahuramazda, but also the other "Ahuras" or princes of heaven (30, 9 and 31, 4). The problem is further complicated by the fact that Zarathustra as a poet frequently prefers to make no distinction between personalities and concepts. As a result, they all appear in his work summed up together as immortal beings who form a unity with Ahura-mazda. An example of this is to be found in the final strophe of the first song (29, 11): "Where are you, divine right, good sense, the kingdom? Receive me then graciously, you immortal, you all-wise." — A later age gave the name "holy immortal ones," Amesa Spenta's, to these beings, six in number, and with Ahura-mazda as the seventh, made all of them heavenly beings, divinities. This development does, of course, form part of the unhappy story of the interpolation of the Zarathustra faith which eventually led to the Zoroastrianism of the era of the Sassanids (224-650 A.D.).

The proper interpretation of the Gathas depends upon our ability to distinguish between personal heavenly beings and abstract poetic personifications when we explain the nature of the "immortal ones." In addition to Ahura-mazda, the following "immortal ones" are frequently named: Holy Spirit (*spenta mainyu*), good sense (*vohu manah*), obedience (*sraoša*), right order (*aša*), kingdom (*chšathra*), piety (*armaiti*),

---

taken up battle with the prince of this world (12, 31). He has broken his power and cast him from his position of power. Cf. also Jn 14, 30; 16, 11; Lk 11, 21ff.; Eph 2, 2.

15. W. Hinz, *Zarathustra*, 102-105 serves as the basis for the following.

healing and immortality (*hauratât* and *amrtât*). — This enumeration of the heavenly spirits must be completed by the powers of darkness; these are the "evil spirits" (*aka mainyu*), the "delirium of death" (*aêšma*).

Of all these "immortals," the following are represented as persons in the Gathas: Ahura-mazda, the creator of all individualities; next, the "holy spirit," the "good sense" and the "evil spirit"; perhaps also "obedience" as the brotherly companion of the angel of revelation, "good sense," and finally the "intoxication of death" (*aêšma*) as the primordial demon and the chief tempter [16] together with his master, the "evil spirit" (*aka mainyu*). All the other "problem words" in the Gathas refer, however, not to real beings, but only to concepts; they are not individuals, but mere abstractions which the poet Zarathustra frequently enough personifies. Kingdom, divine right, piety, sensitivity, remuneration, visitation — no matter how frequently they appear as speaking or acting in the Gathas, they are and remain mere concepts within the prophet's edifice of didactic poetry.

It would seem to follow that there are undeniable similarities between Zarathustra and Daniel. For both, the history of this world is not simply a political struggle; it is even more a contest between the spirit princes. For Daniel, standing in the biblical tradition, faith in the existence of heavenly powers goes without saying; that this faith in personal, immortal heavenly beings surrounding the presence of the supreme God also clearly shows in the case of Zarathustra is, for the Iranian culture, a new concept. Both prophets think of the heavenly beings, not as being removed far beyond the stars, but rather as operative within the confines of earthly history, taking part in the determination of human history. The classical passage for Zarathustra's concept of history is the third Gatha.[17] It is here that history is interpreted as a contest between two spirits, good and evil. When these two spirits first came into hostile contact, they created life and death. The spirit of deceit accomplishes evil, while the holy spirit effects divine right. Both spirits court humankind. A most wretched existence awaits the servants of deceit, while the best sense and judgment awaits those who believe rightly. At the end of history the kingdom (*chšathra*) of Ahura-mazda will dawn (3, 8). Then the realm of the slaves of deceit will collapse (3, 10). Damnation and suffering will be the lot of the servants of deceit, while blessing and paradise await those whose faith is right (3, 11). In their eagerness to achieve this end, the orthodox constantly call upon God and his angels for help in the decisive battle: "Come, Ahura-mazda, and all you princes of heaven with all your allies" (3, 9).

---

16. Cf. the demon Asmodaeus in the Book of Tobit.
17. Translation from Hinz, *loc. cit.*, 169-171.

The one God and all-wise Lord, the heavenly immortal princes, the evil spirits and their attacks, the kingdom to come, the covenant, the confrontation and the final judgment — are these concepts which a student of the Book of Daniel can simply pass by without mention? One might almost get the impression that Daniel was called to be a prophet in order to take up the battle with the Zarathustrian concept of a God over the kingdom. The angel of revelation in the inaugural vision had to struggle explicitly with the "prince of Persia" before he had free access to Daniel. The vision is a more compact unit if we excise the Maccabean interpolation "and also the prince of Greece." On one side we have the "prince of Persia," and on the other side the angel of revelation and the angelic prince Michael. Both are concerned with the kingdom to come. In his inaugural vision, Daniel is given the certain knowledge that the kingdom of God which prevails will not be cast in Zarathustrian concepts; it will be the kingdom of Yahweh of Hosts. The figure of the "great prince Michael will arise" (12, 1).

3) DATE OF THE INAUGURAL VISION

The Maccabean interpretation of this Scripture is clear from the finds in the Dead Sea Scrolls. It was not the historical past that interested them, but rather their own time of crisis. Accordingly, they read a verse of Scripture in reference to the present time, and always added an interpretative note: "That is, that means." This style of Scripture interpretation has been called *pešer*, exegesis or reinterpretation.[18] In the prophetic texts discovered at Qumran it is always possible to distinguish clearly between original text and interpretation. In the Book of Daniel the two elements have become so interwoven that they are difficult to distinguish. Upon closer examination, however, one can hear the ancient prophecy of Daniel on the one hand and its Maccabean interpretation on the other.

The nucleus of the three vision chapters is formed, in my

---

18. The most important *pešer* from Qumran is the commentary on Habakkuk. Eissfeldt, EinlAT 813-816 gives full bibliography.

opinion, by the inaugural vision of the prophet. It is constructed on a pattern similar to the call of the prophet Ezekiel. The account is introduced by a dating formula, "on the 24th day of the 1st month" (10, 4). The year in which the vision took place is mentioned in verse 11, 1a, a sentence whose content and continuity have been destroyed: "In the first year of Darius the Mede." [19] Since this Darius the Mede is none other than Darius the Great, as we shall later demonstrate, we can date the vision May 7, 521 B.C., an era in which the Persian Empire was on the brink of complete dissolution, and every thinking man would have to ponder the significance of "these terrible experiences" (12, 6). Daniel was attempting to control this crisis from a religious point of vantage. Like Ezekiel, he made his way to the river to pray (10, 4). It was there that this nameless creature of fire appeared to him and all but annihilated him. It was there that he received the prophetic consecration. The heavenly being touched his lips (10, 16). The new element in this revelation consists in the fact that Daniel recognizes demonic and heavenly powers at work behind the political struggles of his day: but the demonic powers cannot possibly withstand the kingdom and power of God, and surely they cannot prevail against it. The champion for the people of God is Michael, one of the first princes. When he asks how long this catastrophic period must last, the prophet receives an answer which is for us a riddle: "A time, two times, and half a time" (12, 7), which can be interpreted as half of the sacred number seven. Is this to be understood as meaning that the history of the world is in midcourse and rapidly approaching the end appointed by God? From this inaugural vision, Daniel derives the triumphal consciousness that the people of God is not alone and abandoned at this crisis of history; God comes to their aid through his heavenly warriors.

This inaugural vision was read by a man living in the Maccabean era, and he read it as a Hebrew concerned with the crisis of his own day. Accordingly he reinterpreted the traditional text,

---

19. The dating "in the third year of Cyrus" (10, 1) is, in my opinion, the work of the Maccabean editor and has no historical value.

and the inaugural vision, which now stands with only slight re-touchings in chs. 10 and 12, was torn from its original place. The whole of ch. 11 is a retrospective analysis of history, from the Maccabean point of view, and we shall treat it accordingly, in the section devoted to the "age of Hellenism." [20]

B) THE SEVENTY WEEKS OF YEARS (Dn 9)

As the reader might now suspect, the content of Daniel 9 is divided into two strata, the ancient prophecy of Daniel himself and its Maccabean re-interpretation. The distinction between the two strata is not difficult, since the text expressly introduces the interpretation of the numbers (*pešer*) with the exclamation "Know therefore and understand" (9, 25).

1) DARIUS THE MEDE

The prophecy of Daniel on the 70 years has the same date as his inaugural vision: "In the first year of Darius, the son of Ahasuerus, by birth a Mede, who became king over the realm of the Chaldeans" (9, 1). Previous commentators have been unable to evaluate this dating. Noetscher [21] decides simply that the problem is without a solution. The most serious problem has been posed by the person of Darius the Mede.[22] In my opinion, this dating formula is based upon an historical situation which, by reason of its strange and short-lived character, was quickly forgotten. We must return briefly to our previous discussion of the confusion attendant upon Darius' accession to power. Within a period of two years, 522-520, Darius, according to the in-scription at Behistun, had to capture nine kings and fight 19 battles. Among these, two kings of Babylon are mentioned, both of whom claimed the title *Nabukudurriussur* (Nebuchadnezzar). Historians refer to them as Nebuchadnezzar II, the destroyer of

---

20. Cf. below, pp. 231ff.
21. EB III, 638.
22. H. Rowley, *Darius the Mede and the four World Empires in the Book of Daniel*, (1935). Cf. RB (1936), 130.

Jerusalem, Nebuchadnezzar III, and Nebuchadnezzar IV. Although both of them could have reigned for no longer than half a year, it must have seemed for a while that the Babylonian kingdom was destined to rise again in all its ancient glory. Nebuchadnezzar III laid claim to the throne of Babylon from October 6 to December 18, 522. His private name was Nidintu-Bel. Darius regarded him as an upstart and declared war against him. On December 13, 522, he dealt him a first defeat along the Tigris, and on December 18 he all but annihilated his army at Zazannu. On December 22, 512, he made his victorious entry into Babylon and became "king over the kingdom of the Kasdim" (Chaldeans, Dn 9, 1). Darius' throne in Babylon rested, however, upon a most shaky foundation. His first Babylonian kingship lasted from December 22, 522, to September 8, 521. It was at this point that Nebuchadnezzar IV (Araka) seized power and, as the son of Nabonidus, which he claimed to be, attempted to rebuild the Babylonian kingdom. Once again Darius marched from Babylon, this time to Media, in order to put down the revolution which had broken out under the leadership of Fravartis (*Hšatrita*). The decisive confrontation took place in the battle of Kurundni on May 7, 521. The victory was such a surprising one that it is certainly not surprising that his contemporaries gave the victor the honorific epithet "the Mede." [23] It is this title that explains the dating formula in Daniel. It was only in the Maccabean era, when the historical circumstances were no longer understood, that this victorious title "the Mede" was understood as a genealogical reference, "by birth a Mede," with the result that Darius becomes the legendary son of Ahasuerus. The following table explains the dates for the turbulent years:

Cambyses' death, rebellion all over the Persian Empire	July 522
Bardiya's rebellion in Persia	Mar. 11 522
Conquered by Darius, executed	Sept. 22 522

---

23. Just as G. Julius Caesar (not the great Caesar, but the adoptive son of Emperor Tiberius) actually did not become a German by receiving the surname "Germanicus" upon his successful completion of the campaign against the Germans: "Darius the Mede" means simply Darius who triumphed over the Medes.

Nebuchadnezzar III, revolt in Babylon .... Oct. 6 522
    Conquered by Darius, executed .... Dec. 18 522
Darius' first reign in Babylon .... Dec. 22 522 — Sept. 8 521
    Year of accession .... Dec. 22 522 — April 13 521
    First year of reign .... from April 14 521
Median revolt under Fravartis .... May 7 521
    Daniel's call .... May 7 521
    Prophecy of the weeks of years .... between May 7 and Sept. 8 521
Nebuchadnezzar IV, revolt in Babylon .... Aug. 25 521
    Conquered by Darius, executed .... Nov. 27 521
Darius' second reign in Babylon .... from Jan. 25 520
    Second year of reign .... April 3 520 — Mar. 22 519

These dates are based upon the famous inscription at Behistun, the work of Darius himself, as well as Babylonian sources.[24] The scant attention paid to these Babylonian tablets has kept the chronology of the Book of Daniel from being properly understood.

2) THE MESSAGE OF THE ANGEL GABRIEL

Not every passage in Scripture has the same urgency of meaning for every era. In the turbulent years 522-520 not only was Daniel at work in Babylon, but the prophet Zechariah was at work in Jerusalem with the 70 years' prophecy of Jeremiah (Jer 25, 11; 29, 10; Zc 1, 12; 2 Ch 36, 2, 1).[25] In both cases there is a clear and redeeming awareness that the crisis of the 70 years will come to an end. The world empires had begun to totter; surely the hour of God's own kingdom must be approaching. Daniel combines prayer with his study of Scripture. In a most moving prayer of penance (9, 4-19)[26] he confesses the whole

---

24. G. Brunner, *Der Nabuchodonosor des Buches Judith*, (1959) — the critical edition of the Behistun inscription is in Weissbach, *Die Keilinschriften der Achämeniden*, (Leipzig 1901). Brunner presents further literature on the problem. The precise dating is taken from Parker-Dubberstein, *Babylonian Chronology 626 B.C. — A.D. 75*, Brown University Studies, vol. XIX (1956).

25. Cf. Vol. IV, pp. 332ff.

26. The prayer of penance forms a literary unity. It has many points of contact with Solomon's prayer of dedication in the Temple (2 Ch 6; 1 K 8) as well as the prayers of Ezra and Nehemiah (Ezr 9; Ne 1).

crisis of his day: The land is laid waste, the people carried off, without king, without sacrifice, the temple still lying in ruins. Sin, guilt, and sacrilege could only call down God's punishment. But is there no end to the suffering? Are the 70 years of crisis to continue forever? It is in the midst of this prayer that the angel Gabriel appears with the good tidings of salvation.

"While I was speaking in prayer, the man Gabriel, whom I had seen in the vision at the first, came to me in swift flight at the time of the evening sacrifice" (9, 21). He announces to Daniel the good tidings of the end of the 70 years of crisis: "The 70 years, yea the 70 [27] against your people and against the holy city are at an end.[28] (The time has come) to finish the transgression, to put an end to sin, and to atone for iniquity, to bring in everlasting righteousness, to seal both vision and prophet, and to anoint a most holy place" (9, 24). Zechariah proclaimed the same message: The 70 years of wrath are passed; Yahweh turns again to Jerusalem full of pity (Zc 1, 12-17).

The angel Gabriel announces the beginning of a new era of salvation for Jerusalem ("eternal justice"); he points to a new rebuilding of the temple ("to anoint a most holy place"); this promise seals the doom of the threatened prophecy of a 70

Still, it does bear such a personal stamp that it can hardly be ascribed to anyone other than Daniel; it is the negative counterpart to the positive message of the angel.

---

27. If the Hebrew consonants *šb'ym šb'ym* are read without any foregone conclusions, one more naturally presumes that they are to be vocalized in the same way. Accordingly, I have read it as "seventy, seventy." The locution appears to involve emphasis: "The seventy, aye the seventy are past and gone." The reference to years is obvious to any reader if only because the context is referring to Jeremiah's prophecy of years.

28. The current translation "70 (weeks of years) are established," is far from certain; it can appeal only to the LXX. The Hebrew verb *ḥtk*, which occurs only in this passage, means originally "cut off," and in a transferred sense, "decide, establish." The basic meaning "to cut off, to be at an end," is to be found in Theodotion, in the Syrian and Latin translations (Vulg: *abbreviatae sunt*). There are several other readings in the critical apparatus in J. Ziegler, *Septuaginta*, vol. XVI, pars 2, (Göttingen 1954), 189.

years' crisis. God's mercy will triumph over sin, guilt, and sacrilege, all of which are thus finished, "put end to, atoned for, sealed." Daniel, like Trito-Isaiah, proclaims a "year of grace and liberation" (Is 61, 2). Words like these might well have been destined to comfort the Jews who had still remained in Babylon after Cyrus' edict of liberation (539) and strengthened their faith in Zion. The first party to return home accomplished only a sorry beginning of their task. The Temple still lay desolate; the nation had become a mockery among its neighbors. Daniel's prophecy of the 70 years thus carries the same message as the prophets Haggai and Zechariah. With the latter he shares the privilege of having the gospel of the salvation proclaimed to him through the agency of an angel. In this final epoch of prophecy, the prophetic vision breaks through to include angels and devils; God's kingdom and dominion is established not only on earth but also in the spirit world. Thus the prophecy of 70 years in the Book of Daniel is carried back to its original source. It offers an answer to the burning questions of the day, the collapse of the Persian empire. In the crisis of the Maccabean era, the prophecy is taken up once again, and the numbers are reinterpreted as we shall explain below.[29]

C) SON OF MAN (Dn 7)

"Daniel 7 is just as important for the history of biblical revelation as it is laden with difficult questions. It is this chapter, in the midst of which we find the testimony of the son of man, that has exercised such a far-reaching effect upon Jesus' own preaching on the subject of his mission and his majesty. Thus, it touches upon a central mystery of biblical theology." [30] Here too, the ancient prophecy of Daniel must be clearly distinguished from its reinterpretation in the Maccabean era. The Maccabean rereading does not involve any falsification or any departure from the revelation made to the prophet Daniel; it signals, on the

---

29. Cf. above, pp. 363ff.
30. W. Kessler, *Zwischen Gott und Weltmacht*, CalwK 22 (1956), 91.

contrary, the application of the traditional body of faith to a new era, which cried for direction and comfort. The living source, from which the "church" of the Maccabean era drew, was Sacred Scripture. That their interpretation of Scripture is itself Sacred Scripture is made possible only by the fact that one and the same Holy Spirit is the source of light and illumination to both, to the prophet and to his interpreters.

I) *The Prophecy of the Son of Man in Daniel*

In a night vision, Daniel beholds the sea whipped up by the four winds, and four creatures arising from it. From the very beginning the vision is addressed to universal proportions; four is the number of the four directions, the whole world. The singular point here is the fact that four land animals are rising from the sea, something that is possible only in a dream vision. We recognize, accordingly, that the vision must be dealing in symbols. Now in ancient biblical and Ancient Near Eastern think-ing,[31] the sea is the symbol of uprising and rebellion against God (Is 17, 12; Jer 5, 22; Ps 46, 4, 7; 89, 10). Thus, the four creatures who rise from the sea must be hostile towards God.

The first three beasts have recognizable names: lion, leopard, and bear; the fourth is without a name but it is the most terrible of all predatory beasts. As predatory beasts, all of them together are hostile to man, especially feared by shepherds. The lion is the first to rise; he has the wings of an eagle, symbolic of his nature which is capable of storming the skies.[32] The bear was raised up only on one side. Is this some indication of its lesser power? The three ribs between its jaws testify to its insatiable appetite. The ribs are the last remnants of his prey: he is an in-satiable predator, always hungry for a fresh kill. The leopard has four wings and four heads, an impossibility in the animal world, but a perfect image for his dominion over the four ends of the earth. The fourth beast is a monster, similar to no known animal. It has great iron teeth and paws of bronze, symbolic of its

---

31. Cf. Enuma-elish epic (Babylon); Baal's fight with the sea (Ugarit), Vol. I, pp. 183ff.
32. Cf. Jer 50, 17; Ezek 17, 5; Is 14, 13.

power to trample and devour everything in its path. All four creatures are given power. From whom? From God! Their devouring and trampling and predatory attacks are thus directed by the will of God (Hos 13, 7).

"This scene of wild confusion in the world below with the monstrous creatures rising from the turbulent sea is contrasted by our author with a heavenly scene of sublime and perfect repose. Verses 9, 10, 13, 14, are set in the rhythm of poetry; thus the very language takes on something of the measured and lofty tone that is characteristic of the world of heaven." [33] The scene in heaven is described as an act in progress: Daniel beholds God's throne hall. Thrones have been set up in the judgment hall. The "ancient of days" (*'attîq yômîm* 7, 9) appears, a venerable and aged old man, supreme judge and king of heaven. But his throne is no ordinary throne. It consists of flames of fire, and it has fiery wheels, like the cherub throne in Ezekiel. Not only is the throne made of fire, however, but a stream of fire emanates from it (cf. Ps 50, 3, 4). Fire is the element of God by way of contrast to the sea and its godless monsters. Surrounding the throne are the hosts of serving beings, thousands upon thousands. Then the judges take their place and the books are opened in which everything which has ever happened is duly recorded. The beasts have been given power only for a limited time; the power is now revoked. Who shall inherit it?

Then there appears upon the clouds of heaven the son of man; more properly we should say a creature who was "like a son of man" (*kᵉbar 'ᵉnaš* 7, 13). Who is he? For it is to him that is given the dominion formerly entrusted to the beasts. His kingdom is an everlasting kingdom that shall not ever be destroyed.

Daniel cannot understand the enigmatic drama which unfolds in his vision. He turns to one of the creatures standing around the throne (cf. Zc 4, 4) and asks for an interpretation (*pešer!* 1, 16). The angel's answer is not addressed to individual details; it paints only the broader outlines. The four powerful animals are the four kings who will rise upon earth.[34] After the beasts

---

33. Kessler, l. c. 95 .

34. Dn 7, 17 reads *malkim,* "kings," rather than *malk wan,* "kingdoms."

have been deprived of power, the "saints of the most high" (*qad-diśê 'elyônîn* 7, 18) will receive the kingdom (*malkûtā*). Daniel needed to hear nothing further. The magnitude of what he had seen in vision and symbol — the kingdom of God would replace the empires of this world — that he himself and all who were given to despair in those terrible days could find comfort sufficient in this faith. The gates of hell would never prevail against the foundations of God.

II) *The Maccabean Interpretation*

In the Maccabean crisis, the foundation laid by God in Jerusalem was fighting for its very life. The interpreter of this passage recognizes the traits of the terrible fourth beast in the godless persecutor Antiochus Epiphanes. It is against this ruler that he sets his sights and directs his reinterpretation. The textual development is immediately obvious. Verse 8 says this very explicitly upon the appearance of the fourth beast: "And I saw, that is, I became aware," that among the ten horns a little horn arose, and before it three other horns were plucked up by the roots. This horn had eyes like the eyes of a man and a mouth speaking great things. Verse 11 describes the judgment upon this blasphemous beast. Verses 19-27 all refer to the Maccabean persecutions. The little horn [35] represents the climax of rebellion against God. It does violence to the holy ones of the Most High, lays violent hands upon the holy ordinances, the days and festivals and times. God will countenance this for a while; but the violence of this horn is circumscribed as to time and hour: "A time and two times and half a time" (25, c); that is, for three and a half years the holy ones of the Most High will be delivered to the fury of this horn, and then will occur God's sentence of judgment. The horn will be once and for all annihilated. The final phase will then follow, the delivery of power into the hands of the holy ones of the Most High. A kingdom of

---

35. S. Morenz, *Das Tier mit den Hörnern, ein Beitrag zu Dn 7, 7ff.,* ZAW 63 (1951), 105-114. The kings on Seleucid coins are represented as having horns!

everlasting duration shall arise, and all earthly powers will be subject to it.

III) *Consequences in Biblical Theology*

The narrative of the vision of the son of man appears to be so clear and simple as to need no further interpretation. Yet this is clearly not the case.. The angel says neither who the creature is who appears as a son of man nor what the concrete interpretation of the four creatures is. Are they kings or kingdoms following each other in succession, or do they occur all at the same time? Accordingly, we must attempt to understand these ideas from the chapter and indeed the book as a whole.

1) THE SON OF MAN

Although Daniel uses the expression "son of man" as a comparison, the phrase has given rise to various investigations in the field of religious history. Did Daniel find this concept in the pagan world about him, or is it a borrowing from the early prophetic literature?

a. *Mythical derivation*: In the time between the two World Wars scholars attempted to derive the biblical concept of the son of man from the so-called Iranian first man.[36] Although there can be no objection on the basis of influence from the world outside the Bible, still, with respect to an Iranian derivation, we must be very skeptical in view of our only fragmentary knowledge of Iranian religion at the time of Daniel. The idea of the Iranian first man is a clearly comprehensible concept only in the Manichean writings which have absolutely nothing to do with Daniel. According to these sources, the two primordial principles of light and darkness are involved in a hostile conflict. "With respect to this threat, the father of goodness is, precisely by reason of his goodness, deprived of every medium for counter-action; he decides not only to set up the eons who surround him for his defense, but to fight for himself. He emanates a first figure from himself, the mother of life. This mother then projects

---

36. Especially, Bousset, *Kyrios Christos*, (Göttingen 1921); Gressmann, *Die Erlösererwartung in den östlichen Religionen*, (Gütersloth 1938); Reitzenstein-Schaeder, *Studien zum antiken Synkretismus aus Iran und Griechenland*, (Leipzig 1926).

from herself the first or primordial man. This creature then proceeds to the frontier with his five sons (air, wind, light, water, fire), where he is overcome by darkness and his sons are devoured by the demons. This mission and this defeat are the beginning of the commingling which then takes place. The primordial or first man is nothing more than an hypostasis of the father of the universe, God himself. The primordial man or God who has fallen into this commingled state can be redeemed by being delivered from the commingling." [37] These statements are sufficient to demonstrate the lack of continuity between the biblical and the Iranian concept of the "son of man."

Accordingly, Rost [38] turned to the Canaanite backgrounds and attempted to adduce points of reference from this source. From the Ugarit epics we know that the ancient god El retired and handed over his power to the youthful Ba'al. The son of man in Daniel would be thus simply a fragment from an ancient myth. But, granted the inexorable struggle of our prophet against the Ba'al cult it is hardly conceivable that precisely such a Ba'al myth could have figured prominently in his concept of the son of man. The dissimilarities are simply too great.

b. *Son of man and Ezekiel*: Feuillet [39] has attempted to derive the concept of the son of man from the traditional corpus of biblical literature. In this attempt he falls back upon Ezekiel's description of the apparition of the majesty of Yahweh, where that appearance of Yahweh is described as similar to that of a man: "Seated above the likeness of a throne was a likeness as it were of a human form (*'ādam*)" (Ez 1, 26). The son of man in Daniel would thus be nothing more than the visible apparition of the invisible God. If, then, the power of kingship is entrusted to this son of man, this means simply that God himself takes over the rule. The kingdom of the son of man would be, accordingly, identical with the kingdom of God himself. — It must, however, be objected that in Daniel's description there is always a sharp distinction between God and son of man. "The dominion has been given to him" (7, 14). By whom if not by God? Moreover, the son of man approaches the ancient of days, a further clear expression of their separate identities.

c. *Son of man and wisdom*: Coppens [40] attempts to demonstrate at

---

37. H. Ch. Puech, *Die Religion des Mani, Christus und die Religionen der Erde*, II, 526.

38. L. Rost, *Zur Deutung des Menschensohnes in Dn 7, Gott und die Götter, Festgabe für E. Fascher* (1958), 41-43.

39. A. Feuillet, *Le Fils de l'Homme de Daniel et la tradition biblique*, RB (1953), 192.

40. J. Coppens, *Le Messianisme Sapiential et les Origines Littéraires de Fils de l'Homme Daniélique*, VT Suppl. 3 (1953), 33-41.

least a relationship between the personification of wisdom and the son of man. Even though it is difficult to determine whether or not Hokmah (wisdom) is an independent person or a personification of the wisdom of God, at all events wisdom stands very close to God and thus immediately subject to God, very like the son of man. — On the other hand, we must also admit that the typical salvation-history mission of wisdom is entirely lacking in the case of the son of man; accordingly, the concept of the son of man cannot possibly be derived from the idea of wisdom. Such a singular concept must have a spontaneous origin.

d. *Son of man and angel of Yahweh*: Stier [41] proposes a quite different methodology which leads closer to the objective. It is not in the wisdom literature, but in the figure of the *mal'ak yahweh*, the angel of Yahweh, that the model for the son of man is to be sought. This figure is certainly the form of apparition, literally the "mission" of Yahweh, and thus identical with God. There are sufficient passages in which the *mal'ak* is clearly distinct from Yahweh. It was he who led Israel out of Egypt, who functions as judge and avenger over his people (Ex 23, 21; Jg 2, 2-3). He is called the "prince of the host of Yahweh" (*sar sebā' Yahweh*). He appeared to Joshua as a human warrior (Jos 5, 13). Stier is of the opinion that the *mal'ak* is the biblical counterpart of the office of *vizier,* a concept familiar throughout the Ancient Near East to describe the position of the friend and representative of the supreme king and the gods, charged with the office of accomplishing and making possible their supreme will. — This approach does indeed lay some understandable foundation for the religious history interpretation of the *mal'ak,* but there is no eschatological trait to argue for the existence of a direct relation. In Daniel's time the figure of the angel of Yahweh already seems to have lost much of its popularity. Perhaps Is 63, 9 is to be understood as a polemic against over-stressing this figure: "It is not a messenger or the *mal'ak,* but Yahweh himself who has redeemed you." If this is the case, then it is the prince Michael and not the son of man who is the genuine successor of the bold biblical concept of *mal'ak yahweh;* for just like the *mal'ak* in times of old, it is now Michael who fights in behalf of the people of God.

e. *The son of man as "prince" of the final kingdom*: Already from the inaugural vision (ch. 10) we are familiar with the great nameless "man" (*'iš*) who had to fight with the prince (*sar*) of Persia. He is the "son of man" (10, 16: *ben-'ādam*), who touches the smitten Daniel with his hand and raises him up; he is the "lord" (*'adon, kyrios,* 12, 8) who gives a message re-

41. Fr. Stier, *Gott und seine Engel,* (Münster 1934), 61.

garding the ultimate fate of the people of God; he is the "man" (*'ādam,* 8, 16) who gives Gabriel the command to preach. This would lead to the likely conclusion that the son of man is to be numbered among the "princes" (*sārîm*). Various spirit powers (*sārîm*) have been established over the kingdoms of earth, but the "prince" (*sar*) of the kingdom composed of all peoples, tongues, and nations, a kingdom which shall have no end, is the son of man. His kingdom is not identical with Israel, over which Michael has been established as prince. Here we clearly touch upon something new, something that cannot be derived from the past, something that depends directly upon revelation.

This son of man comes upon the clouds of heaven, which regularly form the path for Yahweh. All nations, tongues, and peoples do homage to him. The Aramaic text employs the verb *yiphlᵉhûn,* which is otherwise used for the adoration paid to God in general. The son of man in Daniel is, accordingly, a creature standing very close to God, exalted above all the other princely powers, the ruler of the everlasting kingdom at the end of all earthly kingdoms. What is new in this figure with respect to the ancient messianic promises?

The Messiah of the older prophets is also a gift from God (Is 9, 5), filled with the spirit of God (Is 11, 2), chosen by God (Jer 23, 5), and operating in the power of God's spirit. But the connection with the house of David has lent a dynastic stamp to his figure and led to the growing preoccupation with earthly-national hopes. In Daniel, we have a clear picture of a reaction against these earthly-dynastic lines of development. It is true that he too speaks of a dominion over all the peoples; but this dominion comes down from heaven in the person of the son of man. It would be possible to picture this heavenly son of man and spirit ruler upon earth exercising his dominion through a descendant of David, just as the other "princes" exercise their power through earthly kings.

It is precisely this point at which revelation requires a further interpretation (*pešer*). In Daniel there is absolutely no mention of the incarnation of this creature; the possibility does not lie within his scope of reference. This new and unheard of reinterpretation is the work of the Gospels. Jesus was particularly fond of referring to himself as son of man. He combined the promise of the coming son of David with that of the son of man. He clearly confessed to being the son of David (Mt 22, 41-46), but he led the captious question of the Pharisees into an insoluble dilemma by demonstrating that the Davidic derivation of the Messiah does not begin to express the fullness of his mission and essence. The Messiah is more, son of David and son of man. It was precisely because of his claim to be the son of man that he was finally condemned (Mt 26, 64).

In this we have gone far beyond the prophecy of Daniel. But once again we must point to the singular structure of the prophecy regarding the son of man. The kingdom is, on the one hand, handed over to the son of man (7, 14), but at the same time it is entrusted to the "holy ones of the most high" (7, 18, 27). This last expression is a Maccabean reinterpretation. "The holy ones of the most high" [42] are the faithful remnant of pious Israelites (hasîdîm) which have stood fast in time of persecution. The Maccabeans thus interpreted the son of man as the type for the holy people of God, although in Daniel the concept bears a very personal stamp. We are dealing with the same kind of corporate personality that we discussed in the case of the servant of God.[43] But with the son of man, the dominion is also entrusted to his people.[44]

2) THE WORLD KINGDOMS

The creature standing in the presence of the throne gave Daniel a short and lapidary answer: "These four great beasts are four kings who shall arise out of the earth" (7, 17), without

---

42. In the ancient literature the "Holy ones" obviously refer to angelic beings; in the course of linguistic development, the word eventually comes to mean "faithful." Thus St. Paul likes to call the Christians "holy ones." M. Noth, *Die Heiligen des Höchsten*, (Mowinckel-Festschrift 1955), 146-161. — R. Koebert, Bibl 35 (1954), 270-272 (kādôš = Angel).
43. Cf. above, p. 34.
44. Further developed in NT: Mt 19, 28; Lk 22, 28-30; 2 Tim 2, 11; Acts 3, 21; 5, 10.

offering any word of explanation. It is only the Maccabean interpreter who recognized the traits of this fourth beast in the kingdom of the impious Epiphanes. In keeping with this interpretation, the three other beasts are identified with oriental kingdoms: 1. the Babylonian lion; 2. the Median bear; 3. the Persian leopard; 4. the apocalyptic kingdom of Greece (Alexander the Great and his successors). Or: 1. the Babylonian lion; 2. the Medo-Persian bear; 3. the leopard Alexander the Great; 4. the kingdom of the Seleucids. These and similar interpretations are all left hanging in the air because they are impossible to the contemporary vision of the historical Daniel. Unless we are very much mistaken, Daniel must have seen these four beasts as the symbols of kings who were rising from the turbulent sea of history in his own day, only to disappear as rapidly as they had arisen. The key for the solution of this riddle is presented by the dating formula which precedes the inaugural vision: "In the first year of Belsazar (Belshazzar)" (7, 1).

Without exception, the commentaries on this passage all take the name as a reference to the Belsazar, son of Nabonidus, who, while his father was living in the oasis of Tema, maintained control of Babylon and was then forced from the throne by Cyrus, together with his father, in 539. Cyrus' entry into Babylon was accomplished in a most orderly manner. Let us refer briefly to the Cyrus-cylinder:[45] "Without any battle, he (Marduk) made him (Cyrus) enter his town Babylon.... He delivered into his (Cyrus') hands Nabonidus." There is no evidence for the fact that Nabonidus and Belsazar were done away with at the conquest of Babylon in the year 539. On the contrary, Cyrus seems to have treated them as honored prisoners. There is some indication that Nabonidus was killed on his flight from Babel,[46] but there is no evidence of Belsazar's death around the year 539. Accordingly, it is quite possible, and even likely, that at the collapse of the Persian empire in 522 he once again seized royal power in Babylon.

The first reign of Darius collapsed in September of 521.

---

45. ANET 315.
46. EncMikr II, 137.

According to the inscription at Behistun (49) we know that a certain Araka, who seized power in Babylon, called himself Nebuchadnezzar (IV) and claimed to be a son of Nabonidus. It is certainly possible that he was not the only usurper. In a similar historical situation in Babylon, during the confusion attendant upon the death of Darius, in the brief period between August 5, 484 and April 3, 483, there were no fewer than four kings, whose names figure in the dating of business accounts from that era (Belšimanni, Šamašeriba, Akšimakšu, and Šikušti).[47] Without these accidental discoveries we would have known nothing of these four "kings for a day." Historical probability thus speaks for the conclusion that during the confused circumstances surrounding the beginning of Darius' reign the first year of the reign of Belsazar would be dated in the fall of 521.

From this point of view the vision of the four beasts and four kings takes on a precise historical background. Darius claims to have overcome nine kings before he had secure control of the government in Babylon. Daniel restricts his reference to the typical number four.[48] Certainly it is possible to interpret the first three beasts as three rebellious kings, perhaps Nebuchadnezzar III of Babylon (the lion whose wings were torn off), the insatiable Bardiya, who contended the succession to the Persian throne with Darius (the bear with the three ribs between his jaws) and finally Fravartis, who quickly enkindled a rebellion in Media shortly after order had been established (the leopard). The fourth and most terrible animal which tramples down everything in his path would then be King Darius himself. The vision is thus replete with contemporary historical events which, by reason of their brief duration, were soon forgotten. But it is not only the contemporary historical events which give a lasting value to the vision of Daniel; it is the history of salvation

---

47. A. Ungnad, *Neubabylonische Privaturkunden aus der Sammlung Amherst*, AFO XIX (1959/60), 74ff.
48. A. Caquot, *Sur les quatre bêtes de Daniel VII*, Sém 5 (1955), 5-13, presupposes an astrological derivation. The Iranian kingdom is supposed to be assigned to the protection of a constellation with the name of an animal.

which is visible behind these events. All earthly kings and kingdoms will be once and for all dissolved by the son of man and his kingdom.

D) DANIEL AS INTERPRETER OF DREAMS

Side by side with the great visions (chs. 7-12) there is a second bloc of narratives (chs. 1-6) which introduce Daniel as an interpreter of dreams and a wise man in the Babylonian royal court. Just as in the visions, here too the Maccabean reinterpretation is clearly visible.

I) *Daniel and Nebuchadnezzar*

1) DANIEL AS PAGE IN THE BABYLONIAN ROYAL COURT (1, 3-21)

This section reproduces a scene from Daniel's youth. Together with other Jewish boys, he is instructed in the writing and language of the Chaldeans so he can later enter into the court service. On this occasion he showed great religious conviction and refused the foods which, by reason of the legal canons of purification, were forbidden to the Jewish diet — a resolution which won both the blessing of God and earthly success as well. On the basis of this narrative we are not justified in concluding that Daniel was trained at the court of the great Nebuchadnezzar. The text speaks only in general terms, as is the case in popular narratives, of "the king" (1: 3, 5,[2] 8, 10,[2] 13, 15, 18, 19[2]); only in 1, 18 is there mention of Nebuchadnezzar, and this can be explained as a later addition.

Furthermore, it is generally asserted that Daniel was deported from Jerusalem by Nebuchadnezzar, on the basis of 1, 1: "In the third year of the reign of Jehoiakim king of Judah, Nebuchadnezzar King of Babylon came to Jerusalem and besieged it." Verse 2 describes the deportation of the Temple vessels, but not the deportation of Daniel and the other expatriates. Even apart from not mentioning Daniel, the dating occasions considerable difficulties. In its present state it is impossible: Nebuchadnezzar became king only in the fourth year of Jehoiakim

(605/4). A siege of Jerusalem for this era cannot be substantiated. Some form of correction must be introduced into the text. I would propose the reading: "In the third *month* of the reign of Jehoiachin. . . ." Jehoiachin reigned only three months and, after the first conquest of Jerusalem (597) was carried off into exile and the Temple vessels with him.[49] Since the principal object of these two verses is reference to the stolen Temple vessels, it would seem that they originally belonged to the story of Belsazar's banquet (ch. 5), in which the sacred vessels were used for sacrilegious purposes. Accordingly, they are silent on the subject of Daniel's being deported from Jerusalem at any time. The special training of promising boys as pages for the Babylonian court could have occurred only around 560 after the liberation of Jehoiachin. At this time Daniel would already have been born in Exile and reared at the Babylonian court. After the conclusion of his education he remained in the service of the court until the first year of Cyrus (539). With the deportation of the Babylonian king, his service was also concluded (1, 21). But his official duties were reestablished as soon as there was another Babylonian king, namely Nebuchadnezzar IV (521).

2) THE DREAM OF THE GREAT STATUE (2, 1-49)

Experiencing dreams and having them interpreted appears to have been very much in vogue. Nabonidus records the fact that he accomplished his temple building as a result of dreams.[50] The interpretation of dreams had developed into a real science. Daniel puts all the Babylonian dream interpreters to shame because he can draw upon a higher wisdom. Surely the dream is a very apt avenue for revelation. Nebuchadnezzar will not disclose what he has dreamed; it is up to the wise men to discover. They cannot do so, and accordingly they are threatened with death. Only Daniel is equal to the task, by reason of his superior source of inspiration. His recounting of the dream is at once an inter-

---

49. Cf. Vol. IV, pp. 349f.
50. The inscription of Nabonidus in Harran: Bibl 49 (1959), 89-109.

pretation. The king had beheld a huge statue; the head was of
gold, the breast and arms of silver, the belly and thighs of
bronze, and the feet of iron and clay. Then suddenly a stone,
cut by no human hand, broke loose from the mountains,[51] shattered
the statue into bits, and then became a mighty mountain (2,
29-35). For Nebuchadnezzar this was not a pleasant message;
its meaning was simply that his kingdom would dissolve in ruins
and be replaced by another.[52] This dream proclaims the same
message as the vision of the four beasts and the son of man.
It is dated in the second year of Nebuchadnezzar (2, 1). The
text does not need to be corrected to "in the 12th year," [53] since
the Behistun inscription speaks of two Nebuchadnezzars, whose
brief reigns could easily be counted as the first and second years
of Nebuchadnezzar. Absolute certainty is impossible in dealing
with the turbulent years 522-521. But if our calculations are
correct, then Daniel's interpretation takes on a more impressive
setting. He was announcing to the usurper Nebuchadnezzar IV
the imminent collapse of his reign. The "stone from the mountain"
could, within the framework of that contemporary history, easily
refer to King Darius, who was to come down from the Iranian
mountains and do away with the usurper. But in the larger
framework of the book as a whole it is the history of the end-
time that is visible behind the history of time.

The erection of a golden statue as the symbol of his imperial
power, an image to which all his subjects were forced to do
homage, fits in well with the picture of the usurper who seeks
to shore up his failing power by such theatrical display. Three
faithful Jewish men refused to show divine honors to this statue.
They were immediately cast into a burning furnace, but through

---

51. E. F. Stiegmann, *The Stone Hewn from the Mountain*, CBQ 18 (1956),
    364-379. Rock, in the ancient texts, is a reference to God, and thus
    here it quite logically refers to the kingdom of God.
52. Section 2, 36-45 is a retrospective reconstruction of history from the
    Maccabean era.
53. BH bases the correction on a reference to 1: 3, 5, 18, that is, the
    great Nebuchadnezzar — but this can hardly be maintained.

God's miraculous intervention they were rescued unharmed (3, 1-30).[54]

3) THE HEWN TREE (4, 1-34)

Despite the manifold content of this fourth chapter [55] it deals primarily with the anxiety felt by the usurper Nebuchadnezzar before his demise. He saw a great tree which was being hewn down; only the rootstock was left, bound with a band of iron and bronze (4, 15). He considered himself secure in the possession of his power: "Is not this great Babylon, which I have built up by my mighty power as a royal residence and for the glory of my majesty" (4, 30). Nonetheless, his days were numbered; he was destined to bow before a greater, Darius, who, after the capture of Babylon, would have him impaled.[56]

II) *Belsazar's Banquet* (5, 1-30)

We have already discussed the most essential details concerning the possible historical framework of Belsazar's reign in Babylon.[57] In the perilous years 522-520 both he and Nebuchadnezzar IV, and perhaps others as well, attempted to seize their lost power. It is in such a situation that we can best understand the banquet scene, with the trophies of former victory, the sacred vessels from the Temple in Jerusalem,[58] being used in the midst

---

54. The Septuagint introduces the following elements into the narrative: Prayer of Azariah (3, 25-45), Hymn of praise to God's majesty (3, 51-56), Hymn of praise of the three youths in the fiery furnace (3, 57-90).

55. The Maccabean interpretation (*pešer*) seems to begin already with v. 15. For Nebuchadnezzar's prayer (4, 31-34), a similar prayer has been discovered in Qumran, in the name of Nabonidus. It is possible that the account of Nebuchadnezzar's life in the wilderness is also patterned on Nabonidus. D. N. Friedmann, *The Prayer of Nabonidus,* BASOR 145 (1957), 31; Cf. RB 63 (1956), 407-415.

56. Behistun Inscription 50.

57. Cf. above, p. 74ff.

58. The mention of Nebuchadnezzar (5: 2, 11, 18) might well be only the addition of the Maccabean editor, and thus unimportant for history.

of the general carousing. But the merry company, drunk with their success, are made to hear the voice of impending doom. A hand appears writing on the wall. The Babylonian interpreters do not know how to explain it. Daniel is sent for. He can both read and interpret the message. "And this is the writing that was inscribed: $m^e n\bar{e}$' ($m^e n\bar{e}$') $t^e q\bar{e}l$ $\hat{u}$-$phars\hat{n}$ (5, 25). And this is the interpretation of the matter: $m^e n\bar{e}$': God has numbered the days of your kingdom and brought it to an end. $T^e q\bar{e}l$: you have been weighed in the balances and found wanting. $P^e r\bar{e}s$: your kingdom is divided and given to the Medes and Persians" (5, 25-28). Many interpreters have believed that it was not entire words written upon the wall, but only the initial letters which could easily be interpreted as current abbreviations for units of money or measure, such as: "mina, shekel, and (two) half shekels," or "unit of measure, unit of weight, and fractional units." [59] Whatever the case may be, the message prophesied by Daniel suddenly came to pass during that very night. Darius, fresh from his victory over the Medes, from which he bore the triumphal title "the Mede," put an end to the reign of the usurper in Babylon and seized his power.

III) *Daniel in the Lions' Den* (6, 1-29)

The dating formula at the beginning of this chapter— "And Darius the Mede received the kingdom, being about 62 years old" (6, 1) — is, in its present form, the result of an attempt to interpret this mysterious statement. If the entire formula is reckoned in terms of shekels, we have this result: one mina equals 60 shekels, which, increased by one shekel and two half-shekels gives the number 62.[60] Belsazar's destruction would thus precisely coincide with the 62nd year of Darius, and this would be the mysterious hidden meaning of the message. But this involves a deliberate reworking of the original date, which, in

---

59. O. Eissfeldt, *Die Menetekel-Inschrift und ihre Deutung*, ZAW 63 (1951), 105. — A. Alt, *Zur Menetekel-Inschrift*, VT 4 (1954), 303.
60. K. Galling, *Die 62 Jahre des Meders Darius in Dn 6, 1*, ZAW 66 (1954), 152.

my opinion, must have stated simply "in the second year of Darius," and served as introduction to the section that follows.[61] Such a solution fits perfectly into the course of history as we know it. For it was in the second year of his reign (spring 520 to spring 519) that Darius, after conquering all his enemies, began the reorganization of his empire. He divided it into large administrative districts and set up trustworthy officials, the satraps. Their name Kšatra-pāvan, "protector of the rule," is of Median derivation. It is not surprising that Daniel should have enjoyed such a position of trust. Later, too, another Jew, Nehemiah, was privileged to function in the important court office of cupbearer. It is also quite possible, historically, that there was considerable public sentiment against Daniel, and that his enemies, unable to convict him of any irregularities in the function of his official office, attempted to bring about his downfall on the basis of his religious convictions. They based their argument on a point of law, namely that a Persian royal edict is irrevocable (cf. Est 1, 19; 8, 8), and managed to secure an edict that for the next 30 days only the king could be prayed to. Daniel's practice of religion would thus prove to be his undoing. As was customary, he thrice daily turned his face towards Jerusalem and prostrated himself in prayer.[62] On the grounds that he was showing contempt to the royal edict he was immediately thrown into the lions' den, but miraculously rescued. His rescue was a demonstration of power on the part of the God of Israel in the midst of the pagan world. After this rescue, Daniel continued to live in the service of the Persian king Darius.[63] The date of his death is unknown.

The Greek Bible and, influenced by the Greek, all the other translations also contain a few legendary narratives from the life of Daniel: the history of the chaste Susanna, who was

---

61. In terms of text criticism, this can be easily established: bisnat tarten (in the second year) has been amplified to read kᵉbar šᵉnîn šittin wᵉtartēn (a son of 62 years).
62. This reading might well have appeared in the course of the Exile.
63. In Dn 6, 29 the words "and under the sovereignty of the Persian Cyrus" are a deliberate amplification.

rescued from death by the clever mind and old energy of a youthful Daniel (13, 1-64); the narratives about the deceitful priests of Bel, whose activity Daniel unmasks (14, 1-22), and the story of the killing of the Babylonian dragon (14, 23-32). While their historical value is much contested, their faith content is established beyond all question. They are an everlasting witness to the faith in Yahweh's victory over the Babylonian dragon. In terms of the history of tradition, these narratives are best understood if they are classified as midrashes, didactic narratives composed for the purpose of exemplifying and bringing to life a truth of the popular faith, but midrashes with some possible historical nucleus.

E) THE LITERARY PROBLEM OF THE BOOK OF DANIEL

The literary puzzle of the Book of Daniel can be clarified by a comparison with the Book of Isaiah, which clearly betrays three strata of composition (Proto-, Deutero-, Trito-Isaiah). The situation is much the same in the Book of Daniel; here too one is justified in speaking of Proto-, Deutero-, and Trito-Daniel. What is more, in the case of Daniel the three strata can be identified linguistically (Aramaic, Hebrew, and Greek). Eissfeldt [64] has clearly demonstrated that the Book of Daniel as we know it, which received its final form in the Maccabean era, was preceded by individual smaller collections. Literary criticism, however, has not generally hit upon this proper interpretation of the history of the Book of Daniel, largely by reason of doubting the historicity of the prophet Daniel. Eissfeldt insists upon reckoning with the possibility of the existence of such a person, whose career would fall within the sixth or fifth century, somewhere in the eastern Jewish diaspora. Since the arguments presented above are sufficient to answer the historical problems concerning

---

64. EinlAT 648: argues that chs. 1-6 are a collection from the middle of the third century; the original individual accounts derive from the East. In the visions in 7-12 there are many very ancient elements preserved.

the actual existence of the prophet Daniel and have, furthermore, fixed his career upon the more precisely determined period around the stormy years 522-520, it is now possible to approach the literary history of his book.

1) PROTO-DANIEL (Aramaic)

In the present form of the Book of Psalms, after Ps 71/72, 20, stands the surprising notice: "The prayers of David, the son of Jesse, are ended." There is a similar statement in the middle of the Book of Daniel: "Here is the end of the words" (7, 28). The original text of Daniel must once have concluded with the vision of the son of man. The primary content of this book is thus preserved in the Aramaic chapters 2, 4b — 7, 28; originally they were preceded by the inaugural vision and the prophecy of the 70 years, which can still be recognized, in their elaborate form, in chs. 9-12. The Book of Daniel thus began in a manner similar to the Book of Ezekiel, with the inaugural vision; this was followed by the events and words from the extremely brief interval of his prophetic activity.

2) DEUTERO-DANIEL (Hebrew)

A man from the Maccabean period came upon the Aramaic original of the Book of Daniel. He determined to rework the ancient prophecy and make it relevant to his own day. The most obvious material for his *pešer* (interpretation) was afforded by the inaugural vision and the prophecy of the 70 years.[65] He translated the Aramaic original, elaborating it by his own interpretation of history, and moved it from the beginning of the book where, on account of the characteristic crisis of the Maccabean period, it no longer belonged, to the end of the book. The new dating formula, the "third year of Cyrus" (10, 1), is also to be ascribed to his authorship, since it is possible that

---

65. The original text and the interpretation are thoroughly distinguished in Kruse, *Compositio Libri Danielis et Idea Filii Hominis*, VD 37 (1959), 198ff.

Cyrus is meant to refer to Epiphanes. The original dating, the "first year of Darius," is still retained in the corrupt sentence (11, 1). After this transformation of the original text, he found it necessary to provide the book with a new introduction, this time written in Hebrew. For a beginning, he chose the introduction to Nebuchadnezzar's campaign against Jerusalem (1, 1-2), which, in my opinion, belongs with the banquet of Belsazar, thereby introducing confusion with Nebuchadnezzar II and upsetting the entire chronology. Instead of the inaugural vision, he gives the story of Daniel's life as a page at the imperial court (1, 3-21). In order to create a transition to the original Aramaic text of Daniel, he composed the Hebrew introduction to the dream of the great statue (2, 1-4a). The vision of the ram and the he-goat (8, 1-27) also derives in its entirety from the Maccabean era; hence the general dating: "In the third year of Belsazar" (8, 1). The reinterpretations and adaptations which occur in the Aramaic text were also composed by him, are smaller in scope, and likewise in Aramaic (2, 36-45; 4, 15-34; 7, 8, 19-27).

3) TRITO-DANIEL (Greek)

After the conclusion of the Aramaic-Hebrew Book of Daniel, the Greek Bible contains the legendary accounts of chapters 13 and 14, which have been inserted into the hymn sung by the three men in the fiery furnace (3, 26-45, 51-90).

Thus the literary problem of the Book of Daniel would seem convincingly settled on the basis of historical criticism. In the Hebrew Bible the book is found not among the prophets, but among the "writings" (kᵉtûbîm), since it has taken on its present form only after the canon of the prophets was closed. In the case of Isaiah, there is no such intimate connection between the prophetic words and their reinterpretation and adaptation (pešer). It is precisely this circumstance that gives the Book of Daniel its own individual stamp and value. In this book we can appreciate how the Scriptures were read and understood: not as a book of past history, but rather as an answer to the crisis of each succeeding period. Scripture was a living word that could always be adapted to a contemporary time.[66] It is precisely in this repeated adaptation of Scripture that we can best appreciate the progress of revelation. The themes of the ancient prophecies were interpreted and given new depth of meaning from the common fund of the nation's faith. A full understanding of the history of salvation can be achieved only in retrospect.[67] Revelation proceeds from faith to a still greater faith, from light to an always brighter light. In the New Testament era the prophets were read in the same way. The New Testament Scriptures are precisely the *pešer*, the adapting reinterpretation, of the Old Testament.

---

66. In the further development that follows, the decisions of the Councils and the Holy Father, insofar as he speaks as head of Christianity, are simply new actualizations and re-interpretations of the traditional body of faith.

67. On the "re-presentation of the Old Testament in the New," cf. G. von Rad, TheolAT II (1960), 329ff.

CHAPTER V

THE BOOK OF JUDITH

THE Book of Judith takes its name from the heroine Judith
($y^ehûdît$ — "Jewess"), who, by her bold daring, brought freedom
and redemption to her people in a time of extreme national
crisis. The book presents a series of absolutely insoluble problems.
Is the content of the story really history or simply a narrative
with historical nucleus (pseudo-history) or simply a free composition? Fr. Stummer feels that honest scholarship must admit
that, in view of the manifold problems and attempts at solution,
the question cannot be answered with anything approaching
positive certainty. The overall opinion of Eissfeldt[1] is not essentially different: "This narrative, as filled as it is with fanatic
chauvinism and religious passion as with lofty poetic movement,
can hardly make a claim of historicity." He feels that the only
solution lies in reconstructing the historical milieu behind the
origin of the book, and not attempting to examine the historicity
of the narrative itself; this would simply lead to an insoluble
labyrinth. There are more than 20 distinct attempts at interpretation.[2] The book has been tentatively dated anywhere from
the seventh century before Christ to second century after Christ,

---

1. EinlAT 726.
2. L. Soubigou, *Judith*, ClamB IV, 490.

in an attempt to fit the primary elements of the book into the course of known history.[3] The effort is tiresome and unrewarding. There is considerable evidence that the Book of Judith is not an historical work at all, but rather "an historical novel with a strong national-religious tendency," [4] composed in the passionately disturbed era of the Maccabean wars, somewhere in the middle of the second century before Christ. In order to do justice to the book, our interpretation must accordingly inquire into the national-religious leit-motifs and not be embarrassed at the historical impossibilities.

Barucq [5] thus classifies Judith in the proximity of the apocalyptic literature. In images of a freely reconstructed past situation, the outlines of the future are didactically drawn. The theme of the apocalyptic battle of the end-time is unrolled; the people of God, threatened by an overpowering opponent, will still be saved by God's intervention at the last hour. The scenes and themes are all drawn from various epochs of Old Testament history.

Even if it were actually proven that Judith is a religious-national novel, the edifice of faith would hardly collapse. Even in this case, the Book of Judith would retain its power of religious presentation. But it would seem to me that the historical possibilities are not so completely exhausted as to permit one to conclude with perfect conviction that the Book of Judith cannot possibly claim a true historical origin. The Ancient Near East must have many new discoveries waiting for us, some of

---

3. Pfeiffer, IntrOT 293ff.
4. Eissfeldt, EinlAT 727.
5. JerB, *Judith* (1952), 14. — E. Haag, *Studien zum Buche Judith, Trierer Theologische Studien* 16, (1962): "The literary genre of the Book of Judith should be characterized as a free, parable-form presentation of history, not the empirical history of the people of God, but the type of historical writing that uses free composition and ideal expression to exemplify the powers and forces that are at work in determining the empirical history of the people of God" (133). In terms of Biblical theology, there are some very worthwhile concepts here, but, in my opinion, they are left rather hanging in the air, since the attempt at any historical re-ordering of the events is, *a priori,* simply excluded.

which might well make the historicity of the Book of Judith appear vastly more probable. It is wise to be somewhat reserved as to the final verdict in this case.

The following discussion will explore new paths along which the Book of Judith can be brought into closer connection, both in time and in literary history, with the Book of Daniel. The turbulent events of Darius' accession to power have found a clear precipitate in this text. The shattered Babylonian Kingdom appears to experience a sort of ghostly afterlife, before it succumbs definitively to the power of the Persian. This drama of world history is profoundly influenced by a woman, Judith, to whose story the book of that same name is entirely devoted.

A) THE JUDITH NARRATIVE

The very beginning of the book casts us immediately into the framework of world history. There is a definitive confrontation between powerful political opponents. Two rivals face each other. The one is introduced as "Nebuchadnezzar, who ruled over the Assyrians in the great city of Nineveh" (1, 1); the other Arphaxad, King of the Medes and builder of the city of Ecbatana (1, 2ff.). On the side of Arphaxad there were the mountain peoples of Armenia, as far as India, while Nebuchadnezzar could count on the allegiance of the nations of the west. When the war breaks out, Nebuchadnezzar defeats Arphaxad in battle, conquers Ecbatana, and pursues the defeated enemy into the mountain country of Ragae, where Arphaxad is taken prisoner and killed with hunting spears (1, 1-6).

Nebuchadnezzar thereupon sends his captain Holofernes against the western countries who had refused allegiance (2, 1-18). The point of departure for the military operation which ensues is the city of Nineveh. One campaign is directed towards the west, against Cilicia; it was here that the "people of Rassis," as well as Lud and Phud were destroyed. After these successes, Holofernes turned towards the south. The cities of the Phoenicians and Palestinian coastal plains declared themselves subject to him and willingly paid tribute; the tribes of the Arabian desert as far as Midian and Epha did the same. It seemed that the western countries were secured. A third campaign led across the Euphrates to the fortress cities along the Habur River, which were conquered in their turn, and from there to the east, across Babylonia and as far as the sea. The general victorious march of Holofernes in the west, however, came to an unexpected standstill in the country of Israel along the Plain of Esdraelon (2, 19 — 3, 10).

Since Holofernes, along his path of conquest, took no concern for the religious prerogatives of the individual peoples and cities, but rather made it his habitual practice to destroy temples and sacred groves alike (3, 8), even the Israelites, newly returned from captivity, began to fear for their freedom. The high priest Joiakim, who was in Jerusalem, called for a time of prayer and fasting. He sent messengers "to every district of Samaria, and to Kona, and Beth-Horon, Belmain, and Jericho, to Choba, Aesora, and the Valley of Salem" (4, 4), and called for general support in resisting the invasion. He wrote to the inhabitants of Bethulia and Betomesthaim, instructing them to seize the mountain passes and thus hinder the further progress of the enemy towards Jerusalem. This the Israelites did, in perfect obedience to the commands of their high priests and the council of elders who sat in Jerusalem (4, 6ff.).

In the camp of Holofernes the Israelite attempts at resistance caused considerable surprise. Accordingly, the captain summoned the leader of the Ammonites, Achior by name, and asked him why it should be precisely this tiny mountain people, among all the inhabitants of the western countries, that dared to offer resistance. Achior explained that this people was unconquerable so long as they remain faithful to their God. But if they had transgressed his commands, then they would certainly be delivered into the hands of their enemies. It would be wise, accordingly, to ascertain whether the people had incurred any guilt; if they had not, there was no point in forcing the issue in battle (5, 1-24). Achior's message so enraged the captains that he was bound hand and foot and delivered before the fortress city of Bethulia, where he was taken in by the Israelites (6, 1-21).

After Holofernes had drawn up his ranks on the Plain of Esdraelon, he prepared to attack the mountain country. He occupied the Plain of Bethulia, took control of the water sources and completely surrounded the city. He hoped that the fortress, forced by thirst and hunger, would fall into his hands without a battle. For 34 days Bethulia withstood. The water supplies in the city's cisterns eventually gave out. There was not enough for another day. Despair was everywhere. The assembly of the people demanded that the first steps be taken towards capitulation. Uzziah, who was in charge of the city, proposed that they hold out for five more days, in the prospect that some help would come from God (7, 19-32).

The help did come from a completely unexpected direction. It came in the form of a widow, Judith, whose husband had been dead for three and a half years. She upbraided the captain and the people for their lack of courage and declared herself ready to make her way into the hostile camp. She promised, further, that even before the five days had passed she would bring salvation (8, 1-36). Thereupon she prayed to "the God of her father Simeon," that is, the great patriarch Simeon who had taken up the sword of vengeance against the city of Shechem (Gn 34), and, together with her maid, made her way into the enemy camp where she was determined herself to accomplish the work of vengeance and judgment (chs. 9 and 10). The Assyrian outposts took the two fugitives and led them before Holofernes, who was immediately struck with Judith. Judith stayed in the camp for three days. Until midnight she would sleep in her own tent, but towards the approach of dawn she would arise, leave the camp, and go into the Valley of Bethulia, ostensibly to pray (12, 1-9). On the fourth day, Holofernes gave a huge banquet. When the wine had begun to flow in abundance, he ordered his eunuch Bagoas to bring in the Hebrew woman. "Then Judith came in and lay down and Holofernes' heart was ravished with her and he was moved with great desire to possess her" (12, 16). Since it had already grown quite late, the servants all withdrew at once and Bagoas closed the tent from the outside. Judith was thus left alone in the tent. Holofernes lay stretched out upon his couch, completely overcome with the wine. Thereupon Judith seized the sword which was hanging at the head of the couch and, taking hold of the captain's hair, struck his neck twice with all her strength, completely severing his head (12, 10 — 13, 10). Concealing Holofernes' head in her food bag, Judith made her way back to Bethulia on the morning of the 5th day. The city, overcome with joy, opened wide its gates. Holofernes' head was displayed from the city walls. The besieged Jews prepared themselves for a final battle; the besieging forces, however, were overcome with panic when they learned of the death of their captain and they fled in all directions. The Israelites fell upon them and pursued them all the way to Damascus (13, 11 — 15, 7). The high priest and council of the elders came from Jerusalem to congratulate Judith upon her deed of heroism (15, 8-13). After plundering the hostile camp, the victorious inhabitants of Bethulia formed a triumphant procession. Women were dancing in the streets, with palm branches in their hands and crowns on their heads. "And Judith went before all the people in the dance, leading all the women, while all the men of Israel followed, bearing their arms and wearing garlands and with songs on their lips" (15, 13). They made their way as far as Jerusalem, where they offered sacrifices of thanksgiving. Here Judith dedicated the entire furniture of Holofernes' tent as a votive offering to the Temple (16, 18-20). They then returned to Bethulia, where, after a long and peaceful life, Judith died in the 105th year of her life (16, 21-25).

B) JUDITH AND HISTORY

The scholar who attempts to fit the neatly and artistically constructed narrative into the framework of Ancient Near East history finds himself faced with irreconcilable contradictions. The name Nebuchadnezzar will strike the naive reader as a reference to Nebuchadnezzar II (604-562), the builder of the Babylonian empire and destroyer of Jerusalem. In the Book of Judith, however, he is called King of Assyria, and has his residence in Nineveh the great city (1, 1). Now Nineveh was so completely destroyed in 612 that it never again revived. Moreover, a siege of Bethulia cannot be substantiated by any other biblical or extrabiblical sources. Must we accordingly conclude that Nebuchadnezzar, Nineveh, Judith, and Bethulia, are simply pseudonymous references to other historical persons and places which actually existed, or are they perhaps symbolic names in an allegorical narrative? Before we resort to such extremes of interpretation, we must once again attempt to take the historical references in their literal sense. Perhaps the resultant picture would not be quite so unhistorical as it would appear on first sight.

1) WHEN DOES THE STORY OF JUDITH TAKE PLACE?

At all events not in the era of the kings. In 4, 3, we find the information "they (the Israelites) had just returned home from captivity, and shortly before the entire people of Judea had held an assembly and the sacred vessels, the altar, and the temple itself had been cleansed from their desecration." The return from captivity began with Cyrus' edict of liberation.[6] This points to the time after 538. As head of the Jerusalem community we find the high priest Joiakim (4, 6). He was son and successor of the high priest Jeshua, who had come to Jerusalem with the second caravan of repatriates, where he had reestablished the official cult (Ezr 2, 2; 3, 2; 4, 3). In the list of high priests (Neh 12, 10) the name of Jeshua is followed by his son Joiakim. From the prophet Zechariah (1, 7) we learn that Jeshua was still alive in the 2nd year of Darius. When Jeshua died and when his son Joiakim became his successor as high priest we do not know. A conjecture around the year 520 could not miss the date by very much. Moreover, we must not exclude the possibility that Joiakim entered upon his public career while his father was still alive.

Together with the high priest, the council of elders passed on decisions in Jerusalem (4, 8). This information is in perfect keeping with the circumstances of the return from Exile and the era of reconstruction. It was not first under the influence of the Hellenistic administration that the council of elders came into importance; it was an essential element in the government set up by the repatriates immediately upon their return from

6. Cf. above, p. 37.

Babylonia; according to the information contained in the edict of Cyrus, the heads of the families (Ezr 1, 5) assembled in order to organize the return home. It is quite probable that this assembly would also be heard on matters of prime importance even after their return to Jerusalem.

The Book of Judith represents an extreme national and religious crisis, a time at which the high priest and the council of elders were forced to act. Their action does not necessarily presuppose the fact that all of Samaria was subject to the control of Judea, nor even that Joiakim, as temporal regent, was in a position to make commands binding upon these various cities. Still, he might well be called the soul of the resistance; for it was he who sent out the messengers and letters and the call for resistance against the attacking enemy. There is no mention of his personal hand in organizing the army. The geographical locations mentioned in the text are either crossroads fortresses or mountain passes. The primary concern was to slow down and possibly halt the attack upon Jerusalem. For the high priest to have turned to Samaritan cities [7] — Samaria, Choba, Betomeshaim, and Bethulia — is certainly possible in the era before 520, since at that time the schism had not definitely occurred. The Samaritan population felt a considerable unity of faith with the repatriates and even wanted to assist in rebuilding the temple at Jerusalem. This presupposes the fact that they recognized the high priest as a religious superior. The rapid advance of Holofernes, destroying temples and sacred high places as he came, appeared as a serious threat to their recently recovered religious freedom. Joiakim's call for help can be explained simply in terms of his position as high priest. It does not at all presuppose any later political situations, such as existed in the era of the Maccabees. The gigantic army of the invading enemy could not possibly be met by a like force of Jewish troops, but it might appear a very wise counsel to put as many obstacles as possible in the path of his troops marching against the capital.

---

7. For an identification of the places named in the narrative, cf. Fr. Stummer, *Geographie des Buches Judith*, (1947); Simons, GTT § § 1606, 1607, 1612.

Accordingly, there is no historical impossibility involved in fitting the historical data into the era of the high priest Joiakim.

2) WHO WAS NEBUCHADNEZZAR?

G. Brunner has discovered a new approach to this question, one which deserves to be examined in some detail, even though his book *Der Nabuchodonosor des Buches Judith* [8] was accorded a rather negative reception by scholarly criticism.[9] The point of departure for his investigation is the inscription of Darius at Behistun.[10] Among the 19 kings conquered by Darius there are two kings of Babylon who bear the name Nebuchadnezzar. Can one of these two possibly have been the Nebuchadnezzar in the Book of Judith? The question revolves primarily about Nebuchadnezzar IV — Araka.[11]

The inscription at Behistun [12] reads as follows (49): "Thus speaks the King Darius: While I was in Persia and Media, the Babylonians revolted from me for a second time. A man by the name of Araka, an Armenian, son of Haldita, arose against me in Babylon. There is a territory called Dubala, and it was there that he based his revolt. He enticed the people to follow him by saying: 'I am Nebuchadnezzar, son of Nabonidus.' Thereupon the people of Babylon revolted from me, going over to this man Araka. He seized Babylon and became king in Babylon." — (50): "Thus speaks King Darius: Thereupon I sent an army to Babylon. A Persian by the name of Windaparna, my servant, him I made my commander and gave him these orders: 'Go on your way! Smite this Babylonian army that refuses to be mine.' Accordingly Windaparna and his army marched on Babylon.

---

8. Berlin 1959.
9. Cf. CBQ 23 (1961), 341; Greenfield, JBL 80 (1961), 298.
10. Cf. above, pp. 48f.
11. Fr. Stummer cannot understand how such a political fly-by-night could possibly have been involved in such a far-reaching enterprise as that described in the Book of Judith.
12. The Elamite, Persian, and Babylonian text, together with a German translation are to be found in Fr. H. Wiessbach, *Die Keilinschriften der Achämeniden*, Vorderasiatische Bibliothek, (Leipzig 1911), 55ff.

Ahura-mazda brought me help. According to the will of Ahura-mazda, Windaparna struck the Babylonians and took them prisoner. It was on the 22nd day of Margagana that he took this Araka who called himself Nebuchadnezzar and the men who were his chief followers. Then I gave the following orders: This man Araka and all the men who were his chief followers were impaled in Babylon." — (51): "Thus speaks King Darius: This is what was accomplished by me in Babylon."

These very short references are sufficient information to describe the bolder outlines of the rise and fall of Nebuchadnezzar-Araka.

a. *Araka, the Armenian*: Nebuchadnezzar does not make a sudden appearance as pretender to the throne in Babylon; he is presented as an Armenian (Persian: *Arminiya*) or as an Urartaean (Babylonian: *u-ra-aš-ta-a-a*). This gives a reasonably clear picture of his origin. We are dealing with a man from the kingdom of Urartu, always hard pressed by the Assyrians and eventually yielding to them. The inscription goes on to relate that Araka launched his rebellion from a district by the name of Dubala.[13] This could refer to no other territory than the biblical Tubal or the Assyrian Tabal.[14] From their original homes along the northeastern coast of the Black Sea, the people of Tubal (Tabarenes) had forced their way to the south. Under Tiglath-Pilesar and Sargon they are classed among the neighboring tribes of Cilicia.[15] Dubala is thus not a city in Babylon,[16] but a province or administrative district in Armenia. For the name Araka is certainly Armenian; it is, however, not a personal name, but a title. Araka means: "young man, crown prince." [17] The name of his father Haldita might also be a throne name rather than his personal name. The Armenian rulers of Damascus all referred to themselves as "son of Hadad," while those who ruled in the Armenian mountains called themselves "son of the national God Haldi." [18] But

13. Persian *dahyaus* means "territory, landscape, valley," and not "city."
14. The fact that in the inscription Dubala is written with a soft *d* presents no difficulty, since other common names like *parsa* are also written *ba-ir-sa*. Cf. Weissbach, *op. cit.*, 108: Inscription from Persepolis.
15. ANET 282-284.
16. W. Hinz, *Das erste Jahr des Grosskönigs Darius*, ZDM6 82 (1938), 162, attempts to locate Dubala south of Babylon, modern Debeleh on the Euphrates.
17. W. Brandenstein, *Der Ursprung der Armenier, Zeitschrift für armenische Philologie*, (Vienna 1961), 692. — V. Banateanu, *Studia et acta orientalia I* (Bucarest 1958), 65ff., 79.
18. On the basis of an oral communication from Prof. Brandenstein, the

what were the real names of this "crown prince" and his royal father? Darius reproaches Araka for having laid false claim to the title "Nebuchadnezzar son of Nabonidus." In the smaller inscriptions from Behistun [19] the same charge must have been made against nine other kings. Modern scholarship admits that Darius made considerable use of deceit and defamation as political weapons.[20] As a result, Araka's claim to be the true son of Nabonidus must not be simply dismissed without a hearing. If he is justified in this claim, then Araka's path from the Armenian mountains into the capital city of Babylon is a logical conclusion. After the collapse of the Persian sovereignty he was simply attempting to recoup the heritage of his dethroned father and thus reestablish the Babylonian empire. This also explains why he began counting the years of his reign as successor of Nabonidus from the year 539.

b. *Coup d'état in Babylon*: The Behistun inscription records only what is favorable to Darius. There is no mention of any political successes in the west. Only the final chapter in Babylon is more closely described. Babylon appears to have gone over to Araka without a battle. On August 25, 521, business papers in Babylon were already being dated after Nebuchadnezzar.[21] Moreover, his sovereignty was not restricted to the district of the city of Babylon; the ancient Sumerian metropolis of Uruk also reckoned dates in terms of his name. All this could certainly give the impression that the Babylonian kingdom had rearisen in all its former glory. Nobody could possibly foresee that this powerful structure was destined to collapse like a house of cards. Darius was occupied in Media during the time of Araka's *coup d'état*. It was from here that he sent his captain Windaparna, who marched into Babylon on November 27, 521. Nebuchadnezzar was taken prisoner and impaled. And thus a mighty dream proved, in the end, illusory.

c. *Araka — the Nebuchadnezzar of the Book of Judith?* Can this statement be made without doing violence to both biblical and Persian sources? Indeed it can. First of all, Araka is a contemporary of the high priest Joiakim. Secondly, the dates "in the

---

ending -ita has not received sufficient attention: the above translation is the most probable one. Cf. Brandenstein, l. c. 693.

19. Weissbach, *op. cit.*, 77ff.
20. According to Herodotus (3, 72) Darius is supposed to have made a speech in which he realistically defends the use of deceit in politics. H. S. Nyberg, *Das Reichder Achämeniden*, HistM III (1954), 76.
21. Parker-Dubberstein, *Babylonian Chronology*, (1956), 16.

17th and in the 18th year of Nebuchadnezzar" (1, 13; 2, 1) can be understood. If Araka regarded himself as the legitimate successor to Nabonidus, then there is some substance to the presumption that he would have begun to number the years of his reign, not with the actual accession to the throne of Babylon, but rather with the end of the reign of Nabonidus, whom Cyrus had deposed on October 29, 539.[22] The 17th and 18th year would thus coincide with year 522/21 and 521/20 (reckoning from spring to spring), and thus the precise time in which the Behistun inscription dates the rise and fall of the usurper Araka-Nebuchadnezzar IV.

If we accept this solution, then the military accounts presented in the Book of Judith are easily enough understood. They portray Asia Minor in a state of political transfiguration. A new master appears and demands the subjection of the western countries. In the narrative described above, the general directions of the military operations are already outlined. The campaign of Holofernes is simply an attempt to secure the western territories for his new lord Nebuchadnezzar. The first decisive confrontation took place in the native country of Araka, in Cilicia.[23] The mention of battles against Lud,[24] that is, the kingdom of Lydia (2, 23), are certainly not surprising in this context. Cyrus had defeated Lydia in 536; but upon the collapse of the Persian Empire there was rebellion. After the victory won by Holofernes on the plateau of Cilicia against the people of Rassis [25] the rest of the campaign was a triumphal procession. The Phoenician cities offered no resistance (2, 28). Even the cities along the Palestin-

---

22. The time from October 539 to New Year, spring 538, was counted as the year of accession. Year one is reckoned from 538/37.
23. Jdt 2, 21: "left of Upper Cilicia": looking from the east to the west, left would be to the south. The great plain of Bectilah ("house of murder") probably refers to the plain of Issos, where Alexander the Great later defeated the armies of Persia.
24. Lud is not to be identified with a site in North Africa; it is a clear reference to Lydia. W. Brandenstein, *Festschrift* A. Debrunner, (1954), 58. *Bemerkungen zur Völkertafel der Genesis.*
25. The name survives in the village of Arsus on the Gulf of Iskanderum. Stummer, *Geographie,* 25.

ian coast [26] which had belonged within the Phoenician sphere of influence, Okina (Acco), Jamnia, Ashdod, and Ashkelon, all bowed before their new master. Inland, the territory of the Chelaeans [27] between the oasis of Palmyra and the Euphrates, was quickly subjected. The territory around Damascus was put to the torch. Military divisions made their way into the territory of the Arabian tribes of Midian and Epha.[28] It was only a matter of time before the conqueror would lay claim to Egyptian territory; three years earlier Cambyses had incorporated Egypt into the Persian Empire.

The military operations in the west were entrusted by Nebuchadnezzar to his general Holofernes, which also is, perhaps, to be interpreted not as a personal name, but rather a title meaning "splendor of his majesty." [29] Holofernes was the grand vizier, and the "second after the king" (2, 4). Araka himself took charge of the campaign against the capital city of Babylon. "He followed the Euphrates and passed through Mesopotamia and destroyed all the hilltop cities along the Brook Abron as far as the sea" (2, 24). The clay tablets already mentioned clearly confirm his rule in the south of Babylonia, in the city of Uruk.

3) ARPHAXAD, KING OF THE MEDES IN ECBATANA

Is it possible to fit in the campaign against Arphaxad of Ecbatana in the career of the usurper Araka-Nebuchadnezzar? It is by no means historically impossible. According to the testimony of the Behistun inscription, 19 usurpers arose upon the death of Cambyses. The empire built by Cyrus was breaking apart. One of the greatest areas of unrest lay in Media. Here Darius had to fight with Bardiya; hardly had he conquered Bardiya, when

---

26. Cf. *Atlas Israel,* Jerusalem, (1956), IX, with a geographical outline of the era.
27. Modern el-Challe, north of Palmyra.
28. The Japheth in the Greek text is probably an error for Epha.
29. Oral communication from Prof. Brandenstein, Graz. The name Holophernes is of frequent occurrence in the older form Orophernes in Cappadocia. F. Justi, *Iranisches Namenbuch,* (1895).

Fravartis raised the banner of revolt. The Book of Judith makes reference to a similiar revolution (1, 6). As allies, Arphaxad the Mede could count upon the mountain countries along the upper course of the Euphrates and the Tigris as far as the Indian Hydaspes. Mentioned by name are Elam, Arachosia,[30] and Chele'ud;[31] all of them provinces which, according to the Behistun inscription, rebelled against Darius, but were quickly controlled by military intervention. Why does Darius not boast in this inscription of a victory over Arphaxad of Media? Perhaps because it was not his own campaign but that of his son Nebuchadnezzar.

Up to this point scholarship has not succeeded in proving the existence of a ruler by the name of Arphaxad in the series of kings of Media. In my opinion it never will succeed, simply because Arphaxad is not a personal name, but rather a Median title of rule. The name is composed of the two elements *arpa* and *kšad*. The same name is handed down in the Hebrew table of nations (Gn 10, 21). The second element *kšad* is a Median dialectal form from the old Persian *kšatra*, "possessing the sovereignty," and appears, e.g., in the name Arta-kšatra. The first element *arpa* can be understood on the basis of the customary Indo-Iranian division of a people in terms of age groups. We are indebted to Herodotus (IV, 5-7) for this knowledge, which he records in his description of the tribes of the Scythians.[32] The Scythians derive their ancestry from three brothers. The oldest was called Lipoxais, the middle Arpoxais, and the youngest Kolaxais. The ending -*xais* is the Greek form of the word *Kšatra-kšad,* which is to say "having dominion or sovereignty." But who has dominion over whom? Kolaxais means "leading the young men" or "leader of the body of young men"; Lipoxais "leader of the older men," Arpoxais "leader or ruler of the middle (age class)." [33] According to the legend, the symbol of the middle age group was the

---

30. The Plain of Arioch has nothing to do with King Arioch (Gn 14, 1); it is a reference to the Land of Arachosia (*a-ru-hat-ti*), which, according to the Behistun Inscription, 45, also revolted against Darius.

31. According to Fr. Stummer, like Karman, in southeast Iran. Here Nabuna'id had been installed as governor by Cyrus. The province kept faith with Cyrus' son, Bardiah, and fought against Darius' claims to power.

32. W. Brandenstein, *Die Abstammungssagen der Skythen*, WZKM 52 (1953-55), 183-211.

33. *Ibid.*, 201, 203.

battle ax,[34] which had, in times primordial, fallen down from heaven. This middle class was privileged to appoint the king and general. Brandenstein freely translates the word *Arpa-kšad* as "lord of the knights."[35] There is evidence to demonstrate that the divisions of the population into three age groups was a matter of law not only among the Scythians, but also among the Medes and Persians. The young manhood represented generally that enterprising element which, as the *Ver sacrum*, the sacred springtime, went out bent upon conquest. The middle class selected the king who was forced to surrender his rule to a younger man at the age of 52.

This is why it would be pointless to look for the name of an Arpaksad in the lists of the Median kings. Arpaksad is not a personal name; it is the designation of the "knightly order" together with its leader, the "lord of the knights." Precisely which "lord of knights" is meant by name must be determined on the basis of other data. In the Book of Judith there are two references to a battle on the Plain of Ragae (1, 5; 1, 15). Does this mean that there were two distinct Arpaksads who were conquered? Or do both reports refer to one and the same event?[36] The text lists two different dates: "in the 12th and in the 17th year of Nebuchadnezzar" (1, 1; 1, 13).

a. *The "Arpaksad" Bardiya*: The first dating, which in the traditional Greek form of the text represents an incomplete sentence, is best resolved as a synchronism: "In the 12th year of the reign of Nebuchadnezzar ... Arpaksad became king of the Medes in Ecbatana" (1, 1). Does this synchronism present an historical meaning? The 12th year of Nebuchadnezzar IV would coincide with the year 527/26 B.C. In the course of this year, accordingly, a change in power must have taken place in Ecbatana. After the death of Cyrus the Great his son Cambyses (ancient Persian: Kambudshiya) would have taken over control in summer of 530. His primary interest was the campaign against Egypt. Late in 526 he marched from Ecbatana. At the end of that same year he had pushed as far as Pelusium, knocking on the gates of Egypt. It is certainly quite probable that, before undertaking this daring enterprise, he would have installed his

34. *Ibid.*, 183.
35. W. Brandenstein, *Bemerkungen zur Völkertafel der Genesis*, Fs. A. Debrunner, (1954), 60.
36. According to Fr. Stummer Jdt 1, 5 is the same as 1, 16: the first reference simply anticipates the actual course of events.

brother Bardiya (Greek: Smerdes) as his administrator in Ecbatana, where Cyrus had already established his residence. Political considerations made the naming of an imperial administrator
absolutely necessary. In Median terms, Bardiya, the "Lord of
the knights," was the real possessor of the kingly power, thus
"Arpaksad."

The task of building up the city of Ecbatana (1, 2-4) to be
the imperial capital was entrusted to Bardiya; he was simply to
continue the work already begun by Cyrus. Cyrus had reigned
not in Persepolis, but in Ecbatana. This building project presupposes a few peaceful years. It was only "in those days" (1,
5) that the great war began. After the death of Cambyses, Bardiya
became the legitimate successor to the throne. Business accounts
in Babylon from April, 522, are already dated in terms of his
name.[37] But he was opposed in this purpose by Darius, who derived his ancestors from a secondary line of the Achemenids, and
claimed throne and kingdom for himself. On the basis of our
present knowledge of the course of history we must say that
it is not Bardiya who was the usurper, as Darius hopes us to
believe on the basis of his inscriptions, but Darius himself. He
succeeded, however, in forcing Bardiya back into Media and
there defeated him in the mountain fortress of Sikayahvatis [38]
on September 29, 522.

Darius was not permitted a long enjoyment of this victory;
upon hearing that the legitimate successor to the throne had been
deposed, a general rebellion flamed up throughout the empire.
Parties to this rebellion were Persia, Elam, Media, Assyria, Egypt,
Parthia, Margiana, Sattagydia and the country of the Sakaes (Behistun inscription: II, 6-9). It is at this point that the second
dating of the Book of Judith refers: "In the 17th year of Nebuchadnezzar" (522/521).

b. *The "Arpaksad" Fravartis*: In the 17th year of Nebuchadnezzar a certain Fravartis rose to the head of the Median nobility; in Babylon Nidintu-bel began to claim that he was the

---

37. Parker-Dubberstein, *Babylonian Chronology*, (1956), 15.
38. In the vicinity of modern Kermanshah, not far from Behistun.

son of Nabonidus, Nebuchadnezzar (III); in Persia General Wahy-azdata was fighting to succeed Bardiya on the throne, and in Elam Ašina claimed legitimate power. The most dangerous of these "rebels" against Darius was Fravartis. In these turbulent days the faith of language was broken. Everyone was accusing everyone else of lying and breach of faith and justice. Fravartis is described as follows in the smaller Behistun inscription: "This Fravartis lied, and this is what he said..." [39] In the greater Behistun inscription (1, 15-17, 24): "This man said: I am Kšatrita from the line of Hvahšatra (Cyaxares!). Accordingly, those of the Median nobility who were in my service at court defected from me and went over to Fravartis." This makes it clear that Fravartis belonged to the serving nobility, that is, the middle age class who were alone justified in laying claim to the rule. The old Persian word Kšatr-ita might well correspond to the Median dialect form kšad-ita in the meaning "son of power," "ruler, legitimate ruler." [40] Arpa-kšad and Kšad-ita are thus on the same level. From this it would follow that the Arpaksad against whom Nebuchadnezzar had to fight in his 17th year was none other than Fravartis. The more precise details we know concerning the death of Fravartis also fit into this reconstruction. "He captured Arpaksad in the mountains of Ragae and struck him down with hunting spears; and he utterly destroyed him, to this day" (1, 15).

According to the Behistun inscription Darius sent his general Widarna against Fravartis. Near Marus, in the neighborhood of Sikayahvatis, Fravartis was dealt his first defeat (January 12, 521). He thereupon withdrew to Ecbatana. The Persians entered winter quarters and awaited the arrival of Darius. On May 7 came the second and conclusive battle. Fravartis fled with a small detachment towards the northwest, probably in an attempt to join forces with the equally rebellious Parthians and Hyrkanians; he was overtaken at Ragae, however, [41] and sent

---

39. Weissbach, *op. cit.*, 77.
40. This identification was suggested by W. Brandenstein. Cf. Fs. A. Debrunner, (1954), 60.
41. Not Ragai = Ra'i near Teheran (Tob 1, 14; 4, 20; 9, 2), but in

back captive to Ecbatana. His nose, ears, and tongue were cut off, and he was displayed at the city gates for the caprice of the mobs. Finally he was impaled (24, 25, 31, 32).

  c. *Nebuchadnezzar and Darius*: Both narratives of the war agree on the essential points, although there are some embarrassing differences. According to the Bible, Nebuchadnezzar was the conquerer of Ecbatana and victor over Arpaksad at Ragae; according to the Behistun inscription it was Darius. Is there any trustworthy explanation for this variance? It would not be the first time in history that the palm of victory over a commonly attacked enemy has been claimed by more than one of the victorious allies. But this would presuppose the fact that Nebuchadnezzar had fought as the ally of Darius against the Medes. One striking element of the Behistun inscription is the lack of explicit mention of any uprising in the western country of Syria. Does this mean that the satrap of this territory fought on the side of Darius? After the victory over Media, however, this alliance fell to pieces. After the campaign against Media, Nebuchadnezzar withdrew into his original camp in "Nineveh" where he stayed 120 days, that is, four months (1, 16). The victory over Fravartis is dated on May 7, 521; four months later, August 25, 521, Nebuchadnezzar enters Babylon as king. The interval is taken up by the wars in Armenia. The Persian armies are supposed to have won victories over the Armenians in three battles at Zuzu, Tigra, and Autiyara. These were not, however, lasting successes. The most successful of the "Armenians," the man who began the battle against Darius from Tubal, was Araka (Nebuchadnezzar IV). He broke with Darius and began to build his own world empire in the 18th year (521/520). "He called together all his officers and all his nobles and set forth to them his secret plan" (2, 2), that is, he began his rebellion. He called upon the western countries to do homage to him. "But all who lived in the whole region disregarded the orders of Nebuchadnezzar King of the Assyrians, and refused to join him in the war; for they were not afraid of him, but looked upon him as only one man,

---

Northern Iran in the neighborhood of Nishapur.

and they sent back his messengers empty-handed and shame-
faced" (1, 11). Thereupon Nebuchadnezzar committed his entire
military strength to the generalship of Holofernes. He himself
turned against Babylon. Nebuchadnezzar's demise is not mentioned in the Book of Judith, since here it is only one small fragment from these tumultuous events that is concerned, namely, the
siege and liberation of Bethulia.

4) NEBUCHADNEZZAR, KING OF "THE ASSYRIANS IN NINEVEH"

This one sentence seems to give the lie to the whole preceding
discussion: "Nebuchadnezzar, who was king of the Assyrians in
Nineveh the great city" (1, 1). Nineveh was so completely destroyed in 612 that it has since lain in ruins and been condemned to complete oblivion. The terrible splendor of the great
dragon was once and for all destroyed. In order to understand
the reference to Nebuchadnezzar as "King of the Assyrians in
Nineveh" we must turn not to the old Assyrian Empire with its
capital city at Nineveh, but rather the terminology proper to
the Persian era. In the course of a century which was filled with
newly formed empires, old names could very well take on a new
geographical application.[42] After the destruction of Nineveh (612)
the ancient Assyrian heartland north of the Tigris was added to
the Median Empire and hence referred to as Media. The name
"Assyria" migrated towards the west. It is generally agreed
that the "Assyria" of the Behistun inscriptions is really "Syria." [43]
Herodotus (III, 155; I, 178; VII, 63) substantiates this fact;
he describes the "Assyrians" in the army of Xerxes as follows:
"These are called Syrioi by the Greeks, but Assyrioi by the
barbarians." Language is a further consideration. For the Persian
imperial administration the "Assyrian" language was not the
tongue spoken in ancient Assyria and written in cuneiform, but
rather the Aramaic language of Syria which was written in alpha-
betical script. "Assyrian," Syrian, and Aramaic thus refer to
the same thing. From the point of view of history, accordingly,

---

42. Compare the Austrian form of the name Styria (Steiermark), originally
    the "Mark (march) of Steier."
43. For more information, cf. Brunner, op. cit., 75.

"Assyria" refers to that territory which was added to the new Babylonian Empire upon the dissolution of the Assyrian Empire in the year 612, that is, territories in northern Mesopotamia as well as the whole of the western countries across the Euphrates, including Palestine, but with the exception of ancient Assyria, which now became the property of the Median Empire. This form of reference continues throughout the Persian and Hellenistic eras. The Persian imperial administration refers to this name, with only few exceptions, as " 'Abar-nahara," that is, "the (territory) across the river (Euphrates)."

If Nebuchadnezzar is, accordingly, called "King of Assyria," he has a right to this title. The geographical territory occupied by Holofernes actually embraces the Syria of Persian and Hellenistic geography. But what about his residence city "Nineveh"? The Assyrian Nineveh no longer existed at this time. Ancient sources, however, give one hint which must not be disregarded. Among the allies of Pompey, Lucan [44] mentions, in addition to Damascus, Gaza, and Sidon, also the city of Ninos. In the fourth century after Christ, *Ninos vetus* was a great city,[45] better known under the name Hierapolis-Bambyke, modern Memdij. It is situated along the ancient caravan route between Aleppo and Carchemish, about 20 miles straight south from Carchemish along the Syrian side of the Euphrates. There is hardly a more favorable location from which to embark upon a campaign into the western territories, or for that matter, into Mesopotamia itself. The narrative in Judith 2, 21 reads: "They marched for three days from Nineveh to the Plain of Bectileth, and camped opposite Bectileth near the mountain which is to the north of Upper Cilicia." This is a reference to the famous Gulf of Iskenderum, in which Alexander the Great fought the important battle of Issos (333), one of history's ancient battlefields; this concept is further developed in the symbolic name Bet-qtileth, "a place of slaughter." From the Assyrian Nineveh this battlefield cannot possibly be reached in three days, although it can from the Syrian Nineveh. The distance, in a direct line, is over 100 miles.

---

44. Pharasalia III, 215.
45. Ammianus Marcellinus XIV, 8, 7.

Whether Holofernes marched up the Euphrates by way of Carchemish or southward by way of Aleppo, we do not know; at all events, the distance cannot be much more than 120 miles, a distance which can certainly be covered within three days.[46]

This concludes the course of our investigation. Of all the proposed hypotheses [47] for the identification of the Nebuchadnezzar of the Book of Judith, the person of Araka-Nebuchadnezzar IV from the Behistun inscription offers the greatest historical probability. There is no need to intrude any symbolism into the text. It means precisely what it says.

5) THE BATTLE FOR BETHULIA

a. *The location of Holofernes' camp*: Since the "Israelites who dwelt in Judea" (4, 1)[48] refused to obey orders to recognize Nebuchadnezzar as their new master, Holofernes had to prepare for battle. "He appeared before Esdraelon,[49] near Dothaim,[50] which lies before the great slope of Judea, and pitched his camp between Gabai [51] and Scythopolis;[52] there he remained for an

---

46. In 1945 I myself escaped from Vienna at the approach of the Russians and made my way about 65 miles by foot in two days.
47. Pfeiffer, HistNTT 295 presents a list of kings with whom Nebuchadnezzar has been identified: Adadnirari, Merodak-baladan, Assurbanipal, Samas-sum-ukin, Kandalanu, Nebuchadnezzar II, Cambyses, Darius I, Xerxes I, Artaxerxes III, Ochus Seleucos I, Antigonos Cyclops, Antiochus IV Epiphanes, Demetrius I, Trajan, Hadrian. The possibilities brought to light by the Behistun inscription are not even discussed here.
48. The term "Judea" is no longer equivalent to the Province of Judea. The people who returned from Exile began naming their country where the kingdom of Judah had ended. King Josiah had annexed the territories of the Northern Kingdom, so that Samaria also belonged to the territory of the Kingdom of Judah. The boundary ran from Carmel to the great plain. The "Israelites" are here distinguished from the foreign ethnic groups settled in Samaria by the Egyptians.
49. Cf. Vol. IV, pp. 42ff. Esdraelon is the same as Jizreel, the winter residence of the Northern Kingdom.
50. In Hebrew Dotan or Dotain: modern tell-Dotan.
51. Tell-'Amr, near el-Haritiye, on the western end of the Plain of Esdraelon, an old pass from the valley, settled already in the Bronze Age.
52. Beth-shan.

entire month, in order to muster the entire striking force of his army." A glance at the maps shows that Holofernes located his headquarters along strategically important points, along the ridge of the watershed between the Plain of Esdraelon and the Plain of Beth-shan. From this centrally located point, he could hold both plains in check and at the same time prepare for a push into the mountain country.

b. *The march*: Two routes of attack can be determined. The primary column was under the control of Holofernes himself. From his principal camp in Esdraelon, his army set out and occupied a position along the low Plain of Bethulia (7, 3). The front had two wings; the one stretched from Dothaim as far as Balaam,[53] the other from Balaam to Kyamon [54] (7, 3). Bethulia itself was completely invested. A division of Ammonites and 500 (As)Syrians marched into the Jordan Plain and made their way through the ancient gateway of Wadi Far'a as far as Egrebel.[55] Holofernes was employing the familiar tactics of a pincer movement. From two sides, north and south, he meant to control the mountain route that led onward to Jerusalem.

c. *The siege of Bethulia*: The arrival of Holofernes completely cut off the mountain fortress of Bethulia. Whereas the other locations, such as Dothaim and Balaam, are sufficiently well known, the name and position of Bethulia can be found in no other biblical or profane source. Does this mean that Bethulia is the product of free imagination? Even locations which are verified in only a single source can still be quite historical. Since, moreover, the details furnished by the text are extremely precise, we can indirectly ascertain the position of Bethulia. One of the peaks of Gebel al-'Asi, probably the dome of šēch-šibel (about 1600 feet above sea level), is a likely location.[56] But the Old Testament settlement which is supposed to have been situated here was called bêt-'Eked (1 K 10, 12). How can the same place also have the name Bethulia?

---

53. Jibleam (Jos 17, 11; Jg 1, 27), modern Khirbet Bel'ame.
54. Not Jokneam, but el-Jamun (Simons, GTT 499).
55. Modern Khirbet el'Akrabaniya, in the spring country of Wadi Far'a, not far from ancient Tirzah.
56. Cf. Stummer, *Geographie* 7; Brunner, *loc. cit.*, 123; a definitive answer as to the existence of an ancient settlement here can only come from excavation.

The difficulty lies in the fact that the name Bethulia has not been handed down in its Semitic form, but rather in its Greek vocalization: *batulia, batulua, batylua* (Latin: *Bethulia*). Since the Semitic guttural has no counterpart in Greek, the original form may have been *bêt-'ul, -hul, -hul, -'ul;* since, furthermore, the prefix *bêt* can be abbreviated as *be-*,[57] it is also possible to divide the word as *be-tul, -tul:* there are thus six possible derivations. Presupposing that ancient *bet-'Eqed* is identical with Bethulia, then the form which approaches closest to the ancient name will have the greatest probability. The full name is *bêt-'Eqed haro'îm,* that is, *bêt-'Eqed* of the shepherds (2 K 10, 12). The Targum of Jonathan [58] translates: "House of the Assembly of the Shepherds," no doubt because the root *qd,* "to bind, to join," means something like "group, assembly." But this does not seem to be the proper direction for a solution. In the Jacob narratives, the same word is used to describe a type of sheep (*'aquddîm:* Gn 30, 35, 39f.; 31, 8, 10, 12): *bêt-'eqed* would thus mean "sheep-house." In much the same connection, Genesis also speaks of *telû'îm,* another species of sheep. In Aramaic, the word *talya* means "lamb," and *tilluya* means "the offspring of young animals"; [59] *bêt-tilluya* would also mean something equivalent to "sheep-house." The two names would thus be practically synonymous, and Bethulia or *betylua* would belong to the more recent, Aramaic era. An ancient shepherd's settlement would, accordingly, have been built up as a center of resistance during a time of crisis. These and similar derivations [60] have only a conjectural value, it is true; but they are sufficiently strong to demand that the identification of Bethulia with *bêt-'Eqed* be seriously considered. Perhaps a new population gave a new name to the location.

Judith and the city commandant Uzziah boast that they are descendants of the tribe of Simeon. When the promised land was first divided, the tribe of Simeon was settled in territories south of Judah. But they were unable to assert their claim. Soon there ensued a general

---

57. Hatch-Redpath, *Concordance to the Septuagint,* Supplement, Eigennamen 34.

58. A. Sperber, *The Bible in Aramaic,* II (1959), 294.

59. Levy, *Chaldäisches Wörterbuch,* (1959), 303. The derivation of the word from *bet-'ul* (house of the young bull) points to the same direction.

60. Other possible derivations: Köhler, LexVT suggests, for *'eked,* the meaning of "pile of sand" (with question mark). If this is correct, the obvious association is the Hebrew word *hol, holah, hawilah,* "sand." This would give the original form of the word as *bet-hol, -hûl (ya)* "house of sand." — Or perhaps the center of resistance was called simply *bet-hel* ("fortress"). EncMikr III, 212. It could also have been an abandoned site (tell) that was newly occupied and fortified. Perhaps it was simply *bet'el, -elôah,* "house of God."

emigration. There is, accordingly, nothing strange about these "sons of Simeon" appearing far from their original territory. In the account of the reforms of King Josiah, the tribe of Simeon is not mentioned together with Judah, but in the same formula with Ephraim and Manasseh. The appearance of Simeonites in the Samaritan mountain country, and thus also in Bethulia, would not be extraordinary (2 Ch 34, 6). There is considerable evidence that within the ancient tribal territory of Simeon there was a place called Betul [61] (Jos 19, 4). It was certainly possible that the name emigrated along with the inhabitants when they moved north. These are questions which must remain open.

The lifeblood of the city of Bethulia was its spring, and this description certainly fits *bêt-'Eqed* (1 K 10, 14). Holofernes did not wish to resort to force of arms and storm the city. A frontal attack upon a well fortified position always entailed considerable loss. He had the springs occupied and thereby cut off the life supply of the city. The besieged populace held out for 34 days before the cisterns were empty. Then they determined to surrender the city unless help was forthcoming within five days.[62] It was at this moment that Judith entered upon the scene.

The fact that the cisterns were nearly empty in Bethulia points to the late summer. At the same time Nebuchadnezzar had advanced towards the east. On August 25 he made his way into Babylon. A mighty dream, the reestablishment of the Babylonian world empire, appeared to have been fulfilled. On November 27, 521, Nebuchadnezzar was captured and impaled by the generals of Darius. What the military power of Persia accomplished in the east the hand of a woman accomplished in the west. The murder of Holofernes meant the dissolution of the army, which immediately fled through Damascus and dispersed (15, 5). Darius dealt with the remnant. For those who had returned home from

---

61. The pilgrim Theodosius visited the site, called Bitolion, and — though this is impossible, in the south — identified it as the location of the narrative of Judith. Stummer, *Geographie* 9.

62. J. M. Grintz, *Sur la source du motif fondamental dans le livre de Judith,* *Môlad* 17 (1959), 564-66, states that the city of Lindos on Rhodes, under siege by one of Darius' generals, determined to capitulate in five days if there were no rain (Inscription of Lindos). Grintz holds that the author of Judith took this story for his narrative, around 360. More than doubtful!

Exile there was now a long time of peace, described at the end
of the Book of Judith. The reconstruction in Jerusalem could
now begin under the impulse of the prophets Haggai and Zechariah.

C) THE TEXT OF THE BOOK OF JUDITH

The historical difficulties presented by the Book of Judith can
be partially explained by the fact that the Hebrew or Aramaic
original of the text has been lost. The surviving ancient translations are markedly different from each other and are thus
evaluated in quite different terms. The Greek text is preserved
in three versions.[63] It is followed rather closely by the Syriac
and old Latin translation. Jerome originally was unwilling to
translate the Book of Judith, since he considered it non-canonical.
But his friends prevailed upon him to translate it. For the text
history of the Book of Judith, it is important to note that he
translated it from a "Chaldean" original. Furthermore, by his
own admission, he worked rather freely. As a result, any attempt
to reconstruct the Aramaic original on the basis of the Vulgate
is extremely difficult. The Vulgate is, on the one hand, signifi-
cantly shorter than the Greek tradition. Thus, for example, at
the end of the first chapter, Nebuchadnezzar's war plan is completely missing, while the long speech to Holofernes (2, 5-13) is
restricted to a few verses, and difficult geographical names have
simply been omitted. These abbreviations, however, are balanced
by rather significant elaborations. Such great differences in the
ancient translations make the attempt at reconstructing the original text extremely difficult. We can say with certainty, however,
that all the translations are based upon a Semitic original. This
is clear from both the sentence structure and the word forms,
which sound foreign in Greek, but which are proper to a Semitic language — whether Aramaic or Hebrew cannot be determined.[64]

There are, as a matter of fact, several Hebrew forms of

---

63. For more detail, cf. A. Miller, *Das Buch Judith*, HSAT (Bonn) 1940,
    17ff. The three Greek versions are: a. a so-called vulgar text (Codices
    BAS), b. the text of Lucian (Codices 19 and 108), c. a recension

the Book of Judith. Their historical value, however, according to A. Miller,[65] is null, since they represent later reworkings in a very late form of the language. The extant Hebrew texts are not the original text, but a retranslation based upon the ancient versions.[66] The claim has been made that they are primarily dependent upon the Vulgate. But the matter does not seem to be so simple as that. Dubarle has made a very thorough examination of the extant Hebrew texts, with surprising results.[67] In the Hebrew texts of Judith it is possible to establish some influence from both Vulgate and Septuagint, but, beyond this influence, the texts represent an autonomous recension, independent of the ancient translations.[68] How are we to explain these differences in the Hebrew texts? Do they all go back to one Hebrew prototype? This would seem most improbable, since it would not explain the considerable variety within the Hebrew tradition. More convincing is the claim that the Hebrew texts, just like the Greek and Latin translations, are the result of a translation and free elaboration (adaptation and reinterpretation!) of an original Aramaic text. The Chaldean text which, unfortunately, Jerome treated with a very free hand, might thus have been closest to the original text. This brings the Book of Judith close to the Books of Ezra and Nehemiah in terms of literary history.

that is related to the text of Lucian (Codex 58).

64. Numerous examples of the Semitic character of the Book of Judith in EncMikr III, 516.

65. A. Miller, *loc. cit.*, 21: The Hebrew composition begins only with ch. 4; Ahior has only a small role to play; the high priest Joiakim is not even mentioned; there is no song of praise by Judith and no mention of her death.

66. A modern comparison might be the new Hebrew translation of the Book of Judith by Y. M. Grintz, *Sefer Yehudith. A Reconstruction of the Original Hebrew Text with Introduction, Commentary, Appendices and Indices*, (Jerusalem 1957). Grintz bases his translation on a critical Greek text.

67. A. M. Dubarle, *Les Texte divers du livre de Judith*, VT 8 (1958), 344-373. Four types of text: a. text of *Osar haqqodeš*, b. manuscript from the Bodleian in Oxford, c. printed version from Venice 1651, d. midrashic fragments.

68. There are traces even in 1 Cor 10, 1-10. Dubarle, *loc. cit.*, 371.

Various individual points of consideration would suggest a time of composition within the Persian rather than the Hellenistic era.

An argument for the Persian era is the division of the army into foot soldiers, chariot soldiers, archers, and horse (2: 5, 15, 16, 22), just as we find in Herodotus (VII, 61-83). The weaponry is also Persian in style. The sword of Holofernes is described by the Persian loanword *akinakes* (13: 6, 16, 9), a small saber which the Persians carried in the belt.[69] Persian, too, is the custom of demanding "earth and water" (2, 7) as a sign of subjection.[70] Persian is the reference to the deity as "god of heaven" (Ezr 1, 2 — 2 Ch 36, 23; Ezr 5, 11-12; Neh 2, 20). Finally, the title "great king, lord of the entire world," the geographical and historical data all point to the Persian era. The schism between Judah and Samaria did not yet exist. Upon the return from Exile, not only was the territory of Jerusalem settled, but a wave of repatriates established themselves in the territory of Nebrakta, which must be sought somewhere in Samaria.[71] If the high priest Johannan later comes to the assistance of the Jews settled in Samaria, and if even the Pharisees persecuted by Jannaeus sought refuge in this same territory, this presupposes the fact that there was an ancient Jewish population there.[72] The territory newly settled by the repatriate Jews was thus greater in scope than the province of Jahud as established by the Persians. The geography of the Book of Judith points to the Persian era.[73]

By way of conclusion, we might thus describe the text history of the Book of Judith:

a. *The text*, which, on the basis of language and content, would point to the Persian era, was actually written in Palestine during the Persian era, composed in the popular Aramaic speech.

---

69. Cf. Herodotus VII, 54; IX, 107; Xenophon, Anabasis I, 2, 20.
70. Herodotus V, 17-18; VI, 48-49; VII, 133-136.
71. EncMikr III, 514.
72. Flavius Josephus, *Antiquitates XIII*, 10, 2 — *Bellum judaicum I*, 4, 5.
73. A fuller account in the monumental *Atlas Yisrael*, (Jerusalem 1956), IX/6, with illustration of the Jewish settlement in the Persian Era.

It is impossible to assign any precise dating for its composition.[74] At all events, the date cannot be far removed from the events described. The time of Ezra and Nehemiah, which was a decisive time for the codification of Old Testament Scripture, could hardly have refused to acknowledge the popular Judith narrative if it had already been existing. As in the case of the prophets Elijah and Elisha, the popular narrative was then re-edited and fitted into the framework of history. This explains the variety of elements in the Book of Judith: popular, enthusiastic narratives about the heroine Judith and a sober organization within the framework of history. A copy of this Aramaic original was probably the text employed by Jerome.

b. *Maccabean adaptations*: In the Maccabean era, the ancient Hebrew literature experienced a renaissance. As we clearly saw in the book of the prophet Daniel, ancient Aramaic texts were re-edited in Hebrew and adapted to the contemporary crisis. In this time the various Hebrew recensions of the Book of Judith might well have their origin. The Greek revisions also date from the same era. The Greek editors are responsible primarily for the lengthy additions — Judith's prayer (9, 1ff.) and song of victory (16, 14). Judith became the ideal type of Jewish piety. The landscape descriptions were all romanticized. Only the Greek editor recalls that the territory around Bethulia is inaccessible and full of narrow ravines (4: 5, 7; 5, 1; 6: 7, 12; 7: 1, 4, 10, 13; 10, 13; 15: 2, 3, 5, 7). All the exaggerated statements are lacking in the Vulgate and in the Hebrew versions.

The text history thus represents a very complicated picture, but hardly more complicated than the text history of many other biblical books. Amid all this uncertainty, one point is sure: the Book of Judith was composed during the Persian era, but then under the impulse of the national-religious renewal of the Maccabean era it was readapted and elaborated in keeping with contemporary taste. That it was never accepted into the Jewish canon of Sacred Scripture might well be owing to the overemphasis on

---

74. The date suggested by Grintz, 360, is too early, since he dates the events only in the time of Artaxerxes II, VT 8 (1958), 346.

the *hebraica veritas,* the use of Hebrew as a sacred language; the Aramaic parts of Daniel and Ezra were transmitted only because they were fitted into the midst of a Hebrew text. The infant Church did not hesitate to receive this book too into her canon.[75]

D) THEOLOGICAL CONTENT OF THE BOOK OF JUDITH

Once the historical foundations for the Book of Judith have been clearly examined, it is possible to attempt some new appreciation of the theological content of the book. It is not the theological content of an historical novel, or a pious legend, but that of actual history. Accordingly, what stands in the foreground is not the theological question about the morality of killing a tyrant, but rather the wonderful deeds of God in human history.

1) THE GOD OF ISRAEL

The picture of God presented by the Book of Judith reminds one of the God of the prophets. He is called simply "God of Israel" (4, 12; 6, 21; 10, 1; 12, 8) or "Kyrios, God of Israel" (13, 7). Everything is subject to his power (9, 8) and his might (9, 11). He is ruler (δεσπότης) over heaven and earth, creator of the waters, king of the whole creation (9, 12), truly the *kyrios pantokrator,* God of Sabaot (cf. LXX, 2 S 5, 10). He is the all-powerful God, and in his hand rests the past, the present, and the future (9, 5f.). His "name," that is, his person, is enthroned in the Temple at Jerusalem (9, 8), from where he passes judgment upon Israel and the nations of the world. He is passionate like the God of Elijah (7, 30), he is the helper of the weak, the protector of the oppressed, the savior of those who have no other hope (9, 11). His presence in Jerusalem means for Israel, not a secure source of protection, but rather a threat of judgment. Because of her sins he gives Israel over to her enemies for punishment (5: 18, 20; 11: 10, 15). On the other hand, he

---

75. There is a fuller account in A. Miller, *op. cit.,* 23ff.; the first Christian citation of the Book of Judith occurs in Clement, *Letter to the Corinthians* 55, 3-5.

stands up for Israel when there is no lawlessness within her (5, 21). Since Israel had been completely purified of her allegiance to idolatry through her settlement in Babylon, she can count all the more securely on help from God (8, 17-20).

The picture of God in the Book of Judith is just as unsettling, stirring, and threatening as that of the prophets; but on the other hand it is grandiose and victorious, so long as Israel preserves her covenant (5, 17; 13, 11; 16, 3, 6). The idea of covenant determines the whole Book of Judith, as a result, coloring it with all the uncertainty resulting from this bilateral relationship. In the Book of Judith, Israel stands in a position of risk with respect to its God. Opposed to God's claim upon his people, the claim of the pagan king, even with all his divine airs, is doomed to failure. The God of Sabaot proves himself to be the Lord of history.[76]

2) THE CHARACTER OF JUDITH

The ideal of this narrative is not the deceitful woman who achieves success by her erotic allure. Judith's heroic deed, the killing of Holofernes, is only a single episode from her long life. She found the strength for this extraordinary deed only because her life habitually surpassed the measure of the ordinary. After three years of marriage she remained faithful to her husband to the age of 105.[77] She led a life of penance, fasting, and self-control. Unshakable faith in God was her strength. This is why she appeared as the strong, God-fearing woman, who in the hour of crisis was equal to an extraordinary deed of heroism. It is fear of God that Judith, in her triumphant song, celebrates above all manner of sacrifice (16, 16). She can point to the earlier example of the resolute Jael (Jg 4, 17ff.), who struck down the enemy captain Sisera when he had fled into her tent, and whose heroic deeds are sung in the song of Deborah. In order to

---

76. Cf. Pfeiffer, HistNTT 301ff.
77. Symbolic number: Judith lived for two jubilees and one week of years: (2 x 49) + 7 = 105.

understand this "murder of a tyrant" in its historical context, we must briefly mention the law of blood vengeance and tribal awareness. Judith then appears not so much as the murderess of an enemy general, but rather the blood-avenger of her fellow tribesmen who had been killed by the enemy. At all events, her deeds are evaluated and praised by her contemporaries as heroism.[78]

---

78. The picture of the woman victorious over the evil enemy was also the basis for the liturgical adaptation, which casts Judith as the type of the Virgin Mary, mother of the Lord. Especially 13, 18, 20, 23-25; 15, 10 have been used in the Office of the Blessed Virgin, in the Vulgate form.

CHAPTER VI

GOD'S BUILDERS

WITH the rise of the Babylonian Empire under Nebuchadnezzar IV, it must have seemed that the reconstruction of Jerusalem which had begun so promisingly under Cyrus' edict of liberation must all come to naught. The uncertain years from 522-520 seriously dampened all enthusiasm. Many simply abandoned the reconstruction. Then there appeared in Jerusalem two prophets who so shook up the lukewarm and despairing spirit that finally, almost 30 years after the first return, work on the Temple was once again begun.

A) THE PROPHET HAGGAI (Aggeus)

We know nothing concerning the person of the prophet Haggai apart from his mention in the Book of Ezra (5, 1; 6, 14) and the little information which can be gleaned from his own prophetic writings — only two chapters. His name is interpreted to mean "festive" (Festus). "He was a man given over neither to ecstasy and visions nor to logic and subtle reasoning, nor to the rapture of poetry and impassioned speech, nor of any great intuition into the fundamental principles of life; he was a man of action. His speech is objective and sober; where he touches upon deeper realities, his style is so obscure that it is difficult to determine the continuity between his words and concepts. He is frequently sharp, even ironic, always aiming at some clear objective, whether he is scolding, encouraging, or rejecting. It is the temple of God that needs to be built, salvation that needs to be seized upon. What he leaves to his contemporaries is the impression of a man sent to deliver a message. And his words are calculated to arouse." [1]

The book presents four dated discourses, all of them coming from a period of three months within the second year of Darius. Like a slow-motion picture, they form a powerful fix upon some of the most agitated hours of Old Testament history:

On the first day of the 6th month of the 2nd year of Darius (August 29, 520): Haggai, with his popular form of speech, asks a most telling question: Why are things going so poorly? "You have sown much and harvested little; you eat but you never have enough; you drink but you never have your fill; you clothe yourselves, but no one is warm" (1, 6). The reason is obvious: the house of Yahweh lies in ruins. You must build it up in order to enjoy God's blessing once again. These words were successful. On the 24th day of the same month (September 21, 520) the prince Zerubbabel and the high priest Joshua took the reconstruction work in hand (1, 1-15).

On the 21st day of the 7th month (September 23, 520): the building project reawakens thoughts of the old Temple. Some of the builders had actually seen it. In comparison, the new Temple is a sorry sight (2, 3). But as a contrast to the misery of the present time, the prophet announces the glory that is to come. Yahweh himself will fill this house with his glory and all the nations will come on pilgrimage to visit him (2, 1-9).

On the 24th day of the 9th month (December 18, 520): another sober reflection, and a casuistic question to the priests: If

---

1. H. Frey, *Das Buch der Kirche in der Weltenwende* (*Die kleinen nachexilischen Propheten*), CalwK 24 (1954), 16. — R. T. Siebeneck, *The Messianism of Aggeus and Proto-Zacharias*, CBQ 19 (1957), 312-328. — Fr. Sp. North, *Critical Analysis of the Book of Haggai*, ZAW 68 (1956), 25-46.

a person carries holy flesh in his garment and touches bread or pottage or wine or oil or any kind of food, does it become holy? The answer: no! The next question: If one who is unclean by contact with the dead body touches any of these, does it become unclean? The answer: It does become unclean. Conclusion: Thus it is with you: your uncleanness has made the entire land unclean, so that it no longer bears any fruit. But from now on God will give his blessing because you are building up his house (2, 10-12). On the same day, Haggai recounts a messianic oracle to Zerubbabel. The reconstruction of the Temple had also awakened the ancient Davidic hopes. The prophet confirms their reliability and proclaims that Yahweh has chosen Zerubbabel to be his signet ring (2, 20-23). A world empire had fallen to pieces, but the kingdom of God was shining its promising light into the world of time.

B) THE PROPHET ZECHARIAH (Zacharias)

"After Ezekiel, Zechariah is one of the strangest prophets. He receives his visions mysteriously at night. Their abundance overwhelms him with an uncanny power, until exhaustion claims him, and he falls asleep until new visions rouse him. The images he beholds are uncanny and bizzare like the confusing products of a terrified imagination. A whole series of figures crowd the stage: angels, mounted armies, war chariots, smiths with axes, women with storks' wings, etc."[2] If Haggai was a man of action, Zechariah is a priest and seer. His name means "Yahweh is mindful." His genealogy is carried back through Berechiah to Iddo, who was the head of a priestly family that returned from Exile (Ezr 5, 1; Neh 12, 4, 16). As a priest he studied the earlier prophets and reinterpreted the ancient thinking in keeping with his own time. His words are full of powerful originality and artistic genius. But his visions do not dissipate into mere imagination; just like Haggai's sober words, they are a call to action.

---

2. H. Frey, l. c. 41.

The Book of Zechariah is divided into two parts: chs. 1-8 are the work of Zechariah himself; they are a precipitate of his prophetic preaching; the rest of the chs., 9-14, are, like Deutero- and Trito-Isaiah, the work of a later era. They are generally described, as in the case of Isaiah, by the name Deutero-Zechariah.[3]

The primary bloc of the Book of Zechariah is formed by the eight night visions (1, 7 — 6, 8), preceded by an introduction (1, 1-6) and followed by some final additions (6, 9-15; 7—8). The appearance of three dates in the text makes it possible to fit the writing into the course of history. Zechariah's first call came on the 8th month of the 2nd year of Darius (October/November 520). He preached to his contemporaries on the subject of God's fidelity and their fathers' unfaithfulness. Yahweh had carried out his plan for history and would continue to be at work (1, 1-6). The eight visions are dated on the 24th day of the 11th month of the 2nd year of Darius (February 3, 519) (1, 7). They are arranged according to a symmetrical pattern, proceeding by pairs:

1 + 8: four horsemen (1, 7-17) and four chariots (6, 1-8, 15).
2 + 3: four horns and four smiths (2, 1-4) and the man with the measuring line (2, 5-9).
4 + 5: the dress of the high priest and the prince (3, 1-10); lamps and two olive trees (4, 1-6a, 10c-14).
6 + 7: flying scroll (5, 1-4) and woman in the ephah (5, 5-11).

In the years 522-520, when the Persian Empire was threatening to burst, many people might have looked in hope to the dawn of God's kingdom on earth.[4] When Zechariah began to speak, Darius had a firmer grasp on the sovereignty than any of his predecessors. The kingdom of God had not appeared. The four

3. Robert-Feuillet, IntrAT 564ff. and 580ff. — M. Delcor, *Les Sources du Deutéro-Zacharie et ses procédés d'emprunt*, RB 59 (1952), 385-411, dated c. 300 B. C. on the basis of its anthological style: *Les allusions a Alexandre de Grand dans Zach IX, 1-8*, VT 1 (1951), 110-124. — K. Elliger, *Ein Zeugnis aus der jüduschen Gemeinde im Alexanderjahr 332 v. Chr;* ZAW 62 (1949/50), 63-115.
4. K. Galling, *Die Exilswende in der Sicht des Propheten Sacharia*, VT 2 (1952), 18-36.

horses which had been sent into the four corners of the earth, symbolic of the rapid messenger service, came back and reported: "We have patrolled the earth, and behold, all the earth remains at rest" (1, 11). What of the promised 70 years? What of the threatened wrath of Yahweh? And the answer for this time of crisis in the faith: Yahweh's zeal is afire for Jerusalem; his wrath is flaming against the nations; he will surely take pity upon Zion and once again choose Jerusalem (vision I). He will send out the four chariots which bear his wrath upon the earth, and then will begin the world kingdom of Yahweh (vision VIII). No power on earth, symbolized by the four horns, can withstand the plans of God; the four smiths are already at work destroying the horns (vision III). The representatives of spiritual and temporal power are already prepared; the high priest Joshua takes off his dirtied clothing and arrays himself in new priestly garments, and the name of the "shoot" (semaḥ) from the house of David is engraved upon a stone with the seven eyes of God.[5] Under his rule, every man will dwell in peace beneath his vine and fig tree (vision IV). The same two powers are symbolized by the two olive trees and the seven-branched candelabra (vision V). The flying scroll which hovers over the land is destroyed (vision VI), and sin, symbolized in the woman who is sitting in the ephah, is carried away and destroyed in the sinful city of Babylon (vision VII).

All these night visions, whose images form a confused tumult, proclaim one and the same thing: Though the entire world has grown peaceful and there appears to be no indication of the dawning of God's dominion, Yahweh will still establish his kingship in Jerusalem. Messianic faith was so strong that the prophet's encouragement was sufficient to have the people forge a golden crown and set it on the head of the "shoot." [6] Under the two powers, the priestly and the royal, the land was destined to

---

5. In 3, 9 we are to read Zerubbabel instead of Jeshua. Robert-Feuillet, IntrAT 564. – Pfeiffer, IntrOT 605.
6. In 6, 11 it is once again Zerubbabel who is meant. – L. Waterman, *The Camouflage of three messianic Conspirators*, JNES 13 (1954), 83-87. The three conspirators would be Haggai, Zechariah, and Zerubbabel. Zc 6-8 would be the literary precipitate of the failure of the enterprise.

sprout forth into new blossom. That a new era had actually dawned is evident from the prophetic decision taken in the 4th year of Darius (December 7, 518) by which the former day of fast in commemoration of the destruction of Jerusalem was to be transformed into a day of festival (7, 1, 18).

The new work on the temple is the result of the powerful prophetic impulse. The temporal power of Persia, which, under Cyrus, had magnanimously given consent for the construction, surely does not figure here. Only when peace had returned to the kingdom did the Persian officials take note of what was happening in Jerusalem. The resistance came from the ruling class in Samaria who wanted to help with the construction of the temple but who had been rejected by Zerubbabel (Ezr 4, 1-5). Finally, Tattenai, the Satrap from 'Abar-Nahara, the land "across the river" (Syria and Palestine) was called in. He first asked in Jerusalem by whose permission the building was being continued. The edict of Cyrus was produced. Tattenai referred the matter to the imperial chancellor in Ecbatana. It is evidence of the precision of the Persian administration that the earlier edict could easily be produced. The satrap's official answer was that he should assist the temple building in Jerusalem and do nothing to hinder its progress (Ezr 5, 1 — 6, 12). It is interesting to note that Zerubbabel has already disappeared from the stage. We do not know whether he had meantime died, whether he had been removed as successor to the throne, or whether, upon the accomplishment of his mission, he simply returned to Babylon of his own free will.[7] At all events, he was the last governor of the Davidic line. On the political plane, the house of David had now completely lost its significance; but the messianic expectations of the future assume a growing importance.

In March 515 the construction of the second Temple was finished. Its dedication was celebrated with the greatest jubilation (Ezr 6, 13-18). A beginning had been made. The people had restored its religious center about which it could gather. Within the closely knit Persian Empire, this tiny religious community in Jerusalem under the leadership of a high priest hardly deserved

---

7. EncMikr II, 940.

attention. Politically Jahud was only a tiny administrative district in the province of Samaria. Great things had been hoped for in this time of political collapse and restoration, the advent of God's kingdom upon earth; what resulted was simply the "church" of the Old Testament.[8]

C) THE PERSIAN WORLD EMPIRE

The era around 500 B.C. was involved in many more events than the reconstruction of the Temple in Jerusalem. The Persian bear was poised to sink its claws into India, Europe, and Egypt. After the end of the revolution and the restoration of a united kingdom, Darius spent the first years of his reign seeing to the interior reconstruction of his empire. A little to the south of Pasargada, where Cyrus had made his grave, Darius began the construction of his imperial jurisdiction. Following the native usage, he called it simply by the name of his land and people, Parsa (Persis), in Greek, Persepolis. This new magnificent residence was the monumental expression of his royal will as ruler and his grandiose dreams of an empire. Even today, its ruins are a mute testimony to the glory of what was then the capital of the world.[9] Beginning with his 4th year (518) Darius had begun to completely reorganize the administration of his Empire, thereby proving himself to be one of the ablest organizers in the history of the world. The Empire was divided into twenty satrapies, with members of the highest Persian nobility administrating each dis-

---

8. W. Eichrodt, *Vom Symbol zum Typos. Ein Beitrag zur Sacharja-Exegese*, ThZ 13 (1957), 509-522.
9. In Persepolis the foundation of bedrock had to be leveled before the principal buildings could be erected: Adapana (colonnade), throne room, palace, treasury. All the buildings were surrounded by a wall. Outside the wall lay the residence of the people; 3½ mi. NNE, in the rocky cliffs of Naksi-i-Rustam, the royal graves were located. Persepolis was excavated from 1931-1939 by the Oriental Institute of Chicago. The monumental work on the subject is by E. F. Schmidt, *Persepolis*, I. Structures, Reliefs, Inscriptions; II. Contents of Treasury. The Univ. of Chicago Orient. Inst. Publ. vol. LXVIII (1953) and LXIX (1957). — Illustrations by von der Osten, *Welt der Perser*, tablets 47-63.

trict, among them the princes of the royal house. This gigantic Empire was thus possessed of a very sensible division and line of command, in which the peculiarities of the individual provinces could be properly taken into account. In order to hold the entire edifice together, however, Darius inaugurated an administration center in Susa with a chancery system capable of overseeing even the finest details. Moreover, the Persian king did not hesitate to take over Aramaic as the heretofore current official language, so that scholars speak of a so-called imperial Aramaic or official Aramaic [10] which also figures in the Bible. Communications circulated within Persia itself were also written in Elamitic while the official proclamations of the king were also written in Persian. Among the many languages represented in the vast Empire, Aramaic represented the best instrument for communicating with the peoples of Asia Minor, until it yielded to Greek. Hand in hand with the organization of the administration, we note the development of the financial system. Darius introduced a gold system, with the daric (Dareikos) as the monetary unit, thereby establishing the entire economic system on a new basis. In order to facilitate rapid communications between east and west he built the royal highway from Susa diagonally through Asia Minor as far as Sardes. Darius well deserves the honor of having created the best organized and greatest world empire throughout the Ancient Near East.

Darius' great campaigns of conquest can be only briefly described in this connection.[11] But it is precisely with reference to this political reorganization of the world that the condition of the religious community in Jerusalem appears all the more impoverished. The heart of the world beat not in Jerusalem but in the Persian royal palace. We must next turn our attention to the attempt upon the continent of Europe itself, Darius' campaign against the Scythians (516). It may well be that Darius planned

---

10. The Persian language was little suited to becoming the official language of the Empire since it was only under Darius that a Persian cuneiform was developed. W. Hinz, *Zur Behistunischrift des Dareios*, ZDMG 96 (1942), 326ff.

11. On the Persian imperial administration, cf. E. Kornemann, *Weltgeschichte des Mittelmeerraumes*, I (1948), 29-34.

to incorporate the tribal territories of the Scythians and the other horse peoples north of the Black Sea as far as the Steppes of Asia into his growing kingdom, and thereby rid himself of the constantly threatening danger from the north; at all events he set foot upon European soil and left his stamp upon the fate of Hellas, thereby fundamentally influencing the structure of the Europe that was to be. From the extreme west he then turned to the extreme east, to India, which he incorporated into his kingdom. It would seem that he was primarily motivated by economic considerations, a fact which has earned Darius the mocking name of shopkeeper. Economics he understood well. This left only the southern area to be secured, Egypt. With Egypt Darius pursued a more friendly policy than had his predecessor Cambyses. He had himself crowned Pharaoh and made a tremendous contribution to the Egyptian economy by promoting the construction of the "Suez Canal," which joined the Nile Valley with the Red Sea. He thus effected a direct sea communications between Egypt and the Persian Gulf.[12] The measure of Darius' success is best appreciated by the fact that the first stroke against the Persian sovereignty came from the most distant west, the very quarter from which 200 years later an annihilating force would be unleashed against the Persian Empire. The course of this history can be given by a few headlines, as it were: 500: Ionian revolt on the coast of Asia Minor; 490: the light-armed Persian forces, without mail armor, succumbed to the armored Greek citizen soldiery at Marathon; 486: death of Darius, accession of Xerxes; 480: Persian punitive expedition, battle at Thermophylae, destruction of the Persian fleet at Salamis; 479: destruction of the Persian land forces at Plataea and expulsion of the Persians from Greece.[13]

---

12. A. Servin, *Les stéles de l'Isthme de Suez, I. Stéles persanes,* Bull. de la soc. d'études hist. et géogr. de l'Isthme de Suez, III, 75-96. The fragmentary Persian passages are restudied. Ramses II carried the canal as far as Tell-el-Mašhuta, Necoh continued it to the Gebel Marjam, Darius joined it with the Bitter Lakes, which were then filled with fresh water.

13. For fuller detail, cf. H. Bengtson, *Griechische Geschichte,* (1950), 117ff. — E. Kornemann, *Weltgeschichte des Mittelmeerraumes,* I (1948), 34ff.

Darius was, at all events, a most extraordinary ruler, a man of exceptional mental endowment and disciplined body. On the façade of his grave, he had his final decrees engraved,[14] a perfect illustration of his spiritual portrait: "By the grace of Ahura-mazda I am such a man as to be a friend of the just man but never a friend of the evil man. It is not my pleasure that the poor man suffer injustice from the powerful, nor is it my pleasure that the lofty suffer injustice on behalf of the lowly. What is justice is my pleasure . . . . So long as my body has strength, I am, when it comes to war, a good warrior . . . , practiced in hand and foot. As a rider I am a good rider, as a shooter I am a good shooter, at foot and on horse, as a lance-thrower I am a good lance-thrower, on foot and on horse. Moreover, I have had the strength to use and enjoy these capacities with which Ahura-mazda has fitted me out. By the grace of Ahura-mazda I have accomplished what I set out to do, relying upon the capacities which Ahura-mazda has given to me. — Thus speaks Darius . . . ." Darius' successors were not made of the same spiritual mold as the tough old warrior who forged a new kingdom from the collapse of the old. Though his seizure of power may be over-shadowed, he still belongs among the most significant rulers upon the Persian throne. It is with perfect justice that history refers to him with the title "the Great." His name, in ancient Persian, *Darayawahush,* means "he who upholds the good." [15] It is with his reign that the building of the second Temple is inseparably bound up, the inauguration of a new phase in salvation history. For the vast Persian Empire, the tiny province of Jahud (Judea), with its capital city of Jerusalem, represents only a small border territory which is hardly reckoned in the overall political and economic picture. In the shadow of Ahura-mazda, however, the Jewish religion, apart from a few isolated instances of interference, was free to develop along its own course. The spiritual life of this time concentrated along two separate foci; the one was and continued to be the diaspora, as described in the Books of Esther and Tobit, while the other, just coming into its own right, was the center of Jerusalem.

---

14. von der Osten, *Welt der Perser,* 80.
15. H. S. Nyberg, *Das Reich der Achämeniden,* HistM III, 75.

THE JEWISH RELIGION IN THE PERSIAN DIASPORA

CHAPTER VII

THE BOOK OF ESTHER

THE Book of Esther is one of the most contested books of the Old Testament. The judgment of Luther is particularly hard:[1] "I am so much opposed to the book and to Esther that I wish it had never existed; there is too much Jewish propaganda and too much pagan mischief." Nonetheless, the Council of Trent [2] decided for the canonicity of this book. It thus belongs to the treasury of Sacred Scripture. It is, however, very much in need of precise historical and literary investigation.

A) HISTORICAL NOVEL?

We must begin with a literary-critical judgment which, while it takes little account of the theological content of the Book of Esther, is still quite characteristic for its evaluation: "The Book of Esther — one of the most successful novels in world literature — is not without its effect upon the reader even today. It tells of Esther, the Persian Queen. Ahasuerus, King of the Persian Empire, gives a feast in the royal gardens. The couches are gold

---

1. Weimarer Ausgabe, vol. 22, 2080.
2. EnchBibl No. 58.

and silver, the serving vessels are gold, and the canopies are white cotton curtains and blue hangings caught up with cords of fine linen and purple to silver rings and marble pillars. On the 7th day, in high good humor, the king sends for Vashti the Queen. But Vashti refuses to come. The king is angry and repudiates Vashti. He calls all the fairest maidens in the country in order to choose a new queen. Among the maidens is a Jewish girl by name of Esther. She finds favor before the king and is made queen. Haman, who had been set in charge of all the princes of the court, feels that he has been slighted by the Jew Mordecai. He is determined to have him punished by death, and begins erecting a gallows in the court. But his vengeance goes further: he manages to obtain a royal edict that all Jews in the Empire should be killed. Esther now becomes the savior of her people. She appears before the king, unsummoned, and is thereby liable to sentence of death. But she finds favor in his eyes: Ahasuerus extends the golden scepter to her. She begs him to spare her threatened countrymen and he listens. It is Haman who suffers death; Mordecai is placed in charge of the princes; a new royal edict goes out through the entire country: it allows the Jews to take vengeance on their enemies. The Jews accomplish this grisly privilege, and then in joy and triumph they organize a festival to commemorate their salvation.

"The narrative is plain and impressive, clearly constructed and full of colorful images. It is difficult to leave the story and turn to the voices of the critics who have attempted to fix its date and interpretation. For here we are faced with a confusing variety. Theologians, philologists, and historians have been at work for decades. Nonetheless, we are still without a final, valid verdict." Thus the literary-critical judgment of R. Stiehl.[3]

The explanation of this problem can only proceed from a proper appreciation of the literary genre (*genus litterarium*) of the Book of Esther. If the majority of the evidence leads us to conclude that Esther belongs in the genre of national-religious novels or legends, our faith in Holy Scripture is not affected, or

---

3. R. Stiehl, *Das Buch Esther*, WZKM 53 (1956), 4f.

rather, it is enriched and made more profound. Just like the parables in the Gospels, novels and legends can be inspired and thus the bearers of truths of revelation.

In support of the novel genre [4] for the Book of Esther the following arguments can be advanced:

1. *Chronological inconsistencies*: Mordecai is supposed to have been brought back to Susa with the other prisoners at the time of King Jehoiachin (597) (1, 3). If now Ahasuerus is identical with the Persian King Xerxes I (485-465), during whose reign the whole story is to have taken place, then Mordecai must have been already 120 or 130 years old. At all events we are faced with an abbreviation of the historical perspective.[5]

2. *The testimony of the Greek historians*: From the narratives of Herodotus [6] we know that Xerxes' consort was named neither Vashti nor Esther, but rather Amestris. Despite some apparent resemblance, the name Esther cannot be equivalated with Amestris. Esther was a Jewess, while Amestris was the daughter of a Persian general. She was married to Xerxes not only in the 7th year (216), but already in the 3rd year of his reign [7] (1, 3). The character of the biblical Ahasuerus might indeed coincide in many respects with that of the historical Xerxes; even the Greek historians paint him as anything but a reasoned person; they see him as an unpredictable despot, quite capable of rash and precipitate action. On the other hand, we cannot possibly pass over the historical "impossibilities" which are introduced incidentally into the text; they might well be ascribed simply to the novel writer's attempts to create suspense, rather than his genuine desire to recount historical facts. His statement that all Persian royal edicts are irrevocable (1, 19; 8, 8) cannot be substantiated by any profane sources. The same is true for his claim that anyone who appeared before the king unsummoned was courting the death sentence (4, 11). These are all tools from the arsenal of the novel writer.

3. *Exaggerated numbers*: On the occasion of the royal feast (1, 3) all the civil and military authorities of the entire Persian Empire received invitations; the festival lasted for six months (1, 4); the maiden selected by the jury received a beauty-treatment that lasts for over a year

---

4. Pfeiffer, IntrOT 737 is strongly in favor of the novel interpretation.
5. O. Eissfeldt, EinlAT 626.
6. VII, 114; IX, 112.
7. Herodotus VII, 6; *Ktesias* 38b.

(2, 12). Haman promised, in the event that the Jewish question was finally settled, to pay 10,000 talents ($18,000,000) to the state treasury. The gallows are 50 cubits high (5, 14). All the nations tremble before the Jews who murder 75,510 gentiles on a single day with impunity (9, 6-16).

4. *Artistic symmetry in the narrative*: The impression of the novel form is considerably strengthened by the artistic construction of the narrative. The players in this drama are divided into two perfectly corresponding groups. The beginning triumph ends in disgrace, while, from the other side, the beginning crisis ends in triumph. Vashti is repudiated while Esther is elevated! Haman is hanged while Mordecai becomes grand vizier. The anti-Jewish decree is transformed into a pro-Jewish edict, while the annihilation of the Jews becomes a slaughter of the gentiles. Surely this is a perfect example of the proverb "he who digs a ditch for another will fall in himself" (Prov 26, 27).

These and other arguments are, accordingly, advanced in support of the novel character of the Book of Esther. Are they actually sufficient to prove the point? The name of God occurs in the Hebrew version not even once. We might thus seem justified in assigning the Book of Esther not to the religious, but to the national or even nationalistic literature of the Jewish culture. It would thus deal not with actual events of history, but rather with types, functioning in fact as the great song of the national Jewish movement in its time of life or death crisis, the story of its salvation and revenge.[8] But the arguments in question, although they are certainly not without foundation, tend to cast the entire Book of Esther in a false and one-sided perspective. The novel character can be definitively established only after every interpretation on the historical plane has proved to be completely impossible — and this is certainly not the case.

B) THE HISTORICAL FOUNDATIONS FOR THE BOOK OF ESTHER

In terms of form, the Book of Esther appears to be history. Moreover, for centuries it has been considered an historical nar-

8. R. Stiehl, l. c. 6.

rative, without any claim to the contrary, and in the strict and most proper sense of the word. The arguments which have been adduced against its historicity lose much of their force when they are countered by evidence from new sources. It is obvious that the text of the Book of Esther, as we shall shortly examine, has had a not uneventful history. Only one thing can be said with certainty: the events described must be fitted into the early Persian era and not the Hellenistic era.

According to the Hebrew text, during the lifetime of Esther, Ahasuerus was king, but in the Greek translation it is Artaxerxes. The Hebrew reading is older and thus to be preferred over the Greek.[9] Philological investigation [10] has shown that Ahasuerus is the Elamite form of the Persian royal name Kšayarša, written in Greek as Xerxes.[11] The name alone points to the territory of Elam and its capital city of Susa. The same is true of the Queen's name, Vashti. Susa was the residence of the Achaemenids in the spring of the year, and also the capital of ancient Elam. It is in this royal city that the events of the Book of Esther are portrayed as taking place. If we now approach the three dates, not as the trappings of novel form, but rather the testimony of true history, a quite different picture begins to emerge.

1) IN THE SECOND YEAR OF AHASUERUS
(March 26, 484 — April 13, 483)

Mordecai Discovers the Conspiracy

There are two versions of this narrative: G 1, 1-17 and M 2, 21-23. The narrative presupposes the fact that Mordecai had some business in Susa at the royal court. On this occasion, during

---

9. How the Greek transliteration of the name Artaxerxes came about is not entirely clear. The simplest explanation would be that the long Hebrew name was to be reproduced with an equally long Greek name; this at a time in which the events themselves were all being dated in the remote past.

10. R. Stiehl, WZKM 53 (1956), 9-13.

11. On the derivation of the name Xerxes, cf. M. Mayrhofer, Altpersische Späne, Or 33 (1964), 87. Xšayaršan = "ruling over heroes."

the night, he overheard the plans of two eunuchs, who were preparing an attempt upon the life of the king. He carried the news to the king, who immediately organized an investigation, soon discovering the truth of the charge. The conspirators were punished, and Mordecai was rewarded by an elevation in rank.

This brief biblical narrative must now be compared to texts from profane history, dating from the 2nd year of Xerxes. These are primarily cuneiform tablets which were uncovered in the ruins of some private dwellings in Barsippa and the vicinity, mostly business accounts from various firms.[12] Since these sober business texts are precisely dated, it is possible to get a very accurate picture of the events accompanying King Xerxes' accession to power.

Darius had died in November of 486. His son Xerxes immediately followed him upon the throne, under peaceful circumstances; for the year of his accession and for the first year of his reign, the dating formulae all use his name. But in the 2nd year rebellion flared up. His name disappears from the business accounts. In its place we find four usurpers: Bel-šimanni, Šamašeriba, Akšimašku, and Šikušti. It must have been a truly turbulent era, with four kings occupying less than half a year (August 5, 484 — March 5, 483). These internal problems produced a disastrous effect upon the business world. The next crisis was the vengeance exacted by the irate king of Persia. As a result, the business firms known to us from Barsippa could no longer maintain their position; they all went under, and their accounts simply cease. It is possible that Barsippa itself was destroyed. The title of Xerxes, "King of Babylon," also stops during this era. Babylonia became a province and lost its personal union with Persia.[13]

From profane sources we thus learn that the 2nd year of Xerxes was a year of conspiracies and rebellions. While the business texts, with their sober and simple dates, cast some light upon the course of events, the Book of Esther describes one of these conspiracies in greater detail, the one discovered by Mor-

---

12. A. Ungnad, *Neubabylonische Privaturkunden aus der Sammlung Amherst*, AFO 19 (1959/60), 74-82.
13. *Ibid.*, 76.

decai. Is it simply chance, or perhaps a reference to the biblical
Mordecai, that one of the business texts from Barsippa [14] contains
the name of a certain Marduka? The text involves a bill sent
to some highly placed persons. Some Persian dignitaries had
come from the capital at Susa on an inspection tour, to Barsippa.
Their travel expenses had to be remunerated. Marduka, the financial administrator of Prince Ustan,[15] was given half a mina as
recompense for expenses. The tablet dates from the year 485.
If this Marduka is actually to be identified with the biblical Mordecai, and this is a possibility that cannot be excluded,[16] it
would follow that he already had a position in the Persian court
before the great revolution and was thus in a perfect position
to discover a conspiracy. This certainly not insignificant chance
event deserved to be recorded in the annals of the king (G 1, 15;
M 2, 23). The reference to the return from captivity under
King Jehoiachin (G 1, 3; M 2, 6) does not mean to say that
Mordecai had been alive at the time, but that he was a descendant
of the repatriates. The genealogy is carried back to the great-
grandfather, and this is a sufficient span to cover the years between
597 and 474.

2) IN THE THIRD YEAR OF AHASUERUS
(April 14, 483 — April 2, 482)

The Great Banquet

Once the narrative of this great banquet (M 1, 1-22) is fitted
into the framework of world history, it is quickly removed from
the alleged fantasy of the Thousand and One Nights. It was not
merely the willful caprice of an Oriental despot that summoned
the nobles from the entire kingdom of the Medes and Persians
into the capital, nor was it the private disobedience of King

---

14. *Ibid.*, 80-81; Amherst No. 258.
15. *sipir, seperu* = court official in charge of the services and maintenance
    of the Temple; *seperri makkûri* = financial minister, treasurer, chan-
    cellor. Ungnad, *loc. cit.*, translated "privy councillor."
16. Ungnad decides in favor of identity of the two persons.

Vashti that lay behind this banquet; there were many circumstances that demanded an exhibition of power to the entire kingdom, and the banquet was symbolic of this. Shortly before this time, Xerxes had succeeded in suppressing a great revolution, doing away with the four usurpers one after another. As a sign that he now held the power fast in his own hands, he summoned the governors of the provinces, the nobility and the military from Media and Persia (1, 3). Babylonia is not even referred to, since it was politically non-existent. The festival thus takes on the character of a coronation banquet:[17] "In those days, when King Ahasuerus came to the throne of his kingship in the fortress of Susa . . ." (1, 2). People and nobility alike rejoiced, and the capital city was in a holiday mood; wine flowed freely among the crowds (1, 7), like the imperial coronations from the Middle Ages. Since in the Orient the sexes were kept separate even on most solemn occasions, the queen gave a banquet of her own, in her palace, for the ladies. As the festival neared its climax, on the seventh day, Queen Vashti was invited to appear before the people and the princes in full state dress, with her crown upon her head (1, 10-22). She refused, however, to do the bidding of the king. Accordingly, she was deposed as queen. The biblical account stresses the private aspects of her conduct. What would the wives do throughout the empire if even the queen refused obedience to her husband? There is evidence to support the sus-

---

17. This solution is favored by Talmud, Megillah 11b: "When he rose to the throne," IntB III (1954), 835. — The magnificence of the festivals celebrated by Oriental kings is amply attested by the inscription of Assurnasirpal II discovered in the excavations at Kalchu in 1951: he had invited everyone of any rank or position to assist at the dedication of his new palace in 879. The feasting lasted for ten days. The entire city of Kalchu was invited: 47,074 working-men, 500 ambassadors from the Hittites, Sidon, etc., 1500 palace officials, a total of 68,574 people. The guests were regaled with 72 different dishes; the animals slaughtered included 2200 beef, 16000 sheep, 34000 fowl, 500 deer, 5000 antelope; 10000 fish, 10000 eggs, 10000 loaves of bread, 10000 skins of wine. E. Vogt, *Convivium regium populi urbis Kalchu*, Bibl. 38 (1957), 374-375. Compare also a statistic from our own times; at a huge pilgrimage festival in Mecca, 120,000 sheep were slaughtered.

picion, however, that there were political grounds behind her behavior: "Not only to the king has Queen Vashti done wrong, but also to all the princes and all the peoples who are in all the provinces of King Ahasuerus" (1, 16). Female intrigues were not uncommon in the Persian court. It might well be that the deposition of Vashti as queen represented the final checkmate in putting down a court revolt.

The invitation of the leading men of the kingdom had also become necessary by reason of the fact that Xerxes was about to prepare for his mighty invasion of Greece: "The preparations that Xerxes had been making for the campaign against Hellas since the year 483 are of a measure to overshadow everything that had ever occurred in the past. They give a most imposing picture of the strength and organization of the Achaemenid kingdom, now at the climax of its military capacity. In order to secure the provisions for the troops, a number of depots were established in Macedonia and Thrace. Particular emphasis was placed on the closest possible cooperation between the land forces and the fleet; conscriptions took place throughout the entire kingdom; this was no mere border skirmish that Xerxes meant to embark upon; he was planning a full-scale war of conquest." [18]

3) IN THE SEVENTH YEAR OF AHASUERUS
(March 31, 479 — April 18, 478)

Esther Crowned Queen

Returning from the Greek campaign, Xerxes raised Mordecai's ward Esther [19] to the dignity of queen, replacing Vashti.

---

18. Bengtson, *Griechische Geschichte,* 154.
19. Perhaps with reference to the Babylonian goddess Istar (morning and evening star); Persian *sitarch* = star; the Hellenistic Jews would think in terms of the Greek word *aster,* "star," — as seen from a funeral inscription in Beth-shearim: "Esther, also called Amphaitha," i.e., "the shining (star)." EncMikr I, 492. — Esther's original name Hadassa is supposed to mean "myrtle." M. Haller, *Die Funf Megilloth,* HAT 18 (1940), 121. But there is some likelihood of its being a derivation of the Accadian *hadašatu* = bride. EncMikr II, 796.

The marriage took place in the 10th month (Tebet) of the 7th year (between December 22, 479 and January 20, 478). As was customary on such occasions, the king granted immunity from taxes, gave copious presents, and put on a magnificent wedding feast. Esther's elevation to the position of "Queen" in Susa does not mean that she also became "empress" of the entire kingdom, a position which, according to Herodotus, Amestris alone enjoyed. Our narrator is primarily interested in the events which occurred at the royal court in Susa.

It was probably in connection with the new orientation of his domestic policies that Xerxes entrusted the office of grand vizier to a man named Haman: "He advanced him and set his seat above those of all the princes who were with him" (3, 1-15). The fact that Haman could now demand obeissance from his peers is an important factor in the development of the story. In his religious policies, Darius was very magnanimous. He allowed the greatest possible measure of political and religious freedom to his subjects. It may be that the defeats suffered in Greece led to a strengthening of the national-Persian sentiment. The demand of obeissance seems to point in this direction. In itself, the act of prostrating oneself before a dignitary might well be interpreted as a purely civil act of recognition of the state's power; but since this homage before the supreme power of the state, in such a definite and explicit form, was equivalent to an act of homage to the official state gods, Mordecai and the other Jews refused to comply with the demand out of religious considerations. They thus became suspect of hostility towards the state.

4) THE TWELFTH YEAR OF AHASUERUS
(April 5, 474 — April 21, 473)

Massacre of the Jews

Haman's injured personal vanity may well have prompted the first steps towards a full-scale massacre of the Jewish population. After all the military expenditures, the state treasury was depleted. Drawing upon confiscated Jewish property, Haman, the original "Jew hater" (3, 10), hoped to enrich the state treasury by some 10,000 silver talents, approximately $18,000,000.[20] It would appear that the affairs of the exiled Jews had prospered considerably during the Exile. This may also have been the case with other repopulated ethnic groups, without their prosperity provoking any general persecution. In the case of the Jews, as it happened over and over again in the centuries that followed, the religious element was an added factor. The situation of the diaspora is here perhaps properly appreciated for the very first time. The wording of the anti-Jewish decree, which is contained in the Greek text of the Book of Esther,[21] establishes the following foundation for the general hatred expressed against the Jews: "Among all the nations in the world there is scattered a certain hostile people, who have laws contrary to those of every nation and continually disregard the ordinances of the kings, so that the unifying of the kingdom which we honorably intend cannot be brought about. We understand that this people, and it alone, stands constantly in opposition to all men, perversely following a strange manner of life and laws, and is ill-disposed to our government, doing all the harm they can so that our kingdom may not attain stability. Therefore we have decreed that those indicated to you in the letters of Haman shall all with their wives and children be utterly destroyed by the sword of their enemies without pity or mercy on the 14th day of the 12th month, Adar, of this present year" (13, 3-6).

Those authors who evaluate the Book of Esther as a novel and date it in the Hellenistic era are of the opinion that a decree so filled with hatred of the Jewish nation and religion is unhistorical in the Persian era, since the Achaemenids are known for their liberal religious policies. But it is the mission of the historian to include in his history not only what appears probable to him, but what actually happened. Prior to the discovery of the Elephantine-Papyri [22] no one would have considered

---

20. IntB III, 851.
21. Insertion into the Hebrew text after 3, 14.
22. See below for a fuller description.

it an historical fact that in Egypt, at the end of the fifth century, in the course of a hate-filled Jewish massacre, even the Temple of Yahweh was destroyed.

Haman had prepared this devastating blow against the Jewish population far in advance. When Scripture records that he cast the lot from the first to the last month, this means to say that he inquired into the most favorable moment for his attack. Decrees with the ordered massacre went out to the governors of the provinces. They were composed in the name of King Ahasuerus and sealed with his ring. In Susa itself the decree was posted in the palace. The massacre was set to begin on the 13th day of the 12th month (March 8, 473), with an intercalary month (April 8, 473).

The credit for having stalemated this extreme crisis belongs to the courageous Esther alone (ch 4ff.). By appearing before the king, and thereby endangering her own life, she turned the crisis away from her people and back upon the arch enemy. It is not Mordecai who is hanged, but the villain Haman. Mordecai enters upon the position of Haman. The tables have turned. "The fear of Mordecai" (9, 3) went throughout the land. The Jews were in a position to strike back. Haman's ten "sons," that is, those who shared his responsibility, were all condemned. Fuller examination [23] reveals the fact that all ten bear daevic names; that is, they worshipped not Ahura-mazda, but the ancient Iranian divinities (*daeva*). Since the discovery of the daeva inscription [24] in 1935, we know that Xerxes had forbidden and attempted to extirpate this cult. The Jews, with their belief in the one God of heaven, were much closer to the Ahura-mazda faith of Xerxes than to the worship of daeva. Is it simply chance that the enemies of the Jews all have names reminiscent of daeva worship? Is it perhaps possible that, in allowing free course to the "fear of Mordecai," Xerxes meant to strike a blow against the hostile daeva followers? We can go no further than conjecture here, since the

---

23. R. Mayer, *Iranischer Beitrag zu Problemen des Daniel- und Esterbuches,* Lux tua veritas, Fs. für H. Junker, (1961), 130-135.
24. Text ANET 316; E. F. Schmidt, *Persepolis II. Contents of the Treasury and other Discoveries,* (Chicago 1957): Magnificent photograph.

decree against daeva is not dated. An historical connection between the massacre of the Jews and the decrees against daeva is certainly not unhistorical. In Susa 500 human beings are reported to have been killed (9, 6; according to 9, 15 only 300), and 75,000 in the provinces (9, 16). Never has hatred been repaid with such consummate hatred. One thing is certain: it must have been a bloody day without parallel, with even the Jews suffering heavily, although there is no record of their losses. The attempted massacre had turned into a victory which deserved to be celebrated for all times to come.

5) THE FESTIVAL OF PURIM

The Book of Esther concludes with an account of the inauguration of the Purim festival. From Susa, Mordecai (9, 20ff.; according to 9, 29 Esther too) sent the Purim letter (*'iggēret happûrîm*) to the Jews settled throughout the entire Persian Empire, stating that, for all the generations to come, they were to celebrate the 14th and 15th of Adar every year as a joyous commemoration of the liberation of the Jewish people from their mortal crisis. The name of the festival, Purim, is based on the fact that the "Jewish persecutor" had cast the lot (*pûr* 9, 24-26) over the Jews, in order to destroy them. The "lot-day" had become a festival of joy.

This would appear to be a proper and sufficient explanation of the Purim feast on the basis of an historical situation. This does not exclude the fact that there had previously been a pagan Purim festival, which the Jews had cleansed of its nature-worship characteristics and turned into a typical festival of commemoration. The Purim festival actually does contain traits characteristic of the spring-new-year festival. The date always coincides with the full moon of Adar 14/15 (February-March), one month before the full moon of the Easter festival. Presents were exchanged (9, 22), which is characteristic of the new year festival among the Persians, Egyptians, and Indians.[25] According to Esther 3,

---

25. H. Cazelles, *Note sur la composition du rouleau d'Esther*, Lux tua veritas, Fs. H. Junker, (1969), 18.

7 and 9, 24, Purim is the festival of the "lot" or the "casting of lots." In this too is a typical new year's custom especially in the Babylonian Akitu new year's festival.[26] On new year's day people believed that the gods were assigning the fates for the year to come. Scholarship has been unable to explain the word *pûr*, which cannot be derived from a Hebrew source, prior to the discovery of the cuneiform tablets from Kiltepe.[27] In these tablets the word *pûr* appears in the uncontested meaning of "lot." It follows that the Jews in Mesopotamia must have taken over the Assyrio-Babylonian word into their own vocabulary. Many exegetes [28] go so far as to interpret the entire Book of Esther on the basis of a mythological Babylonian background. In the Babylonian new year's festival the victory of the creator god Marduk over the powers of chaos is annually celebrated. In the Book of Esther, the name Mordecai stands for the creator God Marduk, while the name Haman represents the powers of evil. But the very simplicity and directness of the narrative are opposed to such mythologizing. Other scholars have suggested the Persian festival of Farvardigan as a pattern for the Purim festival, but this is a festival of the dead and not a festival of joy. The Persian new year's festival Nauruz is also eliminated, since it is celebrated in the fall. Finally, some similarities are claimed with the festival of the Saccaeans, in which the roles of master and subject were reversed, in a sort of Mardi Gras celebration.[29]

---

26. S. A. Pallis, *The Babylonian Akitu-Festival,* (Copenhagen 1926), 183ff.
27. A. Bea, *De origine vocis pûr,* Bibl 21 (1940), 198. — V. Christian, *Zur Herkunft des Purimfestes,* Fs. Fr. Nötscher, BBB 1 (1950), 33-37. From the root *prr* = shake, shake out: *puru* thus means "the shaking out, the lot." — Pfeiffer, IntrOT 746, however, claims that Purim is a deliberate formation, like Kodak.
28. The various opinions of scholarship are discussed in Eissfeldt, EinlAT 627. Also considers the conquest of the Elamite gods Human = Haman and Masti = Vashti by the Babylonian gods Marduk = Mordecai and Ishtar = Esther.
29. H. Cazelles, l. c. 28. — H. Ringgren, *Ester und Purim, Svensk Exegetisk Arsbok* 20 (1950), 5-24 goes into the cultic origins of the Purim festival and assembles all the available material from Persian and Iranian sources. Result: none of the existing festivals can be identified

We are thus forced to the conclusion that none of the known or poorly attested Ancient Near Eastern festivals is a clear model for the Purim festival. There is, however, great probability that an originally profane spring festival gradually lost its true-worship characteristics by being joined with an historical event, until it became a typical commemoration of an event in the history of salvation. Such a process would obviously require considerable time, thus accounting for the relatively late appearance of this festival in Palestine (2 Mac 15, 36).

A sober comparison with the Hellenistic romance literature shows that Esther is composed in a quite different style. The Hellenistic novels are all constructed according to the same outline. Hero and heroine must be beautiful beyond all measure, accomplish miraculous deeds, and be absolutely in love with each other. In order to prolong the happy ending as far as possible, all manner of antagonists appear upon the scene, with the result that the two lovers must first make their way through the most improbable adventures in the most remote parts of the civilized and barbarian world.[30] In terms of structure, the Book of Esther is essentially different from these novels. In Esther, sex appeal is certainly not in the foreground; the description of the wedding is much more sober than sentimental. Moreover, the place in which the drama takes place is not in the romantic distance, but in the capital city of Susa itself, which is sufficiently well known by excavation. The theme of the book is not the happy end of two lovers, but the salvation of a people in mortal crisis. These structural differences are further heightened by the problem of dating. No matter how late a date is assigned, as we shall explain below, the Book of Esther is older than the fashionable love-novels of the over-civilized Hellenistic world.[31]

---

with Purim; there is, moreover, some element of a new year festival in all of them.

30. The characteristic traits of Hellenistic novel form in J. Maillon, *Les Ethiopiques d'Heliodore*, (Lettres 1935), XVI. Comparison with the Book of Esther in H. Cazelles, *loc. cit.*, 20ff.
31. "We can attest this form [the love romance] only in the second century after Christ, in the Syrian Jamblichus; it is probable that the genre is of much earlier origin." R. Helen, *Der antike Roman*, (1956),

Conclusion: The events of the Book of Esther, within the limits of the previous discussion, can be fitted into the course of Persian history without difficulty. The Book of Esther can, accordingly, hardly be called the "most successful novel of world literature," [32] nor can it be characterized as a free historical novel with some sort of historical nucleus; the reign of King Ahasuerus-Xerxes does not lie "in a distant past veiled with the mists of saga," [33] but it is actually what it claims to be: history.

The book bears the name of a woman who plays the primary role. But this is certainly insufficient evidence for evaluating Esther as Hellenistic novel literature. It might well be true that "the Hellenistic narrative literature made greater room for the erotic than it had formerly enjoyed. Love becomes the soul of every narrative presentation . . . . The Jewish literature of late Hellenism could then hardly have gone counter to the tastes of its times. In Josephus and Philo the Old Testament narratives are given an erotic treatment. It is the woman in her erotic aspects, in her sex appeal, that becomes the heroine and savior." [34] But all these claims apply only indirectly to the Book of Esther. We could certainly admit that this extremely contemporary story has, in the course of history, in keeping with the varying tastes of the times, taken on some coloration; but this does nothing to change its essentially historical character.

C) THE LITERARY PROBLEM OF THE BOOK OF ESTHER

The Book of Esther is contained in two textual recensions,

---

32. Together with a considerable survey of the Hellenistic love romance with a discussion of the contents and an evaluation, 32-52.

32. R. Stiehl, WZKM 53 (1956), 5. — Pfeiffer, IntrOT 732: "Esther a brief historical novel"; 737: "not history but fiction"; — Eissfeldt, EinlAT 626: "Historischer Roman, Prosadichtung mit historischem Kern." — Robert-Feuillet, IntrAT 691: "Plus dramaturge que historien." — Stummer, EB 558: "Geschichtlicher Kern." — Haller, Esther, SAT 114: "Meisterhafte Erzählung, aber keine Geschichte."

33. Eissfeldt, EinlAT 630.

34. Stiehl, l. c., 8-9.

Greek and Hebrew. The Greek version contains over a hundred verses more than the Hebrew. Even in those sections which are common to both, the Greek text frequently exhibits startling diversions. This is the textual problem in briefest outline. It turns upon the dilemma [35] of whether or not the Hebrew version is an abbreviated excerpt from an older original which has been preserved complete in the Greek version, or whether the Greek version is simply a free elaboration (paraphrase) of the extant Hebrew text. It is impossible to deny that the text of the Book of Esther has had a long history, and one which cannot be easily traced in every detail. In my opinion, the problem can be solved not by a painstaking comparison between the Greek and Hebrew texts, but simply by a careful examination of the Hebrew text itself.

1) DOUBLE NARRATIVES

H. Cazelles [36] was the first to call attention to the double narratives in the Book of Esther. His presentation suggests the following outline:

Banquet:
a. 180 days for the representatives of the 127 provinces (1, 1-4).
b. 7 *days for the people in Susa* (1, 5ff.).

Councillors:
a. 7 princes of the Medes and Persians (1, 14).
b. 7 *Eunuchs in Susa* (1, 10).

Esther:
a. Account of genealogy (2, 15), prohibition against disclosing popular origin (2, 20), dated in the 7th year (2, 16).
b. *Hadasa = Esther, without mention of father's name* (2, 7), *prohibition against disclosing popular origins* (2, 10), *no date.*

Womens' Quarters:
a. The second womens' quarters under *sa'asgaz* (2, 14).

---

35. B. W. Anderson, IntB III, 823.
36. *Note sur la composition du rouleau d'Esther*, Lux tua veritas, Fs. H. Junker, (1961), 17-29.

b. *Womens' quarters in Susa under Hegai* (2, 8).

Selection of maidens:
a. The second selection (2, 19).
b. *Many maidens in Susa* (2, 8).

Conspiracy:
a. Discovered by Mordecai at the gate, reported to the king by Esther, entered into the annals (2, 21-23).
b. *"Second account": the king knows nothing of the conspiracy* (6, 1-3).

Haman:
a. Enemy of Jews all over the empire (3, 6), dated: "12th year."
b. *Enemy of Mordecai at the gates of Susa* (3, 1-4), no dates.

Esther's Intercession:
a. On Esther's intercession, the house of Haman is given over to destruction (8, 3-8), emergency decree (8, 9-13) with date! Mordecai in his glory (8, 14-17).
b. 1. *Banquet* (5, 1-8) *Haman's decision to persecute Mordecai* (5, 9-14): *king's sleepless night* (6, 1-4), *Mordecai's honoring* (6, 4-15), *Esther's intercession* (6, 14 − 7, 6).
2. *Banquet and Haman's Execution* (7, 7-10), *Mordecai's signet* (8, 1-2).

Destruction of the Enemy:
a. On Adar 13 in the provinces (9, 1-5), in Susa execution of the sons of Haman (9, 6-10), 500 people killed (9, 6).
b. *Adar 14, in Susa, Haman's sons impaled* (9, 13), *300 people killed* (9, 13).

Purim Letter:
a. Sent by Mordecai (9, 20-28), references to Chronicle (10, 1-3).
b. *Sent by Esther* (9, 29-32).

On the basis of these facts, Cazelles reaches the conclusion that we are faced with two independent lines of tradition; one of them, more liturgical in its orientation, concentrates primarily upon Esther and the provinces, while the other, more politically oriented, is primarily interested in Susa, the victory of Mordecai, and the defeat of Haman. In my opinion, the situation is much simpler. There need be no distinction between liturgical and political points of view; the riddle of the Book of Esther lies in the fact that it is a combination of popular narrative and historical chronicle.

a. *The popular version*: Popular narratives take little note of the affairs of world politics. They are interested only in what is close at hand and germane to the story. If we combine the elements in the one column, we produce a unified picture. The activity takes place in Susa, with its royal palace. It is here that Hadassa is chosen queen. In her position as queen she brings new salvation to her oppressed people. The enmity of Haman is directed concretely against Mordecai at the city gates of Susa. In order to increase the suspense, there is a description of two banquets in which Esther intercedes successfully. Mordecai is elevated and put into a position where he can take revenge. Haman is hanged, and his sons are impaled; 330 men are killed. The Jewish population is rescued from a most serious threat. Esther inaugurates the Purim festival.

b. *The Esther chronicle*: A narrative oriented towards history naturally attempts to organize the events within the historical course of time. Hence the dates. At the same time, the narrative aims at a broader horizon. It is concerned not only with a local event in Susa, but with whatever is happening in all the provinces of the kingdom. This Esther chronicle presents a compact and unified picture so that, even without the popular narrative about Esther, we would be in a position to understand the essential course of events. To his royal banquet the king invites not only the people of Susa, but the ruling class of the entire empire. The discovery of the conspiracy by Mordecai is entered into the royal annals. Haman is the enemy of the Jews and the entire kingdom. Esther's intervention is compressed into a single audience. The decree which saves the Jews from their crisis and the elevation of Mordecai are her work. Haman and his sons are condemned. The Jewish counter-offensive in Susa and in the provinces claims 500 victims.[37] The losses among the Jewish

---

37. These numbers are within the range of possibility: but the reference to 75,000 dead (9, 16) is historically impossible. There may be some gematria here, in which the number would be taken as the

party, which must also have been considerable, are not mentioned. In 10, 2 there is express mention of the fact that the heroic deeds of Mordecai have been recorded "in the chronicles of the kings of Media and Persia."

If the division into a popular narrative and a chronicle can be substantiated, it is a perfect explanation of the riddle of the Book of Esther. At the beginning there is the historical event of the salvation of the Jews of Susa and the near environs from the massacre threatening them in the 12th year of Xerxes (474/73). This salvation was to be celebrated every year. The commemorative celebration, however, did not immediately generate the "festival legend." This took time. The historical events were permanently recorded in the chronicles. But the popular memory did not forget the magnificent deeds of Esther; on the contrary, they were repeated over and over again. Eventually, both lines of tradition were combined in the work of a redactor who was interested in the liturgy of the Purim festival. In his work, just as we note in the Pentateuch, motivated not only out of reverence for the tradition, but also in an effort to create an historical framework for the popular narrative, he allowed all the double narratives to stand. In much the same way, at an earlier era, the popular narratives concerning the prophets Elijah and Elisha were incorporated into the chronicle sequence of the Books of the Kings.

The date at which these two traditions were fused cannot be accurately determined. It would probably be incorrect to assign a date later than the Persian era or the beginning of the Hellenistic era. The typically Elamite name forms [38] argue for the fact that the Book of Esther owes its present form to the location described in the narrative — Susa. But it required a new historical impulse for this liberation festival of the Jewish diaspora in Babylonia and Persia to be accepted into the Palestinian festival calendar. In the days of Antiochus IV Epiphanes not only the Jews in Palestine but those in the eastern diaspora were threatened with

point of departure for mystical speculation.

38. R. Stiehl, WZKM 53 (1956), 13ff.

a peril much worse than that which occurred at the time of Xerxes. A Book like Esther was full of contemporary relevance and, in keeping with the religious needs of the new era, it was adapted and elaborated.

2) THE GREEK ADDITIONS TO THE BOOK OF ESTHER

The Septuagint contains the following additions to the Book:

A. The "dream of Mordecai" which precedes the first chapter of the Hebrew book.

B. The content of the anti-Jewish edict of the Persian king, which follows after 3, 14a in the Hebrew text.

C. The prayers of Mordecai and Esther, introduced after 4, 17.

D. The description of Esther's audience with the king which replaces the Hebrew version in 5, 1-2.

E. The counter-edict of the Persian king which revokes the anti-Jewish edict, inserted between 8, 13a and 8, 13b.

F. The interpretation of Mordecai's dream, together with an appendix to the entire Book, added at 10, 3.

A cursory examination is sufficient to reveal the sections as typical additions and elaborations.[39] The wording of the decrees, the prayers of Mordecai and Esther, which are lacking in the Hebrew text, are filled out, and Esther's audience with the great king is marvelously elaborated. Mordecai's dream is a didactic allegory and not a genuine dream at all. The key for properly understanding these additions lies in the so-called adaptation. The Persian sovereignty had long since been replaced by that of Macedon, and Susa itself was considerably Hellenized; its name was now Seleucia on the Eulaios. At the same time, the Maccabees had broken into rebellion in Palestine against the perse-

---

39. Jerome was aware of these Greek additions, but did not incorporate them into the common Vulgate text; they are treated as an appendix. A = 11, 2-12; 12, 1-6; B = 13, 1-7; C = 13, 8-18; 14, 1-9; D = 15, 4-19; E = 16, 1-24; F = 10, 4-13; 11, 1; 15, 1-3 however, is an independent piece of unknown origin.

cutions of Antiochus IV Epiphanes, and a national rebellion had
flared up in Elymais. The common enemy of the "Persians and
Jews" was now "Macedon." It is no surprise that in reworking
the Book of Esther the Jewish persecutor Haman is introduced
as a Macedonian (G 8, 12k). We see here the same tendencies that
are operative in the Habakkuk scroll from Qumran, in which the
ancient texts are adapted to fit the contemporary situation. The
Greek additions and adaptations all point, accordingly, to the
Hellenistic age, more precisely, to the Maccabean era. This explains why Ben Sirach, writing around the year 190 B.C., does
not mention either Esther or Mordecai in his "Praises of Great
Men" (44 — 50). The first reference to the Purim festival occurs
in the Book of Maccabees (2 Mac 15, 36), where the newly
introduced festival of Nicanor Day is dated on the 13th day of
the 12th month, "One day before the day of Mordecai."

There is one final problem: can we possibly assign any precise
time and place for the translation of the Hebrew version into the
Greek. In an epilogue to the Greek translation there is a statement to the effect that "Lysimachos, the son of Ptolemy from
Jerusalem, translated the above letter on the Phrurai festival into
Greek." [40] The priest and Levite Dositheos could then have
brought it to Egypt in the 4th year of the reign of Ptolemy and
Cleopatra (114 B.C.). There is no grounds for doubting the
authenticity of this evidence.

This makes the history of the Book of Esther relatively
simple. The liberation of the Jews from foreign peril in the era
of the Persian king Xerxes was recorded and passed on both
in the chronicle of Mordecai or Esther as well as the popular
narratives about Esther. Both streams of tradition were then joined
together, somewhere in the eastern diaspora, probably in Susa
itself, into the festival legend for the celebration of Purim. This
explains the double version of the story. It was probably in con-

---

40. The Greek word φϱουϱαι = "watch, post," deliberately chosen in
reference to the Hebrew pûr. The Hebrew word hanukkah might be
related to the Indo-European root(s) enek = "achieve, accomplish,"
or "satisfaction": this would suggest the geographical origin of the Book
of Esther. M. Fraenkel, Chanukkah, VD 40, (1962), 30.

nection with the Maccabean freedom movement that the Book of Esther became popular in Jerusalem too. It was here that the Hebrew text was translated into Greek and enlarged by the addition of new material which applied its message to the contemporary crisis. From here the Purim festival made its way into Egypt and the western diaspora.

3) THE THEOLOGICAL CONTENT OF THE BOOK OF ESTHER

The previous discussion has made it clear that Pauschal's contention that the "Book of Esther is not an historical book" is quite untenable.[41] The book's theological content can be understood without having recourse to the literary genre of the religious novel, legend, or historical novel. The historical content is proclaimed by the reliably recorded course of history itself. It is the mystery of Israel surrounded by the nations of the world.[42] An ancient new year's nature festival is transformed into the celebration of Israel's liberation. People exchanged presents, and there was considerable merry-making, not only because a new year was beginning, but because a new era of salvation was dawning, which was given a new expression in the annual renewal of the festival. Because of her faith in God and her law, Israel was distinct from the pagan nations. By her very existence, accordingly, Israel was a challenge to the nations of the world who refused to bow before the one God and his law. Political, economical, and national antitheses, and perhaps even some measure of guilt on the part of the Jews themselves, might well have provided the occasion for her neighbor's hatred to come to a head so frequently and erupt in savage pogroms. But the underlying cause of all this is the mystery of Israel's election. This people cannot be annihilated because it bears the stamp and seal of the living God. That is why, in times of extreme crisis, God always sends a savior. The enemies are overcome and pass into oblivion, while Israel continues its course among the nations

---

41. R. de Vaux, *AT Lebensordnungen* II, 379.
42. Cf. my article: *Bund und Erwählung. Das Mysterium Israel in geschichtstheologischer Schau*, ZkTh 80 (1958), 493-515.

of the world, bearing God's own burden, incapable of finding rest until it has fulfilled its mission. That is why the Book of Esther has become *the book* (*megillah*) of Jewry: the solemn song of the Jewish nation, the solemn song of their mortal peril, their redemption, their vengeance.[43] It is precisely this book which keeps alive the eternal miracle of Israel's survival.

Since, however, the Church of the Messiah Jesus has entered upon the heritage of ancient Israel as the new and "true Israel" (Rm 2, 29), the mystery of Israel lives[44] on in Christianity. Persecution and martyrdom can never annihilate the Church. The situation of Jewry and Christianity as the one Israel of God has not changed since the days of Esther. It is thus quite incorrect to do away with the Book of Esther as Luther wanted to, "because it is too Jewish in its propaganda and full of pagan mischief"; the Book of Esther has become Sacred Scripture as the book of the persecuted Church in both the Old and New Testaments. It is a clear expression of the mystery of God's people in opposition to the nations of the world.

The theological content of the Book of Esther is expressed most succinctly in the symbolic dream of Mordecai.[45] History is the struggle of two dragons, two great forces, the people of God and the nations of the world. The spring which rises up and becomes a mighty stream is symbolic of God's help. God holds the fates of the nations in his hand and guides the course of history, despite darkness, clouds, and tempest, to the goals he has foreordained.

---

43. R. Stiehl, WZKM 53 (1955/56), 6.
44. B. W. Anderson, *The Place of the Book of Esther in the Christian Bible*, The Journal of Religion, 30 (1950), 32-43. Esther is the literary precipitate of that community sense which sought an answer to the meaning and purpose behind Israel's tragic history. The same is true of the question of the tragic history of the Church as the People of God in the midst of the nations of the world.
45. E. L. Ehrlich, *Der Traum des Mardochai. Zs für Religions und Geistesgeschichte* 7 (1955), 65-74. Points up parallels with the Babylonian myth of chaos: the images might come from anywhere: the question is their focus of attention.

CHAPTER VIII

THE BOOK OF TOBIT

THE Book of Tobit (Tobias) belongs to those writings of the Old Testament which have exercised a far greater effect upon a considerable circle of the people than many other books whose significance for the history of salvation is, objectively considered, of much greater importance. Its content, as an essential part of "biblical history," has been preached to millions of people at a very early age. Preaching, too, has made constant reference to this book, while Christian art has illustrated many of its themes. And yet, even more than the narrative of the Moabite Ruth, the ancestor of King David who was so important for the political and religious development of Israel, the Book of Tobit is simply a family history. The hero of the narrative is, after all, one of the nameless Israelites whom historical catastrophe has torn away from their native land and forced to live in the diaspora.

In the Greek Bible the book has this title: "Book of the words of Tobit." The Hebrew original title must, accordingly, have been *sepher dibrê-ṭobî*. It is thus quite similar to the Book of Chronicles, *sepher dibrê-hayyāmîm*, "Book of the words of the days." According to the title, the Book of Tobit was obviously taken as an historical narrative. But criticism poses a problem here: is the Book of Tobit an historical work in the strict sense of the word or only a free narrative with an historical nucleus, or, for that matter, a free invention? What is the literary genre?

A) CONTENT OF THE BOOK OF TOBIT

In attempting to reproduce the content of the Book of Tobit, one is confronted with a difficult choice as to which of the various versions of the text is to be preferred. In order to have some point of departure, we shall at first follow the form of the text as recorded in the Codex Vaticanus (B) and Alexandrinus (A),[1] and then consider the various problems of text criticism.

a. *Reminiscences of home*: From the book's title we learn that Tobit belonged to the Tribe of Naphtali. The Assyrian King Enemessaros (Vg: Salmanassar) had deported him from his home in Thisbe [2] in Upper Galilee and had him sent to Nineveh. His grandmother Deborah had thoroughly instructed the boy in the law of his fathers, since his parents had died at an early age. Even in his home country, while the entire Tribe of Naphtali went over to the worship of the Baals and sacrificed to the golden bull of Jeroboam in Dan, he remained faithful to Yahweh and his law, made the annual pilgrimages to the Temple at Jerusalem, and paid the tithes to the priests, Levites, and poor. He married a woman called Anna, a member of the family, who bore him a son Tobias (1, 3-9).

b. *Buyer of provisions for King Enemessaros*: Even in the diaspora, Tobit held to the dietary precepts of the Jewish law.

---

1. Stummer follows the text of BA: H. Bückers, *Tobias*, (Herderbibel 1953).
2. Thisbe is apparently a translation error for *tôšebê* = "inhabitant of ..." Vulgate 1, 1 has preserved the name of the place as Naasson = Nahson. BA both describe the location rather fully: "to the right of (south of) Kydios (= Kades, Cadesh), above (in the mountain country) of Asor (Hazor)"; Vulg. says, more simply: "behind (west) the great route to the west, with Sephet on its left (north)." — Despite these precise details, the site cannot be located. At all events, it is not *teitaba*, some 3 miles NW of Saphed (Simons, GTT, 1614), but rather to the south of Saphed, perhaps in the vicinity of Akbara.

This observance did not prevent his quickly achieving a favorable position. He was made provisions' buyer (ἀγοραστης) for the king (1, 13). In this capacity he was obliged to travel considerably. On one trip he came to Ragai in Media, where he deposited ten talents of silver with his relative Gaba'el. Wherever he could, he brought assistance to his expatriate countrymen. "I would give my bread to the hungry and my clothing to the naked; and if I saw anyone of my people dead and thrown out behind the wall of Nineveh, I would bury him" (1, 16).

c. *Loss of position*: A transformation occurred when Sennacherib came into power. His unsuccessful campaign against Jerusalem produced fateful consequences for the expatriate Israelites: "In his wrath he had many killed" (1, 18). Tobit observed the last rites for the victims and buried them secretly. His actions, however, were reported to the king. Tobit himself had to flee and take cover. His property was confiscated. Nothing was left him excepting his wife Anna and his son Tobias (1, 18-20).

d. *Return to Nineveh*: After the murder of Sennacherib, Sacherdonos became king. This provided Tobit with an opportunity to return home to Nineveh. Sacherdonos had set up the son of his brother, Ahikar, in charge of the entire treasury and administration. It was he who interceded for Tobit with the king. Tobit was permitted to return to his home in Nineveh (1, 21-22). The joy at his return occasioned a banquet during the time of the Pentecost festival. As the dinner was about to begin, Tobit was informed that one of his countrymen had been strangled and was lying unburied in the marketplace. Tobit immediately left the table, hurried to the marketplace, and brought the victim to his own home. He ate his bread in sorrow, and buried the man after the sun went down. Weary from his efforts, he lay down for a brief rest by the wall of the courtyard. His face was uncovered. There were sparrows on the wall and their fresh droppings fell into his open eyes, causing white films to form on his eyes. He went to the physicians, but they were unable to help him and he became completely blind.

e. *Tobit's trial*: Tobit's wife now had to supply their daily bread. She took in knitting and sewing as long as there was work. One day she brought home a young kid as wages. The animal began to bleat. Tobit supposed that it had been stolen and refused to eat it. This led to a family quarrel. Finally Anna pointed out to her blind husband that all his charitable deeds had profited him nothing. Weary and disconsolate, Tobit withdrew and began praying to God to release him and bring him into the house of eternity (2, 11 — 3, 6).

f. *Sara's trial*: At the same time, a similar family tragedy was taking place in distant Ecbatana in Media. Raguel's daughter Sara was being mocked by her father's slave girls because she had been married to seven men and all of them had been murdered on their wedding night by the demon Asmodaios. She too prayed to God to deliver her from this earth, so that she would no longer have to listen to such mockery and reproach (3, 7-15).

g. *Tobias' journey to Media*: Faced with the prospect of imminent death, the aged and blind Tobit one day called his son Tobias and made arrangements to give him his inheritance. The first and most precious heritage was to be "the wise instruction" (4, 3-19); he next instructed his son to call for the money which had been deposited with Gabael in Ragai (4, 20). He did not like the idea of sending such a young man all alone on such a long journey; he searched for a reliable companion. A suitable choice appeared in the person of the angel Raphael, who pretended to be Azarias, the son of the great Ananias, one of his relatives. After settling upon the wages, a drachma per day, the two set out upon their journey (5, 1-23). As they were preparing to camp at the banks of the Tigris, and Tobias was washing his feet, he was attacked by a giant fish. Raphael called to Tobias to seize the fish and drag it up onto the land. He did so, and the two of them prepared the fish for dinner. Upon Raphael's advice, Tobias took the heart, liver, and gall as a defense against demons and for a medicine (6, 1-9).

In Ecbatana the two were hospitably received by Raguel. After a brief conversation it was learned that, on the grounds of his family relationship, Tobias had first claim to the hand of Sara. Raguel, as patriarch of the family, consented to the marriage in words and symbolic activity. He said to Tobias: "Take her right now, in accordance with the law. You are her relative, and she is yours. The merciful God will guide you both for the best" (7, 12). Thereupon he called his daughter Sara, took her by the hand, and gave her to Tobias as wife: "Here she is; take her according to the law of Moses, and take her with you to your father." He blessed the two of them. Then the contract was written on a scroll and sealed (7, 14-17).

The wedding night passed without incident. Tobias burnt the heart and liver of the fish they had captured. The demon As-modaios thereupon fled to the northern parts of Egypt, where an angel bound him. Raguel had already prepared a grave for the new bridegroom. That night he sent a maid servant into the bridal chamber; shining her light upon the bridal bed she found the couple happily asleep. The joy at their salvation was great. For 14 days the wedding was celebrated (8, 1-21). Meantime Raphael made a journey to Ragai, recovered the deposited money, and brought Gabael himself back to the wedding (9, 1-6).

h. *Return and healing of Tobit*: After the wedding cere-monies and festivities, Tobias asked his father-in-law Raguel to send him and his new wife to Nineveh, since his parents would certainly be concerned over his long absence. His mother Anna kept looking day after day in the direction from which he would return. When she finally saw him coming, she rushed out to meet him, fell upon his neck, and exclaimed: "I have seen you, my child, and now I can die" (11, 9). The aged Tobit heard this. He felt his way to the door and stood there waiting until the younger Tobias ran to him and embraced him. He smeared the fish's gall over the blinded eyes and the white scales came away: Tobit could see once again. Full of joy, he intoned a song of praise. Then a second wedding feast was held, with Achiachoros and his nephew Nadan as guests (10, 1 — 11, 19).

i. *Raphael's self-revelation and departure*: When Tobias at-tempted to find a suitable recompense for his traveling companion

— he offered him half of everything that he had brought home — Raphael revealed his mystery: "I am Raphael, one of the seven holy angels who present the prayers of the saints and enter into the presence of the glory of the Holy One" (12, 15). Then they all fell prostrate upon the ground and were exceedingly frightened. But the angel spoke to them: "Do not be afraid! Peace be with you, bless the Lord!" Then he commanded them to write everything in a book. When they arose they no longer saw him (12, 1-22). Tobit then intoned a solemn song of praise (13, 1-18).

j. *The outcome*: After this miracle they all lived happily together for many years. When Tobit realized that death was near, he ordered his son Tobias to move into Media since, according to the words of the prophet Jonah, Nineveh was destined for destruction. As a warning he pointed to the fate of Achiachoros and then departed in peace at the age of 158 years. When his mother Anna died in her turn, Tobias buried her at his father's side. Then he and his family moved into Ecbatana, where he himself died at the age of 127 years. Before his death he received word of the destruction of Nineveh (14, 1-15).

B) THE TEXT OF THE BOOK OF TOBIT

"In place of the lost original text of this book we are faced with a considerable series of translations. These bear eloquent testimony to the fact that the Book of Tobit was popular and widely spread throughout antiquity. But they also indicate the considerable development and internal transformation through which the text has passed. It was perhaps its very popularity that has sealed the fate of its text transmission." [3] Without considering the particularly difficult details of the problem, we can speak of three fundamental types of the Greek text: a. The longer form: This is the text of Codex Sinaiticus and the Old Latin Translation; b. The shorter form: This is the text of Codex Vaticanus and Alexandrinus, as well as the Syrian Translation; c. The middle form: This is the text of the manuscripts and papyrus fragments.

---

3. Miller, l. c. 15f.

There are diametrically opposed opinions as to which text is closest to the original.[4] The solution of this problem is intimately bound up with the question of the source and date of the Book of Tobit. At all events scholarship is faced with the problem of explaining how the longer form of the text contains 3100 words more than the shorter form. The difference can hardly be explained simply in terms of mere additions to the original text, since the shorter version also contains some 700 words that have no equivalent in the longer form. The relationship between the two can hardly be that of mother and daughter.[5] It is much more likely that these differences should be traced to the history of the original writing.

St. Jerome records that he translated the Book of Tobit, with the help of a Jewish rabbi, from a Chaldean original. Since Jerome, with his unwarranted preference for the "*hebraica veritas,*" did not regard the Book of Tobit as canonical, he translated "more according to the sense" than the strict letter of the text.[6] As a result, this translation, which later passed into the Vulgate, loses something in text criticism, but it does point to the possible original language of the Book of Tobit.

In cave IV along the Dead Sea, three fragments of the Book of Tobit were discovered,[7] one in Hebrew, written on leather, and two in Aramaic, one on leather and the other on papyrus. Obviously, versions in both languages were current among the sect at Qumran shortly before the birth of Christ. Which version has the greater authority? One might suppose it would be the Hebrew. This was the era of the Aramaic Bible translations (Targumim). But this could hardly be the case.

The dating for the Book of Tobit fluctuates between two extremes: either a time shortly after the events described [8] or as

---

4. Miller bases his commentary on Sinaiticus, while Stummer uses Vaticanus and Alexandrinus.
5. EncMikr III, 376.
6. *Praefatio in Tobiam,* Kritische Vulgata-Ausgabe (Rome 1950), 156.
7. Barthelemy-Milik, *Qumran Cave I,* (Oxford 1955), 47; RB 63 (1956), 60.
8. Cf. EncMikr III, 369.

late as the year 100 B.C.[9] The truth lies somewhere in the middle. The contents would seem to argue more for the Persian than the Hellenistic diaspora.[10] This would point to the years between 500 and 300 B.C. The memory of the Assyrian diaspora was still very much alive among the people, even though it lay in the distant past. This made it possible to approach the historical material from a point of retrospect, and to give it a new form corresponding to the demands of the contemporary situation. Since the material dealt with vivid popular traditions, they were composed in the popular Aramaic language.[11] This Aramaic original text of Tobit made its way, very much like the Book of Esther, from the eastern diaspora into Palestine, where, in the religious and national crisis of the Maccabean era, it was given a new orientation and translated into Hebrew. This might well be the age that produced the additions to the text which are very effective as the supplement [12] to the patriarchal narratives, but are not preserved in the shorter version.

The text of the Book of Tobit has thus had a history, which has not been explained down to the least detail. Only some new discovery could yield a complete answer to our problem. The present condition of the various forms of the text, at all events, makes it clear that the book is the result of a gradual process of growth. The place of origin lies in the eastern diaspora during the era of Persian world sovereignty. This relatively quiet period was not unfruitful in literary productivity; these days produced the literary works which, in the era of the Hebrew Renaissance in the second century before Christ, were given a new orientation and literary form. This fact can explain, on the one side, the historical and geographical inaccuracies in the text, while,

---

9. Rost, EinlAT 181; Eissfeldt, EinlAT 725 pre-Maccabean.
10. The elements that should suggest Persia are to be found in EncMikr III, 371.
11. Aramaic original: Pfeiffer, HistNTT 272; — Hebrew: P. R. Saydon, *Some Mistranslations in the Codex Sinaiticus of the Book of Tobit,* Bibl 33 (1952), 363-365; J. Lebram, *Die Peschitta zu Tobit 7, 11-14, 5,* ZAW 69 (1957), 185-211.
12. Robert-Feuillet, IntrAT 743.

on the other hand, it provides a clearer understanding of the literary genre of the book.

C) TOBIT AND HISTORY

1) DATES AND FIGURES

At first glance it would appear that the dates and figures presented in the text might fit the narrative into the framework of world history. Upon closer examination, however, it appears that the numbers are not meant to record an exact date, but only a symbolic value. Tobit's age is recorded differently in the three versions, as shown in the following table:

Tobit	BA	Sin.	Vulg.
before blinding	58 (14, 2)	62 (14, 2)	56 (14, 3)
blind	8 (14, 2)	4 (2, 10)	4 (14, 3)
after blinding			42 (14, 2)
Total ages	158 (14, 11)	112 (14, 2)	102 (14, 2)

A key to understanding these numbers is available in the Vulgate. Tobit lived 56 years before becoming blind, that is, seven weeks of years and one week of years; in other words, one jubilee and one week of years. Then he was blind for half a week of years — "four," an approximate number — and after being healed he lived for 42 years, that is, six weeks of years, in other words: one jubilee less one week of years. The total age is thus 102 years, that is, 2 jubilees and half a week of years $[(2 \times 49) + 4 = 102]$.

This same system of reckoning in terms of jubilees explains the numbers in the other versions, excepting that the Greek translators figure 50 rather than 49 as the jubilee number. Hence the presentation in BA: Before becoming blind, one jubilee and one week (50 + 8); then blinded for one week; after being healed, two more jubilees (2 x 50); this gives a total age of three jubilees and one week [(3 x 50) + 8 = 158].

The age of the younger Tobias is also presented in terms of jubilees. According to the Vulgate (14, 16) he was 99 years old; that is, he lived two jubilees and died the following year [(2 x 49) + 1 = 99]. The numbers of the Greek version can, in my opinion, all be reduced to the Vulgate numbering. BA: 127 years=99 + (3 x 9) + 1; Sin.: 117 years=99 + (2 x 9).

As a result, the traditional numbers cannot possibly be considered as the basis for historical reference. They are understood most literally when they have been interpreted in their symbolic sense. Just like the symbolic numbers in Genesis, which are based on the same jubilee scheme,[13] they are worthless as the basis for historical computation.

2) THE ASSYRIAN KINGS

According to the narrative, the events of the Book of Tobit take place during the reigns of the Assyrian Kings Enemessaros, Sennacherim, and Sacherdonos. The identification of the last two with Sennacherib — Sanherib (705-681) and Esarhaddon (681-669) presents no difficulty; on the other hand, many exegetes [14] have thought it necessary to identify Enemessaros with Sargon II (721-705); since it was precisely this king who carried out the resettlement of the northern tribes after the destruction of Samaria. On the other hand, however, the Vulgate reading is preferable, on purely phonetic grounds, identifying him with Shalmaneser (728-722). It is true that, after conquering the Northern Kingdom, Sargon carried out the resettlement of the northern tribes on a grand style;[15] but we are surely justified in assuming that Shalmaneser, who had besieged the obstinately defended citadel of Samaria for three years, would have deported

---

13. J. Meysing, *The Biblical Chronologies of the Patriarchs*, Christian News from Israel, XIII (1962), 3-11.

14. Clamer, *Tobie*, ClamB IV, 416.

15. Cf. Vol. IV, p. 237: Northern tribes resettled.

the dangerous elements from the already occupied territories in Galilee. As a result, the deportation under Shalmaneser mentioned in the introduction to the book is, historically, quite possible, even though this reference in the Book of Tobit is its only express mention.

It is, furthermore, only obvious that Sanherib's failure before the gates of Jerusalem [16] must have had fateful consequences for the expatriate Israelites. The defeated king took revenge for his defeat on the defenseless expatriates. Furthermore, it is generally known that Esarhaddon, upon his succession to the throne — and this took place under some mysterious circumstances [17] — embarked upon a policy quite opposed to his father's, who had always sought to promote the best interests of the expatriate Israelites.

It follows that the general outline of the Book of Tobit is not the product of imagination, but rather the mirror of an actual historical situation. It is the book of Israel's fate in Exile, just as the Book of Esther is the book of the Judaean fate in Exile. There is considerable divergence of opinion as to whether or not the individual fates are to be interpreted as personal or merely typical.

3) MYTH, FAIRY TALES, AND SPIRITS OF THE DEAD

In order to give an adequate interpretation of the origin and content of the Book of Tobit, scholars have searched the neighboring cultures for similar motifs. Many are of the opinion that the Book of Tobit is simply the biblical transformation of the fairy tale of the grateful dead. In terms of principle, there is no objection to this point of view; even the literary genre "fairy tale" can serve as the vehicle of inspiration. What, however, upon critical examination, proves to be the relationship between myth, fairy tale, and the Book of Tobit?

a. *A dead man with a message*: The Greek poet and philosopher

---

16. Cf. Vol. IV, p. 236: Sanherib's western campaign.
17. Cf. Vol. IV, pp. 294ff.

Simonides of Ceos (556-468)[18] recounts that he found a dead man lying along the roadside and gave him a decent burial. Sometime later when he was about to board a ship, the dead man appeared to him in a dream and warned him not to board that ship, since it was about to be destroyed in a storm. He stayed home, and the ship did indeed founder. Deeply impressed by this extraordinary sequence of events, Simonides composed an epigram which had considerable effect upon posterity. Even Cicero appealed to this narrative in his work on "divination." [19] The relationship with the Book of Tobit is supposed to consist of the fact that a dead man, who had been honored with a decent burial, appears to his benefactor, helping him in time of peril, and thereby demonstrating his gratitude. If this is the case, then there must be thousands of parallels to Tobit. The comparison with the epigram of Simonides bears little if any weight.

b. *Apollo, champion of weddings*: For Greek mythology it goes without saying that gods walk upon the earth in human form. Legend recounts [20] that Apollo himself, in the form of a mortal man, assisted King Admetos of Pherai to win his bride Alkestis. Alkestis' father Pelios had promised to give his daughter as wife to the man who should succeed in yoking a lion and a bear or wild boar to his chariot. It was Apollo who accomplished this heroic deed for Admetos. At the wedding ceremony, however, they forgot to offer sacrifice to the goddess Artemis. When the bridal couple entered their wedding chamber, they found it filled with serpents. Apollo argued with the fates and secured the promise that Admetos might be saved from death provided someone was found to voluntarily die in his place; this would appease the wrath of Artemis.

The point of comparison to Tobit is supposed to lie [21] in the fact that a heavenly person appears in the role of wedding champion and turns aside some dire threat on the wedding night. This is the motif which the biblical author is supposed to have taken over, cleansed of its mythological elements, and adapted it to his own spirit world. But according to this methodology, it is possible to look to each and every wedding-night narrative as a source for Tobit, since even primitives regard the first night as surrounded by tabus.

---

18. Author of the famous epigram on the Spartans at Thermopylae. Cf. also W. Christ, *Geschichte der griechischen Literatur. Handbuch der klass. Altertumswissenschaften,* VII, 161ff.
19. *De devinatione* I, 27, 55.
20. *Apollodorus Mythographus,* Bibliotheke I, 11, 15. J. G. Frazer, (London 1921) (Neudruck 1954).
21. T. Fr. Glasson, *The Main Source of Tobit,* ZAW 71 (1959), 275-277.

c. *The possessed princess*: An Egyptian inscription [22] in the temple of the god Honsu in Thebes (Karnak), dating from the time around 500 B.C., tells of the Princess Bentresh, who lived in the land of Bechten, and was a sister to the Egyptian princess Nofrure. Bentresh was possessed by an evil spirit. She turned to her father in Egypt, seeking aid. Then "Honsu, the councillor, the strong god who drives away the evil spirit," was sent to Bechten and the possessed princess was healed by him.

The only point of comparison with the Book of Tobit is the expulsion of the evil spirit. But on the basis of this reasoning, all similar narratives involving the expulsion of evil spirits could be adduced as sources for Tobit.

d. *The story of the grateful dead*: Closer points of comparison would seem to exist with the narratives of the grateful dead, a theme which is known to world literature, and particularly at home in the territory of the Caucasus and Armenia. In the Armenian version [23] the story goes like this: A rich merchant, on a journey, sees how strangers are violating the corpse of a dead man because he still owed them money. He himself paid the debt and thus provided the dead man with an honorable burial. Later he himself was involved in a serious crisis. He succeeded, however, in marrying the daughter of a rich man. Five, or in some versions seven, men had already attempted to marry her; they were all murdered, however, on their wedding night by a serpent who came crawling out of the mouth of the bride. The grateful dead man, appearing in the guise of his servant, advised his friend not to be terrified at the prospect of this marriage. He was also the one to kill the serpent as it crept forth from the mouth of the bride, thus showing his gratitude.

At first encounter, it would seem that there is indeed some point of comparison between these fairy tales and the Book of Tobit. Both are involved with burial of the dead and a story about a wedding night. "The only difference is that in the narrative of Tobit the hero of the fairy tale is split into two distinct personalities, father and son, and an angel intervenes in place of the grateful dead man." [24] Most famous of all is the version popularized by the Danish fairy tale writer Andersen. But perhaps these conclusions are premature. In questions of literary his-

---

22. Text by J. H. Breasted, *Ancient Records of Egypt*, III, 429-447.
23. The folklore material has been assembled in Simrock, *Der gute Gerhard und die dankbaren Toten*, (Bonn 1896).
24. Eissfeldt, EinlAT 724.

tory, we must exercise the greatest circumspection. In terms of geographical origin (Caucasus-Armenia) and date of composition (extremely late), the two narratives are so far apart that any question of literary dependence is clearly excluded. So long as the fairy-tale cycle cannot be definitively dated as before Christ — and the Simonides story is certainly not sufficient evidence — there is only one critically responsible point of view, namely to abandon the fairy tale in interpreting the Book of Tobit.[25] Despite their apparent similarities, the narratives unfold in two quite different spiritual and intellectual milieux.

4) THE WISDOM OF AHIKAR

In the Book of Tobit we find some reference to a certain Achiachoros (Vg: Achior) which gives rise to the question of whether Tobit might have been influenced by the famous wisdom of Ahikar. The text in question goes as follows: "Sacherdonos appointed Achiachoros, the son of Anael, my brother, over all the accounts of his kingdom and over the entire administration. Achiachoros interceded for me, and I returned to Nineveh. Achiachoros was cupbearer, keeper of the signet, and in charge of administration of the accounts, for Esarhaddon had appointed him second to myself. He was my nephew" (AB 1, 21-22). After the blinding of Tobit, "Achiachoros took care of me until he went to Elymais" (AB 2, 10). At the wedding of the younger Tobias in Nineveh, there is mention of Achiachoros and Nadan (11, 19). Finally, shortly before his death, Tobit alludes to the advice given by Achiachoros: "See, my son, what Nadan did to Achiachoros, who had reared him, how he brought him from light into darkness, and with what he repaid him" (14, 10). There are variations in the individual versions. The overall picture, however, is that the fate of Tobit is closely bound up with that of Achiachoros. Achiachoros is Tobit's influential nephew at the Assyrian royal court.

---

25. M. M. Schumpp, *Das Buch Tobias. Handbuch* 11 (1933), LXXV. — T. Fr. Glasson, ZAW 71 (1959), 275 argues against this position.

The content of the pagan Ahikar story is, in short, as follows:[26] Ahikar, chancellor of Esarhaddon of Assyria, after a long and distinguished period of service, and with the full permission of his king, hands down his office to Nadan his son (?). Unfortunately, Nadan proves to be an ungrateful fellow. He slanders his father in the presence of the king. In anger Esarhaddon sends the executioner Nabusumiskun to Ahikar with orders to kill him. Ahikar is overtaken by the executioner while he is walking in his vineyards. When Nabusumiskun reveals the king's orders, Ahikar prays for mercy and reminds Nabusumiskun that he had once saved him from the prospect of certain death. The executioner lets himself be persuaded to kill a eunuch instead of Ahikar, and then reports to the king that he has fulfilled his orders. The rest of the narrative is, unfortunately, broken off. On the basis of later versions, however, we are safe in concluding that Ahikar eventually was restored to the royal favor. The narrative forms the framework for a collection of adages and fables, which are obviously the whole point of the narrative; in fact the title reads "Sayings of a wise and educated scribe by the name of Ahikar."

The wisdom of Ahikar was widely spread. Fragments of this collection are extant in almost all the ancient languages. The most ancient Aramaic papyrus fragment comes from the island of Elephantine on the Nile (Jeb), and is generally dated around 420 B.C.; the story itself is considerably older. The fragmentary tradition and the demonstrably late additions make it extremely difficult to reconstruct the original form of the narrative. The wide popularity of the book can be explained not so much by reason of the fate of its hero as by the charm and appeal of the wisdom literature it contains. The religious background is, at all events, strictly pagan, since both sun and moon are worshiped as divinities. The Ahikar legend has been the subject of an entire literature.[27] The majority of scholars take the territory of Babylonia-Assyria as the original setting for the book. The literary genre of the collections of wise sayings and fables has its parallels in the Accadian literature: some scholars have even deduced that the story must have been translated from the Accadians.[28] At all events, the wisdom content of the collection is traditional in the Ancient Near East. The names of the persons involved [29] particularly point to the Assyrian royal city of Nineveh. Olm-

---

26. RLA I, 15.
27. EncMikr I, 224.
28. RLA I, 16.
29. Ahi-kar = 'ahum-yaqar = "the true brother, the faithful brother"; Nadan is the short form of nabu-nadin-zer = Nabu had given a seed (a son); nabu-šum-iksum = Nabu has given a name (son). EncMikr I, 224 .

sted [30] has attempted to identify the names with historical personalities. A man named Ahikar is mentioned as a high official in the Assyrian documents of the year 698 B.C.; his nephew Nadan is none other than Nadinnu the scribe, who was active in the royal court under Esarhaddon and Assurbanipal; Nabusumiskun was captain of the chariots under Sanherib.

It must now be obvious that we are faced with the same historical background as in the Book of Tobit. It would certainly be possible that the great "scribe" at the Assyrian royal court was concerned not only with official documents, but also collected the traditional wisdom literature and re-edited it. In connection with the Book of Tobit, there are two important conclusions: despite precise investigation [31] scholarship has not succeeded in establishing a literal accord between the wisdom of Tobit and that of Ahikar. The reason for this probably lies in the fact that both authors drew freely from the general and widespread wisdom literature which was most clearly characterized as coming from the "sons of the east." Tobit and Ahikar, in their sayings and fables, are on different but related paths.

Since the historicity of Ahikar, on the basis of Assyrian documents, has now entered into the realm of possibility, references to him in the Book of Tobit no longer need be explained as a borrowing from the Ahikar romance; they might well have been references to the actual historical experience of his contemporaries. [32]

It would thus appear to have been rather premature to ascribe the Book of Tobit in its entirety to the literary genre of freely invented literature of edification. There is need for considerable caution in this work. "There is certainly no compelling grounds

---

30. Olmsted, EncMikr I, 224.
31. Schumpp, l. c. LXXIV: Many of these wise sayings may have been circulating by word of mouth much earlier, and their incorporation into the text of this book does not necessarily argue for a direct literary dependence.
32. H. Cazelles, Le personage d'Achior dans le livre de Judith, Recherches de science religioeuse 29 (1951), 324-327 claims that the figure of Ahikar is just as fluctuating as that of the Sibyl. Ahikar is thus the pious pagan persecuted by the powerful of this earth. But this

for contesting the presence of an historical nucleus in the essential parts of our narrative." [33] Tobit can be characterized as a faithful witness to the Israelite fate during the Assyrian Exile. This is true primarily with respect to the narratives about the aged Tobit. The person of the younger Tobias, however, has served as a focal point for a body of narratives which must be ascribed to the genre of religious midrash or edifying legend.

D)   THE TOBIAS LEGEND

Midrash is the "attempt" [34] to represent religious ideas in a general and perpetual manner by means of exemplary narrative, whose object can be either historical or freely invented material. Midrash-like narratives generally are bigger than life-size. It is their very improbability which serves to indicate the fact that they are not historical narratives, but simply illustrative types. The reader is not expected to stop at the content of the story; beneath this external form lies religious ideas and truths which are the primary reason for the narrative. There are three particular ideas which determine the narrative of the young Tobias: faith in angels and demons, the tabu of the wedding night, and the law as a norm of life.

1) FAITH IN ANGELS AND DEMONS

Faith in the help that comes from angels and the harm that comes from demons is not expressed for the first time in the Book of Tobit. It is evident throughout the course of the entire Old Testament, but it finds its most explicit expression in the Book of Tobit. Even though Raphael is one of the seven angels

---

generalization of the figure could hardly explain all the remarkable affinities with an historically verifiable name. Moreover, such narratives do not simply grow up without any historical point of contact.

33. Miller, *loc. cit.*, 8.
34. From *daraš*, "seek, examine, explore."

around the throne (12, 15), he makes his way along the streets of men. He put aside his glory and appeared like a man. The patriarchal narratives are familiar with the fact that angels appeared to men (Gn 18 and 19); Joshua, Samson's parents, Gideon, and other heroes were honored by the apparition of a heavenly person. But these are scenes that are compressed to a single brief moment, an experience in which the human person is all but overcome by the impression of the superman. For a person from the ranks of the heavenly powers to walk at the side of a weak and helpless human being is the unheard of new dimension in the Book of Tobit. The angel has become "the brother" (5, 13) of the human hero.

Raphael describes his genealogy; he is Azarias, the son of the great Ananias (5, 13). Anyone who has ears to hear knows what the names mean. They are an abbreviated expression of the angel's mission: *Hanan-Yah* — "God has mercy"; *'Azar-yah* — "God helps"; *Rapha-el* — "God heals." It is through the angel that God's saving and helping grace comes to man. The angel himself belongs to the "sons of God" (cf. Job 1, 6; 2, 1; Ps 88/89, 7). As such he has access to the throne of the glory of the Most High and is privileged to bring "the reminder" (12, 13) of human prayers and good works before the presence of God.

These texts present a particularly striking picture of the angel Raphael. He is not only the symbolic incorporation of God's help, but a spirit person, one of the seven who stand before the throne of God, who come and go before the glory of the Holy One. The number seven is explained by the number symbolism popular throughout the Ancient Near East.[35] We are not justified in supposing a derivation from the Ameša spenta's,[36] since these involve purely abstract personifications but never spirit persons.

The later apocryphal literature gives greater insight into the nature of Raphael than any supposed derivation from the contemporary pagan milieu. According to the Book of Henoch (20, 3), Raphael has been set up over "the spirits of the sons of men."

---

35. On seven as a sacred number, cf. Miller, *loc. cit.,* 95. Hence the number of creatures who stand about the throne of God.
36. Cf. a fuller account in the section on the prophet Daniel.

He shows Henoch the place prepared for the souls of the deceased (22, 3). As a result, many scholars [37] have attempted to connect the word Raphael with the *repha'îm,* the shadow-like dead. Raphael would then be the angel of death or simply the escort of the dead. Since Tobit was concerned with the proper burial of the dead on a truly heroic scale, he is supposed to have been rewarded for his activity by having the escort of the dead himself accompany his son Tobias as a companion on his journey. In the Book of Tobias, however, this area of Raphael's activity is nowhere in evidence.

Raphael's antagonist is the demon Asmodaios. In his demonology, too, Tobias makes no essential progress beyond the concepts familiar to the Old Testament picture of the demon world. Asmodaios belongs to the group of *šedim,* those maleficent evil powers who threaten the security of man and whose home is supposed to be in ruins and deserted places (Lev 17, 7; Is 13, 21; 34, 14). In the Tobias narrative there is clearly a considerable body of suspicious popular language.[38] Faith in demons played a considerable role in the late years of paganism and had its effect upon Jewish thought as well. The compelling feature of the Book of Tobit lies not in the fact that it speaks of an evil demon, but rather in the fact that the book was actually written to combat the popular sense of anxiety in the face of such destructive powers. This is the meaning that a Hebrew reader would have immediately taken from the name Ašmodai, which is similar in sound to the *šamad,* "to destroy, annihilate." The possibility of some relation in the name of the Iranian demon *aēšma daēva,* "demon of wrath, devastation and ignominy," is not, in itself, impossible, but neither is there any proof for it. One thing is certain: the whole of the Ancient Near East lived in perpetual dread of demons and attempted to control them by magic and charms.

2) THE TABU OF THE WEDDING NIGHT

The narrative of the wedding night obviously forms a climax

---

37. EncMikr III, 373.
38. Miller, l. c. 29.

in the Book of Tobit; it describes the final encounter between angel and demon, curse and blessing, life and death. Sara had already been given to seven men in marriage; all of them had been destroyed by the evil demon on their wedding night. That is why the household slaves mocked their mistress as a husband strangler (3, 7-10). Something was clearly amiss.

What we here encounter is an underground human experience of life. Even among the primitives, sex, procreation, and birth are surrounded by a tabu which was originally designed to protect and safeguard the mystery of life. In Tobit, however, the picture that emerges is one of terrible anxiety, a world threatened by the demons. Even though the story of the seven husbands reads like something of a burlesque, it is still somehow an expression of the basic anxiety that the wedding night could easily become a night of demons; the demons too have their times and hours to work.[39] Popular horror stories about the wedding night, in this pattern or in similar forms, may well have been handed about. The biblical narrator has taken over this motif not simply in order to tell a story, but in order to break the demonic tabu of the wedding night.

Acting upon Raphael's advice, the young Tobias took the live ashes of incense with him into the wedding chamber, upon which he then laid the heart and liver of the fish, and made smoke. "When the demon smelled the odor, he fled to the remotest parts of Egypt, and the angel bound him" (8, 1-3). Wild and deserted places were, to the ancient point of view, and in some respects, even to the modern popular belief, the normal dwelling places of evil spirits. The burning of the heart and liver is reminiscent of pagan magical rites. It is precisely in this detail that the Book of Tobit would appear to have seized upon the genuine bit of ancient popular belief. But the purpose of the whole narrative is to combat the popular sense of anxiety in the face of demons. The existence of demons is not denied; the demon is a powerful creature, stronger than seven men; stronger

---

39. Cf. Ps 90/91, where the hour of midday is threatened by demons as well as the hours of the dark of night.

than the demon, however, is the angel of God who overcomes and binds him.

3) THE LAW AS THE NORM OF LIFE

In the present condition of the text — we shall never know whether this was the case in the original version — Tobit is represented as a true Israelite, in whom there is no guile. The ideal of later Jewish theology is already outlined in some detail. According to the testimony of patriarchal tradition,[40] the Jewish religion is based upon three basic pillars: the law, divine service, and good works. Tobit, accordingly, must be a perfect observer of the Law. He is not content with paying the first tithe, the one designated for the priests; he also paid the second and third, the tithes for the Levites, and the poor. In the midst of his pagan surroundings, he keeps himself free from dietary impurities. Jerusalem alone is the holy city in which God can be worshiped; the bulls erected by Jeroboam are an abomination in his eyes. When it comes to marrying his son, he must observe the law of marriage among relatives. His mercy and his good works are destined to be his fate.

The Book of Tobit thus paints the ideal picture of the religious Jew living in the midst of the pagan diaspora. It is really remarkable that, despite the most precise observance of all the religious-national precepts of the law, we find a world-wide humanism, which finds its classic expression in the golden rule: "What you hate, do not do to anyone" (BA 4, 15). Tobit stands as the precursor of a later orthodox Jewish theology which is phrased in clearer and harsher terms.[41] In the Christian interpretation, the Book of Tobit is designed to prepare the way for the Son of God, who truly became man, lived among men, and performed his first miracle at the marriage feast in Cana.

In conclusion, it is obvious that the Book of Tobit cannot be described simply in terms of the literary genre of pure historical writing, nor that of free composition. Both genres are here fused

---

40. *Pirqê abôt* I, 2.
41. Pfeiffer, HistNTT 284; Eissfeldt, EinlAT 724.

into a higher unity. The historical character of the expatriate Tobit became the focal point for a considerable body of popular narratives on the subject of wedding night, angels, and demons. The author, who fused all this into one composition, was a master story-teller, and still more he was a theologian; he took away his people's anxiety and, in so doing, created the family book, the most precious literary heritage of the Persian diaspora.

SECTION FOUR

PROPHETS AND REFORMERS
IN JERUSALEM

CHAPTER IX

THE LAST PROPHETS

IT was not only the Jews in the eastern half of the empire, Babylonia and Persia, that were free to develop under the protection of the Persian rule; in the city of Sardes in Asia Minor there may well have been a Jewish community, on the evidence of a Lydian-Aramaic inscription.[1] In Egypt, the Jewish military colony on the isle of Elephantine (in the Nile) enjoyed the greatest possible measure of freedom. They even managed to build a temple in honor of Yahweh and inaugurate a regular cult. But for the world picture of Jewry which was gradually beginning to develop, it was the Temple of the God of heaven in Jerusalem that formed the center and focus. Despite the fact that they possess their own temple, the Jews in Elephantine had exceedingly close ties with their brothers in Jerusalem, but their faith in Yahweh was not pure. Side by side with Yahweh they also worship other creatures, such as *'ešem-bêt-'el,* "the name of the house of God," *ḥerem bêt'ēl,* "the ban of the house of God," and *'anat-bêt-'ēl,* "the sign (?) of the house of God." Even though these names may have been nothing more than abstractions of the one essence of Yahweh,[2]

1. Bright, HistIsr 359; Cf. Obadiah, v. 20.
2. EncMikr III, 439ff.: *Der Glaube der Juden von Elephantine.* — A. Vincent, *La Religion des Judéo-Araméens d'Elephantine,* (Paris, 1937).

they involve the obvious danger of falling into paganism. In Jerusalem, among those who had returned from Exile, things were no different. The religious life of the returnees threatened to sink gradually back into the pagan or half-pagan practices of the world around them. In this hour of peril the last of the prophets arise. Through their powerful word they prepared the way for the reform under Ezra and Nehemiah. After them the phenomenon of prophecy disappears from history; its place is taken by wisdom and law.

A) THE "MESSENGER" MALACHI

(Malachias)

It is possible that this otherwise unnamed prophet Malachi received his name (which means "my messenger") on the basis of his oracle in 3, 1: "Behold, I send my messenger (mal'akî) to prepare the way before me." Since the book has no dating formula, this prophet's activity can only be approximately dated. He probably made his appearance between 470 and 460 and thus prepared the later reform under Nehemiah and Ezra.[3] He thus does truly function as a messenger and precursor of him who was to come.

Malachi's words are a living precipitate of the confrontation with his opponents. Again and again we find the dialogue form: "You say, 'How have we despised thy name?' By offering polluted food upon my altar. And you say 'How have we polluted it?'. . . . You say 'How have we wearied him?' " (2, 17). The prophet answers these questions by revealing God's directions. The points at issue all revolve about the religious life of his day. Malachi gives the impression of a practical pastor, resolving the problems of life in the name of God. He even goes into judgment with the priests who, unfaithful to their office, have been satisfied with the sacrifice of blemished animals (1, 6-14) and have thus made the sacrificial service despicable in the eyes of the people (2, 1-9). Since the people were not paying the tithe, the Levites

---

3. Fr. Nötscher, EB III, 840.

were forced to provide their own sustenance, contrary to their position in society (3, 7-10). In general, there was a widespread feeling that religious observance had little value. Yahweh was not to be wearied by his servants (2, 17), since it was pointless to serve him (3, 13-17). The abandonment of religious obligations necessarily led to the loosening of moral bonds. Divorce was considered a very small matter, even though God had been witness to the covenant between a man and the wife of his youth (2, 13-16). Those who had prospered financially showed no scruple in preying upon the poor (3, 5). The bulwark against the pagan and Samaritan population had been considerably lowered by mixed marriages, so that gradually a religiously indifferent younger generation was growing up (2, 11ff.); the foreign wives secretly brought their foreign gods with them into Judah.

This religiously indifferent society was roused from slumber by this "herald" with his message of the coming day of Yahweh. Yahweh will suddenly appear as judge; he will be preceded by a messenger who is to prepare his way, the herald whose mission it is to announce the coming of Yahweh Sabaot, the God of Hosts. His coming is a coming to judgment. Who can stand before him? He is like a refiner's fire and like fuller's soap. The people will be cleansed through the fire of judgment and made capable of offering proper sacrifices. The agent of this judgment will be both Yahweh himself and "the angel of the covenant" (mal'ak habberît, 3, 1c), both of whom, as in the accounts of the Exodus from Egypt, are identical. The "angel" (mal'ak) is the human apparition of Yahweh who is always present in his invisible form. This messenger was identified, if not by Malachi himself, then by one of his disciples, as the prophet Elijah.[4] Before the great and terrible day of Yahweh Elijah will make his appearance. He will turn the hearts of fathers to their children and the hearts of children to their fathers, that is, he will convert the entire people, so that Yahweh, upon his coming, will not have to smite the entire land with his curse (3, 23-24). This tiny book, while it can claim no great literary pretensions, is vital to the history of salvation.

---

4. Elijah's return. Cf. Vol. IV, p. 92.

It presents a penetrating picture of the "dying Church," [5] which is roused from slumber by the trumpet peals of the coming day of judgment.

B) THE PROPHET OBADIAH

(Abdias)

The Book of Obadiah, with its 21 verses, is the shortest surviving prophetic book. Its content is an oracle of judgment against Edom. Edom-Esau was, in ancient times, the hostile brother of Israel. Amos (1, 11), Isaiah (34, 5-17), Jeremiah (49, 7-22), and Ezekiel (25, 12-14) all had oracles of threat to direct against Edom. On account of this abiding hostility, it is difficult to fit Obadiah's preaching against Edom into a proper historical perspective. But certainly the Jews could never forget Edom's guilt in the destruction of Jerusalem (Lamentations 4, 21-22; Ps 136/ 137). Since some echoings of the earlier prophets are clearly obvious, the Book of Obadiah probably belongs in the post-Exilic era. This is the date which makes it easiest to understand its historical perspective.

After the destruction of the Kingdom of Judah, the Edomites seized the opportunity to penetrate deep into the abandoned territories. For them the crisis of Judah presented a choice opportunity for expansion, particularly since they were themselves being gradually forced out of their ancient tribal territories by the Arab Nabataeans. Around the year 321 their penetration of southern Judah had progressed to the point that the territory has ever since been called Idumaea.[6] It is obvious that there was continuous tension and occasional outbursts of violence between the repatriate Judaeans and the Edomite newcomers. This seems to be the situation to which the Book of Obadiah is addressed. In highly poetic words he proclaims the fall of Edom. Even though she had built her nest high upon the rocks, like an eagle —

---

5. Pfeiffer, IntrOT 615.
6. Ibid., 584. — Bright, HistIsr 361. — J. Gray, The Diaspora of Israel and Judah in Obadiah, V 20, ZAW 65 (953), 53-59.

the capital city of Petra (rock) lay on an inaccessible rocky cliff — it will be shattered to the earth (4); the wisdom of Edom (Job) will come to an end (8). The annihilation of Edom will be followed by the restoration of Israel. The book is afire with a national passion, far removed from the self-sacrifice of the servant of God that was preached by the disciples of Isaiah, and yet the two books are united in proclaiming the mission of Zion (17) for all time to come.

C) THE PROPHET JOEL

The dating of this book fluctuates between two extremes.[7] Some scholars consider it older than even the Book of Amos, which would make Joel the oldest written prophet; others date him later, towards the end of the Persian era, around the year 350; a middle position, representing Joel as a Temple prophet around the year 600, has been greeted with little enthusiasm. The literary unity of the book has also been attacked. Some scholars have divided it into an original text (1, 1—2, 27) and later additions (3, 1—4, 27). The majority of exegetes are inclined to regard the "original text" as Exilic or post-Exilic, while the additions are much later. Accordingly, the attitude of the book would be best understood by interpreting it against the background of the Persian world Empire and the paltry remnants of the community in Jerusalem. Pfeiffer calls Joel the last of the written Hebrew prophets.[8]

Swarms of locusts [9] were destroying the harvest (1, 2-12); the priests were lamenting, the people assembled in the Temple (1, 13ff.). The prophet writes these words: "Alas for the day! The day of the Lord is near." Their sustenance had been taken away from before their very eyes, the ripe grain was ruined, the barns empty, the granaries in ruins; the cattle groan, and the flocks wander without finding pasture (1, 15-18). In the proph-

---

7. Robert-Feuillet, IntrAT 579.
8. IntrOT 573.
9. J. A. Thompson, *Joel Locusts in the Light of Near Eastern Parallels,* JNES 14 (1955), 51-55.

etic vision, this catastrophe becomes the image of the day of judgment to come. Even more fearful than a swarm of locusts, the soldiers shall storm their way against Zion, while the earth trembles, the heavens rock, the sun and moon are dark, and the stars lose their light. Great and terrible will be that day. Let them sound the trumpet and proclaim a fast. Only penance and conversion can induce Yahweh to once again turn with favor towards his people, to give them corn and oil and the juice of the grape (2, 1-20). But the frightening vision ends with a consoling call: "Do not be afraid" (2, 21-27). "You shall know that I am in the midst of Israel, and that I, the Lord, am your God and there is none else. And my people shall never again be put to shame" (2, 27). The second part of the book once again takes up the subject of the coming day of Yahweh and portrays the terror of what will happen at the end. The beginning is the pouring out of the spirit upon all flesh. The spirit (rûaḥ) is God's creative and miraculous power. When this spirit is sent, that means something new is to be created. Awe-inspiring signs will appear in the heavens and upon the earth. The sun will be turned into darkness, and the moon into blood. Salvation will come forth from Zion, to everyone who calls upon the name of Yahweh (3, 1-5). In that day, the great battle of the nations will be fought. The pagan peoples, especially Tyre, Sidon, and the Philistines, who had sold the Jews as slaves to the Greeks, will be annihilated in the Valley of Jehoshaphat (Yeho-šaphat — Yawheh holds judgment), in the judgment of God himself (4, 1-8). The battle itself is then described in inexpressibly vivid terms. The nations are called out to prepare themselves for war, to beat their plowshares into swords, and to assemble in the Valley of Jehoshaphat. Sun and moon grow dark. Then Yahweh roars out from Zion and accomplishes the redemption of his people (4, 9-16). Once again, all the earth will recognize that "I, Yahweh, am your God, who dwells in Zion" (4, 17). The very blessings of Paradise will then stream over the country. Egypt and Edom will be a wilderness; Judah, however, will be preserved forever, and Jerusalem forever and forever (4, 18-21).

Here the message once again touches upon the coming day

of Yahweh's judgment with which the prophet Amos began his message. This is a fundamental element of the prophetic preaching, forming a perpetual credo in Yahweh's invincibility and in the indestructibility of his foundation upon earth. Despite the disturbing overtones of vengeance which characterize the contemporary description of Yahweh's day of judgment, this invincible faith has formed the prophet's heritage to the New Testament Church. The literary style of Joel is first-rate. He understands the use of words, and, despite its grisly images, his language is restrained. He is one of the last representatives of the Silver Age of Hebrew literature.[10]

---

10. Pfeiffer, IntrOT 576.

CHAPTER X

RENEWAL OF COVENANT AND LAW

(Nehemiah and Ezra)

IN the years after 450 B.C. there are two men who left their mark upon the Jewish community newly arisen from the grave of the Babylonian Exile, a mark which, in many respects, it has retained today: Nehemiah as the political and economical organizer, and Ezra, the scribe, as the spiritual and religious reformer. In order to present the necessary historical background to their careers, the following events must be briefly outlined.

The Persian advance into Europe broke against the resistance of the Greeks. In the time that followed it was the Greeks who took the offensive. In the year 466 they defeated the Persian fleet at the mouth of Eurymedon. The defeat sealed the fate of Xerxes. Artabanos, the captain of the bodyguard, seized upon the general public dissatisfaction and murdered Xerxes toward the end of the year 465. His successor Artaxerxes I Longimanus (465-424) was unwilling to be merely a tool in the hand of the favorite, Artabanos. The battle which ensued resulted in a victory for Artaxerxes, but the interior weakness of the Persian Empire was more enticing than ever to its sworn enemies.

In the year 463 the Athenians determined to overcome Cyprus and for this purpose they built a fleet of 200 ships. In that same year Egypt rebelled, under the leadership of the Libyan prince Inaros. The Persian satrap for Egypt, Achaemenes, was defeated and forced to take refuge in the fortress of Memphis. Inaros, who had meantime been acclaimed Pharaoh, turned to the Athenians for help; they were already on their way towards Cyprus with their fleet, but they altered their course and made their way into Egypt. The young Artaxerxes felt himself unequal to the combined attacking forces of the Egyptians and Athenians.

Evidence of the serious crisis threatening the Persian Empire in these years is the fact that Artaxerxes, in the years 459/58, mustered an army of 300,000 men from all his provinces. When the army had been assembled and the 300 ships commissioned expressly for this purpose had been prepared in the year 458, under the command of Megabyzos, the attack was launched against Egypt, on both land and sea. The Egyptians were defeated; the remnants of their army gathered with the Athenians on the Delta island of Prosapitis. Here they managed to maintain themselves for a year and a half. But they were forced to surrender when the Persians diverted the stream and beached the Athenian ships (454). Inaros himself was taken prisoner and later crucified. Egypt was thus "pacified."

In the year 450 the Athenians resumed their expedition against Cyprus. The Persian fleet was defeated. At this critical juncture, Megabyzos, satrap of Syria, revolted against Artaxerxes. As a result, the great king was forced to conclude what was for the Persians the humiliating peace of Callias (448). It was only the reconciliation with Megabyzos in the year 448 that introduced the Persian Empire to a relatively long span of peace and prosperity which was the necessary prerequisite for the activity of Nehemiah and Ezra.[1] What the Persians had lost in war they attempted to recover in the years that followed, by resorting to diplomacy in an effort to sow discord. Their efforts were greatly facilitated by the fact that the Greeks, preoccupied with their hereditary quarrels, were unable to unite. When the Pelponnesian War broke out in the year 431, the Persians simply sat by and

---

1. On the political and economic situatio   cf. V. Palovsky, Bibl 38 (1957), 283ff.

watched the Greeks kill each other off. At the end of the war (404) the Persian position was more powerful than ever.

A) NEHEMIAH THE REORGANIZER

The reconstruction of the Jewish community in Jerusalem runs parallel to the Golden Age of Athens. Here there were politicians, philosophers, poets, and artists, such as Pericles, Socrates, Sophocles, Aeschylus, Phidias, etc., who are famous as the architects of European culture; in Jerusalem there were two men, Nehemiah and Ezra, whose significance for world history must be evaluated in terms reminiscent of the respect in which the Golden Age of Athens itself is held.[2]

1) THE ROYAL CUPBEARER

Nehemiah was a man who knew how to use his opportunities. As a descendant of the Judaeans who had been deported into Babylon, he had risen to a high position, having been named cupbearer to King Artaxerxes in his winter residence at the court of Susa. Although he appears to have been a eunuch, which his position at court would appear to have demanded, he was still a man of tremendous energies. Despite his secure position at court, he continued to think and feel for the fate of his people. His thoughts always went back to Jerusalem. In the month of Kislev, in the 19th year of Artaxerxes (November/December 446), Nehemiah's brother Hanani came to Susa as part of an embassy. Nehemiah inquired about conditions at Jerusalem. The news was devastating: "The survivors there in the province who escaped exile are in great trouble and shame; the wall of Jerusalem is broken down, and its gates are destroyed by fire" (Neh 1, 1-3). The intrigues of the hostile Samaritans had suc-

---

2. F. M. Heichelbeim, *Ezra's Palestine and Peiklean Athens*, Zeitschrift f. Religion und Geistesgeschichte, 3 (1951), 251-253. The harbor city of Dor on the Palestinian coast belonged, in the time between 460 and 450, to the Attic Empire. The Persians promoted Jewish interests in an effort to remove the Greek influence.

ceeded in maintaining Jerusalem in a condition of dependence. There was little that could be done along normal diplomatic channels. Four months later, in Nisan of the 20th year (April/ May 445), Nehemiah the cupbearer made bold to present the crisis of Jerusalem personally before the king (2, 1-8). He was successful. Artaxerxes gave him permission for the reconstruction of the walls of Jerusalem and even went so far as to name him "governor" [3] of Judah (Neh 5, 14; 10, 1). Judah was thus freed from the bonds of Samarian control, and was in a position to develop along its own course.[4] The king gave his cupbearer letters of recommendation to the governors across the great river and sent him upon his way.

2) THE BUILDING OF THE WALLS OF JERUSALEM

From Susa Nehemiah made his way into Babylonia, in order to recruit those of his countrymen who were willing to return home or to make monetary contributions. Negotiations with the officials in the satrapy "across the River" and the provision of necessary building materials occupied a rather long time.[5] When he arrived in Jerusalem, Nehemiah immediately began to take steps to prevent his work from being checked from the very outset. Three days after his arrival, he went out to inspect the destroyed city walls, by night, in order to gain a clear picture of the magnitude of his undertakings. Only then did he unfold his plans before the leading citizens of the community (2, 11-18). A working force had been enrolled from the whole of Judah (ch. 3), and the city walls were then apportioned to the control of various responsible leaders. The building began with feverish haste. After 42 days (6, 15) the walls were substantially complete. The progress provoked considerable opposition. The arch-

---

3. Hebrew *peḥah*, Accadian *pilahatu*, "responsibility." Bibl 42 (1961), 246.

4. A. Alt, *Die Rolle Samarias bei der Entstehung des Judentums*, Kleine Texte II, 316-337.

5. According to Ant. XI, V, 7, Nehemiah arrived in Jerusalem first in 440.

enemy was Sanballat, governor of Samaria (4, 1). Despite his Babylonian name, "May the moon god Sin give life," he was faithful to the cult of Yahweh. This is proved by the names of his two sons Deliah and Sedemiah.[6] He was, moreover, related as son-in-law to the high priest at Jerusalem (13, 28). A second enemy appeared in the person of Tobiah,[7] governor of the Province of Ammon. He too must be characterized as a Yahwist, as indicated by his name and that of his son Jehohanan. From Nehemiah's point of view, however, the faith in Yahweh practiced by the Samaritans and Ammonites was no longer pure, since it had been overgrown with pagan influences. There was to be no compromise in matters of faith: "You have no portion or right or memorial in Jerusalem" (2, 20). Angry with the treatment they had received, these two powerful antagonists determined to offer active opposition to Nehemiah's work. They were joined in their efforts by an Arab Geshem,[8] the powerful sheik from Kedar, a prince to whom even Edom and the southern part of Judah were subject. Enemies arose from all sides. With mockery, intrigue, and brutal force they were determined to stalemate the reconstruc-

---

6. Elephantine, ANET 492.
7. B. Mazar, *The Tobiads*, IEJ 7 (1957), 137-145; 229-238. The Tobiads, an influential noble class who made their home in Judah and in Gilead, "the land of Tobiah," had considerable holdings. The genealogy can be traced in an unbroken line from Antiochus III about 200 B. C. as far back as the time of Sedeciah, about 590. Perhaps the rival to the throne Tob'el (Is 7) is from the same clan. C. C. McCown, *The 'Araq el-Emir and the Tobiads*, BA 20 (1957), 63-76. In the ruins, the name *twbyh* is frequently encountered, cut into the stone. Apparently this was the family seat of the Tobiads. The Arabic name *Qasr el-'abd*, "palace of the servant (of god)" points to Neh 2, 19.
8. F. M. Cross, *Geschem the Arabian, Enemy of Nehemiah*, BA 18 (1956), 46-47, describes three silver vessels, one of which bears the inscription "kaynu, son of gašmu, king of qedar." Dated in the fifth century, Cain's father was thus the biblical Geschem. — W. F. Albright, *Zur Chronologie des vorislamischen Arabien*, BZAW 77 (1958), 1-8. The *gšm* of the Nuran inscriptions is the biblical Geschem, the adversary of Nehemiah. — His residence was apparently in Lachish, where, in level I, a great palace was uncovered, together with a small temple. BA 17 (1955), 9-17.

tion of Jerusalem. "If a fox were to jump upon your stone walls, he would tear them down," was the mocking statement of Tobiah. When Nehemiah refused to be shaken by such propaganda, the raids began. Arabs, Ammonites, and Philistines, all attacked the Judaean settlers (4, 7-12). Nehemiah, accordingly, divided his people into two groups; the first group stood at the walls and worked with feverish haste while the second group seized their weapons and defended the city against attack.[9] In order to increase the population of Jerusalem, Nehemiah had people from the threatened villages brought into the city. When all the attempts to destroy Jerusalem had failed, an effort was made to get rid of Nehemiah, the soul of the resistance. His enemies planned to lure him out of Jerusalem and kill him from ambush (6, 1-4). He was accused of rebellion at the Persian court (6, 5-9). But it was not only the enemy from without who threatened; there was hostility even within the city. Tobiah and his sons had married their way into some Jerusalem families. His new relatives kept him well informed of everything that happened in the city. Threatening letters were sent to Nehemiah (6, 17-19); finally even a prophet was sent against him (6, 10-14). He ordered Nehemiah to take refuge in the Temple in order to save his life. But Nehemiah was not a man to be broken by intrigues. The city walls continued to grow and finally they were consecrated (12, 27-43). The first battle had been won, and the Judaeans returned from Exile could, for the time, feel secure in their fortified city.

3) ECONOMIC MEASURES

The newly formed Province of Judah comprised the territories from Beth-zur, north of Hebron, as far as Bethel, and counted barely 50,000 inhabitants. Nehemiah appears not to have introduced any new administrative system, but rather to have adapted

---

9. W. Luethi, *Die Bauleute Gottes. Nehemia, der Prophet im Kampf um den Aufbau der zerstörten Stadt,* (Basel 1945).
10. Bright, HistIsr 364ff.

the existing form of administration. The economic situation was hopeless. Crop failure and exorbitant taxes had reduced a considerable proportion of the population to a condition of debt-slavery. It was against this abuse that Nehemiah now took energetic steps. He reproached the Jews with the argument that in Babylonia considerable sacrifices had been made in order to redeem the Judaean slaves from the hands of their pagan masters, while here in Judah they were enslaving their own countrymen. At an assembly of the people, to the accompaniment of the most solemn oaths, he proclaimed the emancipation of all slaves (5, 1-12). Nehemiah was a selfless man. Throughout the entire time of his administration, from the 20th to the 32nd year of Artaxerxes (445/44-433/32) he refused the official allowance proper to a governor, although he had a right to claim it (5, 14). In the course of time he grew more and more convinced that his economic reforms had not solved the entire problem. The religious situation called for an energetic religious reformer.

4) NEHEMIAH'S SECOND MISSION

After the course of twelve years, Nehemiah returned to the Persian court (13, 6), possibly because he had not been granted a longer period of freedom. But it is also quite possible that he returned to the east in order to lay the foundations of a far-reaching religious reform, and to inform the court of his plans in this direction. He would appear to have made his second journey to Jerusalem in the jubilee year [11] 430/429. This time he spent only a short time in Jerusalem.

Hardly had Nehemiah left Jerusalem when his opponents gained the upper hand. The priest Eliashib — probably the well known high priest (3, 1; 13, 28) — had gone so far as to prepare Nehemiah's mortal enemy Tobiah a place in the Temple, which had formerly been used for the cereal offering, the incense, and the sacred vessels, etc. Upon his return, Nehemiah immediately had Tobiah's property thrown out onto the street; he then cleansed the chamber and restored it to its original use. He also

---

11. V. Palovsky, Bibl 38 (1957), 440-443.

had to reorganize the portions of the Levites. Since the tithe had not been paid and the Levites were thus left without any income, they had made their way into the countryside. Nehemiah therefore completely reorganized the tithe system (13, 10-14). The sabbath, too, had been completely profaned. "In those days I saw in Judah men treading winepresses on the sabbath, and bringing in heaps of grain, etc." (13, 15). He quickly commanded that the gates of the city be shut on the sabbath. When the merchants presumed that these measures were not to be taken seriously and took their normal places on the first and even on the second sabbath, he had them driven away by force. A further abuse were the mixed marriages with non-Jewish women, whose children were not even able to speak Hebrew. Nehemiah remonstrated with his countrymen to abandon these immoral practices (13, 23). When the son of the high priest Eliashib married the daughter of Sanballat, the avowed enemy of the Judaeans, Nehemiah threw him out of the city, thereby once and for all sealing the hostility between Judah and Samaria [12] (13, 28). How long Nehemiah continued as governor over Judah is unknown. But around the year 411 we find a Jew with a Persian name, Bagoas, acting in this capacity.

Nehemiah was not destined to have the great and lasting effects that King David had produced. Despite this fact, his activity forms a turning point in the history of the Old Testament. It was he who carried through the work of separation and set the definitive norms for the repatriated Judaeans in Palestine. His personal integrity, energy, and steadfast courage make him one of the most sympathetic figures in the Bible. With trowel and sword he built up the Old Testament Church at a crisis in its history.

B) EZRA, THE REFORMER

---

12. According to Josephus, Ant. XI, VIII, 2, the banished son of the high priest is supposed to have built a temple on Mt. Gerizim and there established a schismatic Yahweh cult. There is some doubt as to the truth of the story.

1) "AGENT FOR THE LAW OF THE GOD OF HEAVEN" (Ezr 7, 12)

Just like Nehemiah, Ezra too made his way to Jerusalem with the authority and commission of King Artaxerxes, although his mission is of a quite different character. It was addressed not only to the province of Judah, but to the entire satrapy of *'abar-nahara* (Syria and Palestine). He was to have authority not in civil affairs, but only in matters of religion. Anyone who opposed him is threatened with death, imprisonment, fine, or exile (7, 26). Behind Ezra there stood the entire authority of the Persian royal law. Moreover, by virtue of his plenipotentiary powers, he was in a position not only to exact payments from the Babylonian Jews, but, to a certain degree, he could encumber the state treasury (7, 15-19), in order to accomplish the task assigned to him, the restoration of the divine service in Jerusalem. Nobody before Ezra — under the Assyrian or Babylonian sovereignty this would have been unthinkable — had ever enjoyed such a favorable political situation for the accomplishment of his mission. The plenipotentiary decree is incorporated, in the Aramaic form, into the Book of Ezra (7, 11-26). He appears there under the title "Ezra, the *sāphār* for the law of the God of heaven." The Aramaic word *sāphār* does not here have the later, more familiar meaning of "learned in the law, scribe," but rather the original sense of "scribe-secretary." [13] Ezra was, accordingly, so to speak, the "general secretary for the religious affairs of Judah." The formulation of the decree presupposes the scribe who is well informed on the subject of Judaean religious practices. It would certainly be possible that the text was composed by a Jew at the royal court, perhaps even by Ezra himself and simply approved by the king. This would certainly be in perfect accord with what is known of Persian administrative procedures, according to which the various peoples of the kingdom were allowed the highest possible degree of self-determination.

---

13. H. H. Schaeder, *Esra, der Schreiber*, (1930), 39-59.

2) EZRA'S REFORM

The date at which Ezra began his work of reform in Jerusalem can no longer be accurately determined. The chronological problems will be considered later on. The greatest probability would point to an activity immediately prior to the second visit of Nehemiah, partially overlapping with his stay in Jerusalem. Ezra did not come to Jerusalem alone; he was leading a huge caravan of repatriates (Ezr 7, 27; 8, 36). At the river Ahawaa, a location which can no longer be identified, the caravan made a camp (7, 15). From here, on the 12th day of the 1st month (April 15, 428), after praying and fasting (7, 21, 31), the caravan marched for 4 months (August 2), without any kind of military protection — times were peaceful — all the way to Jerusalem. Here Ezra surrendered the treasures he had carried with him to the keeping of the Temple. The following months he was completely occupied with seeing to the housing and employment opportunities of the repatriates, and with helping them make their way into the community.

a. *Reading of the Law* (Neh 8, 1-18): Since Ezra had come primarily as the champion of the Law of God, he probably seized the first opportunity, the Feast of Huts in the fall, to accomplish his primary mission, the new promulgation of the Law. "When the seventh month had come, the children of Israel were in their towns. And all the people gathered as one man into the square before the Water Gate; and they told Ezra the scribe to bring the book of the law of Moses which the Lord had given to Israel" (Neh 8, 1ff.). A wooden pulpit was erected; Ezra opened the book (the scroll), and said a prayer to which the people, raising their hands, answered Amen. He then prostrated himself in prayer upon the ground. Next came the reading of the law from the book which Ezra had brought to Jerusalem with him. The law he read was nothing new; but his wise selection of passages from the book made a deep and lasting impression upon the assembled community of God. Levites assisted Ezra, probably by translating the Hebrew text into the Aramaic understood by the people (8, 7). Stirred up by this solemn reading of the Law, the people celebrated the Feast of Huts with the greatest possible enthusiasm and read a selection from the Law on every day of the entire week of the festival (8, 13-18).

b. *Regulation of mixed marriages*: Despite the religious enthusiasm which had been set in motion by the reading of the law, Ezra still had some serious hurdles to overcome. In describing the career of Nehemiah, we have already mentioned that he was forced to take a strict stand against mixed marriages, which contributed so heavily to the religious indifference and moral decay of his people. We have described how the unholy practice had already made its way into the family of the high priest. In order to completely uproot this evil, which was envisaged as a dangerous threat to the national faith, Ezra embarked upon a course of almost reckless severity. Two months after the Festival of the Huts, on the 20th day of the 9th month (December 8, 428), he once again called an assembly of the people (Ezr 10, 9; Neh 8, 2). The people sat upon the square before the House of God, shivering with cold, for it was raining; but shivering even more in the face of the powerful sermon they expected to hear on the subject of mixed marriage (Ezr 10, 9ff.). Ezra's inexorable demands were these: "Separate yourselves from the peoples of the land and from the foreign wives" (10, 11). The assembly agreed with him. But since the regulation had far-reaching implications for the stability of the newly established families, creating difficulties which could not be solved in a single day, a commission for the regulation of mixed marriages was established (10, 14). How accurately this commission did its work is evident from the lists of guilty parties still preserved in Ezr 10, 18-44. The purification continued to the 1st day of the 1st month (May 26, 427) (10, 17). The considerations which drove Ezra to these hard measures were not racial, but **purely**

religious. This work of separation, in which he was avidly supported by Nehemiah, firmly established the individuality of the
Jewish race and religion for all centuries to come, and set a final
and insurmountable barrier to the gradual process of fusion with
the Canaanite ethnic and religious elements.

  c. *Documents and signatures*: The climax and conclusion of
Ezra's activity is the formal settlement of the new "state constitution," which was drawn up in document form and signed and
sealed by the leading princes, priests, and Levites. The details
of this story are narrated in Neh 9 and 10.[14] This narrative
is written in the first person plural, probably evidence of the
fact that the success of this great enterprise is owing to the combined efforts of Nehemiah the governor and Ezra the scribe. The
parties to the covenant all swore:
  1. To enter no mixed marriages; 2. To buy nothing from the
merchants on the sabbath; 3. To observe the sabbath year (to
forego the harvest on this year); 4. To pay the shekels to the
Temple every year; 5. To supply the wood for the holocaust; 6.
To observe the first-fruits; 7. To pay the tithes. In conclusion,
they all swore: "We will not neglect the house of our God"
(Neh 10, 39). Ezra no doubt took this document with him to
the Persian court, as evidence of having fulfilled his mission.
  Ezra's activity may have been extremely short — it could
all have been accomplished within the course of a single year —
but it was far-reaching. It was his work which breathed the spirit
of religious reform into the political and economic reorganization
of Nehemiah, and by obligating the people to observe the Law in
its entirety, lent a certain perpetuity to their combined efforts.
Ezra entrusted the preservation of his spirit to the Levites, from
whose ranks he had chosen his closest collaborators (Ezra 7,
24; 8, 15ff.; 8, 30). The letter incorporating his mission had

---

14. Neh 9, 1: "On the 24th day of the month" is an unclear dating
    formula, since it is not certain what month is taken as a point of
    reference. If it actually is the month of the Feast of Huts, mentioned
    in the preceding chapter, then the treaty would have been concluded
    already on October 22, 428; the regulation of the mixed marriages
    would then be a consequence of the treaty.

included a direction to establish judges and guardians of the law who were to instruct the people in the law of the God of heaven (7, 25). "The new teachers of the people needed to be instructed first themselves, and thus it is quite probable that Ezra taught his disciples and fellow-workers not only the Law but also the history of Israel which had long figured as an essential element in the religious instruction of the people. He thus wrote a handbook of Israel's history, a chronicle form of history (1 Ch 1 — Ezr 6). The traditional point of view, which claimed the work of the chronists as coming from the pen of Ezra himself,[15] goes far to explain the individuality of the work: the emphasis which is placed on fidelity to the law, upon the cult, and upon the Levites, and finally its anti-Samaritan tendency."[16]

Ezra's disciples are also the ones who gathered the earlier religious writings and edited them in their present form. The peaceful era which was now beginning might well be termed the cradle of the Old Testament Bible. After all the terrible catastrophes of history, Israel realized that her greatest treasure and privilege was the Law of God. It was during these days that the great hymns to the glory of the Law were composed (cf. Ps 1 and 118/119). The religion of Israel was on its way to becoming a religion of the Law. But in this early era, the word law had not yet taken on its oppressive or restrictive sense; it was still filled with faith in the grace of God and the election of Israel; hence the enthusiastic acclamation: "Blessed the man who walks in the way of God's law" (Ps 1, 1).

C)   PROBLEMS IN HISTORICAL AND LITERARY CRITICISM

1) LITERARY PROBLEMS

Just like the Books of Samuel, Kings, and Chronicles, which are now numbered as two books in the present form of the Bible but were originally a single book, the division of the unified history of Ezra-Nehemiah is the work of a later era. Its division

---

15. Introduction to Chronicles. Cf. Vol. III, pp. 282ff.
16. V. Palovsky, Bibl 38 (1957), 450.

in the LXX is first attested to by Origen.[17] Jerome followed the same pattern. Under the influence of the Vulgate, the division was then introduced into the Hebrew Bible (the edition of Daniel Bromberg, 1517). In order to arrive at a proper evaluation, we must, accordingly, treat the currently divided texts of the Books of Ezra and Nehemiah as one single historical work. Furthermore, they must be taken as a continuation and conclusion to the Books of Chronicles, so that all four books (1 + 2 Chron, Ezra + Neh) represent one unified historical narrative. The individuality of the Book of Chronicles, which proclaims a theology of history in bold outlines from the dawn of creation to the author's own day, has already been described.[18] The manner of composition in Ezr-Neh is the same. The author made use of sources and arranged them about motifs from theology history. The chief distinction between this book and Chronicles lies in the fact that here we have two independent sources which have been taken up and stitched together by the new text.

a. *Nehemiah's memoirs*: Scholars are generally agreed in including: Neh 1, 1—7, 73 together with its title: "Words of Nehemiah, son of Hacaliah," a first-person account of the work of reconstruction; 11, 1-2: increasing the population of Jerusalem; 12, 27-43: dedication of the walls; 13, 4-31: second mission. Nehemiah most likely wrote these memoirs as an official report to the Persian court.

b. *Ezra's memoirs*: In the case of Ezra, there is no such general consensus of opinion. He too recounts his activities and words in the first person (first person accounts: Ezra 7, 27-28: prayer of thanksgiving; 8, 1-34: return home; 9, 1-15:

---

17. The references to the various books are somewhat confusing. LXX counts three, and the Vulg. four books of Ezra. LXX Ezr I = Vulg Ezr III (an apocryphal writing which enjoyed considerable popularity but was never admitted to the canon). LXX Ezr II = Vulg Ezr I = our Book of Ezra; LXX Ezr III = Vulg Ezr II = our Book of Nehemiah. Vulg Ezr IV = Apocalypse of Ezra (apocryphal).
18. Cf. Vol. III, pp. 282ff.

regulation of mixed marriages). Perhaps Ezra also composed an official report on his activity. Careful examination shows that the style and vocabulary of the first person narratives differ very little from the style and vocabulary of the chronist. This fact has led to two quite different conclusions; some scholars go so far as to explain the first person narratives as a literary fiction, and to completely deny the very existence of Ezra.[19] Others see the similarities in language as proof of identical authorship, that is, they maintain that Ezra himself wrote the entire book, which was later reworked by his disciples.[20] Since, however, in addition to the first person narratives, there are some third person narratives (7, 1-26: preparation for the return home and the decree; 10, 1-27: prayer of penance and assembly of the people; Neh 7, 73 — 9, 37: reform), and also a narrative in the first person plural (Neh 10) it is easy to get the impression that, in the case of Ezra, there must also have been a clearly determined source text, in the form of memoirs, which was incorporated into the history sometimes literally, sometimes freely reworded. The precise dating would suggest the style of a journal: Ezr 7, 9 (1st day of the 1st month); 8, 31 (12th day of the same month); 7, 8-9 (1st day of the 5th month); Neh 7, 73b — 8, 18 (the first 8 days of the 7th month); Ezr 10, 9 (20th day of the 9th month); 10, 16, 17 (from the first day of the 10th month to the 1st day of the 1st month). Ezra's official report for the Persian court would thus comprise Ezr 7, 1-10, 44 and Neh 7, 73 — 9, 37.

c. *The author of the history*: In addition to the two memoirs, the historian also had access to other documents from archives, in particular the various lists [21] and these he incorporated into his work. Why he should have split up his two primary sources and

---

19. D. F. Robinson, *Was Ezra Nehemiah?* AnglTR 38 (1958), 177-189, claims that the hero of the Ezra narrative is actually Nehemiah, who, however, as a eunuch, seemed unfit to play such a significant role in the history of the Jewish religion.
20. W. Rudolph, *Esra und Nehemia*, HAT (1949), 165.
21. H. L. Allrik, *The Lists of Zerubbabel and the Hebrew Numerical Notation*, BASOR 136 (1954), 21-27.

arranged them in different order is not particularly clear. At all events, he did not organize his material according to the chronological point of view, a fact which occasions considerable difficulty in the interpretation of his work. "This practice on the part of the author — one we find very difficult to comprehend — has certainly obscured the real course of Nehemiah's and Ezra's careers. But the content of the documents clearly points to the actual course of events." [22] At all events, the Books of Ezra and Nehemiah are the most valuable historical source which we have from the long period between the return home (538) and the era of the Maccabees, an era about which we otherwise know so very little apart from the brilliant light that illuminates this one brief but very vital interval. With Ezra and Nehemiah we see the end of an era, "the heroic-tragic Hebrew history of the Old Testament, and the beginning of a new, the era of the holy community of God, Israel of the law." [23]

2) CHRONOLOGICAL PROBLEMS

The primary question is whether Ezra's activity antedates that of Nehemiah or coincides with it.[24] The problem can be solved by the references to the Persian king Artaxerxes, whose regnal years form the basis of the dating. There were, however, three kings with this name: Artaxerxes I Longimanus (465-424), Artaxerxes II Mnemon (404-358), and Artaxerxes III (359- 338). The last-named need not be considered, since he did not reign for 32 years (Neh 5, 14). The chronist nowhere says whether he is referring to the first or second ruler of this name; he simply calls him Artaxerxes. Now Nehemiah's activity is unanimously established as occurring in the time between the 20th to the 32nd year of Artaxerxes, and this primarily on the basis of the Elephantine Papyri.[25] The same source refers to Jehohanan as high priest

---

22. Palovsky, Bibl 38 (1957), 454.
23. Pfeiffer, IntrOT 838.
24. For a thorough discussion, cf. V. Palovsky, *Die Chronologie der Tätigkeit Esdras,* or *Neuen Lösung,* Bibl 38 (1957), 275-305; 428-456. — Bright, HistIsr 375-386. — H. Schneider, *Die Bücher Esra und Nehemia,* BB (1959), 67-75.
25. ANET 492-493.

in Jerusalem for the year 408. Now Nehemiah came to Jerusalem
under the high priest Eliashib (Neh 3, 1); according to Neh
12, 10, Jehohanan was Eliashib's successor; accordingly, Nehemiah must have come to Judah for the first time under Artaxerxes I, that is, in the year 445. The same papyri for the year
408 witness to the influential activity of the sons of Sinuballit,
who is probably to be identified with the Sanballat of the Nehemiah memoirs (Neh 2, 10 — 13, 28). But if Sinuballit was already an old man in the year 408 and had sons who were already
ruling, Nehemiah must have begun his activity under the reign
of Artaxerxes I. The argument which insists upon Artaxerxes II
would have to posit an Eliashib II and a Sanballat II. But there
are no grounds for such an assumption, and the year 445 can be
counted as definite for the beginning of Nehemiah's career. It is
quite different in the case of Ezra, for whose activity three
separate dates can be argued.

a. *Ezra before Nehemiah, in the year* 458: According to
Ezr 7, 8, Ezra came to Jerusalem in the 7th year of King Artaxerxes. If we read the narrative in what has been generally
presupposed to be its proper chronological sequence, we should
indeed have to assume that the Artaxerxes involved is the same
king whose regnal years are the basis for the dating of Nehemiah's
activity, and would thus arrive at the year 458/57. This would
place Ezra's activity prior to that of Nehemiah. Schneider [26] advances seven arguments in favor of this position. Ezra is supposed
to have come to Jerusalem with his caravan in the 1st years
of Artaxerxes I (Ezr 4, 12). Just as Darius, in 519, had given
orders that the law of Egypt be recorded in writing, Artaxerxes
I would have entrusted Ezra with the codification of the Mosaic
Law. The formal reading of the Law would have followed in
the 7th year, which was also a sabbath year. The activity of the
practical-minded governor Nehemiah was a necessary follow-up,
since the unpractical theological thinking of Ezra had met with
failure. The most serious argument against this position is the

---

26. L. c. 74-75.

circumstances surrounding the year 458, a time at which the Persian Empire was in complete turmoil, so that there seemed to be no opportunity for a peaceful mission such as that of Ezra's.[27]

b. *Ezra after Nehemiah, in the year* 398/97: This argument is supported by literary and historical criticism. The author would not be presenting his account in a temporal sequence. Instead, he had arranged the somewhat earlier events under Darius (completion of the Temple, 515) shortly before the public appearance of Ezra (Ezr 6, 1ff.), while the historically later events under Cyrus, Xerxes, and Artaxerxes, have been anticipated. A similar transposition could well have taken place in the case of Ezra. Accordingly, Ezra and Nehemiah would not be contemporaries. The priest Ezra would then simply have put the finishing touches on the work of Nehemiah, in the year 398/97.[28] But since the measures introduced by Ezra were so close to those promoted by Nehemiah, especially in his second period of administration (Neh 10; 13, 4-31), it hardly seemed justified to treat their two careers separately. The explanation of this position sets the groundwork for the third explanation.

c. *Ezra during and shortly after Nehemiah's second mission* (428/27): Ezra's mission seems to have been prompted by Nehemiah's trip to the Persian court. He was forced to admit that the unpeaceful religious and liturgical situation in Jerusalem could not be handled by a layman. Ezra was thus sent to Jerusalem with the official title of "agent of the law of the God of heaven" to reorganize the administrative system in Jerusalem. Palovsky[29] argues that Ezra had already traveled to Jerusalem together with Nehemiah in the year 430, on a fact-finding tour. After learning of the sad situation, he returned to Babylonia, where he provided

---

27. Palovsky, *ibid.*, 283ff.
28. H. H. Rowley, *Nehemiah's Mission and its Background*, BJRL 37 (1955), 528-561. — N. H. Snaith, *The Date of Ezra's Arrival in Jerusalem*, ZAW 63 (1951), 53-66. — H. Cazelles, *La Mission d'Esdras*, VT 4 (1954), 113-140.
29. Bibl 38 (1957), 443.

himself with the necessary power and then organized a caravan of repatriates in the 37th year of Artaxerxes (428/27). In Ezr 7, 8, accordingly, we must introduce a correction: instead of seven, we must read the 37th year.[30] Even though it seems hardly possible to achieve any current agreement on the subject of the temporal sequence of the reforms of Ezra and Nehemiah,[31] in my opinion the last position, which argues for both men to be working simultaneously, seems to correspond most closely with the historical data.[32]

At all events, it was under the protection of Ahura-mazda that the religious and spiritual life was free to develop in the Persian province of Jahud. The spiritual energies were no longer directed against the eradication of the Canaanite Baal cult; this quiet century afforded all the prerequisites for the formation of the schools of wisdom. Energy was concentrated exclusively upon the investigation and study of the Law. One precipitate of this effort might well be the Book of Job, with its presentation of an individual taking a stand against the traditional teachings. The historical background of the Book of Job is, indeed, a hotly contested issue; but in my opinion it is best dated towards the end of the Persian era. Accordingly, it will be treated in the next chapter.

---

30. On the possibility of miswriting numbers, cf. H. L. Allrik, BASOR 136 (1954), 21-27: the use of letters to designate numerals came into Hebrew only under Greek influence; prior to that time, Hebrew had its own system of numerals, so that the loss of the 30 is easily enough understood. But in my opinion the present dating in the 7th year is not owing to the loss of the 30, but rather the result of a deliberate harmonizing. Numbers are always handed down with the greatest possible accuracy.

31. A. Weiser, EinlAT (1957), 260.

32. For this dating: Palovsky, Bright (HistIsr 386). M. Noth, GeschIsr 289 dates Nehemiah before Ezra, but adds the note that the most scholarship can hope to achieve is a calculated probability.

CHAPTER XI

THE BOOK OF JOB

IN order to explain the basic problem of the Book of Job,[1] let us first examine the following opinions: "The suffering man is the theme expressed in the Book of Job. By reason of its great general-human content and its marvelously elevated form, this book has become a well-known work of world literature and its appeal to the religious temperament and artistic sensitivity is an abiding one. It has continued to find new friends, who are unwearying in their efforts to sound its deepest meaning and to reproduce its artistic form. The difficulty in understanding and reproducing this book is not so much a problem of its thought content, but rather its external composition, as we see it today. In its present form, the Book of Job appears to be a unified piece of work, proceeding along the lines of dramatic development. Upon closer examination, however, and deeper study, we realize that what appears to be the work of a single hand actually dates from various periods of history and has been put together from a great diversity of material. This deeper understanding of the inner structure of the Book of Job does indeed destroy its dramatic unity. But the beauty of the individual sections is not in the least diminished; rather it is increased, while the interpretation

---

1. P. Volz, *Hiob und Weisheit*, SAT (Gunkel) (1921), 1-2.

gains considerably. One might compare it to a European cathedral which owes its origin to various periods of construction and concepts of style: there is no genuine artistic unity, but the individual members thereby invite a closer contemplation, and the resultant history of its construction is richer and closer to life." [2]

What must occupy us here is an analysis of the "building history," that is the origin, development, and present form of the Book of Job. Then, on the basis of this historical appreciation, we must study the structure of the book and evaluate its basic principles.

A) THE HISTORY OF THE BOOK OF JOB

1) THE JOB OF PRE-HISTORY AND THE LITERARY JOB

If we explained the name Job on the basis of its current Hebrew form *'iyyôb,* it means "the persecuted," or perhaps even "the persecutor." [3] It would hardly seem possible to find a better name for a man who constantly attacks both God and men, and who is himself attacked down to the very end. Yet, it does not seem to be a literary symbolic name; the name Job can, it would appear, easily be fitted into a series of Canaanite, or more properly "Amorite" personal names which date back to the patriarchal era. The Amarna letters mention a certain *A-ya-bu,* prince of *Pi-hi-lim* (Pella) in Transjordania.[4] This certainly does not mean that this prince is to be identified with the biblical Job.

---

2. All critics are united in their admiration of the Book of Job. One American has called it "the Matterhorn of the Old Testament." V. E. Reichert, *Job,* SoncB (1958), XIII.

3. Nominal formation for vocational names from the basic form *qattal* — *quittôl;* the corresponding form is *'iyyob* = "the accuser." By comparison with the form *yillôd* ("the one born, the child"), we derive *'iyyôb,* as a passive in the sense of "the one attacked." Fr. Horst, *Hiob,* BK XVI/1, 7. — The passive form also survives in the name of Niobe, whose children were destroyed because of the hostility of the gods. Phoenician *ne'eyobah* = Nioba = "the one attacked." EncMikr I, 244. Greek and Latin *Job,* Syrian *Iyub,* Arabic *Ayyub;* the form that has been common in German since Luther, *Hiob,* arises from the fact that the initial aleph was written with the letter H.

4. Knudtzon, El-Amarna Nos. 256, 817.

It simply means that the name Job was widely spread already in the middle Bronze Age. The original form of this name *'ayya-'abu*, contracted to *'ayyabu*, gradually developing into the form *'iyyôb*, means, "who is the father?" [5] Tradition has preserved the record that one bearer of this name had withstood a severe trial to his faith. When and where this man lived can be determined only in the broadest outline.

Job's land was the country of 'Us which belonged to the greater territory of Kedem. Both names point to the area of Transjordania; either in the Aramaic district of Hauran in the north, or the Edomite settlements in the south. Both districts were famous for the wisdom of the "sons of the east" (Ob 8; 1 K 5, 10f.; Bar 3, 22f.). The territory of Edom is suggested by an addition to the Greek version of Job (48, 17ae), where Job is identified as the second king of Edom (Gn 36, 33). His predecessor was called Bela' ben-Be'or (Gn 36, 32). Tur-sinai [6] maintains that Bela' is simply a variant for Bil'am ben-Be'or, who was killed in a battle against the Midianites (Nb 31, 8). This ben-Be'or would be the man who expelled Job(ab) from his property and made off with all his possessions; after the victory of Israel Job was free to return to his former possessions. The story of Job would thus preserve an episode not fully described in the Torah, a story dating from the era in which Israel was occupying the promised land. According to the Talmud,[7] it was Moses himself who composed the Book of Job. But all this is pure speculation, which cannot be supported by competent criticism.

The figure of Job can be fitted into the patriarchal era. Job's great wealth is described in terms that are used in reference to Isaac's riches (Gn 26, 13f.); Job offers sacrifices very much like the patriarchs do. What is more, he bears a name that was current in the northwestern area of the territory settled by the Semites. The story of his trial and steadfastness has its closest parallel in the story of Abraham's trial and fidelity.[8] Job, like the patriarchs, would thus be a figure from the earliest history, a man whose reverent memory was handed down from generation to generation.

The opposite opinion, which is also represented in the Talmud, maintains that the Book of Job is simply a didactic fiction (*masal*),

---

5. W. F. Albright, *Northwest-Semitic Names in a List of Egyptian Slaves*, JAOS 74 (1954), 222ff.
6. EncMikr I, 244.
7. Baba bathra 14b.
8. Fr. Horst, *Hiob*, BK XVI/1, 9.

and that there never was a man by the name of Job.[9] The historical and geographical details are meant to serve simply as an ornament. It would be idle effort to attempt to identify the country and origin of a figure who was simply invented. For the prophet Ezekiel, however, Job was a figure from early history, on a par with Noah and Daniel (Ez 14, 14-20). Noah points to the time before the great deluge, while Daniel refers, not to the Biblical prophet, but to the wise king Dani-il in the Ugarit epic.[10] In a similar manner, Ezekiel's mention of Job is not a reference to the Book of Job, but to the living figure of the great and patient Job from pre-history, as preserved in an oral tradition.

As a result, we must clearly distinguish between the literary figure of Job and Job of pre-history. "The book pretends to be a recounting of events that were actually witnessed by its author, who, however, knew Ijjob only by word of mouth, from the living voice of legend, which had grown up around the earlier historical figure. The speeches of Ijjob are thus the author's own speeches, just as the speeches of Hamlet are really the words of Shakespeare." [11] The literary Job is thus no less historical than the Job of pre-history. The author was so taken up with the familiar narrative that he made it his own. The essential problem is not to determine when, where, or how the Job of pre-history actually lived; ancient popular traditions generally develop around a genuine historical nucleus.[12] What needs study and interpretation is the Job who speaks to us from the present book. "The parties to this dialogue appear to be Ancient Near Eastern nomads, but actually Job and his friends are expressing the thoughts of the post-Exilic wisdom literature." [13] Just as in Goethe's *Faust,* it is not the thoughts of the *Urfaust,* but the Faustian thoughts of Goethe himself which are expressed, so we must clearly distinguish between the "ur-Job" preserved by popular tradition, and the dramatic literary work of the Book of Job. The "popular Job" is to be seen in the writer's prologue (ch. 1 — 2) and in the epilogue

9. Baba bathra 15; Gn rabba 57.
10. A. Jirku, *Kanaanäische Mythen und Epen aus Ras Schamra-Ugarit,* (1962), 115ff.
11. Fr. Stier, *Ijjob* 261.
12. H. Junker, *Das Buch Job,* EB IV, 316.
13. *Ibid.*

(42, 7-17). Linguistically, it is reminiscent of epic prose.[14] The
principal bulk of the work, whether we call it dialogue or drama,
is in clearly marked rhythm, in language that is elevated poetry,
powerful, and even primordial.

Since the Book of Job unites two distinct elements, the ancient popular tradition and a heated, almost passionate argument
on the subject of the traditional faith, the problem of literary
criticism needs to be posed. Was this fusion of two elements the
work of a single powerful poet, or does it result from a process
of gradual growth and accretion?

2) PRE-HISTORY AND COMPOSITION OF THE BOOK OF JOB [15]

Many and various attempts have been made to understand
this erratic bloc formed by the Book of Job in the midst of the
Old Testament. Scholars have repeatedly cut the book into small
pieces, only to recognize, at the end, its well-established unity.

a. *The background story*: No single attempt to solve the literary
problem of the Book of Job has ever drawn a line between the
introductory narrative and the debates; on the contrary, the legend
of Job sets the entire scene for the coming drama. The poet
came up with the ancient tradition describing the sufferings of
Job, his argument with his wife and relatives, and a decisive
word of judgment from God. This original story is, therefore, not
simply an ornamental introduction or setting to the book; it is
a point of crystallization, about which the two great debates are
developed. The poet did not take over the traditional story word
for word; he reworked it freely into the construction of his writing.[16] Instead of relatives, he introduces three friends who make
three separate attempts to convict Job of wrongdoing.

---

14. N. M. Sarna, *Epic Substratum in the Prose of Job*, JBL 76 (1957),
    13-25.
15. G. Fohrer, VT 6 (1956), 249-267.
16. G. Fohrer, *Überlieferung und Wandlung der Hioblegende. Erlanger
    Forschungen* A 10 (Fs. F. Baumgärtel), 41-62, discovers several
    original strata in the framing narrative.

b. *The dialogue, its original form and later additions*: In his brief description of the history of interpretation of the Book of Job, Eissfeldt [17] makes it very clear that the book itself has not been spared. Scholars have established gaps and tears, patchworks, elaborations, and additions, in their effort to uncover the original form, the basic outline of the poet. Their conclusion is that, of the whole book, only the basic organization of the first dialogue and the imperfectly preserved monologue of Job which follows in chapters 15 – 31 are original. "In their conversation, Job's friends insist there can be no suffering without guilt (Eliphaz), that Job must pray to God for favor and he will then get back his health and prosperity (Bildad), that God knows who are the evildoers and that Job has only one recourse, penance (Zophar). But Job vigorously rejects his friends' attacks and holds fast to his certainty that he is in the right with respect to God, and that he will receive justice from heaven. In the monologue he once again gives free course to his indignation at the injustice he has experienced, but he grows closer and closer to the certainty that God is not his enemy but his friend and that God is about to prove this publicly. He concludes in a truly royal burst of pride with an expression of confidence that he is still in the right. The original poem is thus "the cry of a pious man from the depths of despair to which he has been forced by the obligations which are a heavy burden upon his piety" (Baumgartel), that is, his belief in divine retribution. "In a terrible personal struggle this pious man contests the justice of God insofar as he can within the obligations imposed by his faith; he clings to a faith in God that is without limit, severely put to the test, but not to be snuffed out: he calls upon God in bold and certain hope" (Baumgartel). But the original form of the poem does not pose a problem. Thus, the original Job-dialogue would be simply a lament, but not an argument, closer to the confident prayer of an unjustly persecuted man than to a theological debate. It is only the historical process of development that introduces the element of argument.

Tur-Sinai [18] suggests the interesting if not completely demonstrable possibility that the first outline of this poem was composed by a leading thinker, a priest or prophet, during the time of Exile, where it was written in the Aramaic language, that it was then brought back to Jerusalem by the repatriates where it was translated into Hebrew, reworked and amplified. The editor arranged his composition on loose sheets of paper,[19] which were, unfortunately, not put together in the proper order.

---

17. Eissfeldt, EinlAT 560-567.
18. EncMikr I, 248.
19. R. Tournay, *L'ordre primitif des chapître* XXIV-XXVIII *de Job*, RB 64 (1957), 321-334 claims that the lack of order results from mis-

Pfeiffer,[20] on the other hand, attempts to locate the home of the poet not in the Babylonian Exile, but in Edom. The old legend is dated around the eighth century, the great unified outline is the work of an Edomite poet around the year 600; the final form of the book dates from 350 to 300.

In these attempts to reconstruct the original outline the three separate dialogues have all been reduced to one single dialogue; but even those scholars who argue for an original three-fold debate almost unanimously interpret the speeches of Elihu (32 − 37), the hymn to wisdom (28), the natural-history description of the hippopotamus and the crocodile (40, 15 − 41, 26) as later additions. But the criterion of the composition − unity of thought and interior structure − remains unassailable.[21]

In their attempt to determine the proper point of origin and thus the appropriate literary form for this poem, other scholars have argued that many portions which have been rejected as additions actually belong to the essential and original content of the book. This has occasioned a new approach to the literary problem of the Book of Job. If it is really to be identified as the genre of lawsuit,[22] the following would be the stages of its composition: the presupposition of the lawsuit (1 − 3), the preliminary arbitration between the three friends and Job (4 − 14), the judicial process (15 − 31), the resumption of the process by Elihu after the failure of the earlier process (32 − 37), God's eventual judgment (38 − 42).

Even though this legal and judicial interpretation of the Book of Job does much to illuminate our understanding, there are many difficulties it does not explain.[23] The Book of Job is not exclusively a lyrical lamentation, not exclusively an ancient historical epic, nor a problem drama, nor a piece of didactic fiction, nor simply a solitary meditation. Like other great poets, Job combines poetic genius with a high degree of learning.[24] He had mastered the combined knowledge of his day and made liberal use of it whenever it served the purposes of his work. For him,

placing the loose pages.

---

20. IntrOT 678, 684.

21. New position of the entire problem in H. H. Rowley, *The Book of Job and its Meaning*, BJRL 41 (1958), 167-207.

22. H. Richter, *Studien zu Hiob. Der Aufbau des Hiobbuches, dargestellt an den Gattungen des Rechtslebens*, Theol. Arbeiten XI (1958), 7-147.

23. Pfeiffer, IntrOT 684.

24. *Ibid.*, 687.

knowledge was not an end in itself, but rather a weapon in his crusade which combined both a complaint against God and defense of God. But despite all its learning, the Book of Job is not a didactic poem; it is "the document of a struggle with God," [25] which is not simply a literary portrayal, but is actually fought by a nameless Job in the name of uncounted rebels. The battle is all the more breathtaking in that Job has to fight not with the dragon of primordial times, but with the "angels of light," who press him to the utmost with weapons from God's own armory that have been finely honed in the theological schools. But Job is fighting against God and against theology, so that both God and theology will remain true.

The problems outlined in the Book of Job have certainly bothered more than one single man and one single generation. The problem of the innocent sufferer is one of the eternal problems of humanity. Israel particularly, after the destruction of the Temple, after the loss of her national independence, abandoned to the caprice of the pagans, certainly had to confront this vexing problem of human suffering. It is no mere accident that the songs of the suffering servant of Yahweh were developed in the Exile. Job too, both in the prologue and in the epilogue, is addressed as "my servant" ('ebed). This would rank the Book of Job alongside the songs of the servant of God.

Now it would certainly be historically possible as Tur-Sinai [26] has proposed, that already during the Babylonian Exile the first reworking of the ancient Job narrative into a theological problem story had already taken place, perhaps in an Aramaic version. This first outline could easily have made its way into Palestine with the repatriates. It was here that the post-Exilic community was formed, and the theology of the wisdom schools took firm root. Ezra and Nehemiah brought the law to its completion. The carefully protected system of the wisdom teachers, however, was shattered by a Prometheus who once again took up the Job theme and worked it into its present form. The Book of Job could not be the work of some impersonal evolution. It is not

25. Fr. Stier, *Ijjob*, 261.
26. EncMikr I, 248.

simply an outgrowth of the years; the grandiose scheme of the book could have been achieved only by a living personality who had himself experienced much suffering. We might call him simply the "poet of Job." He has managed so completely to clothe himself in the figure of the Job of ancient history that we, today, are in a position to suggest only the barest outlines of his personal history, his home and the time at which he composed.

As a consequence, we must recognize the fact that it is not Ancient Near Eastern nomads who speak in the Book of Job, but sedentary teachers of wisdom who are shaken from their security by Job's misfortunes. Even granting the fact that several eras have still attempted to complete the work of the poet of Job, perhaps with a view towards toning down the scandalous passages, achieving a deeper grasp of the basic lessons taught, making the religious content even more religious — even with the addition of all this supplementary effort, Job's argument with God remains equally striking, stirring, and at the same time redeeming. Since, however, textual and literary criticism are not unanimous in identifying the later additions, it would perhaps be best to let the book speak for itself, in its present state, as it is contained in the canon of Sacred Scripture. The following outline shows the structure of the work:

Prologue ch. 1-2
The Nine Dialogues
of the three friends in three series

I. Eliphaz	Job answers
4-5	6-7
15	16-17
22	23-24, 17 + 24, 25
II. Bildad	
8	9-10
18	19
25 + 26, 5-14	26, 1-4 + 27, 1-12
III. Zophar	
11	12-14
20	21
28, 13-23 + 24, 18-24	19-31

Praise of Wisdom: 28
Elihu's Words: 32, 1—37, 24

God's Decision   Job's Answer
38, 1-40, 2   40, 3-5
40, 6-41, 26   42, 1-6

Epilogue: 42, 7-17

B) THE THEOLOGY OF THE BOOK OF JOB

In no other book of the Old Testament is a theological problem developed so stubbornly down into its ultimate possibilities as in the Book of Job. The theology of this book is best studied by following a brief outline of the spiritual battle.[27]

1) THE CASE OF JOB

"Job from Us, a highly esteemed man, richly blessed with material goods, suddenly, in a rapid sequence of catastrophes, loses his family and his slaves, his house and his property, all he has. His misfortunes are climaxed by a blow which touches his own person, leprosy. Suddenly and without warning, his very existence as a man is threatened to the ultimate.

Catastrophes like this have befallen other people as well. It is a story that can be told many times over. Only a few cases survive the general process of oblivion, and remain solidly established in the memory of all mankind, by finding their poets and interpreters: Croesus, Polycrates, and Job.

The recollection of Job's history is far older than the book which describes it. What kept this story alive was not so much the magnitude of the misfortune which befell Job as rather the scandal that it should have touched upon precisely him — a man so well known for his justice and piety, God's most faithful servant. In some inexplicable way, injustice has been done in the case

27. Fr. Stier, *Ijjob*, 217-251 serves as basis for the following.

of Job, and God himself appears to be its author — who else, since it is God who brings all things to be. And God is the All-just — the question is why?" [28]

This is a brief and precise statement of the problem. The three friends, and later Elihu, act as defenders of God. It is unthinkable that God should have acted unjustly; he would then no longer be God. As a result, the man himself must be the cause of his own misfortune. But Job defends himself against this charge, on the basis of his clear conscience. Since he cannot receive justice from men, he dares the unthinkable move of addressing God himself. God is supposed to answer his charges, point for point. "We eliminate the really monstrous element of the book, that is, man entering into judgment against God, if we see this official legal charge and action as nothing more than a literary form." The "case of Job," which could just as well be the "case of Everyman," is now open for discussion. The court action can begin. It begins in heaven, enters upon an insoluble continuation upon earth, and finally listens in dumb astonishment to the answer that comes from heaven.

2) SATAN, THE ASSAILANT IN HEAVEN

The long and tiresome arguments of the wise men on earth follow an overture, the grandiose assembly in heaven. God is not the only one who occupies a throne. All about his throne are gathered the "sons of God," [29] assembled to present themselves before the Lord (1, 6). This presupposes the fact that, acting upon Yahweh's command, they have made their way all over the earth and, as the "eye of God," see everything that men are

---

28. *Ibid.*, 217.
29. "Sons of God" must be understood not unqualifiedly as a reference to a divine generation, but simply as belonging to the heavenly beings. In the Canaanite pantheon there was a conception of the generation of sons of the gods, but the biblical concept has been completely demythologized. "Sons of God" means belonging to the sphere of God; cf. "sons of the prophets" as belonging to the community of the prophets.

doing.[30] They also report on the case of Job. God's judgment, that Job is a "blameless and upright man, who fears God and turns away from evil," they can only corroborate. But then appears the opponent, the tempter, the "satan." Here satan still belongs among the sons of God, which must be taken as evidence for the very ancient theology of the Book of Job; just as in the case of the prophet Ezekiel, the annihilators (*mašhît*) belong among the angels (Ez 9, 5ff.). "Satan" here has its original simple meaning of "enemy, opponent, assailant," in the juridic as well as in the political frame of reference. But still we must regard this as a theological point of origin from which, with the development of revelation, the figure of satan developed more and more clearly as the great opponent of God. He does not contest God's judgment on Job. Job is indeed "blameless and upright, fearing God and turning away from evil." This cannot possibly be argued. But the assailant adds one single consideration which catches everyone's attention and puts the case of Job suddenly into a very different light: *Hinnam*, "free, gratis, without recompense, without remuneration." Satan's charge, neatly formulated, states that Job's whole piety is not really a service of God, but simply a case of self-interest. He honors God so that he will receive good things from God, a religion of *quid pro quo*, a concept unworthy of either God or man. In order to prove the falsity of this satanic thesis, God gives satan a free hand (2, 7f.).

Job loses all his property and possessions, and is struck with leprosy in his own body. Deprived of all earthly goods, he sits upon a pile of rubbish scratching the scabs from his sores with a potsherd, a striking picture of ineffable human misery, *Ecce Homo!* Nor is this all. External misery can be bearable, so long as the inner man is not affected. But now his friends come and, one after another, shatter Job's inner certitude so that a final

---

30. Similar conception of a council in heaven is to be found in the vision of the prophet Micah in 1 K 22, 19ff. — Parallels in the study of religion history are to be found also in the assemblies of the gods in the Canaanite myths from Ugarit. Cf. Fr. Horst, *Hiob*, BK XV/1, 12.

cry to God himself is the only alternative left. Job has lost everything that could possibly be considered a recompense from God. No earthly thing can have any meaning now: it is only a question of God himself.

3) THE DISPUTANTS: DEFENDERS AND ACCUSERS OF GOD

Eliphaz, Bildad, and Zophar: three men, three names, three places of origin, but in their speeches they all fuse into one, they all come from the same spiritual background. They all profess "wisdom," the ancient traditional "inquiries of the fathers" (8, 8-10; 15, 2, 18f.; 12, 2-12; 26, 2). Wisdom is the spiritual power whose authority afforded them the defense of a secure knowledge and instruction.

The primary points of their teaching: God, the One, Creator of all, all-powerful, all-just Lord of humanity. Wisdom is the teacher of humanity, since wisdom knows what is good and evil, and wisdom instructs what is to be done and what is to be avoided. Wisdom teaches that God recompenses the good with good and the evil with evil, for God is "just." This is a clear and simple teaching, a "teaching on God," which understands and rationalizes God's essence and activity in moral and legal terms, and also a "teaching on salvation," in that it claims to know the "way of life." This simple theology, too reasonable to be true, makes the defenders of God deaf against the cries of the innocent, for the theologically impossible conclusion that even the All-powerful has wrongfully harmed a just man, can never be true for it. If Job is in the right, then God is in the wrong — an unpleasant consequence, in fact a blasphemy. All four have become lost in the same *cul de sac*. Unshakably Job holds to the testimony of his own conscience, and we know that this testimony is a true one, although the conclusion that God is treating him unjustly is a false one. Just as unshakably his three friends hold to the justice of God. The two sides of the argument are drawn hard and fast: humanly speaking, there is no solution.

The arguments that ensue are not well weighed. Job calls his friends "miserable comforters" (16, 2) and "quacks" (13, 4), while their words are "humbug," "deceit" (21, 34), and their

teaching is "grubbing around in the ashes" (13, 12). His three
opponents are not sparing in their rebukes either: Job is "full
of words, full of babble" (11, 2), "the words of your mouth are
a great wind" (8, 12; 15, 2; 20, 3) — "Ten times you have cast
reproach upon me" (19, 3), and, most serious of all, a charge
of impiety and blasphemy against God (15, 4). It would be
a serious mistake to compare the coarse dialogue of these men
with the finely polished speech characteristic of the Platonic dialogue and make it an argument for charging them with a lesser
degree of civilization. It would be incorrect precisely because the
speeches of men who are arguing do not belong to the literary
genre of dialogue and conversation. The speakers here are ac-
cusers and defenders, accused and judge. It is a courtroom situation rather than a dialogue. The question is guilt or innocence,
and it will be decided by their argument.

The defenders of God cannot find any escape into blind
fate, *fatum*. Neither for them nor for Job does there exist any
power who can work beside or against the All-powerful. Nor is
there any refuge to the other alternative, to ascribe the injustice
simply to an evil power, the anti-God. For their decision they
must turn to the most fundamental of the Ten Commandments:
". . . visiting the iniquity of the fathers upon the children and the
children's children, to the third and the fourth generation" (Ex
34, 7). The prophet Ezekiel had, on the one hand, rejected this
all too simple doctrine of retribution, while, on the other hand,
he gave it greater precision: "It is not because our fathers had
eaten sour grapes that the teeth of their sons are on edge"; each
individual is responsible for his own actions and has to face the
consequences that result from them. Neither do the disputants have
the enlightening knowledge of a resurrection to come and a retribution after death. No one returns from sheol, the underworld
of the shadows (26, 5; 7, 9-10; 10, 21-22; 4, 10-12; 16, 22).
The three defenders of God cannot find the cause of evil in God
himself, which is precisely why they repeat their monotonous
reasoning nine times over: Job is himself guilty for the evil that
has befallen him, and he must have sinned against God. But
Job is not prepared to agree with s   solution to the problem:

"Till I die I will not put away my integrity from me" (27, 2-5).
The defense rests, the three defenders having been unable to convince Job; even Elihu,[31] called in as arbitrator, can advance no new arguments. There seems to be no further bridge between the true testimony of human conscience and the wisdom teaching of God, between the assertion of the defense that "God is like this" and the denial of the plaintiff: "God cannot be so." It is God's place to decide. Job appeals to the living God, as opposed to the God "of faith." The real God has become an inexplicable riddle for him. It is not the task of the exegete to weaken the strong words of Job. God has closed his net about his servant, God has done him violence, God has despised law and justice. God has walled up his path, robbed him of his honor, crushed him, burnt him in the fire of his wrath; God is his attacker, his besieger (19, 6-12); on the other hand, this same God is the final guarantee of hope in justification. This is a hope that must be cut into living stone with hammer and chisel:

"For I know that my Redeemer lives,
And at last he will stand upon the earth;
And after my skin has been thus destroyed,
Then shall I see my witness, God.
Whom I shall see on my side,
And my eyes shall behold, and not another.
My heart faints within me" (19: 25, 27).

In the Hebrew text, this passage is very obscure, and has given rise to the most diverse interpretations.[32] The Vulgate regards this as the *locus classicus* for hope in the resurrection.[33] In

---

31. G. Fohrer, *Die Reden des Elihu*, AFO 19 (1959), 83-94.
32. The various readings proposed are to be found in Fr. Stier, *op. cit.*, 297-300.
33. "I know that my redeemer lives and on the last day I will arise up from the earth; once again I will be covered with my skin and I shall see God in my own flesh. I myself shall see him and my own eyes will behold him, and not another. This hope clings fast to my inmost heart." — It is the faith of the Christian Church that

the mouth of Job, however, it is an expression of faith in God's final judgment. Condemned by men, Job must turn in expectation to the redeeming judgment of God, since God is himself the "ransomer" (*gô'el*). A term from family and property law has thus been introduced into the process.[34] "Ransomer," that is, redeemer of a pledge, could not be just anyone; the law set up various degrees of competence, with respect to the law of property and the marriage law. In the case of Job there is no "ransomer" other than the "final ransomer," that is, God. Men have failed, and only God can be at once witness and helper. Whatever was alien in Job's image of God will one day lose its alien character; he will behold him and — perish. Whether Job, in these words, looks forward to the restoration of his rights still during his lifetime or only after the resurrection which is to come upon death can no longer be determined from the current condition of the text; but one thing is certain: this text contains the seed of the Old Testament hope in a resurrection.

4) THE TRANSCENDENT QUESTIONS OF GOD

God's answer takes on the form of a question addressed to his human interrogators. Three kinds of questions appear: a. "Do you know" (38: 4, 18, 21, 33; 39, 1f.); b. "Are you able to" (38: 12, 20, 31, 32, 34, 35, 39; 39: 10-12, 19, 20, 26, 27); c. "Who is able to" (38: 5, 25, 28, 36, 37; 39, 5) It is through questions, and through questions alone, that Job's world of recognized and familiar and known things, the everyday world, is transformed into something strange and different, into an atmosphere in which it appears "alien" to man. Did Job perhaps have an experience of the Wonderful in the midst of all these "Wonders," the Wise and Mighty One, God himself, appearing through the medium of these manifold questions?

It is through these questions that Job is led to true knowledge. We are inevitably reminded of the "tree of knowledge" from which mankind desired to eat at the beginning of their way upon earth.

---

speaks here, not the Job of the Old Testament.

34. Cf. Stier, l. c. 298.

The brief concluding answer of Job (42, 1-5) employs the word "to know" (*yada'*) four times.[35] The debate does not end with a simple commonplace: "the suffering of the just man has this or that meaning": the final solution leads us into much greater human and divine depths. As a human being, Job is forced to admit his limitations, his lack of knowledge: "you showed me wonderful things, and I do not understand; you showed me wonders far above me, and I do not comprehend them" (42, 3). In the recognition of his own limitations Job first has some access to the knowledge of God who is infinitely greater. The solution lies in the knowledge of not knowing, in learned ignorance (*docta ignorantia*). In the case of Job, this new element is operative not only in the knowledge of his intellect, but in his living meeting with God: "Now my eyes have seen you" (42, 5). The solution of the problem of suffering is thus presented by revelation and not achieved by human logic. On the purely human plane, there is no answer to the suffering of the just man; only with reference to the God who reveals himself as always greater and above his human creature does suffering take on any meaning; it is all taken up into God's great plan of the universe. It would thus be foolish to "darken God's plan" with foolish protestation (42, 3). But God's plans are not so simple as the three wise men would have believed. Suffering does not need to bear the stamp of sin. Nor does satan's charge ring entirely true. Job holds fast to the great God of his faith "*gratis,*" even from the midst of his misery. And thus the divine judgment pronounced in the heavenly court at the beginning of the book remains true: "Job, a servant of God, a blameless and upright man, who fears God and turns away from evil." The case ends with an exoneration of Job. The man who suffers is not a sinner; he is God's servant and slave (*'ebed*); for suffering too is included in God's masterplan (*'esah*).

What God means to do with the suffering of the just man

---

35. "Job thus sees himself called to a decision, whether he will make bold to surpass the original limitations of the human condition — to want to be like God himself (Gn 3, 5) — or whether he will shrink before this ultimate abyss." G. Fohrer, *Gottes Antwort aus dem Sturmwind,* Hi 38-41, ThZ 18 (1962), 23.

becomes evident only in the epilogue. It is precisely the suffering
Job, characterized as a sinner by God's three defenders, who is
called upon to act as intercessor and intermediary for the others.
The man condemned by men is raised up by God's grace and
restored to his former glory. Even though the conclusion of the
book sounds something like a fairy tale — after surviving the test,
everything the hero has lost is restored, house and property, flocks
and possessions, wife and children, beautiful daughters, and a
long life besides — still this restoration of fortune is not restricted
to the plane of fairy tale or the three wise men's doctrine of
retribution: it is to be understood on the level of grace. According
to God's plan, suffering must not end in despair, but in glory
together with God. None of this, in the last analysis, will ever
be clear to men. Even though the Book of Job has a clear claim
to be the most human of the Old Testament, still it is not man
who forms the point of focus, but God himself. In terms of salvation
history, this obstinate debate prepares for the understanding of
the servant of God who, although there was no sin in him, went
to his death for the sins of all and was raised to the right hand
of the Father. In this connection, Job has no spiritual relatives
throughout the whole world of the Ancient Near East, in which
the original theme of Job has undergone many transformations.
In retrospect, we might reconstruct the following outline:[36]

     the three — Job
     the preservers — the tested
     the certain — the shaken
     the unassailable — the assailed
     the knowing — the asking
     the possessing — the seeking
     the defender — the accuser
     the case for God — the case about and against God
     words about God — words to God
     .... — God answers Job
     teaching on God — God's teaching.

---

36. Stier, l. c. 251.

C) THE THEME OF JOB OUTSIDE THE BIBLE

The meaning of evil in the world has been questioned so long as there has been a human race. The question becomes all the more serious when the evil afflicts a man who is obviously just. "The suffering just man" is an eternal scandal, a problem that the Babylonian teachers of wisdom attempted to solve almost a thousand years before the time of Job. The "Babylonian Job" is extant in three different versions, none of which have any literary connection with the others.

1) THE SONG OF THE SUFFERING JUST MAN

The kingdom of the great Hammurabi was shaken to its very foundation during the time of his third successor Ammidi-tana. Such periods of upheaval are a stimulus for questioning the why of suffering. The cuneiform tablet AO 4462, preserved in the Louvre, contains a song on the subject of the suffering just man, in nine strophes, with ten lines each.[37] The peculiar element of this poem lies in the fact that it is not the suffering man himself who breaks out in lament and accusation, but rather his friend who assumes the role of the defender and intercessor before the divinity. The first strophe characterizes his suffering: "His heart is fire (fever), in his anguish he lies sick; his spirit is darkened, seized by the night of death." Misfortune has fallen upon him even though not a single fault could be found in him (2 strophe). But despite his suffering, the just man holds fast to his faith in God (3 and 4 strophe). In the 5 and 6 strophe the friend and advocate contrasts the present suffering with a former state of happiness and, in the 7 strophe, appeals directly to God: "Appear to him, and make his heart light. Look upon him and let his health be restored." Hereupon God answers the suffering just man and his advocate: "Your heart is innocent. You have experienced anxiety, dread fear in all its measure (fullness). The way was

---

37. J. Nougayrol, *Une version ancienne du "Juste Souffrant,"* RB 59 (1952), 239-250, Cuneiform text with translation and introduction.

barred, but it is opened for you; the path is smoothed, the grace is bestowed. But in the future you must not forget your God, your creator . . . . They stand open, the gates of salvation and of life (*abul šulmin balaṭim*),[38] you are free to come in and go out. You are healed" (9 strophe).

"This is obviously a problem song; but it is less taken up with the problem of the innocent sufferer as with the miracle of unhoped for restoration. The man who had been forced to feel the heaviness of God's hand upon him is even more devout after his restoration to health; for he has now experienced that suffering too has its place in the plan of God. One surprising element is the fact that in the entire song there is no mention of any pagan God by name. The climate is monotheistic, suggestive of the patriarchal era." [39]

2) THE DRAMATIC MONOLOGUE

In Nineveh and Assur tablets have been discovered which also treat the problem of Job. They are named for their opening lines *ludlul bêl nêmeqi,* "I shall praise the Lord of wisdom." [40] Here too a man is suddenly plunged from prosperity into misery. "The fury of my enemy has annihilated me . . . . From the midst of my dwelling place I have been carried off. The day is misery, the night is weeping, the month is quiet, the year is lamentation. Like the dove I lament all my days, my eyes are filled with weeping. I cried out to my God, but he veiled his countenance." The obscurity of the entire problem lies in the fact that what appears to be good to man is bad in the eyes of God, and conversely. Hence the question: "Who can learn to understand the will of the gods in heaven?" (tablet II, 5). What follows is a description of the sufferings which is reminiscent of Job: "My flesh falls away from me, my blood disappears, my bones are cut to pieces" (II, 90). The third tablet describes the transformation and healing. A powerful personage, sent from Marduk, appears to the suffering

---

38. Hebrew corresponding form: *šālôm,* which means not only "peace," but being whole in every respect.
39. Nougayrol, l. c. 250.
40. Translation in Gressmann, AOT 274-281; ANET 434-437.

man in a dream and pronounces an oracle of restoration. All the evil powers are driven out, the terrible headache is gone, the fevered eyes shine again, the stopped ears are open, the closed nostrils find air again, the stammering lips begin to speak, the mouth opens once again, the clenched teeth are relaxed, and the bond on his tongue is loosened. "He wipes off the rust, purifies his splendor; his restored beauty is magnificent" (III, 75ff.). After his restoration the healed sufferer is free to make his way into the "gates of salvation, of life, of sunrise, of freedom from sin, of praise, of pure water," all of which lead him into the sanctuary of Esagila. "Then all the Babylonians saw that Marduk had given him his life, and all their mouths praised his greatness" (III, 145). Here too the problem of suffering is solved, not in philosophical terms, but in a religious-existential atmosphere. Marduk's wisdom, which also signifies strength and power, is most openly manifest in the salvation and restoration of the suffering just man.

3) DIALOGUE ON THE INJUSTICE OF THE WORLD

In Gressmann's edition [41] this poem is entitled: "Lament of a wise man over the injustice of the world." Meantime, scholars have recognized the fact[42] that this powerful song, 27 strophes with 11 lines in each, is not a monologue, but a dialogue. In the odd-numbered strophes it is the suffering just man who speaks, while his friends speak in the even-numbered strophes. The lines of the individual strophes each begin with the same initial letters (acrostic) which yield the following sentence: "I, Saggil-kinam-ubbib, the conjurer, praise God and king." Thus we learn the name of the poet — and this is infrequent in the literature of the Ancient Near East — as well as the purpose of his literary work. His name means: "O Esagila (Temple of Marduk in Babylon), declare the just man to be pure."

The basic position of this long and unfortunately not entirely preserved dialogue is reminiscent of Job. The just man, un-

---

41. AOT 287-291.
42. ANET 438-440.

expectedly cast into deepest misery, is attacked by his friends from an unassailable position. But the suffering man, whose name is Baltatrua, continually protests his innocence: "More than any other man on earth have I been concerned with the plan of God, and yet I am forced to bear a heavy burden without profit as my yoke. Instead of riches, God has rewarded me with poverty and wretchedness" (VII, 70). The song ends in a terrible cry of anguish, without suggesting any solution. It is possible that the lost fragments described the restoration of the suffering just man.

"These three (Babylonian) versions do indeed contain a common theme, but their dissimilarities will not permit us to conclude that they are a development of a common source. Much less are we justified in claiming any literary connection between Job and the Babylonian versions. . . . From this era of great historical upheaval, from the ruins of social and political life, the voice of the eternal Job will ever rise, in every country, at every age." [43]

---

43. Fr. Stier, *Ijjob,* 265.

THE HELLENISTIC ERA

CHAPTER XII

FROM ALEXANDER THE GREAT TO
THE MACCABEAN WAR OF LIBERATION

WHEREAS the destruction of the Assyrian and Babylonian kingdom was accompanied by the trumpet notes of the prophets,
the transition from the Persian to the Macedonian world Empire
hardly occasioned a single notice. There is no great prophetic
figure to mark the approach of Alexander the Great, probably
because of the fact that his accession to power did not occasion
any threat to religious freedom. In terms of salvation history, the
rise of Alexander signals neither a breach in history nor a new
beginning. This explains the meager references in Sacred Scripture to the person of this heroic king. The historians of the
age of Daniel refer to him only as a point of origin for the Maccabean crisis. The huge blasphemous horn which trampled the
holy ones of the Most High sprang from the horn of the goat.
The vision of the ram and the he-goat does indeed do justice
to the true historical, and indirectly the salvation-history, significance of Alexander (Dn 8, 3-8). The ram with the two horns

is symbolic of the Medo-Persian world empire. From the west comes a he-goat with only one horn between his eyes. He makes his way across the country without touching the ground; this is a reference to the irresistible triumphal procession of Alexander. The ram and he-goat come together in battle; the he-goat overcomes the ram and shatters his horns; there is no one to rescue the ram from his power. The he-goat grows stronger and stronger. But when he is at his strongest, the large horn breaks off and in its place grow four other horns, towards the four corners of the world. This is the briefest possible description of the history of the empire of Alexander and its successor states. The history assumes real importance only at the moment in which the struggles of the individual horns involve the chosen land of God in suffering and misery. The closer the Maccabean era, the more explicit the historical narrative.

The most explicit account of the events which take place from Alexander the Great up to the time of the Maccabean wars of liberation is to be found in ch. 11 of the prophecy of Daniel, although it is partially in the form of symbolic and figurative language. It is precisely this chapter which has occasioned the greatest amount of scholarly attacks against the historicity of the Book of Daniel. The chapter pretends to be true prophecy, that is, the foretelling of future events, but it is actually only a prophecy after the event (*vaticinium ex eventu*). Hartenstein [1] speaks of the "wooden poker of prophecy." Incompatible elements have been united here, a prophecy of lies instead of a genuine prophecy. A more sober sense of literary criticism would not phrase the problem in such lapidary terms since, as has been explained above, the Book of Daniel is made up of prophecies from two eras. Chapter 11 actually does not belong to the Babylonian prophet Daniel; it is the prophetic contemplation of history after the spirit of the great master. But what is the vision of history that it affords?

The Persian Empire is disposed of with a single verse (Dn.

---

1. Hartenstein, *Der Prophet Daniel*, (1938); quoted in W. Kessler, *Das Buch Daniel*, CalwK 22 (1956), 17.

11, 2). The heroic king Alexander receives two verses (11, 3-4). But the closer the Maccabean era, the more explicit the narrative. Antiochus III receives 10 verses, and Antiochus IV 24 verses. The primary interests of the interpreter (*paršan*) are directed towards his main objective. Since, through the division of the kingdom after the death of Alexander, Palestine became a battleground between the Ptolemies in Egypt and the Seleucids in Syria, the various phases of this struggle between the kings of the north and the kings of the south are more accurately portrayed.

A) BATTLES BETWEEN THE KINGS OF THE NORTH AND THE SOUTH

1) WARS AND POLITICAL MARRIAGES (Dn 11, 5-9)

Alexander's sudden death had left the world situation in a quite unexpected tangle.[2] None of the generals who seized power over the various parts of his world had really meant to abandon the dream of a unified empire that Alexander had begun to outline. But the reality of political factors proved stronger. The dream of unity had to be given up; the territory of the great kingdom of Alexander turned into a succession of warring principalities. In Egypt, Ptolemy Lagi I (323-285) became ruler. Seleucus I Nikator (312-281) served under him for a time, but then declared his independence and became the founder of the Seleucid Empire. This development established an international tension which has once again appeared in modern politics. The Ptolemies in Egypt were bent upon regaining their lost property in Syria, in a peaceful or hostile way. It is against this background that Dn 11, 6 describes a political marriage. Antiochus II (261-246) had been married first to Laodike. Political intrigues succeeded in forcing Antiochus to repudiate his first wife and marry in her place the Egyptian princess Berenice, the daughter of

---

2. Based on H. Bengtson, *Griechische Geschichte. Handbuch der Altertumswissenschaft*, 3, 4, *Zeitalter des Hellenismus*, (1950), 273-490.

Ptolemy II (285-246). The marriage took place in the year 252, and was celebrated as an expression of fraternal affection between Egypt and Syria. But when Antiochus II died in 246, the bonds were severed. In his final will and testament, Antiochus had not, as the Egyptians had anticipated, named the son of Berenice as his successor, but rather the son of his first wife Laodike, Seleucus II Callinicus (246-226). Berenice, who had thus been passed over, refused to acquiesce to this situation. She determined to contest her son's hereditary right by force of arms. In her brother Ptolemy III Euergetes (247-221) she found a ready ally. Egypt's position had been extraordinarily strengthened by the acquisition of Kyrenaika. Events, however, took a quite different course than had been anticipated in Egypt, where victory appeared certain. Berenice and her young son were assassinated. The retaliatory campaign of Ptolemy took on the proportions of a triumphal march. Antioch was taken and plundered, but the Egyptians did not succeed in establishing a permanent control over Seleucid Syria. Quite the contrary, around the year 242 Seleucus II undertook a counter-offensive against Egypt which was destined to have no more lasting effect for Syrian control. "He shall come into the realm of the King of the south but shall return into his own land" (11, 9).

2) ANTIOCHUS III THE GREAT (Dn 11, 10-19)

A new era of Seleucid sovereignty began in the year 223 with the succession of Antiochus III (223-187), who was only 18 years of age. Supported by wise advisors, the young king deliberately set about reestablishing the great days of the empire under Seleucus I and Antiochus I. In this effort he exhibited a truly remarkable energy. A strong Seleucid Empire could not be formed and maintained without the support of the territories in Southern Syria and the cities along the Phoenician coast. Revolts in Babylonia and Persia, as well as the defection of a king in Asia Minor, could not keep Antiochus from pursuing his plan of restoring the empire. Quite the contrary. In the same year in which Hannibal began the siege of Saguntum (219), Antiochus captured the important coastal city of Seleucia in northern Syria;

Tyre and Ptolemais (Akko) fell to his hand. But all these initial successes were completely undone by the defeat at Raphia (217) along the Egyptian frontier (Dn 11, 9-12). Antiochus then directed his energies towards a great campaign of conquest against the Asiatic provinces, in an effort to recoup his position. His famous anabasis began already in 212. It led him through the whole of upper Asia as far as India. Greco-Indians, Bactrians, and Parthians were forced to recognize him as sovereign. This energetic Seleucid king had thus, in the years 212-205, set up a magnificent system of vassal states throughout the East. His anabasis, which is somewhat reminiscent of Alexander's earlier march, won him the admiration of the entire Greco-Hellenistic world. After thus establishing himself, he assumed the Achaemenid title "great king." Antiochus' final success coincides with the decisive battle between Rome and Carthage in the western Mediterranean. The sudden ascendancy of the Seleucid empire was made possible by the total passivity of the Ptolemies in Egypt. From his new position of strength, Antiochus was now ready to avenge the earlier defeat of Raphia; this time he used diplomatic intrigue rather than force of arms.

An occasion for interference was afforded by the death of Ptolemy IV Philopator (204?). Sosibios, the all-powerful favorite of the king, tried to conceal his death. He feared the possibility of foreign interference, and rightly so, since the successor to the throne was still a small child. As it actually turned out, Antiochus III and Philip V, king of Macedonia, made a secret treaty (winter, 203/02) for a bold and deliberate partition of the Egyptian Empire, in which Syria was destined to receive the lion's share.[3] This bold piece of political thievery had far-reaching consequences which could not have been foreseen.

a. *The Macedonian War* (200-197): When the king of Macedonia attempted to take possession of the newly acquired spoils of Egypt, that is, the islands in the Aegean Sea, he found himself opposed by the trading colony of Rhodes. Rhodes turned to Rome for help. Rome had just defeated Hannibal in the battle of

---

3. *Ibid.*, 400.

Zama (202), and thus became sole ruler throughout the whole of the western Mediterranean. Although Roman historians like to claim that Rome undertook only defensive wars in an attempt to preserve the *Pax Romana,* it is still quite obvious that the Scipios promoted a deliberately imperialistic policy and thus greeted Rhodes' call for help as a most favorable opportunity to initiate their claim to control over the eastern Mediterranean.

b. *The "glorious land"*: Antiochus III had received, as his share in the spoils of Egypt, the former Egyptian province of Palestine, referred to as "the glorious land" in Dn 11, 16. An Egyptian army under Skopas offered resistance, but was defeated in the year 198 in the battle at Paneas at the sources of the Jordan. Palestine was thus incorporated into the Seleucid Empire, thereby setting the historical background for the Maccabean wars of liberation and the formation of the Hasmonean rule, but also preparing the way for the further penetration of the Roman armies into the east.

c. *"He shall turn his face to the coastlands"* (11, 18): The Macedonian party to the treaty had been dealt a devastating defeat by the Romans at Cynoscephelae in Thessaly in the year 197. The victor dictated a Draconic peace treaty and withdrew from Greece. The power of Antiochus III was now on the verge of a rapid and unheard of rise. His next move was to link conquered Egypt to his empire by the peaceful bonds of marriage. The young Ptolemy V Epiphanes (203-180) was betrothed to Antiochus' daughter Cleopatra I in the winter of 194/93. Antiochus' kingdom had thus almost reached the size of Alexander's earlier world Empire. His Oriental Empire extended from the Indus to the Hellespont. The Aetolian League in Greece was justified in referring to him as the supreme commander (*strategos autokrator*).

This sudden increase in power could not be long tolerated by Rome. The situation was made more pressing by the fact that Hannibal, after fleeing from Carthage, had turned to Syria, where, in the summer of 195, he met with Antiochus in Ephesus.

The occasion for a new contest was afforded by the Aetolian League, who were dissatisfied with the order of affairs that the Romans had introduced into Greece. For Antiochus, the war took a tragic turn. His expeditionary corps against Greece was defeated at Thermopylae (191); while the Asiatic contingent was destroyed towards the end of the year 190 in the Sipylos Mountains, near Magnesia. Although Antiochus had twice the strength of the Romans — his 70,000 men faced only 30,000 Romans and allies — he was defeated. Eumenes II of Pergamum made a significant contribution to the Roman victory. His spirited cavalry attack quickly routed the Seleucid cavalry squadrons, and then overran the left wing of Antiochus' phalanx. The Roman conditions of peace were, as usual, extremely hard. Antiochus was forced to relinquish his entire fleet, with the exception of 10 ships, and to abandon his claim to all of Asia Minor, as far as Cape Sarpedonion in Cilicia. The Romans sent a commission of 10 men into Asia Minor, to be responsible for affairs in the east. The power of the Seleucid Empire was thus broken. The hard conditions of peace, especially the size of the tribute payments, weighed heavily upon the land. A chronic lack of finances led to forced measures. In order to raise necessary funds, Antiochus III attempted to plunder even the temple of Bel in Susa, and in so doing lost his life (187). "He shall tumble and fall, and shall not be found" (11, 19).

d. *The exactor of tribute* (11, 20): The son of Antiochus III, Seleucus IV Philopator (187-175) followed his father's example. In order to fill the empty state treasury, he sent his chancellor Heliodorus to Jerusalem to take possession of the temple treasury. But there he was struck down by a mysterious power, an angel (2 Mac 3, 26ff.). Jerusalem was saved for the time. It was the same king who "sent an exactor of tribute through the glory of the kingdom; but within a few days he was broken, neither in anger nor in battle" (11, 20). Seleucus IV was assassinated by his chancellor Heliodorus.

3) ANTIOCHUS IV EPIPHANES (Dn 11, 21-45)

Antiochus IV Epiphanes (175-164) was, beyond doubt, one of the most able men ever to occupy the Seleucid throne, truly one of those powerful ruling figures who can stand in the face of surrounding tragedy, and succeed in stopping the inevitable decay of a declining kingdom while they restore something of its ancient glory.

a. *Further war with Egypt* (170-168): The minority of the successor to the throne afforded Epiphanes an opportunity to interfere in Egyptian politics. He wanted to recoup in the south what Antiochus III had lost in Asia Minor. After a victory at Pelusium (spring 170) he forced his way into Egypt. The whole land, with the exception of the capital city of Alexandria, fell before him. He made a treaty with the youthful Ptolemy VI (181/80-145) and then had him crowned with the double crown of Upper and Lower Egypt in the ancient city of the Pharaohs, Memphis. He attempted to conceal this surprising move. He pretended that he had simply undertaken the regency in behalf of his minor nephew Ptolemy VII. His real plan was to weld together the Seleucid Empire with the Ptolemaic Empire into one united bloc of power against the Romans who were making their way into the east. In the year 168 he once again marched to Egypt. This time he abandoned all pretense. He marched as a conqueror and laid siege to Alexandria. It was at this point that Rome intervened.

The successful career of Epiphanes had long been regarded with anxiety at Rome. Rome was vitally interested in maintaining a certain balance of power in the east. Immediately after their victory over the Macedonian Perseus at Pydna (June 22, 168), the Romans sent Popillius Laenas, of consular rank, into the headquarters of Epiphanes at Eleusis, a suburb of Alexandria.[4]
He delivered an ultimatum to put an immediate end to the war

---

4. The date is definitely established by reason of an eclipse. Bengtson, *loc. cit.*, 461.

and to withdraw from Egypt without delay. When Epiphanes asked for time to deliberate, the Roman ambassador drew a circle around the king and declared that he must give an unequivocal answer before he crossed the line. Epiphanes yielded to the demands of Rome. And thus, a few weeks after Pydna, the Romans had won a second victory, this time with the weapons of a brutal diplomacy. The two victories once and for all sealed the fate of the Hellenistic kingdom.

b. *Internal reorganization in the kingdom*: The Roman ultimatum must have struck Epiphanes like a bolt of lightning. While there was a certain method to his earlier politics, after this unfortunate day at Eleusis, the king appears nervous, strained, and unpredictable. Blunders grow more and more frequent, and with them failure. In order to secure the defenses of his kingdom, he attempted to complete the work that Alexander the Great had begun. Alexander had dreamed of a fusion of the east with Greek culture. The Hellenistic culture was still the predominant element, but the basic substratum of the Oriental population remained aloof. It was to this problem that Epiphanes directed his reorganizing activity. Ancient Babylon was rebuilt into a Greek *polis,* complete with theater and gymnasium. The same objectives were pursued in Palestine as well. Jerusalem, too, the capital of the Jewish nation, was supposed to become a city after the Greek pattern. The sympathy of Hellenistic circles in Jerusalem, reaching as far as the high priest himself, was willing to meet him halfway. Under the high priest Jason, a gymnasium was built in Jerusalem, in which part of the Jewish youth joined the Hellenes in both physical and mental exercises.

In sharpest contrast to the pro-Hellenic element were the pious people of the country, the Hasidim (Hasideans), headed by the Maccabeans who led the battle for national and religious freedom. The course of this struggle is explicitly narrated in the Books of the Maccabees. They opposed any compromise with Hellenism. The conflict reached its climax when, in December of 167, Epiphanes attempted to effect the Hellenization of the Jews by force. The cult of Yahweh was abrogated and all Jewish ritual was forbidden. In the Temple, the altar of Zeus Olympius, the national god of the empire, was erected, and at his side was placed the image of the ruling sovereign, while the official rites of the ruler cult were prescribed for both. The community of Greeks and pro-Hellenes were organized as their own body-politic under the name of Antiochene. This was the climax of the Hellenization of Jerusalem.

c. *The God of the fortresses*: While these religious reforms struck the Jews hardest of all, they also had a considerable effect upon the pagan religious forms that had become deeply rooted in the country. "He shall give no heed to the gods of his fathers, or to the one beloved by women; he shall not give heed to any other god, for he shall magnify himself above all. He shall honor the god of the fortresses instead of these" (11, 37). The foreign god of fortresses is perhaps the Olympian Zeus (2 Mac 6, 12), or, better, Jupiter Capitolinus. The man was fascinated with the irresistible power of the Romans. In an effort to conjure it away, he venerated the power of the Roman god.

d. *The demise of Epiphanes*: The rebuilding of the empire encountered resistance not only among the Jewish Hasideans; even as Epiphanes was celebrating his triumphs in Egypt (11, 42, 43), he was greeted with sudden disturbing reports from the north and the east (11, 44). Withdrawing from Egypt and making his way northwards, he pitched his palatial tents between the sea and the glorious holy mountain (Jerusalem), that is to say, somewhere along the Palestinian coastal plain (11, 45). Yet he still came to his end, with none to help him (11, 45). According to the new regnal lists of the Seleucids,[5] Epiphanes' withdrawal from Egypt falls in late September of the year 169 (1 Mac 1, 20). During the following years he was held in check by the newly awakened unrest along the northeast frontier of the empire. Under pressure from the Huns, who, around the year 200 B.C., had formed their first empire in the Desert of Gobi, tribes from

---

5. J. Schumberger, *Die neue Seleukidenliste BM 35603 und die makkabäische Chronologie*, Bibl 36 (1955), 423-435. — E. Vogt, *Catalogus cuneiformis regum Seleucidarum*, Bibl 36 (1955), 261-262.

the interior of Asia were making their way towards the west and south. They forced their way through the portals of Turkestan into the Seleucid Empire. It was on the occasion of these skirmishes, probably at Gabei (Isfahan), that Epiphanes met his end, between November 19 and December 17 of the year 164. It was precisely this fact that the oppressors were busily occupied in the distant eastern frontier of their empire that made possible the reconsecration of the Temple in Jerusalem.

At this point the historical narrative breaks off. As a result, we are in a position to assign a precise date to the actual writing of the Book of Daniel. The desecration of the Temple by the erection of the "abomination of desolation" [6] is dated in the month of Kislev (December) of the year 167; our historian, however, also records the reconsecration of the Temple in the same month of Kislev, in the year 164.[7] Since he also refers to the death of Epiphanes, the Book of Daniel must have been concluded shortly after the year 164.

It is only from this point of view that the historical retrospective (Dn 11) can be understood at all. The historian, despite the explicit detail of his narrative, has little interest in the history of the Seleucid or Ptolemaic kingdoms.

He is interested in them only because these world powers have involved the "land of glory" in catastrophe, and brought it to the very brink of religious and national destruction. It is only natural that, in such a time of crisis, men would be concerned about the duration of the crisis, the meaning of this visitation.

In this description of the historical background, we have gotten far ahead of our narrative. In connection with the wars we must once again examine the same era, but this time from a completely different point of view. History can be written "objectively" as we might expect it from a trained modern historian; but it can

---

6. Hebrew *šiqqûs šômen,* "abomination of the desolation" (Dn 9, 27; 11, 31; 12, 11; 1 Mac 1, 54) is a deliberate reworking of the words *ba'al haššamayim,* "Lord-god of the heavens," a favorite title of the ancient Semitic storm and thunder and sky god Hadad, who, in Hellenistic times, was identified with Zeus Olympios.

7. On the mysterious days cf. below, pp. 366ff.

also be written with a full and angry heart; it is the very existence
of one's own people at stake. Chapter 11 of the Book of Daniel
belongs to the latter kind of history.

B)   PALESTINE UNDER PTOLEMAIC RULE

1) POLITICAL CONDITIONS IN PALESTINE

The occupation of the Persian province of Jahud (Judea) by
Alexander the Great has left hardly any trace in the biblical books,
because the transition from Persian to Macedonian sovereignty
took place without any political or religious interruption. Samaria,
residence of the Persian governor, did indeed offer resistance and
had to be conquered by force of arms.[8] After the destruction, the
Samaritans fled to Mt. Gerizim, while Macedonian soldiers were
settled in the territory of the capital city. The century under
Ptolemaic sovereignty proved to be a peaceful one for Palestine,
by and large, since the new masters did nothing to violate the
interior structure of Judah. The balance of power in Palestine
remained approximately what it had been during the days of
Ezra. In Transjordania the family of the Tobiads (bêt tobiyah)
continued to enjoy its ruling position under the Ptolemies. Records
from this era have been discovered among the Zenon-Papyri in
Fajjum. They are named after Zenon, minister of finance under
Ptolemy II Philadelphus (285-246). Among them are two letters
from Tobias of Ammon, who was entrusted with the preservation
of order and the collection of taxes in his district. The records also
mention that he used to send the Egyptian king gifts of rare
animals which were developed by scientific cross-breeding ex-
periments.[9] In like manner, the Ptolemies allowed affairs in Jerusalem to remain essentially as they were. The high priest was
responsible to the crown for the payment of tribute. So long as
there were no difficulties, the royal officials did not interfere. The
high priest was the representative of the Jewish people and as

---

8. Eusebius, PG XIX, 489.
9. C. Bradford Welles, Die hellenistische Welt, PropWG III, 535. On
   page 520 there is a facsimile of a Letter of Zenon.

such he was responsible not only for their spiritual, but also for their secular well-being. As a result, his purely spiritual office was gradually turning more and more into the office of a secular prince, much more so than during the Persian era, and gradually it became a bone of contention among rival parties. Meantime, the Jews were free to pursue their own individual religious life without disturbance, but there was no lasting defense against the eventual influence of the Hellenistic culture and civilization.

Alexander the Great's dream had been a cultural fusion of east and west. By the establishment of new cities and colonies, the Hellenistic element made greater and greater inroads into the newly conquered territories. The centers of Hellenistic settlement in Palestine lay along the coast and in Transjordania.[10] The ancient coastal cities of Ascalon and Joppe were Hellenized, while Anthedon and Straton's Tower were new foundations. The most important settlement took place in ancient Acco. Ptolemy II Philadelphus had the city and its harbor considerably enlarged and renamed it Ptolemy. Transjordania witnessed the rise of new Hellenistic cities: Gedara, Pella, Dium, Hippos, and especially Philadelphia, successor to the Ammonite capital city of Rabbat-Ammon. The name, once again, comes from the builder of the city, Ptolemy II Philadelphus. The foundation of these new cities generally followed the same outline. First came the construction of the city walls and a few important buildings, then the formation of the Greek-Macedonian populace from all available sources, partially, at least, made up of veterans or retired soldiers from the army. Then the free-native population, who would be responsible for the economic life of the city, were introduced and enlarged by the addition of slaves and agricultural serfs. These new composite communities arise against an Oriental background, but they are no longer purely Greek or purely Oriental: they are precisely Hellenistic and quickly become the bearers and points of radiation for the new culture and civilization.[11] In the midst of this circle of Hellenistic city building, it was impossible that tiny

10. Schürer, GJV I, 188ff.
11. *Ibid.*, 522.

Judea should manage to offer a successful opposition to the influence of the Greek element. Judea was simply too small and too insignificant to be allowed to go its own way completely cut off from the cultural streams of that era. The reins of economic and cultural life lay in the hands of the Greeks. The simple necessity of survival forced the Jews to adapt to a certain measure of Hellenistic civilization; but the process was never a welcome one.

At the beginning of the second century B.C. Hellenistic penetration of Palestine must have been considerably advanced. This is the only explanation for the fact that the leading Jewish circles, under the leadership of their high priest, were forced to agree with the Hellenizing programs of their new masters. In the melting-pot of this new era, it was not only nations that were fused into a new unity, but also their various gods. Egyptian and Asian cults took on a new, Hellenistic stamp. The question now was whether the God of Jerusalem could also be Hellenized. "If this process had been allowed free rein, it is quite probable that the Jewish religion in Palestine would, in time, have taken on a form in which it could hardly be recognized." [12] But when the Seleucids began to enforce the Hellenization of Palestine, they were met by a sudden flare-up of Jewish national and religious resistance. In this more peaceful century, however, a series of wisdom teachers in Jerusalem, open to the cosmopolitan culture of that day, were attempting a legitimate confrontation with the Hellenistic culture without surrendering anything of their traditional faith.

2) THE JEWS IN EGYPT

The rise of Alexander the Great's city, Alexandria, with its great harbor and international trade center, proved an invitation to enterprising elements from all over the world. There were Jewish colonies in Egypt, and had been for many centuries, spread throughout the country as small settlements. Since, at the founding of Alexandria, Jews were settled with an opportunity to enjoy the same rights as Hellenes, more and more Jews from the other parts

---

12. *Ibid.*, 189.

of Egypt, and even from Palestine, emigrated to this new metropolis of world trade. At the time of Philo two of the five districts of the city were pure Jewish, while the others contained considerable Jewish elements. Alexandria thus became, second only to Jerusalem, a new world capital for the Jewish religion in the Hellenistic world and later in the Roman Empire.[13] It was here, in this new world capital, that the Jewish religion must survive or forever perish.

"Alexandria was the jewel of Egypt with its palaces and open gardens, with its sacred temples of the royal cult and the cult of Serapis, with its museum and library, with its extensive harbors and shipyards and the island of Pharos with the famous lighthouse and the breakwater over a mile long. Practically invincible to hostile attack, Alexandria, with its famous harbor, bound by a system of canals to the Nile River, and a climate that was pleasant almost throughout the entire year, seems to have been destined by nature herself to become a center of world trade and traffic and a city of delights. By establishing the best library in the entire world and by the magnanimous patronage of scholars and literary men from all over the empire, the Ptolemies made Alexandria a center for culture. Athens retained its pre-eminence in philosophy and rhetoric, and continued to be the capital of abstract thought, but it was Alexandria that claimed the teachers of science, scholarship, and literature, and perhaps the arts as well." [14] The Jews who settled in Alexandria predictably enough used Greek as a vernacular. The Hebrew texts of the Sacred Scriptures were gradually no longer understood by the common people and needed to be translated. According to the legendary account in the Letter of Aristeas, the stimulus for this translation came from King Ptolemy II Philadelphus, since his librarian Demetrius Phalerius wanted a copy of the Law of the Jews in his library. Upon his bidding, the Jewish high priest Eleasar is supposed to have sent 72 hand-picked men, six from each tribe, who completed the work in 72 days. Hence the name Septuagint, the Greek word

---

13. *Ibid.*, GJV III, 36.
14. C. Bradford Welles, *Die hellenistische Welt*, PropWG III, 469.

for "seventy." [15] The scientific interest of the royal librarian, who was not in a position to disregard the spiritual heritage of such a large element of the population of his native city, may well have had some historical influence upon the translation. But everything else in the account of Aristeas is pure legend. It was not scientific research, but rather the pastoral concern of the synagogue that stood at the cradle of the Greek version of Scripture. And before the Septuagint reached its final stages, many people in many places must have worked at translating the sacred text into the new vernacular.[16] This translation of the Bible, however, had provided the unexpected and new instrument of spiritual confrontation between the Jews and the Hellenistic-pagan world around them. Sacred Scripture makes its way from the isolation of the Hebrew text into the wide world of Greek culture.

15. Schürer, GJV III, 424.
16. Further discussion of the Septuagint: Eissfeldt, EinlAT 855ff.

CHAPTER XIII

THE WISDOM TEACHING
OF JESUS BEN SIRACH

The Book of Ecclesiasticus

THE books of the prophets were written under the terrible splendor of the Assyrian dragon, under the hammer of Babel, and in the shadow of Ahura-mazda, always as a confrontation with the era that produced them. These words from God are "like silver fired in the oven, like gold purified seven times over" (Ps 11/12, 7); they are a precious wine which has been collected in the wine press of long, pain-filled centuries. When the Macedonian panther bared his claws against the territory of Asia Minor, there were no prophets to hurl their oracles of threat and vengeance against him. A new era of confrontation had dawned. It was no longer the storm birds whose wild flight heralds the advent of catastrophe; quiet scholars are at work establishing the ways of wisdom. The new era is to receive the word of God in a new manner. The manner of this new confrontation is visible in the development of the language of the three wisdom books. The preacher (*Qoheleth*) has always existed in a Hebrew form; Ben Sirach had, until very recently, been available only in a Greek translation; the "Wisdom of Solomon" was originally written in Greek. The fact that the books of the New Testament were written exclusively in Greek is only a continuation of this spiritual and historical development which is already to be noticed at the end of the Old Testament. All three wisdom books are inspired by a Hellenistic atmosphere, but they develop from the inner spirit of the Old Testament. They represent a genuine attempt at spiritual and religious reorientation in a changing era. The word of the prophet has yielded to the teacher of wisdom.

1) BEN SIRACH – TEXT HISTORY

The Book of Jesus Ben Sirach — called the Book of Ecclesiasticus in the Latin Church [1] — can claim a history and discovery that is no less exciting than the manuscripts from the Dead Sea Scrolls. Until the year 1896, Ben Sirach was known only in Greek translation, while the Hebrew text was considered to have disappeared. St. Jerome [2] does indeed claim to have seen the Hebrew original of Ben Sirach. But since he did not regard the Book of Ecclesiasticus as a canonical book, he made no effort to provide a translation.[3] It would be incorrect to suppose that the ancient Jews did not treasure this book; modern investigation proves quite the opposite. In the divine service of the synagogue there are several marked echoes of Ben Sirach.[4] Still,

---

1. The name Ecclesiasticus for the Book Ben Sirach first appears in the course of the second or third century. Since it was used as a sort of catechism instruction for catechumens, it was given the name "Church" book, "Ecclesiasticus" (liber). Rufinus, PL XXI, 374. In the Latin liturgy, no other book, apart from the Psalms, is used so frequently as this, a fact which surely vindicates its name. – Some scholars, however, hold that the name comes from the struggles on the subject of the canon. Ben Sirach could be read in Church, but it was not to enjoy any canonical authority, only "Ecclesiastical" recommendation.
2. In the prologue to the Solomonic books, PL XXVIII, 1242.
3. In the Vulgate we have the Old Latin translation.
4. C. Roth, *Ecclesiasticus in the Synagogue Service*, JBLEx 71 (1952), 171-178.

Ben Sirach never succeeded in being received into the Hebrew canon of Sacred Scriptures. This is explained partially by the peculiar fate of the textual tradition. The Hebrew text was not preserved with the same careful attention as the other, canonical books; it was allowed to remain lost for several centuries.

In the year 1896, two women, A. Lewis and M. Gibson, who had recently returned from a great manuscript discovery in the monastery of St. Catherine on Sinai, bought a sheet of parchment in Jerusalem, which contained the text of Sirach 39, 15 − 40, 7. Professor Schechter from the University of Cambridge examined, translated, and published this discovery. At about the same time, Professor Sayse from Cairo provided seven pages from the same book (Sir 40, 9 − 49, 11) on his return to England from Egypt. These pages contained marginal notes in Arabic and Persian, giving rise to the speculation that the book had been written in Bagdad. Schechter, armed with letters of recommendation, made a trip to Cairo in an attempt to seek out the original home of the manuscripts. He discovered that all the pages had come from Genizah [5] the synagogue of the Caraeans [6] in Fustat, a suburb of the ancient city of Cairo. Among other important new discoveries, his investigations yielded further fragments of Ben Sirach. Thus, around the turn of the century (1896-1900), the textual history of the Book of Ben Sirach had embarked upon a new stage. But this was not all. In the years 1930/32 J. Marcus discovered a new fragment of Sirach in the collection of E. Adler in New York. The various fragments were marked only with large letters. A: 6 pages, eleventh century; B: 19 pages, twelfth century; C: 4 pages, end of the tenth century; D and E, 1 page each, time undetermined.

In terms of content, the pages make up about three-fifths of the Hebrew text; that is, 40 out of 51 chapters, or 1090 out of 1616 verses.[7] In terms of textual history, the text of Sirach is no more poorly attested than is the Hebrew text of the other books of the Old Testament, whose manuscript evidence, prior to the discovery of the Dead Sea Scrolls, had gone back no further than the ninth or tenth century.[8] The discovery of

---

5. genizah, literally "hiddenness"; in a transferred sense it refers to the separate chamber or hidden niches in the synagogue where the worn out or damaged or unclean, or even heretical scrolls were deposited and thus removed from further use.

6. The Caraeans were a Jewish sect who recognized only the reading of Scripture as the sole source of faith. Their name comes from qara' = "to read."

7. On the history of the text, cf. C. Spicq, ClamB VI, 541ff., JBL 74 (1959), 93-95.

8. Eissfeldt, EinlAT 843.

the medieval manuscripts of Sirach was already a great accomplishment. But even this was surpassed by the discovery of a few fragments of Ben Sirach among the Dead Sea Scrolls.[9] This would prove the contention that the wisdom doctrine of Ben Sirach was well known in Palestine towards the end of the Old Testament. While scholars hope to make further finds, it is unlikely that they will have any far-reaching effects upon the history of the text. A comparison between the medieval codices and the manuscripts from the Dead Sea proves that the text of the Bible has been handed down with uncommon accuracy and fidelity.

In terms of language and metrics,[10] Ben Sirach fits very well into the ancient Hebrew poetry of the Bible; he is, accordingly, frequently called "the last representative of the Silver Age of Hebrew Literature."[11] His work quickly spread into the Syrian and Greek world. The history of the Syriac translation is difficult to trace; the only point that seems to be established is the fact that the Syriac translation is based upon the Hebrew original. The Peshitta is thus of considerable aid in establishing the original Hebrew.[12] We are much better informed on the history of the Greek translation.

From the prologue and epilogue to the "wisdom of Sirach" (σοφία Σιράχ)[13] we know that a certain Jesus, son of Sirach, composed the work in Hebrew, in Jerusalem. The grandson of the author traveled to Egypt in the 38th year of King Euergetes and translated the work there. The title Euergetes can only refer

---

9. H. L. Ginsberg, *The Original Hebrew of Ben Sira 12, 10-14*, JBL 74 (1955), 93-95.
10. S. Mowinckel, *Die Metrik bei Jesus Sirah*, ST 9 (1955), 295-296. The work is composed in regular distichs. 1081 readable strophes have been preserved. The strophes are constructed along a metrical pattern, with the predominant rhythm being one of four ictus.
11. Pfeiffer, IntrOT 405.
12. V. Hamp, EB IV, 572.
13. The final *Chi* in the Greek transliteration is simply an attempt at precise rendition of the Hebrew final Aleph. Hebrew Sira' becomes Sirach, just as *chakel-dama'* becomes *akel-damach* (Acts 1, 19). It is also possible that the *Chi* is meant to indicate the indeclinability of a word. Spicq, ClamB VI, 533. This would be then simply an orthographical symbol; it would be thus pointless to continue speaking of Sirach; the man is better referred to as simply the son of Sira, Ben Sira; Cf. Ben Hur; Ben Gurion, etc. The meaning of the name has not been satisfactorily explained. Syrian manuscripts contain the form *'asira*, "the captive," and combine it with a legendary captivity narrative.

to Ptolemy VII Euergetes II, who had the surname Physkon (fat-belly). He ruled as sole ruler from 170-145. This would suggest a date around the year 132 B.C.; in Egypt, probably in Alex-andria, Ben Sirach's grandson found a large Greek-speaking Jewish community, to whom he attempted to transmit his grand-father's wisdom teaching. He himself had described his method of translation: "It seemed highly necessary that I should myself devote some pains and labor to the translation of the following book, using in that period of time great watchfulness and skill in order to complete and publish the book for those living abroad who wished to gain learning, being prepared in character to live according to the law" (prologue). He is well aware of the difficulty of his proposed task. He knows the problem of trans-lating. There is not always a corresponding Greek word for every Hebrew word. But he does not approach his task without considerable preparation. Detailed literary investigation has proved the fact that he turned particularly to the Septuagint version of the Pentateuch as his "dictionary." [14] He thus adapted his lan-guage to the style of the Septuagint Bible that was already cur-rent. Scholarship has indeed pointed out that he failed to under-stand the meaning of many passages, and thus made a faulty trans-lation. But this surely does not undermine the value of his trans-lation which deserves to be ranked next to the Greek Pentateuch. The Greek text served as a basis for the Latin translation. Be-tween the years 200-250 A.D. the old Latin translation was al-ready popular; it was this version of Ben Sirach which, since St. Jerome made no attempt to translate the book, was incorporated into the Vulgate.[15] Since the translators, drawing upon their own collection of wisdom material, made many additions to the text as they translated, their new version has grown so conflated that, in many passages, it has led to variants in the division of chapters and verses, and introduced an element of general confusion. In the discussion that follows, references will be from the edition of V. Hamp, in the *Echterbibel,* where there is always a careful

---

14. J. Ziegler, *Zum Wortschatz des griechischen Sirach,* BZAW 77 (1958), 274-287.
15. On the history of the Latin translation, cf. Spicq, ClamB VI, 544.

distinction of sources, with marginal letters indicating G (Greek), H (Hebrew), V (Vulgate). The final result of any scholarly discussion on the text of Ben Sirach must necessarily conclude that the matter is still very much in a state of flux and needs considerable further investigation.

2) THE PERSONALITY OF BEN SIRACH

If the grandson translated his grandfather's work around the year 132 B.C., then the original writing would have to be dated two generations earlier, approximately 190-180. Furthermore, it can be demonstrated that Ben Sirach was a contemporary of the high priest Simon II (218-192?). The words in praise of the high priest Simon (50, 1-24) are a profusion of the most varied images and metaphors, all in an attempt to resurrect the image of departed glory. Simon was like the radiant sun, the rainbow against a backdrop of clouds, the blossoms on the spring branches, the lilies along the streams of water, the green foliage of Lebanon, the verdure of the olive tree, when, as high priest, he made his way up to the altar of holocaust or, after sprinkling the blood on the day of atonement, made his way from the Holy of Holies. There is nothing in the hymn to indicate the shadow that was beginning to threaten the image of the high priesthood. The covenant with Pincha, the high priestly family of Zadok, is to abide forever. It was only under Simon's successor and son Onias III, that the catastrophe was destined to dawn. The high priestly office became the plaything of political partisanship. The deposition of Onias put a final end to the high priestly aspirations of the family of Zadok, as we shall explain more fully in connection with the Maccabean revolution. We conclude, accordingly, that the activity of Ben Sirach is to be dated shortly before this stormy era. His work still breathes the calm of those calm decades before and around the year 200 B.C., an era in which a peaceful synthesis could still be attempted between Hellenism and Jewish philosophy.

There is hardly another book in the Bible whose author has provided such an explicit portrait of himself as the Wisdom of

Ben Sirach. He comes from Jerusalem (G 50, 27), where he probably spent the greater part of his life and produced his book. He cannot conceal his urban origins. The prophet Amos had taken his images from the milieu of the countryside; in Ben Sirach, on the other hand, it is the life of the city which is predominant, with its various trades and occupations (chs. 19 and 38). His thinking crystallizes about two polarities: the Temple and the synagogue. His love for the Temple goes without saying; it is evident already in his hymn of praise to the high priest. But he certainly did not spend his life as a solitary scholar, concerned only with promoting the study of wisdom; his house turned into a *bêt hammidraš*, a teaching house, a schoolhouse, or, according to the Greek text, a house of formation for the young (οἶκος παιδείας — 51, 23). Young people from the priestly class and from the nobility who were eager for knowledge and learning were welcome in his home. He expresses the hope that they enjoy their experience in his home (51, 29). Whoever passes through his school can count not only on becoming wise, but also acquiring a good position in life (51, 28). Ben Sirach thus formed something like a Greek academy about himself.[16] There was freedom to come and go, and a common sharing of the struggle to achieve proper knowledge of life and wisdom. The master himself was the living center of all this activity. His doctrine on wisdom was worth more than gold and silver. Without pay or recompense, he shared his treasures of wisdom with any man who cared to hear him. The entire house was filled with a spirit of freshness, open to the knowledge of the entire world.

Ben Sirach was a teacher who, in his own youth, had spent much time as a student. Since his boyhood days he had been in search of the sources of wisdom. What he counsels his disciples he has already done himself. "Be ready to listen to every narrative, and do not let wise proverbs escape you. If you seek an intelligent man, visit him early; let your foot wear out his doorstep" (6, 35). The principal source of his wisdom is doubtless the Sacred Scripture (prologue). But this was not enough. The young man

---

16. Spicq, l. c. 535.

must broaden his horizons and learn to know the wisdom of the entire world. Ben Sirach must have undertaken considerable travel in his early years, and thus acquired a good stock of experience (34, 9ff.). It is not improbable that he was active in the service of a foreign king (39, 4). It was this occupation that would have won him his typically Hellenistic breadth of world knowledge, which he then attempted to unite with the traditional doctrine of his faith into one harmonious synthesis. In terms of Jewish society, he belonged, after the establishment of his circle of disciples, to the class of sôferîm, scribes, whose primary occupation was the study, interpretation, and practical application of the law of Moses. The fact that his own individual coterie of disciples quickly formed about him is testimony to the power of his mind. It has been said [17] that the wisdom taught by Ben Sirach is at one and the same time biblical and humanistic. The peculiar needs of that era could be satisfied not by turning a deaf ear to the steady stream of Hellenism, by living in a Jewish ghetto, but rather in an open and ready acceptance of the positive elements offered by this new world culture.

On the basis of scattered references in the text, we are justified in concluding that Ben Sirach must have been an aged and white-haired man (51, 13) when he actually wrote his book. Most likely he had experienced a happy marriage with his wife. "He who acquires a wife gets his best possession, ... Where there is no wife, a man will wander about and sigh" (36, 29f.). His children had been brought up with care and discipline (7, 24; 42, 9). It is possible that he owned some property outside Jerusalem, and could thus enjoy an independent life in the city. This property was administered with prudence and shrewdness. There were those who envied him; but he knew how to keep order in his own house (6, 7ff.; 9, 29ff.; 33, 20-33). Parasites were refused admission, but towards the poor and suffering he showed an open heart and helped wherever he could (12, 1).

Ben Sirach seems to have been a man peculiarly open to everything beautiful and good. He was particularly dedicated to the study of wisdom, but this did not make him a solitary

17. Pfeiffer, IntrOT 368.

ascetic or hermit. He is equally interested in politics, technology, medicine. He had a fine feeling for the beauty of nature (42, 15 — 43, 33). He felt most at home in the society of friends and disciples who were of like mind. Hence his words in praise of festive gatherings where guests ate costly foods and drank choice wine, listened to fine music while displaying congenial flashes of wit. "A ruby seal in a setting of gold is a concert of music at a banquet of wine. A seal of emerald in a rich setting of gold is the melody of music with good wine" (32, 5f.). Ben Sirach, however, was a man to observe moderation in everything he enjoyed; he was a proponent of the golden mean. He knew how to enjoy the beautiful things of this world without being too taken up with them. For this life is ruled and set in gold by the law, and the beginning of the law is the fear of God. Despite his open attitude towards the new Hellenistic culture, Ben Sirach was unwilling to sacrifice a jot or tittle of the law. He was a Jew in religion, and Greek in culture.[18]

Ben Sirach thus belongs somewhere among the predecessors of the Sadducees, who, some years after his death, formed a special party in opposition to the Pharisees. From the New Testament we know that the Sadducees denied the resurrection (Mt 22, 23; Acts 23, 6). It is a surprising fact that in the Hebrew picture of the world, the horizons of the hereafter — judgment, recompense, resurrection of the body — are accorded a place of little importance. In the Greek translation, however, many lines were given a sharper development. The grandson did not make simply a literal translation; he also worked the theological concepts of his age into the finished product.[19] Finally, we must point out the fact that the great messianic hope of Israel is directly dependent upon nothing in the wisdom literature. This does not justify the conclusion that Ben Sirach is opposed to the messianic hope; it is simply that his system was directed primarily towards practical activity, and thus the messianic expectation does not enjoy a position of prominence. On the other hand,

18. Ibid., 371.
19. M. Fang, Che-Young, Ben Sira de novissimis hominis, VD 21 (1963), 21-38.

from beginning to end, his work is permeated with the Law of Moses, the Pentateuch. Wisdom came to him primarily from the study of the Law. "Ben Sirach thus represents the transition from Bible to Talmud, from the authority of scriptural inspiration to the authority of teaching and commentary." [20]

Considerable effort has been made to discover some system in the 52 chapters and some units of thought. The results of this effort have not been encouraging. Formally, at all events, two groups can be distinguished, a collection of wisdom proverbs (2, 1 — 47, 14) and the so-called praises of the fathers (44, 1 — 50, 14). Spicq [21] attempts to prove that the content of the book, in keeping with its being patterned after the five books of Moses, is arranged in five divisions. The individual sections, he claims, exhibit a similar construction. At the beginning of each of the five groups of proverbs stands the praise of wisdom or the God of creation. There is, moreover, a progressive line of development in the teaching of the individual sections. Just like the Book of Genesis, Ben Sirach proceeds from the universal to the election of Israel. This would result in the following outline:

1, 1 — 16, 23: Essence and activity of wisdom.

16, 24 — 23, 27: God and creation, man and his moral activity.

24, 1 — 32, 13: The activity of wisdom in the family and in social life.

32, 14 — 42, 14: The proper conduct of one's life.

42, 15 — 50, 29: The revelation of wisdom in nature and in the history of Israel.

51, 1 -30: Conclusion, prayer of Ben Sirach.

---

20. Pfeiffer, l. c. 369.
21. Spicq, l. c. 553ff.

The entire work was certainly not written at one sitting. The divisions outlined above are perhaps an indication of units of instruction which were gathered together in the course of Sirach's teaching career. Like most other books of the Old Testament, Ben Sirach matured to its final form only gradually. Nor can it be denied that the zeal of his disciples and students has made a significant contribution to the collection.[22]

3) THE TEACHING OF BEN SIRACH ON WISDOM

Ben Sirach, as teacher and instructor, certainly elicits a sympathetic impression. His educational ideal seems to be the harmonious man, the person who knows how to achieve a golden mean between self-indulgence and self-discipline. That is why his writing still enjoys a considerable vogue even today. First we must examine into the guiding motifs of his instruction.

a. *Leader in every situation of life*: The teacher of wisdom needed to prepare his student for every situation in life, and leave him with a feeling for genuine, lasting values: "All elements of human society are to be encountered in these pages: vocation and family, priest and pauper, withered old men and corpses, hotheads and idiots, every kind of human temperament, women, friends and associates, powerful men and princes. The master makes use of all of them to teach his disciples how to maintain that difficult golden mean in their use of the passing goods of this world; for death will spare neither the famous nor the rich nor the powerful. Yet better than the thought of death is the fear of God, which is the last word of all this instruction." [23]

b. *The picture of man*: Every instructor keeps before his eyes an ideal image that he strives to attain, but also a basic and fundamental image upon which he bases his instruction. The basic problem of all *paideia* revolves about the nature of man.

---

22. The gradual development of the book is argued also by Robert-Feuillet, EinlAT 757.
23. *Ibid.*, 758.

For Ben Sirach the norm of human morality is the will of God
(2, 15-17; 15, 11-13; 25, 1; 32, 14 [— G 35, 14], 35, 3
[— 32, 5] etc.). The will of God is known to him not on the
basis of any speculation upon the nature of man, but from the
revelation of the law. His anthropology is already a theology,
since his fundamental sources for knowledge are supplied by
revelation. Ben Sirach is little interested in the many ritual and
cultic precepts of the Pentateuch, affairs which pertain to cult,
Temple, and sacrifice; his interest is centered on the personal,
moral behavior of everyday life. It is here that he must confront
the problem of the origin of evil in human nature. In the solution of
this problem he may well have been influenced by the prophet
Jeremiah, who sees the origin and principle of evil action "in
a stubborn and rebellious heart" (Jer 5, 23f.). Within the human
spirit there dwells a power which drives him on towards evil,
"the drive towards evil" (*yeser hara'*) (Gn 6, 5; 8, 21; cf. Dt
31, 21; 1 Ch 28, 9; 29, 18). But if the human person is impelled
towards evil by some obscure power, is he really master of his
decision? Does not the responsibility somehow fall back upon
God who first embodied this impulse within the human heart?[24]

Against this conception of things, Ben Sirach directs an
energetic argument (15, 11). He stresses the fact that the
will of man is always in a position to make a free choice: "If
you only will, . . . you can fulfill his will" (15, 5). This the human
being can do only when he chooses the law as the measure of his
activity. "Whoever keeps the law controls his *yeser*" (21, 11).
Ben Sirach's vision of man does not involve the uncomplicated
harmony of paradise, but rather his weakened state after the
Fall. Man is dust and ashes, open to the power of his evil im-
pulses (17, 31). There is something demonic about Ben Sirach's
picture of man: "It was he who created man in the beginning, and
he left him in the power of his own *yeser*" (15, 14). Ben Sirach
turns back frequently to the story of the Fall: "From a woman
sin had its beginning, and because of her we all die" (25, 24).
The lack of harmony in man, together with his inclination towards

---

24. Pfeiffer, IntrOT 392ff.

evil, is interpreted in terms of human origin. As a result, evil cannot come from God. God simply has not willed evil. Behind this evil impulse stands the Satan, the despoiler of man (H 15, 14). God, on the other hand, constantly tries to rescue man from his inclination to evil. He destroys the stiff-necked and stubborn man (16, 6-11), but if a man has proper dispositions, he will chastise him and lead him to insight and conversion. The whole teaching on wisdom is closely bound up with the call to repentance (34, 25 [— G 31, 31]; 35, 12 [— G 32, 14], 38, 10). In setting as his goal the description of the truly good man, Ben Sirach has completely abandoned the purely humanistic level. His ethics of education thus turn into a morality of redemption. Man can be freed of his evil inclinations only if he accepts the yoke of the Law. This yoke, in Ben Sirach, implies nothing oppressive; rather it leads directly to the original freedom which was built into God's great plan of creation: it is synonymous with wisdom.[25] Ben Sirach's concept of wisdom is, accordingly, based on a different foundation than the Greek. Sophia, for him, is not the result of human endeavor; wisdom comes from God. Wisdom proceeded from his mouth, took up residence in his creation, and can be shared with man (24, 3ff.). Wisdom is thus equivalent to revelation. But since revelation has found its clearest expression in the Law of Moses, wisdom and Law are practically identical.

c. *The power of example*: As a good teacher, Ben Sirach was familiar with the power of example. Words move, but examples have an impelling power. His teaching on wisdom is thus cast into the form of the "praises of the great men of the past" (44, 1 — 50, 24). The whole history of the Old Testament is presented in outline form. As in a picture gallery, 20 figures from Israel's glorious past parade before our view: Henoch, Noah, the patriarchs, Moses, Aaron, Phinehas, Joshua, Samuel, David, Solomon, the prophets Elijah, Elisha, Isaiah, and Jeremiah. In this meditation upon history Ben Sirach is a disciple

---

25. O. Kaiser, *Die Begründung der Sittlichkeit im Buche Jesus Sirach*, ZTK 55 (1958), 35-92. The Law has no negative note: it is also a promise.

of the prophets. He too believes that it is Yahweh who calls and rejects, and that Israel's history is dependent upon her position with respect to the covenant. It might be that Ben Sirach already recognized the great temptation of defection to Hellenism. The great figures from the nation's past which he calls back to life are thus meant to serve as a warning to the present. Israel can live only from the covenant law, from wisdom, or Israel must perish. It is not only his picture of man that is different from that of the Hellenistic world around him: there is an essential difference in his attitude towards history. Man and history have their beginnings in God. Looking back to times past can only confirm the constant presence of God throughout the course of history. That is why history has a goal, an objective, why it is open towards the future. "May their bones return to life" (46, 12; 49, 10) is the most earnest prayer of this wise old man. If Ben Sirach nowhere makes any direct reference to the messianic hopes of Israel, the praises of men of old are at least a powerful indirect allusion to the messianic perspective.[26]

Ben Sirach was not a genius who forges ahead along a new path; nor was he a philosopher who ruthlessly rethinks every position and shatters the securities of his contemporaries, like Job and the Preacher (Qoheleth); he was a man whose eye was open to the world, a man who appreciated everything beautiful and noble and good, a scribe and interpreter of the Law in the best sense of the word. The wisdom of the world and the faith of revelation unite in him to form that clear precipitate of wisdom which of its very nature turns into a school. In the transferred sense, accordingly, we might refer to his book itself as a bêt hammidraš, a house of instruction, or an οἶκος παιδείας, a house of formation for the young.

In the course of the intellectual and spiritual history of the Old Testament, Ben Sirach stands at a turning point. The confrontation between Hellenistic culture and the religion of the Old Testament had to be somehow overcome. Ben Sirach dared to achieve a new synthesis without either hostility or the surrender

---

26. R. T. Siebeneck, *May their Bones return to Life. — Sirach's Praise of the Fathers*, CBQ 21 (1959), 411-428.

of anything essential to his own faith. It was precisely this confrontation with Hellenism which enabled him to achieve a new and deeper understanding of the inexhaustible depths of revealed wisdom. Shortly after him, however, this bridge was broken. Instead of confrontation there is war and hostility. But the path upon which Ben Sirach embarked remains a valid approach. Almost immediately after the perilous days of the Maccabean wars, his work was translated into Greek and thus introduced to the wide world of culture. His ripe and almost exuberant humanism is the most noble fruit of the Hebrew wisdom literature; it could have ripened only on the tree of fear of God and knowledge of God.

In terms of salvation history, Ben Sirach prepares the way for the philosophy of the New Testament. In the Gospel of St. John, the figure of wisdom is actualized in the person of the Incarnate Word: "In the beginning was the Word...." Just as wisdom existed in the beginning with God, proceeded from the mouth of God, and set up her tent among men (24, 3ff.), so too the Logos was together with God in the beginning, and then set up his tent among men. St. John testifies that he has seen his glory (δόξα), the glory of God himself (prologue to St. John). The Book of Ben Sirach thus points back to the narrative of Paradise and at the same time it points forward to the fullness of time.

CHAPTER XIV

THE WISDOM OF QOHELETH
THE PREACHER
The Book of Ecclesiastes

"THE catechism of pessimism," "the solemn song of scepticism" [1]
— that is what this book has been called. These powerful words
are meant to express the peculiar characteristics of this book,
so out of place with the habitual message of the Old Testament.
It is obvious that Qoheleth, like Job, is a problem book. "His
sayings are like goads, and like nails fixed" (12, 11) which
bore into the flesh and leave deep wounds. The rabbis used to
argue whether or not contact with this book "made the hands
unclean." [2] These simple words meant that many of them contested Qoheleth's place in the canon of Sacred Scripture. Finally,
the book established itself both in the synogogue and in the
successor to the synagogue, the Church, as a holy book, belonging
to the canon, and thus inspired by God.

---

1. H. Lamparter, *Das Buch der Weisheit*, CalwK 16 (1955), 26.
2. Mishna Jadajim 3, 5.

1) NAME AND TIME OF COMPOSITION

There is no completely satisfactory interpretation of the name Qoheleth. The Septuagint translates it as Ecclesiastes, that is, the man of the *ecclesia,* the popular or church assembly. The Greek word *ecclesia* corresponds to the Hebrew *qahal* in the original text, *qahal* being the common expression for the popular assembly of Israel. The final syllable -*eth* is used to designate a function or office, such as *sopheret,* the office of scribe or scripture scholar; accordingly, Qoheleth would signify the office of the leader of the assembly or the speaker in the assembly, hence the word "preacher." [3] In reading the text, however, one does not get the impression that the speaker is addressing any particular assembly; his message is directed to the individual. As a result, it might be preferable to derive the word from the root *qhl* with the meaning "to be contentious, stiff-necked."[4] Qoheleth would then be the contentious philosopher, the critic who attacks everything and carries the argument all the way to its basic premises. For this he needs no assembly; in his solitary study or within a small circle of scholars and disciples he can produce his work. The mere fact that this book could even be written already presupposes an era in which everything threatened to be called into question.

The title "words of Qoheleth, son of David, king in Jerusalem" (1, 1) and the form of the narrative "I was king in Jerusalem" (1, 12) are a poetic invention rather than an argument for dating the book within the Davidic-Solomonic era, a time which surely presents no likely background for such new and revolutionary thinking. Since all direct references to a possible dating of the book are worthless, scholarship has turned to a careful evaluation of the indirect references. The foolish old

---

3. Jerome translates: concionator, preacher. Fr. Nötscher, EB IV, 537, prefers this translation.
4. E. Ullendorf, *The Meaning of* QHLT, VT 12 (1962), 215 considers even a derivation from Arabic *qala,* "to speak." *Qoheleth* thus means "speaker, orator, rhetor." VT 11 (1961), 378.

king (4, 13) has been identified as Antiochus II, while the young king returning from exile would be Seleucus II, and the king before whom the whole people rejoiced (4, 14) would be Antiochus III. Qoheleth would thus be a contemporary of Antiochus III the Great, and would thus have written his book in this glorious period of Hellenism's fullest bloom, about 200 B.C.[5] Even though this proposed solution is subject to objection on some points,[6] this much can be considered definite: the life and activity of Qoheleth do not belong in the Davidic-Solomonic era, but in the Hellenistic era of the third century.[7] Palestine was then enjoying a long period of peace under the sovereignty of the Egyptian Ptolemies, and this political calm was bound to produce literary and artistic advances. Considerations of language and style would point to the same era, especially the clearly evident influence of Aramaic and even Phoenician.[8] Both elements are clearly possible as an explanation. Aramaic had made its way thoroughly into the culture as the language of the people; on the other hand, large sections of the Palestinian coastland had, since the Persian era, been in possession of the Phoenician commercial cities of Tyre and Sidon. This would closely enough delineate the external framework within which it was possible to develop a spiritual confrontation with the forces of that age. Qoheleth's home is thus to be sought in Palestine rather than in Egypt; the entire book is full of allusions to life and activity in Palestine.[9]

2) STRUCTURE AND LITERARY GENRE

Even though he was surrounded by a flood of Hellenism,

---

5. K. D. Schunk, *Drei Seleukiden im Buch Kohelet*, VT 9 (1959), 192-201. — Robert-Feuillet, EinlAT 673 extends the framework somewhat: the atmosphere of the Lagide era (300-170) would furnish the best background for *Qoheleth*.

6. Fr. Nötscher, EB IV, 548 sees no historical references in this text.

7. R. Gordis, *Qohelet and Qumran — A Study of Style*, Bibl 41 (1960), 395-410.

8. M. J. Dahood, *Canaanite-Phoenician Influence in Qoh*, Bibl 33 (1952), 30-52; 191-221; — *Qohelet and recent Discoveries*, Bibl 39 (1958), 302-318.

9. W. H. Hertzberg, *Palätinische Bezüge im Buch Kohelet*, ZDPV 73 (1957), 113-124.

our contentious philosopher did not choose the Greek dialogue form to develop his thinking; he remains closely bound up with the traditional Hebrew manner of thinking and speaking. "For the presentation of his thought he chose the proverb form, as the form of expression most likely to impress itself upon the memory of his audience, and in this genre he proves to be a master. Example and observation from human life are evident throughout his composition, in order to develop a certain insight and experience taken from actual life. The bond among the individual sections is quite loose, and does not argue for any progressive and clearly developed sequence of thought. Every attempt to demonstrate an original progression, an all-embracing outline and organic structure, has thus far been condemned to failure, and will always be so. What we have here are loosely arranged aphorisms, which are all subordinated to a basic guiding thought with the result that they tie in even the most deliberate variations with the theme outlined in the introductory verses." [10]

Even though the work cannot be divided according to a thematic point of view, the text itself does suggest a division into three sections. In chs. 1 and 2 the author presents King Solomon as summing up the whole knowledge and experience of his life. This is followed by a series of proverbs, which lead up to the concluding statement in 7, 23: "All this I have tested by wisdom; I said, 'I will be wise'; but it was far from me. That which is, is far off, and deep, very deep, who can find it out?" — With 7, 25 begins the third series of proverbs: "I turned my mind to know and search out and to seek wisdom and the sum of things, and to know the wickedness of folly and the foolishness which is madness."

Within this basic outline many scholars have attempted to find distinctions on the basis of text criticism and source analysis. That the epilogue (12, 9-14) was written by a disciple of Qoheleth can be considered as definitely proven. Some scholars have gone so far as to claim that Qoheleth, in its original form, was too scandalous for pious temperaments and was thus re-edited by orthodox scholars by the insertion of formulae more

---

10. H. Lamparter, *Das Buch der Weisheit*, CalwK 16, 28.

in keeping with the traditional faith (z. B. 4, 9-12; 4, 17 — 5, 6; 7: 1-12, 18, 22; ch. 10 almost in its entirety; 12, 2-6). But even with these attempts at reediting, the text of Qoheleth is just as full of scandal as before. In terms of text criticism, we are not justified in dismembering the text. "Kuenen is obviously correct when he says that it would be more difficult to attack the unity of the book than to demonstrate it." [11]

In terms of his method, our contentious philosopher does not proceed from one line of demonstration to another, gradually approaching a forceful conclusion; his basic thesis is known from the outset. He attempts to approach the solution by developing his thought in concentric circles.

3) QOHELETH'S MESSAGE

One fundamental point must be established: Qoheleth, unlike the prophets, is not proclaiming an oracle from God: "Thus speaks the Lord." The times have changed. From all appearances, it is no longer the spiritually conceived words of God which are presented here: "Here we have a man speaking out his own thoughts. Within the limits of human reason he reflects on what he has observed under the sun, in the world about him, and within his own self, always with alert perception, with sharp reason, with unassailable judgment, and with his whole heart." [12] The human mind, with all the powers at its disposal, ranges through all the realms of being and is forced to recognize its ultimate dissatisfaction. Vain, completely vain and perishable is everything that man grasps after. But this knowledge does not lead to existential anguish, to a mocking scepticism, to a despairing pessimism, or even to a defiant nihilism; this awareness of existence comes to him from the basis of his Old Testament faith in God, who, it goes without saying, is presupposed in all this search for wisdom. Where the ways of man come to an end, they open

---

11. Robert-Feuillet, EinlAT 672. — Sources in: O. S. Rankin, IntB V, 7-12.
12. W. Vischer, quoted without source identification in H. Lamparter, l. c. 29.

upon God. And thus even these human words, spoken with an extreme measure of irresponsibility, are, in the last analysis, borne along by the spirit of the wisdom of God. That is why Qoheleth must be considered one of the most original, but also one of the most radical thinkers of the Old Testament.[13] His work is an open manifest of war. His attacks are directed not against the foreign Hellenistic philosophy; the enemy must be sought within the structure of contemporary Jewish thinking. Since he himself is a teacher of wisdom, his battle is directed against the self-assured teachers of wisdom whose philosophical structure he shatters and reduces to absurdity.[14]

a. *The vanity of all earthly things*: To those who are constantly involved in the demonstration of order and harmony in the cosmos and the life of man and who attempt to solve the great enigma of the world, Qoheleth opposes the guiding thought of his whole philosophy: *habél habalîm, habél habalîm, hak.kol habél.* This sets the fundamental tone of the entire book. The word *hébel* occurs 72 times in the Old Testament, 37 of them in Qoheleth.[15] The literal meaning is "breath of air, vapor, evaporation," and in its transferred sense: "illusion, disillusion, nothingness, vanity, idleness." How are we to translate the introductory sentence, in which the word *hébel* is used five times? We are faced here with a typical Hebrew form of expression. In order to achieve the comparative or superlative degree of the noun or adjective, two nouns are joined together. The most common example of this is the title of Solomon's Song, *šîr haššîrîm,* "Song of Songs." Since this form of expression is not congenial to our modern vernaculars, we do best to dissolve the compound word something like this: "Breath, only a breath; only a breath is everything." Or, in its transferred sense: "illusion, simply an illusion; everything is an illusion." Man might claim to stand upon a secure foundation; but under the attack of our philosopher

13. Pfeiffer, IntrOT 726.
14. Eichrodt, TheolAT III, 147.
15. Köhler, LexVT 223.

all his securities prove to be vanity and nothingness. Human endeavor is simply "a striving after wind" (re'ut rû^{a}ḥ: 1, 14; 2: 11, 17, 26; 4, 4; 6, 9), all and all it is "an unhappy business" ('inyan ra': 1, 13; 4, 8; 5, 13). Qoheleth ranges through all the possibilities that can provide inner satisfaction for a man. As a type he chooses Solomon in all his glory. Everything that the human heart desires was possible for him: power, riches, enjoyment, women, wisdom, knowledge (1, 12ff.); but the end of it all is death and vanity. This mention of the final inevitability of death is and remains the fundamental presupposition of the entire book.[17] The edict of expulsion from paradise, "You are dust and into dust you shall return," has here been developed to its logical conclusions. The theme which continually recurs in comfortless monotony, "a breath, perishable and nothing is everything," thus looks far back into the original history of humanity. The basic theme-word habél might well have been chosen as a subtle reference to the name of the first man to die upon earth, Abel (Hebrew habél — breath). It is his tragic figure that first exemplifies the true human condition, subject to death: man is simply a short and perishable breath of air. The Book of Qoheleth could thus be called the "book of the man Abel."

b. *The distant God and the wheel of fate*: Qoheleth's concept of God is not developed from the basis of Greek philosophy; it is completely under the impression of the narrative of creation in Genesis. This forms a powerful background against which the human tragedy can be enacted with telling force.[18] Everything else might be questionable to the philosophy of Qoheleth, but not the existence of God. He does not attack God as Job does. The God of creation is the undeniable prerequisite for everything that exists. From birth to death, through all the particulars of existence, everything is determined by God. But Qoheleth does not experience the closeness of God, as the Psalms describe him in glorious poetry; God is far away from him. What characterizes

---

17. Hertzberg, l. c. 223.
18. More detail in Hertzberg, l. c. 227ff.; Cf. C. C. Forman, *Kohel-et's Use of Genesis*, JSS 5 (1960), 256-263.

his theology is his clear knowledge of the distance between God and man (5, 1). That is why the "fear of God" forms a constitutive element in his picture of the deity [19] (12, 13).

But fear is not the only element in his picture of God. Qoheleth has been accused of hedonism and epicureanism, since he has words of praise for the enjoyment of life, eating and drinking, plucking the blossom of the day. But this joy in living would not be possible without the knowledge that it too is a gift from God. Surely there is a dichotomy about his entire work, the awareness of human mortality, but also the happy and moderate enjoyment of life. The dichotomy is hard to resolve. Perhaps it is to be noted already in the first chapters of Genesis. The world created by God was "exeeedingly good," and yet the sentence of death hangs over each individual man. God no longer walks with man as he did in Paradise.

As a result, men frequently have the impression that it is not God, but rather blind laws that determine the course of the universe. Everything happens as it has been foreordained (9, 11f.). "The personal characteristics of the deity are in little evidence. There is some mention of cult and prayer; but there is no evidence of a personal relationship to God, a relationship of prayer." [20] Does this mean that the living God, the Father, has turned into an impersonal force of fate? Is it simply the wheel of fate which determines the course of history? There is one point, however, which gives the lie to what appears to be a deistic and predestinarian image of God, and that is the thought of judgment. Man is responsible for what he does (5, 5; 7, 16ff.; 8, 5). He must appear before the judgment of God. That will be the final decision. After the day of judgment the somber curtain is drawn; the view of heaven and hell is closed. There is no spark of messianic hope here, only the inevitability of death, fear of God, God's judgment, and the doctrine of contentment with the small pleasures of this life. There could hardly be a more moving portrayal of the human condition, man put out of Paradise. This thought has led Hertzberg to conclude: "The Book of Qoheleth,

---

19. Hertzberg, l. c. 224.
20. *Ibid.*, 226.

standing at the end of the Old Testament, is one of the most moving messianic prophecies that the Old Testament has produced." [21] How can this be? There had to be a thinker to approach this book from the fullness of time and recast it in terms of prehistory as a statement of the human condition in its present reality: man is nothingness, condemned to death, abandoned to a meaningless course of fate, unapproachably far removed from God. The Greek translation introduces a slight change in the book's emphasis. In Hebrew, Qoheleth is "a lament over the mortality and vanity of human effort," while in the Greek it is rather an "accusation." [22]

The apostle Paul does not contradict Qoheleth's point of view. He too felt the burden of death: "Wretched man that I am! Who will deliver me from this body of death?" (Rm 7, 24). He admits that all creation sighs and laments because it has been subjected to futility (*mataiotes,* Rm 8, 20). But he has more to say than Qoheleth. In Jesus the Messiah, the second Adam, a new humanity begins. "If the Preacher was not correct in saying that everything is vain and that there is nothing new under the sun, that it is impossible for man either to recognize or achieve justice, that, finally, death is the one certain thing, . . . why is it then that Christ came down to earth from the eternal throne of God above the sun and died on the cross outside the gates of Jerusalem for the salvation of the entire world?" [23]

Since, however, the man baptized into Christ is not taken out of this world, the situation described by Qoheleth continues to hold for him. In the realm of human experience his statements will continue to be valid so long as this heaven and this earth abide. That is why the Book of Qoheleth cannot simply be relegated to the lesser knowledge of the Old Testament with a sigh of relief: it is the universal book of the human condition. That is why the Church has also accepted it into her canon of Sacred Scripture and preserved it.

---

21. *Ibid.*
22. G. Bertram, *Hebräischer und griechischer Qohelet. Ein Beitrag zur Theologie der hellenistischen Bibel,* ZAW 64 (1952), 26-49.
23. H. W. Hertzberg, *Der Prediger,* KAT XVII (1963), 238.

The conclusion of the book suggests a scene from a composition of modern poetry.[24] There is an accumulation of imagery. The almond tree blossoms, the grasshopper drags itself along and desire fails; the silver cord is snapped, and the golden bowl is broken, the pitcher is broken at the fountain, and the wheel broken at the cistern. Dust must return to the earth from whence it came, and the spirit returns to God who has given it (12, 1-8). The author has finished. Qoheleth-Solomon has seen through everything on earth.[25] Nothing survives, there is only a breath of wind in the face of nothingness. The things of earth, upon close examination, are a vast emptiness — or perhaps they are a vast openness. For God remains unchanging and unchanged.

---

24. It is characteristic of our modern situation that Qoheleth's ideas, by a simple shift in accent, largely owing to the suppression of the divine, keep creeping up in our philosophies. Fr. Rudolf Schabl (who died at the age of 27) has, in the one article published by him, "Ein Buch der Bibel und das Nichts," Der Seelsorger, 31 (1960/61), 503-511, closely examined the traces of Qoheleth in Kierkegaard, Jaspers, Heidegger, Sartre. His conclusion: "The philosophical mind is more taken up with nothingness than with existence. The man who seeks sensual enjoyment grows sick (nausée) of its emptiness in the very midst of his enjoyment. The most frightening fact in all this is that we carry this sickness with us to our death. The experience of nothingness is an essential component of human existence."

25. Hertzberg, l. c. 215.

CHAPTER XV

THE BOOK OF WISDOM OF SOLOMON

1) AUTHOR AND DATE OF COMPOSITION

THE Books of Qoheleth and Ben Sirach were conceived and composed in Hebrew; but in the Book of Wisdom of Solomon we can clearly recognize the "aroma of Greek eloquence." [1] Even if Hebrew sources were utilized in the composition, they were so freely translated into the Greek idiom that they are equivalent to an original work in the Greek language. It follows from this that the wisdom of "Solomon" has nothing in common with the great king of Israel excepting for its name. Solomon is the type of the wisdom teacher; it is to him, accordingly, the great master of wisdom at the beginning of the Israelite royal era, that also the last book of the Old Testament is attributed. The name of the actual author has been lost; what remains is his work, which many scholars rank among the most beautiful literary products of the last centuries of the Old Testament, a judgment that can easily be defended. [2]

Ben Sirach's teaching of wisdom led to the lecture room of the teaching house; the wisdom of Solomon, on the other hand,

---

1. Hieronymus, Praefatio in libros Salomonis: "Ipse stilus graecam eloquentiam redolet," Kritische Vulgataausgabe, Rome XI (1957), 5.
2. Pfeiffer, IntrOT 334.

calls us out into the marketplace and arcade, where people are gathered. What it presents is not an abstract form of knowledge suitable only for the scholar; it takes up burning religious issues which involve considerable elements of the Jewish people and also many of their pagan neighbors. The problems are developed in what was a very contemporary form and practice in the Hellenistic world, the diatribe.[3] The appearance of Alexander the Great had consequences not only in the political field; it had intellectual and religious repercussions of considerable magnitude. "With the demise of the Greek city state, the spiritual mooring of the Greek citizen in his polis, which the gods of his fathers had always guarded and protected from every danger, had begun to lose its firm hold. In the hearts of thousands of thousands of men the faith in the power of the heavenly beings, particularly Themis and Nemesis, whose activity also affects the life of men on earth, and especially their faith in what we today are inclined to call a 'moral order in the world,' — all this was collapsing. Only Tyche, blind chance, and raw violence seemed to have any power on earth. In its despair, the Greek soul looks about for a solid point of reference, new and eternally valid criteria for thought and actions; for without this firm point of reference it is impossible for man, in the long run, to preserve his interior equilibrium. All the Hellenistic philosophers, despite some fundamental differences in their picture of the world, have the basic objective, to restore man's interior freedom and peace of soul, his Eudaimonia . . . . This deep need in the souls of the masses was soon met by a 'mass propaganda.' Popular speakers make their appearance, to discuss not the world of politics, but the problems of moral philosophy. These are popular philosophers, men who preach a 'philosophy for every man,' men who mean to act as guides for the Greek mind and spirit lost in a situation that has radically altered, determined to lead people to an interior self-assertion in the face of the chaotic change that is everywhere evident upon earth, to lead them to the secure harbor of Eudaimonia, from which the blows of fortune can never dislodge

---

3. Cf. W. Capelle, *Reallexicon für Antike und Christentum* III (1957), 990-997.

them." [4] These popular philosophers did not choose the classic dialogue form for their message; the new wine needed new wineskins. What they turned to was the so-called diatribe. This form, unlike the dialogue, was not bound to observe the strict laws of logical progression of thought. The diatribe form presupposes a speaker, the "philosopher," and a rather large group of people, his public, who listen to him. It is to this public that he addresses his discussion of a great variety of problems, which he then discusses and resolves in an easily understood manner. Parables, quotations, historical and mythological examples all serve their purpose to make the spoken or written presentation both interesting and informative.[5]

Just like the Hellenistic philosophers, the author of the Solomonic wisdom presents his hearers with an ultimate orientation based not on the treasure stores of Hellenistic culture, but the wisdom of the Bible. Taken as a whole, he is perhaps no more strongly influenced by the Greek philosophy of his day than any other educated Jew of that time.[6] Certain basic philosophical concepts and slogans were in the air. But when he takes them up, he gives them a new and deeper meaning. His real home is in the world of the Law, the prophets, and the Holy Scriptures.[7] He is a man in an age of transition; he is still speaking to his Judaean contemporaries, but his words echo beyond the confines of Jewish culture, and are addressed to the pagans as well. As a result, his book is a precursor of the early Christian missionary sermon.

---

4. *Ibid.*, 990-991.
5. Olof Gigon, *Das Hellenische Erbe*, PropWG III (1962), 673.
6. J. Weber, *Le Livre de la Sagesse*, ClamB V, 391ff. discusses the relationship to Greek philosophy. Technical terms were used, but given a different force and content. The confrontation with Greek philosophical thought had a stimulating and catalystic effect, providing a new light in which to view the traditional body of faith. — E. de Places, *Un emprunt de la "Sagesse" aux "Lois" de Platon?* Bibl 40 (1959), 116-117 however thinks it is possible to demonstrate a direct literary dependence.
7. G. Ziener, *Die Verwendung der Schrift im Buch der Weisheit*, TTZ 66 (1957), 138-151.

When and where did this man live? Everything would seem to point to Alexandria, the Hellenistic metropolis in Egypt with its Jewish elements. It was here that the Hebrew Bible was turned into Greek. This city continued to remain the spiritual center where the faith of the ancient Bible was being transformed into a new set of words and concepts in the Hellenistic spirit. Since the author is attempting to arm his fellow believers against persecution and to protect them from defection, scholars have carefully searched through the second and first centuries before Christ looking for times of persecution. But there is nothing definite to go on. The Third Book of Maccabees [8] does indeed describe a great persecution of the Jews, but this is generally regarded as a legendary midrash. After a victory over Antiochus the Great at Raphia (217), Ptolemy IV Philopator (222-205), on the occasion of a state visit to Jerusalem, is supposed to have wished to enter the Holy of Holies. At the prayer of the high priest Simon, however, he is supposed to have fallen unconscious to the ground, and, upon his recovery, immediately fled from the city. Upon his return to Egypt, he is then supposed to have taken vengeance upon the Jews in Alexandria. Since they refused to accept the cult of Dionysos, he had them all herded into the stadium. He meant to have them trampled by elephants, but the execution of this order for their murder, though he gave the order three times, was prevented by miraculous divine intervention. Flavius Josephus,[9] on the other hand, places the entire history of the elephants in the time of Ptolemy Physcon (170-163 or 145-116).

The historical nucleus behind this legend might well be the "abiding anti-Semitic attitude of many Egyptians," [10] an attitude which frequently flared up in riots against the Jews. Prosperous Jews had attempted to become assimilated into the Hellenistic world, even at the expense of giving up their traditional faith. These emancipated Jews had nothing but contempt for those of their countrymen who still held to the traditional faith. This

---

8. Text in P. Riessler, *Altjüdisches Schrifttum ausserhalb der Bibel*, 682-699.

9. Contra Apionem II, 5.

10. Pfeiffer, IntrOT 327.

is the background against which the Book of Wisdom of Solomon
is best understood. The precise date of its composition can no
longer be determined. The most probable dates fluctuate between
150 and 50 B.C.; individual conjectures, however, have dated
the book either earlier or later. The year 100 B.C. could not
be far from the truth.[11]

On the basis of the historical background the construction
of the book is also easily understood. There are three basic
blocs of thought: a. Invective against the apostate Jews (1 — 5);
b. Defense of the faith (6 — 12; 16 — 19); c. The nothingness
of the pagan gods (13 — 15). A more detailed outline of the
book's content need not be advanced here, since it can easily
be found in works of introduction and good editions of the text;
we shall attempt only to isolate a few of the basic ideas in which
there is something new for the history of salvation.

2) THE THEOLOGY OF THE BOOK OF WISDOM

The basic position of the Book of Wisdom can be described
as a theology of encounter.[12] The author does indeed speak differently than the earlier prophets, who all proclaimed the rights
of God on earth; but he is and remains, even as a wisdom teacher,
a genuine prophet. He too is concerned about God, about his
activity in the world and human history, about the fate of the
individual man, and the nation Israel, and all humanity. Since
he is writing as a believing Jew in the midst of a Hellenistic
world, he pours out his prophetic vocation into words, images,
and ideas which do not sound alien to the Greek spirit. In this
encounter he is not so much the receiver as the giver. Like a
wise steward, he is in a position to take new things and old from
the treasury of the Old Testament and communicate them to
the Greek world.

a. *The picture of God in the Book of Wisdom*: The fact

---

11. Pfeiffer, IntrOT 327; Eissfeldt, EinlAT 743; Robert-Feuillet, EinlAT
    750.
12. J. Weber, *Le Livre de la Sagesse*, ClamB V, 381f.

of God's existence did not need to be proved to the believing Jew, but in the enlightenment of the Alexandrian world this was a proof which had to be presented (13, 1-9). The existence of God is an obvious conclusion for the normal thinker. Ignorance of God is thus the greatest folly. The conclusion from the visible world to the invisible existence of God,[13] from the work to the master (τεχνίτης) is a compelling one. From the beauty and grandeur of creatures the originator (γενεσιουργός) can be clearly seen. There is, therefore, no possible excuse for those who do not recognize the existence of God on the basis of his creation and who stop half-way, with a creaturely goal. Genuine knowledge of God is thus not simply a matter of the thinking and seeking intellect; it is even more a matter of the heart that makes a decision.

The God who has created and who maintains this world is totally and completely above the world (11, 22). The world is for him like a speck that tips the scales, and like a drop of morning dew that falls upon the ground. He has created everything from formless matter (1, 14; 11, 17), and is himself bounded by nothing (11, 21; 16, 24). All-present and all-knowing (1, 6-10), he has ordered everything in terms of number and measure and weight (11, 17-20). That is why he is sovereign Lord whom no one can stand against in judgment (12, 12-18). His deeds are just and unimpeachable. Life and death (16, 13), and all power are dependent upon him (6, 1-11). Neither the little and insignificant nor the great and powerful can escape his providence which plans and maintains all creation (6, 7-8; 11, 26; 12, 12-13). He is the provident father who even directs ships along their course through the waves (14, 13).

It is not the all-power of the creator, not the all-knowledge of the master of the world that most deeply moves the teacher of wisdom; it is rather his incomprehensible love and mercy which extends to simple creatures. God is prepared to pardon anyone who is genuinely converted to him (9, 1; 11, 21 — 12, 2). The Book of Wisdom takes up the message of the prophet

---

13. Deliberate play on the Hebrew for God, Yahweh.

Hosea and enlarges it to universal proportions. God's love and mercy are not for Israel alone, but for every creature upon earth. Here we already catch a glimpse of the theology of St. John: "God is love," and with particular stress on the forgiveness and redemptive quality of that love. The punishments which God sends thus take on the character of *paideia,* education and up-bringing. They are to lead to the knowledge of God. But if a person takes a stand against the call of God, then God will abandon him to his own devices, and eventual ruin.

This living and personal conception of God far surpasses the notions of Greek philosophy. The Greek thinkers did indeed hit upon the concept of a supreme being, but their god remains a philosophical abstraction without any religious appeal, or it is reduced, together with the world, to an all-abiding One. The transcendental god of the Judaeo-Hellenistic philosophers is so far removed from the world as to lose himself in absolute nameless-ness and, on the practical sphere, to give rise to a dualistic in-terpretation of the world. Matter as such is incapable of God and unworthy of God; it is thus reduced to a position of not deserving to exist, a necessary evil. In the Book of Wisdom, on the other hand, it is a living and personal God who speaks, revealing himself both in the world and far beyond the world.

God is nowhere in the entire book referred to explicitly as king, and yet there are some references to the "kingship of God" (βασιλεία Θεοῦ 10, 10). He rules upon his royal throne in the highest heavens (9, 10; 18, 15) and it is from there that he determines the fates of men and nations. In keeping with his secret counsel he directs the just during their life (2, 22); after their death they have a share in the divine kingship of God: "God is their king forever" (3, 8); "They receive kingship and glory" (5, 16) and rule with God forever (6, 21). Division of this kingdom of God has no earthly boundaries. It exists wherever man bows to the will of God. To serve God is to rule.

God is *the* existent (13, 1), while the gods of the nations are nothing. The prophets have already unmasked the wretchedness of the pagan gods, but the Book of Wisdom goes a step further and attempts to give the phenomenon of paganism some ex-planation in terms of religious history. First there were the powers

of nature, which gradually turned into deities (13, 1-9). From
the cult of the dead gradually developed the figures of the gods.
A father once upon a time made an image of his child who had
been suddenly taken away from him (13, 10-14, 13; 14, 14-20).
Thus it happened that men attributed the inalienable name of
God to stone and wooden images (14, 21). Nor was that all.
The confusion in their minds quickly led to a confusion in their
hearts. Immortality, murder, and excess were rampant on so-called
sacred places (14, 23ff.). The folly of this path eventually resulted in the worship of irrational animals (11, 15-16; 12, 23;
15, 18). According to the Book of Wisdom, this was not the
case from the beginning. In the beginning there was universal
belief in one God. That is why a day of judgment shall dawn
upon the gods of the pagans. At the end of human history, however, the one God will once again be recognized as lord and king
by all humanity (14, 11-14). In other words this means that the
author of the Book of Wisdom looks to the coming of God's
dominion. He thus takes a stand essentially different from the
Greek concept of God, which is completely alien to this final
confrontation of the end-time. The Book of Wisdom continues the
prophecy of the coming judgment of God in a new manner. There
is no discussion of this dominion being achieved through the
agency of a messiah; it is wisdom itself through which God will
accomplish his great deeds in the world. But what is this wisdom?

b. *The problem of wisdom*: In the earlier writings of the
Old Testament, and especially in the Book of Judges, all extraordinary deeds are referred to the "spirit of Yahweh." The
Book of Wisdom also uses this terminology and thus affords the
necessary key to a proper understanding of "wisdom." "The
Holy Spirit (πνεῦμα ἅγιον)" lives and works in man (1, 4-5;
12, 1); he is given from on high (9, 17); what is more, he
penetrates all things, forging everything into a unity (1, 7). The
same statements are also made in reference to wisdom (9, 18). It
would seem, therefore, that the author uses both concepts without
distinction. Wisdom and Holy Spirit find evil abhorrent (1, 4
and 1, 5); together they penetrate and hold together all things
(1, 7 and 7, 2-24; 8, 1). Just as the spirit once inspired the

prophets, so it is now wisdom (7, 27). It is, therefore, not surprising that the two concepts are joined together and spoken of simply as the "spirit of wisdom" (πνεῦμα σοΦΐας 7, 7). This manner of speaking is in itself nothing new. It occurs already in the prophecy of Isaiah [14] but upon closer examination, it is possible to recognize new points of departure in this revelation which approach the threshold of the New Testament but cannot manage to cross it.

Wisdom belongs to both God and man. It is God who plans, creates, and maintains the world through his wisdom. Wisdom is thus an attribute of the God of creation, one with him. She shares his divine throne (πάρεϑρος 6, 14; 9, 4), she is the issue (ἀποροεῖα) of the glory of the Pantokrator, the radiance of everlasting light, the unmarred mirror of the divine activity, the image (εἰκών) of his goodness (7, 25f.). That is why wisdom enjoys divine attributes. Wisdom is non-material, all-powerful, all-penetrating (7, 22ff.); since she is together with God she is also initiated (μύστις 8, 4) in God's knowledge, plans, and activity. She was present when God created the world (9, 9-12), and she maintains the universe in existence and providentially directs the path of all that exists (1, 7; 7, 27; 8, 1). It is thus also her task to sanctify the souls of the just (7, 27). All these are prerogatives proper to God alone; they can be shared with no creature. Who is this wisdom? Is it the personification of an attribute of God? If the Old Testament were not followed and interpreted by the New, our knowledge would stop at precisely this point. But looking back from the fullness of time we can recognize the fact that in the concept of wisdom we have not only an attribute of God personified, but an anticipation of the very person of the incarnate Logos.[15]

The activity of wisdom achieves its fulfillment in man. Immediately, in keeping with her divine nature, she builds the bridge between God and man. Not every man is capable of

---

14. Cf. Vol. IV, 267ff.
15. For more detailed treatment of the relationship between Wisdom and New Testament, cf. G. Ziener, *Weisheitsbuch und Johannesevangelium*, Bibl 38 (1957), 396-418; 39 (1958), 37-61.

wisdom. There are prerequisites which must be met on the part of the human agent. He must be free from sin (1, 4-5; 6, 15-16; 7, 27). He has no right to wisdom, but is free to pray for it (7, 1-14; 9, 1-18). Wisdom is a lover of men (φιλάνθρωπος 1, 16), and is willing to share herself with those who desire her (6, 12-16). If a man is open to wisdom, she leads him to salvation, to the kingdom of God (βασιλεία θεοῦ 6, 20). Together with wisdom come all other good things (7, 15-22; 8, 8); she introduces man to the deepest mysteries of God and makes him a friend (7, 14) and son of God (υἱός θεοῦ 2, 18; 5, 5; 18, 13).

The activity of wisdom is directed primarily to the people of Israel (15, 1-6), which has a particular mission to fulfill in the midst of the nations of the world. It is through Israel that the imperishable light of God is to shine in the darkness (18, 4). It was wisdom who guided Israel through all times and perils. Everything that is said of the redemptive deeds of Yahweh in the Book of Moses is here ascribed to wisdom (10—19). Wisdom was, accordingly, already at work from the very beginning of salvation history. It was through wisdom that Yahweh liberated and redeemed Israel.

This leads to the great vision of the future, the coming kingdom of wisdom which recognizes no national limitations and no geographical borders, the kingdom of God itself. The Book of Wisdom does not yet make any statement with respect to the incarnation of wisdom. This lies outside the limits of all human thinking. But this is still the preparation of the line of thinking which, in the later history of salvation, leads directly to the mystery of the *Verbum incarnatum;* for man is to be redeemed through wisdom (9, 18).

c. *The destiny of man*: The Book of Wisdom frequently goes back to the older biblical writings;[16] it is, accordingly, no wonder that the concept of man bears the stamp of the creation narrative from Genesis. Man consists of a body (σῶμα) and a soul (ψυχή),

---

16. R. T. Siebeneck, *The Midrash on Wisdom 10-19*, CBQ 22 (1960), 176-182. In the Book of Wisdom the earlier biblical books are reworked in a Midrashic continuation and given a new interpretation.

which is also called understanding (νοῦς 9, 15) or spirit
(πνεῦμα). All three terms are equivalent in meaning. The body belongs to the normal mode of human existence (1, 4); it is not
a prison for the soul, even though, by reason of its earthly mortality, it does weigh heavily upon the human person (9, 15).
The soul is a sacred trust from God, and man must someday answer for it (15, 11, 16).

What is the final destiny of this creature, who has been
molded together from the dust of the earth and the spirit from
on high? Is there an horizon that stretches beyond death? The
representatives of earth deny this possibility. With death everything is over; thought is only a spark occasioned by the exercise
of the heart muscles; the body turns back into dust and ashes,
while the spirit is scattered like thin air (2, 2). The conclusion
of this vision of life can only be: enjoy what can be enjoyed.
"Let no pleasant meadow fail to share in our revelry, everywhere
let us leave signs of enjoyment" (2, 9).

But wisdom has quite different plans for man. Man is created
not for death, but for life. Death came into the world only
through the envy of the devil (2, 24). But God is prepared to
grant pardon, and thus life (12, 2). New life begins already in
this world of time. Whoever follows wisdom becomes a friend
of God and a son of God (2, 16-18; 5, 5; 9, 4; 7, 1-14, 27).
This life established upon the principles of wisdom leads beyond
the threshold of death to immortality (ἀθανασία 3, 4; 4, 1; 8,
17; 15, 3) and to incorruptibility (ἀφθαρσία 2, 23; 6, 18-19).
But this is a knowledge that no man can reach on the basis of
philosophical reflection upon the spiritual nature of man; immortality and incorruptibility are free gifts of God's grace. Even if the
just man dies early or meets a violent end,[17] death is for him
something secondary, only a transition into what really matters
(3, 1 — 4, 19). The life of the godless, no matter how magnificent it might appear to be in the eyes of men, is actually death

---

17. The figure of the unjustly persecuted just man may have been
    influenced by the Songs of the Suffering Servant. M. J. Suggs, *Wisdom
    of Solomon 2, 10–5; a Homily based on the Fourth Servant Song*,
    JBL 76 (1957), 26-33.

(1, 16); it ends in the darkness of Hades. The *Basileia Theou* is formally opposed by the *Basileion* of Hades (1, 14). The ancient Hebrew concept of Sheol, a place in which the departed spirits must live a shadowy existence, has taken on a tremendous depth; it has become a place of torment for the wicked (4, 19).

Men are divided into two camps,[18] pious and godless. The day of "visitation" will come (2, 20; 3, 7; 4, 15), the day of "examination" (1, 9; 4, 6), the day of "decision" (3, 18). The Book of Wisdom here takes up the ancient prophetic concept of a sermon of judgment, and gives it new form. There is, however, no oracle hurled against the contemporary world powers: the individual, but also the human race as a whole, are all subject to judgment. There is thus an individual judgment after death (3, 1 — 4: 6, 18, 19) and a general judgment at the end of days (4, 20 — 5, 23). The two phases cannot always be clearly distinguished, but they are both present. The description of the final judgment reminds one of the ancient prophets. God makes his appearance as the great warrior: justice is his coat of armor, holiness his shield; he sharpens his sword, and shoots his arrows; his breath ranges across the earth like a powerful storm; the godless are annihilated, while the pious are saved. Although the Book of Wisdom makes no explicit mention of the resurrection of the body, this is a necessary conclusion from its teaching on the nature of God and man. God wants not death, but life (2, 23ff.); he has power over life and death, and can even make his way into the world of the dead, but he will once again give life (16, 13). There is no directly messianic aspect to the expectation of the end of time, just as there was none in the expectation of the coming of the God of the kingdom. It is God himself who holds judgment, without the intervention of any messiah-judge. This is another concept that needed to be made more profound in the fullness of time. But at all events we have here those preliminary conceptions of the endtime upon which the preaching of Jesus on the subject of the last judgment was later to build.

---

18. The same conceptions are to be found in the Dead Sea Scrolls. A. M. Dubarle, *Une Source du Livre de la Sagesse*, Rev. des Sciences Phil. et Theol. 37 (1953), 425-443.

Men, good or evil, are on their way to judgment. Do the people of Israel have a special role to play here? The Book of Wisdom does not attempt the fateful and premature conclusion that the people of Israel as such are equivalent to the just man. The distinction will be made within Israel itself. It is not nationality but justice that is the decisive element in judgment. Still, Israel does have a special mission in the midst of humanity. God chose Israel as his first-born son (18, 3, 13), and made an alliance with Israel (12, 21); God has preserved Israel from idolatry and shown him the way of life (15, 1-6). Always and everywhere Israel stands under the direction of God. Israel is to provide the light of the law for the peoples of the world (18, 4). One day the cult of pagan idols will completely disappear and all nations will worship the one God in Israel (14, 11-14; 18, 4). Messianic horizons make their appearance, but there is no mention of the Messiah as such. The kingdom of God envisioned here could be conceived of even without the Incarnation of the Word. The Jewish religion, which refuses to recognize Jesus of Nazareth in his capacity of Messiah, would then have advanced no further than this concept of a kingdom of God. God's dominion and kingdom are realized in the fulfillment of the law, which is the emanation, mirror, and radiation of the wisdom of God himself. In strict logical consequence, the kingdom of God could come without a Messiah.

This final book of the Old Testament, with the realities of faith that make their first appearance here —kingdom of God, last judgment, human immortality, resurrection of the flesh — can indeed be referred to as the immediate precursor of the New Testament. But it leaves open many possibilities which God, always greater than our human conception of him, has realized in the fullness of time, in an unheard of and truly divine manner.

SECTION SIX

THE MACCABEAN WARS OF LIBERATION

CHAPTER XVI

THE BLASPHEMOUS GREAT HORN

(Dn 8, 9)

AFTER the decisive battle at Paneas at the sources of the Jordan (198) Judah too changed masters. The Ptolemies were forced to relinquish their Asiatic holdings and contained to the Nile Valley, as we have already seen described in the prophetic presentation of history announcing the battles of the kings of the north and the south. This change of rule appears to have been attended by some joy in Jerusalem. The border wars had involved considerable hardship for the country. It was expected that a powerful victor would guarantee more peaceful times. Antiochus III confirmed for the Jews all the privileges deriving from Persian times. The greatest of these was the right of self-administration under the direction of the high priest. He further granted three years' immunity from taxation, so that the country could recover from the ravages of war. Moreover, the tribute to be paid in future years was reduced by one third, and the Temple personnel were completely free from all royal taxation. The king even granted an annual sum, taken from the state funds, for the proper maintenance of the official cult in the Temple.[1] Such

---

1. Thus the account of Flavius Josephus, Ant. XII, III, 3f., whose historicity can hardly be doubted.

magnificent marks of favor and privilege appeared to mark a most promising dawning of a new era under the sovereignty of the Syrian Seleucids.

The Seleucids reformed the ancient, tiny district units [2] into larger administrative units, which were called eparchies. Thus, the eparchy of Paralaia comprised the coastal territory together with the cities along the coast; the eparchy of Samaria counted the territories of Judea, Galilee, the harbor city of Jappho (Joppe) and Bet-Tobiah, east of the Jordan, although it no longer contained the district of Amman-Philadelphia. The rest of Transjordania formed the eparchy of Gilaad. The districts south of Judea, including the cities of Yabneh and Ashdod, belonged to the eparchy of Idumaea. Following the example of the Ptolemies, the Seleucids also demanded the introduction of Hellenistic culture and Hellenistic cities in the newly organized territories.

Where were the new centers of Jewish settlement? Obviously in the Medinah of Judea; but already in the Persian era the repatriates made their way not only into the ancient tribal territory of Judah, but also into the other sections of Palestine and Transjordania. The Jewish settlement was no longer contained within the political boundaries of the province of Judea.[3] At the outbreak of the Maccabean wars of liberation, Palestine represented a colorful and variegated ethnic, religious, and political structure. The province or district of Judea was only a small and insignificant part in opposition to the variety of political powers. Seen from without, incorporation of the Jewish nation was the high priest. But it was precisely the high priesthood that involved the real tragedy of this fated hour. The Temple had become surrounded by too much earthly power and too much wealth, and the spiritual office was quickly involved in a struggle for Mammon.

1) DISPUTE OVER THE MARKET LAWS (2 Mac 3, 3ff.)

The dispute erupted from a quarter in which it was least ex-

---

2. Hebrew *medinah*, literally "jurisdiction."
3. The best maps for this era to be found in *Atlas Jisrael*, Jerusalem 6/IX.

pected. The "captain of the Temple" Simon, from the tribe of Benjamin, split with Onias, high priest of that year, on account of the market laws (ἀγορανομία). Presupposing that the text has been handed down in correct form, it is certainly strange to note that a Benjaminite,[4] who did not belong to the priestly caste, should have attained such a high position in the Temple administration. The precise nature of the office of "captain of the temple" (προστάτης) cannot be determined.[5] At all events, the captain of the Temple Simon was such an influential man that he was in a position to oppose the high priest himself. Under his control came all deliveries to the Temple: grain, oil, cattle, etc. What is more, he might well have exercised an indirect influence upon the Temple treasury. There is no explicit statement to the effect that he misused his position to raise or lower prices. The point of the dispute seems rather to have been a decision as to what belonged to the king and what to the Temple. The high priest was overstepping his authority when he attempted to hold on to properties and moneys that went far and beyond what was necessary for the maintenance of the divine services and the daily sustenance of the priests, delivering it directly into the Temple rather than to the royal treasury. Under these circumstances it is quite probable that Simon actually was a Benjaminite, that he was champion of the king's position against the high priest (ἐξουσία τοῦ βασιλέως, 2 Mac 3, 6). What was involved was the *Exousia,* the full power: what belongs to the king and what to the Temple?[6]

Since Simon, the Benjaminite, made no headway against the high priest, he turned to more highly placed officials. Judea belonged to the eparchy of Samaria and to the larger territorial unit of Coele-Syria, which was subject to Apollonius[7] the governor (στρατηγός 1 Mac 3, 10; 2 Mac 3, 5). Simon turned to

---

4. The Old Latin translation reads Bilga, a priest who returned from Exile (Neh 12, 5); others have suggested a correction in an effort to remove the scandalous element.

5. On the various Temple offices, cf. Schürer II, 325ff.

6. Cf. the questions put by the Pharisees in the Gospel: "Is it allowed to pay taxes?" (Lk 20, 22).

7. Flavius Josephus, Ant. XII, 7, 1 Strategos of Samaria.

Apollonius and informed him of the tremendous treasures which
were being hoarded in the Temple of Jerusalem, though they
properly should have accrued to the royal treasury. On the occasion of a chance meeting with Seleucus IV Philopator (187-
175) Apollonius passed on this disturbing news. For the royal
administration this was an unexpected opportunity to interfere
in the interior affairs of Judea. The king sent his royal chancellor
Heliodorus, who had practical control over the affairs of state,[8]
on a tour of inspection through Coele-Syria and Phoenicia, a
mission which naturally enough brought him to Jerusalem too.
Here he was accorded a friendly reception. In keeping with the
power of his position, he caused inquiry to be made concerning
the points at issue, whether actually funds had been held back
that should have been paid into the royal treasury. The high
priest gave an account of the Temple's financial situation. He
claimed that the great accumulations of capital in the Temple treasury were primarily the contributions of widows and orphans who
trusted the inviolability of the Temple sanctuary. He mentioned
also a very wealthy man, Hyrcanus ben-Tobiah, who had also
deposited considerable sums. The total amounted to 400 silver
talents and 200 gold talents. The imperial chancellor, however,
decided that these moneys belonged to the royal treasury and
set a day for their transport and delivery.

This decision occasioned the most extreme disturbance in
the capital city. People ran together in streets and in houses; the
sanctity of the Temple was in danger of being violated. In the
Temple itself, the priests conducted a rogation and penitential
service (2 Mac 3, 15-22). But Heliodorus was not to be stopped.
With an armed escort he made his way into the Temple treasury
(γαζοφυλάκιον). It was here that something occurred which some
scholars have seen as legend or pious fraud, but which our
historian explains as the saving intervention of heaven itself.
Heliodorus no longer saw the magnificent treasures of silver and
gold; he was seized by a powerful apparition, produced by the
lord of spirits and hosts. He saw a rider on a fearsome horse,

8. 2 Mac 3, 7: ὁ περὶ τῶν πραγμάτων, "He who is (appointed) over
the affairs."

charging towards him. The steed struck at him with his fore-hooves. Heliodorus fell to the ground, and darkness enveloped his mind. The man who had so proudly violated the sacred ground is carried out on a stretcher. Recovering his senses, Heliodorus offered sacrifice and returned to the king who had given him his orders. He had experienced the fact that there is a power from God (δύναμις θεοῦ) at work in the Temple of Jerusalem (2 Mac 3, 38), and that God himself acts as guardian and protector of this sacred place (3, 39). This miraculous event had, for the time being, decided the question of Agoranomia, the rights of the temple versus the rights of the king, in favor of the Temple, but it was not a lasting solution. The enemies of the high priest Onias did not give up the attack.

2) THE VICTORY OF THE OPPOSITION — INROADS OF HELLENISM IN JERUSALEM

Meantime, the situation in Jerusalem remained tense. Simon was intriguing against Onias. Finally it came to political murders. In all his dealings, Simon could count on support and cover from Apollonius the governor. In this desperate situation, the high priest could find no other escape than a direct appeal to the king himself. He went to visit the king at Antioch, in an effort to defend the interests of the common good (2 Mac 4, 1-6). This journey, undertaken with heroic determination, proved to be his condemnation to exile and a tragic death.

Seleucus IV Philopator (187-175) had just died and Antio-chus IV Epiphanes had succeeded him in September of 175. This change in rule was quickly seized upon by the opposition in an effort to gain the upper hand. It is a note of pure tragedy that the man who rose to lead the opposition was precisely Jason, the brother of the high priest Onias. Anything could be achieved by gold and silver, since the state treasuries were depleted from the wars. Jason offered King Antiochus 360 silver talents, most likely from the Temple treasury, and 80 talents from another source, and finally another 150 talents in addition, if he would allow him a free hand in completing the Hellenization of Jerusalem

(2 Mac 4, 7ff.). The king was only too happy to agree to the terms of the offer.

Thus all the privileges granted by Antiochus III, in accordance with which the Jews were to be allowed to live according to their own Torah, were immediately dissolved. This also meant a sentence of death for Onias, who, in his crisis, sought asylum in a pagan temple in Daphne, a suburb of Antioch. Jason returned to Jerusalem as high priest, by favor of the king, and opened the door wide to the new progressive party.

In terms of civil rights, he brought a rich gift to the citizens of Jerusalem. They were now free to be registered as citizens of Antioch. Their legal position would thus be on a par with the citizens of the imperial capital. This was Jason's attempt to give a modern and Hellenistic stamp to the ancient city of Jerusalem. One of the primary embellishments of the Hellenistic city was its gymnasium, the "sports arena." Jason had such a structure built, at the lower end of the citadel. But it was not only the noble art of Hellenistic sports that was practiced here; the pagan culture and mentality also made rapid advances. All the ancient customs were abolished, and newer, progressive practices were introduced in their place. The great rivalry to equal the position and accomplishments of the other Hellenistic cities went so far that, on the occasion of an athletic contest in Tyre, Jason actually sent money for the sacrifice to Heracles. The messengers entrusted with the delivery of the money were, however, over-come with religious scruples and attempted to have the money spent, not for the pagan sacrifices, but for the building of a ship (2 Mac 4, 7-20).

It can only be regarded as a triumph for the progressive powers that Antiochus Epiphanes himself made an official visit to Jerusalem. This visit coincides with larger political events that were in the making. In Egypt, after a long minority during which the rule was administered by a regent (since 180), the 14-year-old Ptolemy VI Philometor succeeded to the rule himself in the year 173/172. On the celebration of his accession to the throne, Epiphanes sent an official directive. He must have realized that the young Ptolemy would once again press Egypt's ancient claims to Palestine. Epiphanes needed to be on guard to anticipate such an attack. He thus made a visit to the important harbor city of Joppe, in order to make arrangements for its eventual defense. From here he made his way to Jerusalem, to determine whether or not he could rely on this city. He was greeted with a torch-light procession and cries of welcome. Under the leadership of the high priest Jason he might well reckon on the support of the Hellenistic-minded Jews (2 Mac 4, 21-22).

3) STILL MORE MONEY — STRUGGLE FOR POWER AND MURDER

After three years [9] (2 Mac 4, 23) there was need for a meeting between the high priest Jason and King Antiochus IV Epiphanes in the capital city of Antioch for the purpose of attending to some state affairs and the transfer of funds. Accordingly, Jason sent Menelaus, a brother of Simon, captain of the Temple, to bring the money to the king. The messenger, however, determined to seize the opportunity for his own purposes. He offered the king more than Jason, and thus managed to win the high-priestly dignity for himself. He returned to Jerusalem as high priest. Jason, who had earlier supplanted his brother, was forced to flee to Ammon. But the new high priest proved to be in no hurry to deliver the money he had promised. Accordingly, both he and the captain of the citadel, Sostratus, were summoned before the royal court. Both men left representatives behind them in Jerusalem, Menelaus his brother Lysimachus; and Sostratus, Crates, the captain of the Cyprian guard. As it happened, the king was also absent from Antioch, since he had to quell a rebellion that had flared up in Cilicia. As his representative he had left Andronicus in the capital (2 Mac 4, 30).

Once again the gold began to flow. Menelaus had stolen some of the gold vessels from the Temple and now gave them as

---

9. The point of reference for the numbers is not clear: apparently it starts not from Jason's accession to office in 174, but actually from the royal visit of 173. "Three years" does not mean three full years in our sense of the word; one full year and two fractional years would suffice. We thus arrive approximately at the year 171/170.

a gift to Andronicus. Andronicus then enticed the high priest Onias from his asylum in Daphne, by dint of many promises, and had him put to death (2 Mac 4, 33-35). When the king heard of this assassination upon his return, and the rebellion of Jews and pagans which it had occasioned, he had Andronicus stripped of his purple robes and led throughout the city, to the very place where he had committed the outrage against Onias, where he was then murdered in his turn (2 Mac 4, 36-38).

Meantime, Lysimachus, the representative left behind in Jerusalem, had made good use of his opportunity to increase his wealth. He had several treasures of gold secretly removed from the Temple. When this became known, rebellion broke out in the city. Lysimachus called upon 3,000 soldiers. The result was barricades and street fighting. Lysimachus himself was struck dead in his treasure chamber. But this proved to be the end of peace in the country.

At the royal assembly which Antiochus IV apparently held in Tyre upon his campaign against Egypt in the year 170/69, there were three ambassadors from the High Council, who had been called to present their accounts, but also to make charges against Menelaus for plundering the Temple. The doom of Menelaus seemed to be certain. But the king made his way into a colonnade, seeking refreshment. Menelaus joined him here, where he promised that he would once again represent the king's cause in Jerusalem, and promised him more money. The king then decided — perhaps for reasons of state policy — in favor of the Hellenistic element, sentenced the three Jewish ambassadors to death, and once again gave Menelaus a free hand. It is understandable that such a development could only embitter true patriots, and provide tinder that was destined to burst into full flame (2 Mac 4, 44-59).

4) ABOMINATION OF DESOLATION IN THE HOLY PLACE

As we have already described, Antiochus Epiphanes attempted to bring Egypt under his sway, in an effort to indemnify himself for the territories he had lost in Asia Minor. The long awaited opportunity for interfering in the affairs of Egypt was offered by the succession to the throne in the year 172. The 14-year-old Ptolemy VI Philometor was declared a major and officially enthroned. His succession to power, however, reawakened the ancient claim to Palestinian territory in the Egyptian court. Epiphanes, the uncle of the successor to the throne of Egypt, reacted to this threat with a massive demonstration of power. Upon his first campaign to Egypt in the spring of the year 169, he made a triumphal entry into Memphis, where he struck an official treaty with his nephew and, in a most unexpected gesture, placed the double crown of Upper and Lower Egypt upon his head. As a protest against this move, the brother of Philometor, Ptolemy the Younger (later Ptolemy VIII Euergetes II) was proclaimed counter-king in Alexandria. For the time being, however, Epiphanes was free to enjoy his laurels, since the Romans were, for the moment, occupied with the Macedonian War. He returned to Syria laden with spoils.

Passing through Palestine, he did not delay in paying a visit to Jerusalem. This time he came as an arrogant victor. It was in the 143rd year of the Seleucid era, September, 169. He made his way boldly into the Temple, demanded to see the treasures, and simply took whatever his heart desired. Among the Jews who were not sympathetic to the Hellenistic culture, he unleashed a violent purge. Unspeakable desolation spread over all "Israel," a title which, in this connection, always refers to those who remained faithful to the Law and covenant. The whole affair served simply to put a sharper edge on the already tense situation in Jerusalem. On the occasion of his second campaign against Egypt, in spring of the year 168, Antiochus IV Epiphanes dropped his mask entirely. He no longer came as the protector of his ward and nephew, but as an open conqueror. When Alexandria offered resistance, he began siege operations. But it was there, before the gates of Alexandria, in the suburb of Eleusis, that he was humbled as never before. On June 22, 168, the Romans had achieved a final victory over the Macedonians at Pydna. Now they were in a position to present a vigorous opposition to the further inroads of Syria. In anger and humiliation, Antiochus was forced to yield.

In Jerusalem, meantime, the rumor had spread that the king was dead (2 Mac 5, 5ff.). The exiled Jason now believed his hour had come. With a thousand men he marched from Ammon towards Jerusalem, in an effort to drive his brother and rival from the office of high priest. Menelaus could not stand before such an attack; he withdrew into the citadel. Jason let loose a relentless slaughter of his fellow citizens all over the city. But Antiochus was not dead. In furious anger he marched back from Egypt, only to learn that Jerusalem was in revolt. He sent his army against the holy city. Jason, the executioner of his country and his fellow citizens (2 Mac 5, 8), was forced to flee to Ammon for a second time, and from there to the Arab Nabateans. King Aretas had him thrown into prison. He succeeded, however, in making his escape to Egypt. Here, too, he was unable to find support, so that he continued his flight to Lacedaemonia, where he died unlamented (2 Mac 5, 8-10). Jerusalem was plundered and burned to the ground, while women and children were carried off into slavery. For three days there was continuous slaughter of young and old alike. The only one who profited from these tragic days was Menelaus, the traitor to the Law of his fatherland (2 Mac 5, 15). He was confirmed by Antiochus in his office of high priest, but the whole of the Temple treasury, 18,000 talents, had to be surrendered. To secure the peace, two royal officials were left behind, the Phrygian Philip in Jerusalem, and Andriochus upon Gerizim in Samaria (2 Mac 5, 22).

After the departure of the king in autumn of 168, peace did not seem to have returned to the country. As a result, in the following year [10] Antiochus sent his chief tax collector (ἄρχων φορολογίας) Apollonius against Jerusalem with a considerable force of men (1 Mac 1, 29; 2 Mac 5, 24ff.). He came with the most friendly assurances. But when he felt himself secure, he immediately began to destroy Jewish Jerusalem and build a Hellenistic polis in its place. He suddenly broke loose upon the city, in a

---

10. This follows from 1 Mac 1, 29 "after two years," which are to be reckoned from the first Egyptian campaign in 143, Seleucid Era, thereby giving the year 145, Seleucid Era (October 168 to October 167).

burst of general slaughter, plundering, and destruction. The city walls were torn down. He then built a new acropolis, the stronghold of Akra,[11] which he surrounded by a thick and lofty wall with strong towers. It was around this new acropolis that the new, Hellenistic Jerusalem grew up. He settled many godless people in this community (1 Mac 1, 34), that is, pagans and apostates, pro-Hellenistic Jews. Those who were faithful to the law were forced to flee. The holy city was turning into a dwelling of aliens.

Side by side with these violent military measures, there came a cultural and spiritual transformation. The king sent an aged Athenian, whose name is not mentioned, to supervise the cultural reorientation of the Jews. It was his objective to make a Hellenistic ethnos out of the Jewish people, and thereby incorporate them as a part of one unified nation. "Then the king wrote to his whole kingdom that all should be one people, and that each should give up his customs" (1 Mac 1, 41). But since the Jewish people, by reason of their religious law, had always led a separate and individual existence, the new cultural prescriptions touched primarily upon the religious law of the Jews. The religious edicts were designed to be the death-blow of the Jewish people and religion.

The first step was the transformation of the Temple of Yahweh in Jerusalem into a temple in honor of Zeus Olympios, together with the erection of a statue of Zeus, which Daniel referred to as the abomination of the desolation (Dn 11, 31). This took place on the 15th day of Kislev, in the year 145 of the era of the Temple (December 4, 167); 10 days afterwards the pagan sacrificial cult began, that is, on the 25th day of Kislev in the year 145 of the Temple era (December 14, 167 — 1 Mac 1, 54, 59). In the same manner, the Temple of Yahweh which the Samaritans built on Mount Gerizim was changed into a temple

---

11. The precise location of the Syrian Akra is not known. Only excavations within the Old City itself could achieve real clarity. Essentially there are two chief positions: either the Akra lay on the southwest hill, on the site of the later citadel of the Hasmoneans, or, more probably, on the southeast hill in the neighborhood of the ancient City of David (1 Mac 1, 3). For a fuller discussion, cf. Simons, *Jerusalem in the OT* (1952), Millo and Acra, 131-157.

in honor of Zeus Xenios. The transformation into a pagan temple also involved the reintroduction of cult prostitution (2 Mac 6, 4). Furthermore, the rite of circumcision, the constitutive element of the Jewish faith since the days of Abraham, was now forbidden under penalty of death. The sabbath and the observation of the annual festivals were also abrogated (2 Mac 6, 10), and the reading of the book of the covenant was forbidden (1 Mac 1, 56). In the place of the old festivals, there were new, pagan holidays, the birthday of the king, and the Dionysia (2 Mac 6, 7). In outward appearances, Jerusalem had become a pagan, Hellenistic city. At the doors of the houses, and in the public squares, incense sacrifices were offered to the pagan gods (1 Mac 1, 56; cf. Dn 8, 9-14, 22-25).

In order to insure compliance with the religious edicts, royal commissions made their way through the villages and forced the inhabitants to offer incense before an altar erected in honor of Zeus (1 Mac 2, 15). This edict applied not only for the province of Judea, but all the Jewish settlements in all the eparchies east and west of the Jordan. Ptolemy, son of Dorymenes, minister of religion in Antioch, issued a directive to the Hellenistic cities to force the Jews who settled in their territories to observe the law of the king (2 Mac 6, 8).

The Jewish nation had never faced such a serious threat to its national and religious existence. It was a time for martyrs. Courageous old Eleazar preferred death to even the appearance of eating pork (2 Mac 6, 18-31). The mother and her seven sons preferred to face a death of torture rather than transgress the traditional laws (2 Mac 7, 1-42). Everyone who attempted to keep faith with the covenant could look forward to persecution and the threat of death.

There were, however, some elements in Judea that welcomed this development; these were not only isolated religious groups that wanted to secure their continued existence, but also the religious leaders of the country, led by the high priest Menelaus, who was joined by many of the priestly class (2 Mac 4, 14). One wonders how these progressive elements managed to combine the ancient faith in Yahweh with the new faith in Zeus. It must have been something similar to what occurred at Sinai, where Aaron believed he had to yield to the will of the people and represent the invisible Yahweh under the form of a golden calf. Did the Hellenistic priestly class actually have such a lax conscience that they believed it was possible to equate the one Yahweh with the supreme God of the Hellenes, even if this meant abandoning practices long honored in history? The phenomenon is too involved to admit of any simple solution. The fact of the matter is that the economic and cultural progress all lay with the Hellenists. The entire world, Egypt, Asia Minor, the whole of the Ancient Near East had opened its arms to the Hellenistic culture, and why should Judea remain the one obstinate province! Once again we hear the cry: "We want to be like the other nations."

But in every case of progress there is a limit beyond which no further step can be taken without too much self-surrender. The religious edicts did achieve one genuine blessing, in that they forced a final decision in a situation that was cloudy and obscure. There was, after all, no other solution for the faithful followers of the covenant than to dare the impossible, to win or lose everything in an open act of rebellion.

CHAPTER XVII

THE SACRED WAR OF ISRAEL[1]

THE signal for rebellion was given by the priest Mattathias ben-Johannan ben-Šimon, from the priestly caste of Joarib, that is, "May God fight." He lived with his family in Modein near Lydda. When the royal sacrificial commission made its appearance here, Mattathias immediately drew his sword and cut down the apostate Jews who were willing to sacrifice before Zeus, as well as the government officials who ordered them to do so. He thus set himself outside the laws of the land. He had no other choice but to take refuge in flight. Hence the battlecry: "Let everyone who is zealous for the law and supports the covenant come out with me." He and his sons fled into the mountains. They left all their property

1. For the history, cf. O. Plöger, *Die Feldzüge der Seleukiden gegen den Makkabäer Judas,* ZDPV 74 (1958), 158-188 (particularly interested in the strategy — the chronology has been now surpassed). For an identification of the various sites mentioned, cf. S. Wibbing, *Zur Topographie einzelner Schlachten des Judas Makkabäus,* ZDPV 78 (1962), 159-170. — Simons, GTT §§ 1096-1224. Of the historical atlases, only two are to be recommended: *Atlas Yisrael,* (Jerusalem 1956), XI/6: maps of the return from Exile up to the Maccabean revolt; XI/7: from the Maccabees to Herod. — P. Lemaire and D. Baldi, *Atlante Storico della Bibbia,* (1956), 176ff. — For the chronology (although it has been partially surpassed), cf. Fr. X. Kugler, *Von Moses bis Paulus,* (1922), 301ff.: Seleukiden, 345.: Makkabäer.

behind (1 Mac 2, 15-28). The wilderness and the inaccessible mountain country had always provided a refuge for the victims of political persecution. It was in this same territory that David had begun his battle against Saul.

There were many who followed the battlecry of the priest. They moved into a life of hiding, with their wives and families and cattle, living in caves in the mountain wilderness. Then the king's party launched a counter-offensive. The troops who were quartered in Jerusalem, in the city of David, were ordered to pursue the "rebels." They were overtaken and surprised on a sabbath, in their hiding places. Not a single one of them offered any resistance to the soldiers. They were all cruelly murdered, obedient to their law (1 Mac 2, 29-38). Under the influence of these tragic events, Mattathias and his followers determined that in the future they would indeed fight on the sabbath, since otherwise the nation would be completely extirpated. The revolutionary movement received its first real support from the addition of the Hasideans,[2] a body of men who were brave and faithful to the covenant and wholly devoted to the law (1 Mac 2, 42; 7, 13). Together with the family of Mattathias they formed small raiding parties, making rapid and unexpected attacks on the villages, tearing down the pagan altars, killing apostate Jews and pagans, and disappearing without a trace into the wilderness. Upon his death in the year 146 of the Temple era [3] (167/66 B.C.), Mattathias named his son Judas, who was also known as "the Maccabee," to carry on the battle. His name [4] most likely does not

---

2. hasîd, generally translated as "pious, faithful." The word is derived from hesed, which was used in the prophetic literature to refer to God's fidelity to his covenant with the chosen people, as well as the people's fidelity to their God; the Hasideans are thus those "loyal to the covenant," and since the covenant is equivalent to the Law, they are "faithful to the Law."

3. In the Books of the Maccabees there are two methods of reckoning chronology. One according to the Seleucid Era for events of profane history, and the other in terms of the Temple Era, for religious events.

4. The interpretations of this name are many. This is largely because of the fact that the name comes down to us in various Greek transliterations, but without any Hebrew or Aramaic form. The middle con-

mean "hammer," — he "hammered down" the enemies of Israel — but simply "leader." It was his dying father himself who raised Judas to the position of *maqqaba*, that is, "designated" among his brothers. Judas, a hero to the death, fulfilled the mission entrusted to him with all his power. "He was like a lion in his deeds, like a lion's cub roaring for prey" (1 Mac 3, 3).

A) THE STRUGGLE PRIOR TO THE CONSECRATION OF THE TEMPLE

Judas continued the battle tactics of his father. In keeping with the established practices of guerrilla warfare, he and his men were everywhere and nowhere. "Coming without warning, he would set fire to towns and villages. He captured strategic positions and put to flight not a few of the enemy. He found the nights most advantageous for such attacks" (2 Mac 8, 6-7).

sonant is in question. The form *Makkabaios* would suggest an original Hebrew *Koph;* hence the derivations from *maqqaba* = hammer; *maqqabî* = the hammerer (cf. the name Charles Martel, the "hammerer," who fought the Arabs in Spain). — But the form *Machabaios* would suggest rather a *Kaph;* hence the derivations *makbî* = the extinguisher, the annihilator of the foe. — Other scholars have supposed the consonants of the name to be merely the initials of the battle-cry (anagram) *m(i)-K(amoka)-B(a'elim)-Y(hwh)* = Who is like you, Yahweh, among the gods? (Ex 15, 11). This derivation seems most improbable. Schürer I, 204, N. 47. — A. Penna, *Libri dei Maccabei*, GarB (1953), 6 suggests *maqqabyahu* = the established, appointed, chosen of Yahweh. — Since the other Maccabee brothers all have surnames which are in keeping with their military tactics and diplomacy, Judas' surname could well be derived in the same manner. Arab parallels would suggest an interpretation of "leader." *Nakib* = leader, chieftain (Wehr, *Wörterbuch der arabischen Schriftsprache*, 879); *manqah* = general (Pfeiffer, HistNTT 462). The same root is to be found in Old Hebrew (cf. Amos 6, 1; Nb 1, 17). — In my opinion the word *maqqaba* is simply an Arabic passive participle Aphel from the root *nqb* and means simply "the one deputed, entrusted with a mission, delegate, leader." Just as the Aramaic form *pharisa* (passive participle I) develops into the Greek form *pharisaios*, so *maqqaba* becomes the current form *makkabaios*. Judas Maccabee is thus equivalent with "Judas, the leader of the rebellion."

What had begun as a struggle against the apostate Jews themselves gradually had to evolve into a battle against those who supported the apostates. The confrontation with the Syrian authorities was inevitable. It was a holy war that flared up, not so much a war of the Jewish nation against a foreign rule as it was a war of faithful "Israel" [5] against apostate Jews and the violent interference of the pagans, a religious war in the truest sense of that word.

a. *The sword of Apollonius* (Winter 167/66): The occupational forces in Jerusalem were the first to take a stand against the disquieting activities of the Maccabees. Apollonius, city commander of Jerusalem, thought that, with the added strength of a division from Samaria, he was in a position to crush the partisans. The place where this encounter occurred is not named, but it was probably not far from Jerusalem itself. Judas and his free-booters won their first victory against the regulars. Apollonius fell on the battlefield. Judas took his sword as a memorial of their victory and used it throughout the rest of his military career (1 Mac 3, 10-12).

b. *The battle at the ascent of Beth-Horon* (166): The defeat of Apollonius had an alarming effect upon the Syrian occupational forces. Apollonius' immediate superior, Seron, Strategos of Coele-Syria, took up the attack. He too underestimated the desperate courage of the opposition and trusted that he would acquire the laurels of victory without any great effort. He assembled his military forces along the coastal plain, from where he marched to the ascent of Beth-Horon, which had always been the gateway to an invasion of Jerusalem. It is quite understandable that "Israel" was in danger of losing their courage at the approach of such an army. But Judas, resolute leader of the opposition, continued to encourage his men. What they were fighting was a holy war. The decision would not be determined by the relative size of the opposing parties; strength would come from God. "They come

---

5. "Israel" in the Books of the Maccabees takes on a new meaning; it refers not to the nation, the people of the Jews as such, but to faithful "Israel"; the apostate Jews are thus no longer "Israel."

against us in great pride and lawlessness to destroy us . . . ; but we fight for our lives and our laws" (1 Mac 3, 21). Judas made a sudden attack from his superior position in the mountains, striking the army while it was in march, utterly routing it, and throwing it back into the coastal plain. Seron himself fell. "Then Judas and his brothers began to be feared, and terror fell upon the Gentiles round about them. His fame reached the king, and the Gentiles talked of the battles of Judas" (1 Mac 3, 13-25). The whole world stopped to listen. These Jewish guerrillas had to be taken seriously. Like it or not, the king himself would have to become involved in the problems of Palestine.

c. *The defeat of the royal army at Emmaus* (165): The Palestinian revolt came at a most unfavorable time for Antiochus IV Epiphanes. He was in the midst of his preparations for a campaign against Asia. The Parthians had made an attack from northern Iran. Arsakas, King of the Parthians, had already occupied Media. Persis was also beginning to shake off the yoke of the Seleucids. Unless Epiphanes meant simply to acquiesce to the loss of the Iranian territories, he needed to march with a powerful army in order to assert the claims of his sovereignty. But the developments in Judea forced him to divert a part of his forces which were so desperately needed for the Asian campaign and commit them to the subjection of Israel. The imperial minister Lysias was entrusted with the conduct of the war in Palestine, while Antiochus himself marched to the east in the year 147 of the Seleucid era (166/65 — 1 Mac 3, 37).

At the approach of the Syrian army, under the command of three generals, Ptolemy, Nicanor, and Gorgias, Israel's fate appeared to be sealed. The objective was to destroy Israel once and for all. The high confidence of the Syrians is demonstrated by the fact that slave dealers had already joined the army, hoping to make an easy profit from trafficking in the defeated and enslaved Jews. What could Judas find to oppose this well-disciplined and well-armed force? Just like Samuel in the days of the Philistine peril, he raised his hands to heaven. His cry of prayer was soon transformed into a battlecry.

The Syrian army had taken up a position in the neighborhood of Emmaus, with a strength of 40,000 foot and 7,000 horse soldiers (1 Mac 3, 39; according to 2 Mac 8, 9, there were only 20,000 men). The situation was extremely critical for the rebels. Judas and his guerrillas had left the territory of Mizpah and occupied the heights south of Emmaus (1 Mac 3, 37). When Gorgias observed the enemy on the heights, he selected 5,000 foot and 1,000 horse soldiers. He made his move at night. He meant to attack the camp of the Jews without warning. But Judas observed all this activity in the hostile camp. The time had come for him to strike. A divided army is easier to fight against than a united force. He abandoned his mountain position and threw himself with all the courage of despair against the rest of the troops who were left in the camp at Emmaus. Deprived of an essential part of his forces, Nicanor was unable to withstand. The Syrian army was defeated and pursued as far as the territory of Ashdod and Jamnia. When Gorgias reached the positions formerly occupied by the Jews in the mountain heights, he found them deserted. He was forced to recognize the bitter fact that the other half of the army had been defeated. Meantime, however, Judas had regrouped his army in order to take up a new offensive position against Gorgias. Gorgias, however, refused the challenge; he quickly withdrew and fled back into Philistine territory (1 Mac 3, 38 — 4, 25; 2 Mac 8, 8-29, 34-36).

d. *The battle at Beth-zur and armistice* (164): The news of the defeat at Emmaus caused general consternation at the court in Antioch: "When Lysias heard it, he was perplexed and discouraged, for things had not happened to Israel as he had intended" (1 Mac 4, 27). Lysias, the imperial administrator, now determined to take personal control of the supreme command. A new army of 60,000 foot and 5,000 horse soldiers was mustered (1 Mac 4, 28). In spring of the year 164, this army began its march southward. Lysias had learned his lesson from the earlier defeats. Judas had always taken advantage of his mountain position to swoop down upon the armies marching against him and deal them a swift and unexpected blow. In order to avoid this danger, Lysias chose to make his attack from the south. Along the heights of the mountain road from Hebron to Jerusalem he could feel secure from unexpected attack. Along the coastal plain Gorgias joined him with the contingent he had saved from the earlier defeat. The approach through Idumaea, a territory which was more or less hostile towards the Jews, passed without event. Lysias soon reached the position of Beth-zur (house of rock) on the border between Judea and Idumaea, 17 miles south of Jerusalem.

This time Judas was able to launch an army of 10,000 men. The battle was a bitter one. But Lysias did not achieve the breakthrough he had hoped for. The Syrian was forced once again to quit the field. Lysias withdrew to Antioch, in order to fill out his troops with new mercenaries. It was in this momentary pause in the fighting that the negotiations for armistice got under way.

e. *Armistice and dedication of the Temple*: In the Second Book of Maccabees we find three dated diplomatic instruments, whose authenticity can scarcely be doubted: [6] the letter from Lysias to the people of the Jews (2 Mac 11, 16-21), the letter of King Antiochus to the Gerousia (High Council) of the Jews (2 Mac 11, 27-33), and the letter of the Romans to the people of the Jews (11, 34-38). We can thus conclude that, after the battle at Beth-zur, Judas sent a delegation to Antiochus in order to achieve a "just peace" (11, 14). The embassy delivered a memorandum to the court. Lysias sent the ambassadors back with a short written reply. He agrees to everything insofar as it is possible within the limitations of his authority. What he means by this is not clear. For what exceeds his authority he refers them to the decision of the king. The letter is as diplomatic and general in tone as possible. If the Jews should remain loyal and well-disposed towards the regime in the future, he is willing to do his best for them. The letter is dated in the year 148 of the Seleucid era (165/64), but the dating of the month is, unfortunately, undecipherable.[7]

---

6. The documents are borrowed from Jason's history: Jason was able to study them in the Archives at Jerusalem.
7. Perhaps, instead of reading "on the 24th day of Zeus Korinthios," we

The king's letter is not addressed, as might be expected, to the victory, Judas Maccabee, but to the Gerousia, the high council. The high priest Menelaus had offered his services as a mediator for peace (2 Mac 11, 29). In the eyes of the Maccabees he was an apostate. Only a dishonorable peace could result from his mediation. What is more, in his letter to the king he managed to reconstruct the facts to his own advantage. He claims to have learned that "the Jews are willing to reconsider" (11, 29), which should probably mean that they are willing to return to loyalty to the king. For those who were willing to make this change, the 30th of Xanthikos is established as the limit within which the amnesty will be observed. Nobody will be called to give an account for the previous hostilities. What is more, the Jews are free to enjoy the practice of their own law and their own worship. Menelaus is entrusted with the execution of these details. Finally the date: year 148 Seleucid era, 15th day of Xanthikos (March/ April, 164).[8]

Epiphanes was quite prepared to take cognizance of the situation, since he was currently involved in a desperate war of defense against the Parthians and needed to have a peaceful situation in his rear. What is more, the Romans were already developing a considerable interest in Palestinian affairs, and this could hardly be a matter of indifference to Epiphanes who had already been humbled by Rome. The Roman letter to the people of the Jews bears the same date as the king's letter. After the Maccabean victory at Beth-zur, diplomacy between east and west was at a rapid pace. Judas, at all events, made good use of this time of armistice in order to arrange matters to his own advantage so far as possible. His march to Zion (1 Mac 4, 37) forms the climax of the Maccabean revolt. His objective was not so much the city of Jerusalem as the holy mountain with its Temple. But what was the result? "They saw the sanctuary desolate, the altar profaned, and the gates burned. In the courts they saw bushes sprung up

---

are to read the "24th day of Dystros," February/March 164.

8. Dating in: J. Schaumberger, Bibl 36 (1955), 432.

as in a thicket, or as on one of the mountains. They saw also the chambers of the priests in ruins. Then they rent their clothes, and mourned with great lamentation, and sprinkled themselves with ashes" (1 Mac 4, 38ff.). Judas was determined to restore the Temple and to renew the interrupted divine services. But in order to be free of the Syrian garrison in the citadel of Akra, he quickly invested the citadel with a small force and began to purify the Temple. The desecrated altar of holocaust was carried away and its stones deposited in a convenient place on the Temple hill until a prophet came to take charge of them. Then they took unhewn stones and built a new altar. On the 25th day of the 9th month, that is the month of Kislev, in the year 148 of the Temple era (December 14, 164), the sacrificial service was once again resumed in the Temple, precisely three years after its desecration by the pagans. The festival of the dedication of the Temple lasted for eight days, and it was then decreed that there should be an annual commemoration for all time to come.[9] In order to protect the Temple mountain from any kind of desecration, Judas surrounded the "mountain of Zion" [10] with a high wall and strong towers (1 Mac 4, 60). — Were all these projects included in the permission granted in the king's letter of Xanthikos 15? At all events, the surrounding settlements looked upon the restoration of Zion with great disfavor. Throughout the Hellenistic territories, the Jews were submitted to hate-filled massacres.

B)   SOLEMN RETURN TO ZION (January — May 163)

Hardly had the echoes of the Temple dedication died away when rumors of alarm made their way to Jerusalem. A letter from Transjordania (1 Mac 5, 10ff.) and messengers from Galilee with rent garments (5, 14) all announced the same sad news: "The Gentiles around us have gathered together against us to

---

9. The beginning of 2 Mac (1 – 2, 18), with its incorporation of legendary material, shows that the festival of the dedication of the Temple was celebrated by the Jews in the Diaspora as well.

10. "Zion" takes on new meaning: it now refers no longer to the ancient city of David on the southeast hill Ophel, but the Temple citadel itself.

destroy us" (5, 10). It is evidence of the strength of the Maccabees that they were able to carry the attack as far as the coastland in the west, as far as Galilee in the north, and as far as Hauran in the north-east, and liberate their oppressed brethren. The operations were carried out in lightning-like maneuvers and great versatility. It is impossible to reconstruct the precise historical sequence of these campaigns.

a. *The ascent of the Scorpions and the towers of the wilderness* (1 Mac 5, 1-5): Judas' first attack seems to have been a bold sortie into the hostile territory of Idumaea, where he liberated the territory of Akrabattene. Along the commercially important ascent of Akrabim (scorpions) [11] on the route that leads from the sink of the Arabah into the mountain country, the Beduin tribe of Baian [12] were established as brigands. Their ambuscades made the entire territory unsafe. Judas vowed the ban (*ḥerem — anathema*) against them, and drove them back into the towers in the wilderness, which he then burned. While this campaign was directed towards the securing of the commercial routes, his intervention in Galilee and Gilead was designed to rescue his Jewish compatriots from mortal peril. The Maccabee brothers divided their various objectives among themselves. Simon was sent into Galilee, while Judas and Jonathan directed their attention to Gilead.

b. *The campaign in Gilead* (1 Mac 5, 24-54; 2 Mac 12, 10-31): After crossing the Jordan and marching for three days, Judas encountered a group of Nabateans along the frontier of the wilderness; they were at that time already in control of the caravan traffic. They reported on the condition of the Jews in northern Gilead.[13] In the cities of Bozrah, Bosor, Alema, Chaspho, Maked and Carnaim, the Jews had been shut up and were in

---

11. Akrabattene might here refer not to the location of that name in Middle Palestine, lying to the east of Shechem along the Jordan, but rather the Ascent of the Scorpions *naqb es-safa* (Nb 34, 4).
12. Perhaps the Benê-Bohan: cf. Josh 15, 6; 18, 17: "Stones of Bohan."
13. Gilead here refers to the Eparchy, not the ancient district.

mortal peril. On the basis of this information, Judas developed a plan of attack. He changed the direction of his march, moved quickly towards the east, made a sudden attack upon the unsuspecting city of Bozrah, and burnt it to the ground. A night march of some 30 miles brought him into the neighborhood of the fortress city of Dathema, in which the Jews had entrenched themselves against the attack of the Strategos Thimotheos of Gilead. Thimotheos was already preparing to storm the town. Ladders and siege machines had already been brought into position against the walls. Trumpets were giving the signal for the final attack. Then the Maccabees suddenly appeared with their storm troops, fell upon the rear of the besieging forces, completely routed the hostile troops, and liberated their threatened brethren.

Now Judas had a free hand to attack and conquer the neighboring cities of Alema, Chaspho, Maked and Bosor. The fortress city of Dathema served as a base of operations for all these campaigns. Thimotheos had meanwhile assembled a new army, but Judas defeated this at Raphon. They threw their weapons away and fled into the temple of Carnaim. Judas pursued them and burnt the temple to the ground. He was thus master of all northern Gilead. He took advantage of the cessation of hostilities to reorganize the persecuted and harried Jewish populace for a triumphal return to Zion. The city of Ephron refused passage to the Jews, and barred its gates; the Jewish forces then made their way by sword and violence. The caravan of returning Jews crossed the Jordan. In the Plain of Beth-shan (Scythopolis) Judas gathered his forces and then, probably following the Jordan Valley as far as Jericho, made his way to Zion, where the caravan arrived before the feast of weeks (Pentecost, April/May 163).

c. *The campaign in Galilee* (1 Mac 5, 21-23): Simon had a similar task to face in Galilee. Here, too, the Hellenistic populace were attacking the Jews who settled in their territory. The individual phases of this campaign have not been recorded. At all events, Simon defeated the hostile forces and pursued the routed enemy to the very gates of Ptolemais. He then gathered the Jewish population and led them into Zion, to Jerusalem.

In Jerusalem Judas learned of the defeat at Jamnia. The forces left in Jerusalem had, upon their own initiative and under the leadership of Joseph and Azarias, undertaken an attack upon Jamnia. The wise old soldier and general Gorgias had defeated them and put them to flight (1 Mac 5, 55-62). After the festival of Pentecost, Judas meant to avenge this disaster. He attacked Idumaea, conquered Hebron and the surrounding territories, and marched up into the coastal plain, where Gorgias was waiting for him. The battle at Marisa was unsuccessful. Judas was forced to withdraw in the direction of Odollam, but Gorgias was afraid to abandon the fortress of Marisa. Judas was thus in a position to make a quick attack upon Azotus (Ashdod), from where he returned to Judea laden with spoils (1 Mac 5, 63-68; 2 Mac 12, 32-45).

These successes were possible only because of the fact that, in December, 164, Antiochus IV Epiphanes had died in the east. His crown, royal cloak and ring he had given, on his death-bed, to his representative Philip, a man whom he could trust, directing him to bring the royal insignia back to Antioch and there raise the young Antiochus V to the throne. But Lysias the royal administrator had anticipated the arrival of Philip. Upon the news of Epiphanes' death, he immediately raised the young Antiochus V to the throne and gave him the throne-name Eupator. These uncertain first months of the year 163, where there was yet no properly confirmed royal power and no one knew whether Lysias or Philip would gain the upper hand, were put to good use by the Maccabees for their victorious campaigns in Galilee and Gilead (1 Mac 6, 1-17).

d. *Second battle at Beth-zur, and the peace of Lysias* (winter, 163/62): Despite these successes, the Syrian citadel of Akra in Jerusalem was like a thorn in the flesh of victorious Judea. The garrisons of the citadel were a constant threat to the security of the Temple. Judas Maccabee thus formed a plan to overcome the Syrian stronghold. In the year 150, Seleucid era (163/62),[14] he invested the garrison within the citadel and began a formal siege.

---

14. 1 and 2 Mac give different dates: in the 150th year (1 Mac 6, 20) and in the 149th year (2 Mac 13, 1). The first date follows the Seleu-

A few members of the garrison succeeded in forcing their way through the besieging forces and fleeing to Antioch. The authorities there had to act quickly if the citadel in Jerusalem was not to be abandoned. Once again there was war (1 Mac 6, 18-27).

Lysias once again was the commander. For reasons of security, he brought the young king with him on this campaign. The approach from the south, through Idumaea, was once again a successful maneuver. The two forces came to a standstill before the gates of Beth-zur, which Judas had fortified. The Syrian army was equipped with the most modern weapons, with war elephants, and far superior in numbers to the Jewish forces. Judas was accordingly forced to withdraw from Beth-zur back to Beth-zachariah. Between these two locations the forces engaged in a battle in which the bold Maccabean Eleazar killed an elephant by piercing it through its belly, and was crushed to death under the weight of the collapsing beast. The sacrifice was in vain. The defeated Maccabees were forced to withdraw to Jerusalem with what was left of their troops. The fortress of Beth-zur was able to hold out for a brief interval. But then, since this was a sabbatical year,[15] the provisions ran out, they were forced to surrender to the enemy (1 Mac 6, 49). After these successes, Lysias committed his entire forces against Jerusalem. The surrounded Jews defended themselves with the courage of final despair. The forces were on the verge of famine and collapse when suddenly an unexpected turn of events rescued them. The internal struggles for power in Syria came to a head at precisely the proper moment to effect the salvation of Jerusalem (1 Mac 6, 28-54).

---

cid Era system, while the second is in terms of the Temple Era. 150 SE = fall 163 to fall 162; 149 Temple Era = spring 163 to spring 162. The expedition thus occurred in the winter of 163/162.

---

15. The sabbath year mentioned here coincides with the familiar sabbath year from autumn 164 to autumn 163, since the sabbath year was reckoned in terms of the business year, beginning in autumn. This led to the poor harvests of 163. The reference to the sabbath year during the siege of Jerusalem thus suggests a date of winter 163/162. J. Achaumberger, Bibl 36 (1955), 430.

Negotiations for peace were immediately undertaken in Jerusalem itself. Under the prevailing circumstances, the peace could only be a compromise. The Syrians agreed not to press the religious edicts and promised complete religious freedom to the Jews; the Jews, for their part, were forced to recognize the sovereignty of the king and to promise no further rebellion against the state officials. Under these stipulations, the besieged populace was ready for peace. The king and the generals took the oath of peace. This was followed by the surrender of the fortified Temple hill. Lysias ordered the destruction of all fortifications and then returned as rapidly as possible to Antioch with the young king (1 Mac 6, 55-63).

Philip had already taken control of the city, but after a short battle he was dislodged and Lysias held the reins of power more tightly than ever before (1 Mac 6, 63). Now the peace treaty with the Jews could be officially recorded in writing. In a letter from the king, in retrospect, we learn of the causes for this long war; the Jews, it is claimed, had not been willing to go along with the "transition into the Hellenistic mode of life" that had been proposed by Antiochus IV; the new regime respected this preference of theirs and would restore them their ancient liberties. They were now free to live according to the law of their fathers, and the Temple was to be returned to them (2 Mac 11, 22-26).

The Maccabees thus lost their last battle, but they won their holy war. Religious Israel was free to live according to the covenant. The attempt to turn Israel into a pagan nation had failed. The goal of the insurrection had been achieved. The Hasideans were, by and large, content. Finally, the king put an end to the career of the high priest, Menelaus, the leader of the Hellenistic element, and made him responsible for the Jewish rebellion. He was found guilty and taken to Beroea near Aleppo, where he was cast into a tower filled with burning ashes, and thus died in torment (2 Mac 13, 3-8).

Could a rebellion, in which religion and national pride were so intimately bound together, possibly halt with the accomplishment of only its first goal, religious freedom? Once the avalanche has been put into motion, it continues to roll along its course inevitably, and the religious war turned into a war for national liberation. Lysias had succeeded in getting the upper hand over his political opponent Philip, and in concluding an honorable peace with the Jews (spring, 162). But his days, and the days of his protegé, the young Antiochus V Eupator, were numbered. In autumn, before the beginning of the winter storms, in the year 151 of the Seleucid era (162/61), the son of Seleucus, Demetrius, who had been kept in Rome as a hostage, made a sudden and unexpected landing on the Syrian coast and claimed crown and throne for himself. The army went over to him. Lysias and Eupator were taken captive. Asked what was to be done with these important prisoners, the young usurper had a short and brutal answer: "Do not let me see their faces." They were immediately killed by the army (1 Mac 7, 2). With the death of Lysias, the peace treaty he had concluded with the Jews was seriously threatened.

C) THE NATIONAL WAR OF LIBERATION UNDER THE LEADERSHIP OF JUDAS

The new master Demetrius was now charged with determining the successor to the office of high priest in Judea. The candidate was Alcimus, who had soiled his career by taking part in the religious massacres (2 Mac 14, 3). In the year 151 of the Temple era (spring, 161), he appeared at the head of a troop of "godless and lawless individuals" (1 Mac 7, 5), which is to say pro-Hellenistic elements, at the royal court, where he was accorded a friendly reception. The time had now come for them to undertake a counter-offensive to the position of the Maccabees and Hasideans. "As long as Judas lives, it is impossible for the government to find peace" (2 Mac 14, 3-11). Whether Demetrius liked it or not, he was forced to interfere in the internal struggles of Judea. He entrusted this delicate mission to Bacchides.

a. *Bacchides on a tour of inspection in Palestine*: Although Bacchides made his way to Jerusalem with a strong military escort, he encountered no resistance at all — thanks to the Peace of Lysias. Together with him came the new high priest Alcimus, whom he installed in his office. He then attempted to make contact with the various parties. Primarily he wanted to win Judas Maccabee over to his side or else destroy the man's power. He sent messengers to him with friendly words. The Maccabee was unwilling to trust this master who came with military force. The Hasideans, on the other hand, felt there was no basis for such mistrust, since Bacchides was accompanied by a priest from the tribe of Aaron, the high priest Alcimus. This disagreement signalled the defection of a large number of scribes and Hasideans to the party of Bacchides and Alcimus, in an effort to achieve a "just solution" to this delicate question. Alcimus assured all parties, in the most friendly words and solemn oaths, that he would do no harm. He then departed and made his camp near Beth-zait, 18 miles south of Jerusalem. From these headquarters he conducted a search among the neighboring villages for men who had "defected," that is, who had fought against the Syrians on the side of the Maccabees. There was no further talk of amnesty and peace. The Hellenistic party, whom the Syrians had now restored to power, were in a position to secure their revenge. Once again fear and terror reigned in the country. Yesterday's warriors for freedom had suddenly been cast in a very dubious light, and their very existence was threatened. Judas, the leader of the rebellion, could no longer be an idle spectator. He began his well-known guerrilla tactics once again. As in the beginning of the revolt, he became the hope of Israel. Even the pious elements of the population were forced to recognize the fact that there cannot be religious freedom without national freedom. The signal for the renewal of conflict was given by the high priest Alcimus, who called for Syrian support against the Maccabees (1 Mac 7, 1-25; 2 Mac 14, 3-11).

b. *Nicanor Day*: Despite his earlier defeat at Emmaus, the general Nicanor was entrusted with putting down the Jewish rebellion. With a considerable force of men he marched to Jerusalem (1 Mac 7, 26ff.). The objective of this campaign was to do away with Judas Maccabee and confirm Alcimus in his position (2 Mac 14, 12ff.). The Maccabees prepared for de-

fense. Their attempt to attack Nicanor along his route of approach
to Jerusalem was a failure. Simon's forces were defeated near
the village of Dessau (2 Mac 14, 16). Nicanor now attempted
to solve the Jewish problem by means of diplomacy. He even succeeded in organizing a confrontation with Judas himself. The
result was a peaceful solution to the whole problem. Nicanor dismissed his army and remained behind as Strategos, Syrian high-com-
missioner, in Jerusalem. Nicanor did nothing contrary to the
law (2 Mac 14, 19-24), and even cultivated a close relationship
with Judas, who was also free to come and go among his own
people.

The expedition had thus taken a quite different direction from
what Alcimus and the Hellenists had hoped. By their intrigue at
the royal court, they managed to have the peace treaty annulled
and orders sent to Nicanor to bring Judas back to Antioch in
chains (2 Mac 14, 26ff.). Judas soon recognized the sudden
change in the political situation and for that reason avoided what
would have been a treacherous confrontation (1 Mac 7, 29ff.),
so that once again the decision was left to arms. At Capharsalama,
some four miles north of Jerusalem, the battle took place. Nicanor
was defeated and fled into the Akra of Jerusalem (1 Mac 7, 29-
32; 2 Mac 14, 27-30). Angry at this defeat, Nicanor applied
considerable pressure on the priesthood at the Temple. He was
able to achieve the immediate delivery of Judas, on the threat that
he would otherwise have the Temple burned to the ground (1
Mac 7, 35).

Meanwhile, he assembled a new army and camped at Beth-
Horon, where a new Syrian army came to meet him. Judas had
set up his people at Adasa, five miles north of Jerusalem. On
the 13th day of Adar (March 27, 160), the hostile forces met
in battle. When Nicanor fell in the struggle, his soldiers threw
away their weapons and fled. The Jews from the surrounding
neighborhood fell upon the fleeing army, and pursued them into
the plain, as far as Gezer, capturing considerable spoils. The extent of the bitter feeling is shown by the fact that Nicanor's
head and right hand were cut off and displayed as trophies in
Jerusalem. His tongue was cut into pieces and thrown bit by bit
to the birds to be devoured (1 Mac 7, 39-50; 2 Mac 15, 1-37).

In order to perpetuate the memory of this victory, the 13th day of Adar was hereafter to be known as Nicanor Day, one day before Mordecai Day, for all time to come.

c. *The treaty with Rome*: Judas was only too well aware of the fact that Demetrius was prepared to answer the defeat of Nicanor Day with a much greater armed force. As a result, he looked about for allies. At the conclusion of a peace treaty on Xanthikus 15, the Romans had provided some assistance. Perhaps they might once more prove willing to help the people of the Jews against their common enemy, "the kingdom of the Hellenes" (1 Mac 8, 18). A Jewish embassy made its way to Rome in order to effect a treaty of friendship and alliance. The Roman senators were very interested in the battle that the Maccabees were fighting against Demetrius, and they were also prepared to enter a bilateral treaty. The wording of the document is quite in keeping with the normal outlines of alliance treaties. The direct military assistance was, however, beyond the scope of the embassy. Still, the treaty did give the Romans a juridic position from which to apply considerable diplomatic pressure upon Demetrius, a pressure, which, unfortunately came too late for the fate of Judas Maccabee, which was already sealed (1 Mac 8, 17-32).

d. *Judas' fall*: Already in the first month of the year 152 of the Temple era (April/May 160), one month after the defeat, Bacchides — and the twilight character Alcimus was once again in his retinue — was marching with a new army towards the south. He followed the ancient military route across Damascus and the sources of the Jordan to the Lake of Gennesareth. At Arbela he faced his first battles. The guerrillas had concealed themselves in the many caves from which they had to be dislodged (1 Mac 9, 1-4). This cleared the way for the march further south.

After laying siege to Jerusalem, Bacchides set up his camp at Beroea, ancient Be'erot, some 10 miles north of Jerusalem. Judas made his camp at Elasa,[16] about a mile to the southwest.

---

16. Cf. *Atlas Yisrael*, 6, IX: Elasa is not a scribal error. Elasa lay on the western edge of the settled district of modern Ramallah, while Beeroth lay on its eastern border.

Their relative positions were such that the opponents could observe each others' movements. When Judas' people saw the tremendous size of the hostile army, 20,000 foot and 2,000 horse soldiers (1 Mac 9, 4), their courage failed. It would be sheer folly to oppose such a superior force. Not even Judas, victor in so many uneven battles, could succeed in holding his army together. Only 800 brave souls stayed with him. He himself realized that the battle was useless, but nonetheless he could find no other alternative than to die heroically in battle for all his brethren (1 Mac 9, 10). He concentrated his attack on the right wing of the enemy, where general Bacchides was fighting. Contrary to all expectation, he managed to defeat the enemy whom he pursued as far as the mountains.[17] But then the left wing pivoted around and fell upon the pursuing army from the rear. "The battle became desperate, and many on both sides were wounded and fell. Judas also fell, and the rest fled" (1 Mac 9, 17ff.). He was buried in the tomb of his fathers at Modein. All Israel lamented his fall: "How is the mighty fallen, the savior of Israel" (1 Mac 9, 21). Judas Maccabee had stood up strongly for the freedom of his people. For a time it seemed as if faith and freedom would both be secured. But his tragic death spelt the end of Israel's short time of freedom. His brother and successor Jonathan, who was surnamed "the sly desert fox," had to begin all over again.

---

17. In the Greek text we have the words "as far as Azotus," the city of Ashdod which lay on the coastal plain — but this is impossible. There has been an error in the translation. Hebrew *'ašed*, plural *'ašdôt* means "abyss, precipice of a mountain." Simons, GTT 1150.

CHAPTER XVIII

JONATHAN, THE SLY DESERT FOX

THE defeat and death of Judas Maccabee meant a free hand for the Hellenistic powers. Denunciation, persecution, prison, and torture forced the Maccabees and their adherents to once again go underground. The "contemners of the law" triumphed. The high commissioner Bacchides brought the land under a strict control. In order to fill up the measure of their suffering, a severe famine broke out in this year. Even the very fields seemed to be offering resistance to the conduct of the faithless and godless rulers (1 Mac 9, 24).

Terror generally succeeds only in strengthening resistance and forcing the oppressed to make a common cause. The Maccabees chose Jonathan,[1] the brother of the fallen Judas, as the new head of the resistance movement. He was given the surname Apphus,[2] which apparently means simply "the sly one" (1 Mac 2, 5). Since he organized his resistance movement from the desert base, he can properly be referred to as "the sly desert fox."

a. *Hideout in the deserts of Judah*: When the high commis-

---

1. *Yo-natan* = Yahweh has given; cf. Theodore, Deodatus.
2. Since there are no gutturals in Greek, the Semitic form *ḥps* is probably the original: *ḥappus* = the sly one. Cf. Fr. Keil, *Kommentar über die Bücher der Makkabäer*, (1875), 58.

sioner Bacchides organized a search for the new leader of the resistance, Jonathan and his adherents had already fled into the desert of Tekoa, southeast of Bethlehem, into the very territory in which David was driven as a fugitive. The focal point of the organization, as it must necessarily be in the desert, was the oasis and ancient well of Asphar.[3] Jonathan's first move was to provide for the security of the non-combatants, the women, children, and old people, as well as the properties and possessions they had saved and brought with them. In this he was following David's example who had sent all of his people who could not take part in battle into the safety of Moab. Jonathan ordered his brother John to bring all the people and baggage into safety in the territory of the Nabateans, east of the Jordan. The caravan was, however, overcome and destroyed by the sons of Jambri in the vicinity of Madaba. John himself was killed. This led to an immediate invocation of the law of blood vengeance, or the avenging of the murder of the innocent. Jonathan did not delay long. With his people he crossed over the Jordan, attacked the unsuspecting sons of Jambri south of Madaba, at the very moment when they were setting out for a wedding festivity, and quickly avenged the innocent blood of their victims (1 Mac 9, 32-34). Just as quickly as he appeared he had once again vanished, this time in the impenetrable territory along the banks of the Jordan. Bacchides received news of the attack and marched down to the Jordan with a strong contingent, in an effort to capture the leader of the resistance. A bitter battle ensued. Bacchides was forced to withdraw. Jonathan took advantage of this favorable opportunity. He and all his soldiers abandoned all their property, swam across the Jordan, and barely managed to return in safety to their hideout in the desert of Judah.

     b. *Fortifications, hostages, and eventual peace*: In order to discourage any further Jewish uprisings, Bacchides began to strengthen the existing fortifications, and also to build new implacements, so that the province of Judea was surrounded with a tight

---

3. Modern *Khirbet bir ez-Za'faran,* 3 mi. south of Tekoa.

ring of security: Jericho in the east, the valley gateway of Emmaus, Beth-horon, and Gezer in the west, Thamnatha, Pharaton, and Tephon in the northern mountain country,[4] and, to the south, the absolutely impregnable fortress of Beth-zur. In Jerusalem itself, the stronghold of Akra still dominated the city (1 Mac 9, 50-53). In addition, the high commissioner had some of the leading Jews arrested and kept as hostages in the Akra, in order to make any further revolution impossible from the outset. In this he was enthusiastically supported by the high priest Alcimus, who even agreed to tearing down the walls of the inner Temple court, so that not even this holy sanctuary could provide a basis for resistance. It was on this occasion that he became so excited that he suffered a severe stroke and died. This happened in the 2nd month of the year 153 of the Temple Era (May, 159). After Alcimus' death, Bacchides returned to the court at Antioch. The land enjoyed two years of peace (1 Mac 9, 57). But Jonathan did not let this peaceful interlude go by without profit.

He reacted to Bacchides' arrests by counter-arrests of his own. He captured 50 men who were "leaders in this treachery" (1 Mac 9, 61), and had them executed. He answered the fortifications with the construction of a stronghold in the desert, at Bet-Bessei [5] southeast of Bethlehem along the border of the desert. When the high commissioner Bacchides, upon his return to Palestine, attempted to capture this fort and actually attacked it with his siege machines, he suffered such great losses that he was forced to withdraw without accomplishing anything. The sly Jonathan seized this opportunity to make an offer of peace. Bacchides, who finally wanted to have peace, acquiesced. Jonathan was offered a personal safe conduct, and the prisoners were released on both sides. After this pacification of the country, Bacchides left Judea and once more returned to the court at Antioch. Jonathan left the desert of Judah and established his residence

---

4. The three places were already in the territory of Samaria, Simons GTT §1160.
5. In the Wadi Umm el-Kal'ah, "valley of the fortress"; the ancient history survives in the name.

at Michmash, north of Jerusalem. The land enjoyed peace. In the five years of peace that followed, Jonathan cleverly and prudently reinforced his position so that he would be prepared to seize the opportunity whenever it was presented.

c. *The rebel becomes high priest*: The fact that the Jewish people were able to achieve their national independence is owing to the situation of world politics and the disunity among the enemy and, in considerable measure, to the clever political tactics of Jonathan who understood how to achieve the most improbable results in every situation.

In the year 160 of the Seleucid era (153/52) there was another revolution in Syria.[6] The power behind the scene lay in Asia Minor. Attalus II, who felt himself threatened by the foreign policy of the Syrian Demetrius who was certainly an energetic but ruthless king, attempted to threaten his adversary's position by sending Alexander Balas,[7] a man of unknown origin, into his country as pretender to the throne. Balas landed in Ptolemais and assembled an army. From here he meant to march directly upon the capital. Now both kings — since the throne of the one was not established and the throne of the other was no longer secure — began to court the good favor of the former rebel Jonathan. This would presuppose the fact that Jonathan already had a considerable military force at his command.

The first move was made by Demetrius who needed military force to oppose his rival who had already landed on the Palestinian coast. He offered Jonathan a treaty of friendship and promised to deliver the hostages if he would offer his forces as *symmachos,* ally. Jonathan did not refuse. He left Michmash for Jerusalem; the hostages were freed; the army was mustered up. The Syrian garrison in the Akra, by and large, simply abandoned their positions. Jonathan had Mount Zion refortified. He thus became master of Jerusalem.

---

6. C. Bradford Welles, *Die hellenistische Welt, zerbröchelnde Dynastien,* PropWG III, 500ff.
7. Probably a Semitic name, Balas derived from *ba'al,* "he who is favored by Baal."

It was now the counter-king's turn to make his move. Alexander Balas made a much more attractive offer than Demetrius had made. In a letter he speaks to Jonathan as "his brother"; he named him high priest and sent him a purple robe and a golden crown. Once again Jonathan was not unwilling. In the 7th month of the year 160 of the Temple Era (October/November, 152), on the occasion of the Festival of Huts, Jonathan functioned for the first time as high priest. Now he turned in earnest to the task of preparing for what lay ahead.

Demetrius, having thus been outbid, tried a countermove which, however, did not find favor with Jonathan. Jonathan had cast in his lot with the younger man, Alexander Balas, and was about to reap the advantages of his cunning. Demetrius lost both the battle and his life. Balas secured his throne by a marriage with Cleopatra, the daughter of Ptolemy VI, whose surname was Thea, "goddess." The marriage took place in the year 162 of the Seleucid era (151/50) in the harbor city of Ptolemais. Even the high priest Jonathan was invited. For him, this marriage meant an important elevation in rank and power. Balas named him *strategos* and *meridarches,* that is, the highest civil and military position in the governorship of Judea. Jonathan was the only real winner in the Syrian struggle for the throne. Balas proved to be an incompetent ruler; after three years his throne was tottering.

d. *The double crown over Egypt and Asia*: In the midst of the warring dynasties, the promise of a united kingdom of Egypt and Syria suddenly flared up, only to sink as rapidly as it had appeared. The adherents of the defeated Demetrius would not rest content without proclaiming his son Demetrius II as legitimate successor to the throne. With the help of mercenaries hired from Crete, he established a foothold in Northern Syria. As his ally in the struggle he had Apollonius, the governor of Coele-Syria, the great southern province to which Judea also belonged. For Apollonius, the old friend and advisor of the former king Demetrius, it seemed an opportune moment to reckon with the crafty Jonathan who had gone over to the rival king. This time

Jonathan did not change coats. He remained faithful to Balas, primarily because Balas was being supported by his Egyptian father-in-law and he must have felt that the Jewish cause would be better advanced by an incompetent ruler on the throne of Syria than a resourceful pretender to that throne.

Jonathan now seized the initiative. He marched to Joppe, where a contingent of Apollonius' forces was stationed, and forced the citizens to surrender the city. Apollonius then made his way into the coastal plain with a strong army. He passed by Joppe unharmed; his objective was to develop an extensive campaign in the plain country and he marched as far as Azotus (Ashdod). Jonathan followed him with his army. The two met in an extremely bitter encounter. Jonathan would have fallen victim to an ambuscade had not his brother Simon appeared in the nick of time with a second army and thus secured the victory. Azotus and all the neighboring cities were burned to the ground. Ascalon was taken without a struggle. Jonathan returned victorious to Jerusalem. In recognition of his services, Alexander Balas sent him a golden brooch and delivered the city of Accaron into his personal possession (1 Mac 10, 67-89).

Now, finally, the Egyptian father-in-law Ptolemy VI Philopator appeared with his army; not primarily in order to support the tottering throne of his son-in-law Balas, but rather to take the crown of Asia for himself. At his approach along the Palestinian coastal plain, the cities all opened their gates to him; as he continued his march, he regularly left Egyptian contingents in the cities at his rear. Jonathan marched to meet the Egyptian, with great pomp and circumstance, at Joppe, and escorted him as far as the Eleutheros River, which formed the boundary of Coele-Syria.[8] He then returned to Jerusalem, to await the further development of this struggle for power.

Ptolemy made his way as far as Seleucia, the harbor city of Antioch, without encountering any resistance. Here he was met by his daughter Cleopatra, who was betrothed to Balas. Now the Egyptian dropped his mask. He declared himself Balas'

---

8. *Nahr el-kebir*, the great brook, north of Tripolis (*tarablus*).

enemy and now offered his "divine" daughter as wife to Demetrius. Balas was forced to flee from Antioch. In Cilicia he assembled an army with which he marched against the capital. On the plain before Antioch there was a battle which ended in victory for Ptolemy. Balas fled to the Arabs, by whom he was murdered. Ptolemy entered into Antioch and placed the crown of Asia upon his head. "He thus wore two crowns, the crown of Egypt and the crown of Asia" (1 Mac 11, 13). But three days later he died of the wounds he had suffered in the battle. Now the way was once again free for Demetrius, the Seleucid. The double crown had been broken. The Egyptian garrisons were driven from the cities. In the year 167 of the Seleucid Era (146/45) Demetrius II Nikator became king (145-138).

Once again the crafty Jonathan was the real winner. It is true that Demetrius had a firm grip upon the reins of government, but he preferred to have the powerful Jonathan for his friend rather than his adversary. Jonathan had taken advantage of the confusion of the times to lay siege to the Syrian citadel of Akra in Jerusalem, in an effort to be rid once and for all of this thorn in his flesh. Then Demetrius made his appearance in Ptolemais, demanded the immediate cessation of the siege, and invited Jonathan to explain his activities. Jonathan dared to make the extremely risky journey to Ptolemais. Not only was he confirmed in his position as high priest, Strategos, and Meridarch; the three territories of Ephraim, Lydda, and Ramathaim were taken from the province of Samaria and joined to Judea. What is more, he was also granted tax indemnity on a grand scale. In recognition of these privileges, Jonathan had to pay 300 talents (1 Mac 11, 20-37).

e. *Maccabean auxiliaries and the tottering throne*: When Demetrius felt himself firmly enough established in his position of power, he began building his army. His first step was to release all the veteran troops. This proved to be his undoing. The army revolted. Demetrius found himself in a desperate position. He turned to Jonathan for help. Jonathan demanded, as a condition of his assistance, the definitive withdrawal of the Syrian garrison in Jerusalem. The promise was made. Jonathan thereupon marched to Antioch with a Jewish auxiliary corps of 3,000 men. The city was in a state of uproar. There was revolution: the streets were barred, the king was besieged in his palace. The Judaean troops fought to free him. After the king had been rescued and peace restored, the auxiliary corps was called back to Jerusalem. But now that Demetrius was restored to power, he had no further memory of his promises. This was a sign to Jonathan that there was no further hope from Syrian assistance. A political change of course was clearly directed (1 Mac 11, 38-52).

Demetrius' adversary was not idle. Tryphon had been active in Chalcis, in the neighborhood of Aleppo, where he proclaimed Antiochus VI Dionysos, the little son of the fallen Balas, as legitimate successor to the throne, and himself as administrator of the government. The soldiers who had been dismissed by Demetrius joined his party. At the approach of this counter-king, Demetrius abandoned his capital and withdrew to the harbor city of Seleucia. From here he could maintain control over the whole coast. But once again the fate of the Syrian dynasties was dependent upon the political position of the Jewish high priest. Demetrius had proved false, while Tryphon was lavish in his gifts. He confirmed Jonathan as high priest, gave him the title "friend of the king," promised to increase the territorial possessions of Judea by the addition of yet a third district, Acrabattene, and finally named Jonathan's brother Simon as strategos of the Eparchy of Paralaia, the whole of the coastal territories. Jonathan decided in favor of Tryphon and now intervened with considerable energy in the struggle for the Syrian throne.

Jonathan was thus practically the supreme ruler over the ancient province of Abarnahara, Transeuphratania (1 Mac 11, 60). It was here that he was to establish the authority of the new regime. After a few preliminary campaigns along the coastal territories, against Ascalon and Gaza, he turned back to Damascus and assembled a considerable force. But Demetrius' generals were not idle. They had occupied Upper Galilee and taken a position near Cades. Jonathan concentrated his army along the Lake of Gennesareth. From there he marched to the north as far as Hazor. Here he suddenly found himself confronted by the enemy. The battle was extremely hard. Only the personal valor of Jonathan achieved the victory. The enemy was thrown back, the camp at Cades captured, and the army severely beaten (1 Mac 11, 67-74). But Demetrius did not consider his crown lost. Though the invasion of the south had failed, he made a second attempt towards the north, in the country of Hamath. At the approach of Jonathan, however, the army disbanded without a fight (1 Mac 12, 24-30).

The Maccabeans thus controlled the entire territory of Coele-Syria, from the boundary of Egypt to the Eleutheros River. Tryphon still held the capital city of Antioch under occupation, but Demetrius was the recognized master along the Syrian coast and in Upper Asia, insofar as these territories had not yet been overrun by the Parthians. It was to the east that Demetrius felt he still had another chance.

f. *The empire of the Parthians*: Antiochus III the Great had succeeded, in his now famous Anabasis, in renewing the kingdom of Alexander the Great in Upper Asia. But even under Epiphanes this situation had completely changed. He was forced to wage a series of defensive struggles along the eastern boundary of his kingdom, a venture in which he lost his own life. The focus of the unrest lay in Inner Asia. It was from here that the Huns were exerting tremendous pressure not only upon the Chinese Empire in the distant east, but also along the steppe-dwellers of the west, and they in turn were forced to give way. Once the stone was set in motion, it continued to roll inevitably and devastatingly across the face of the Ancient Near East.

"It is against this violent transformation of the political situation in the east that the Parthian conquest suddenly bursts. After a series of battles in easten Iran, Mithradates I, relying upon the brilliant discipline of his cavalry troops, fought an extremely successful campaign. With the exception of the middle and lower Indus Valley, where Hellenistic sovereignty continued to assert itself for a few decades more, the whole of eastern Iran and northwestern India fell to the armies of the victorious allies. The Hellenistic cities of the coast, as far as the frontiers of India, were forced to recognize Parthian sovereignty. Mithradates had thus almost duplicated the frontiers of the great kingdom of the Achaemenids. He accordingly took for himself the glorious title of 'great king of kings' which had not been used since the destruction of the Persian Empire. On the basis of new numismatic inscriptions, it has been established that the conquest of the east took place between the years 150 and 145." [9]

When Demetrius II, in the year 172 of the Seleucid Era (141/40), assembled his forces for a campaign into Media, he did so not only in an attempt to score a military defeat against his rival Tryphon, but even more so in an attempt to recover what was already a lost heritage. Shortly before this time, the Parthian advance had reached the territory of Mesopotamia. In the spring of 141, the capital city of Seleucia on the Tigris had fallen and shortly after that Susa. Mithradates I (171-139/37), proudly took the title of Basileus Megas Arsakes Soter (Great King Arsakes, the Savior). In the midst of this triumphal journey, he was overtaken, in December of 141, with the news of an invasion of the steppe-dwellers in the territory of Turkmen, which served as an open gate from Inner Asia. He was forced to commit all his military strength to the threatened northeastern frontier. This was Demetrius' ideal opportunity to launch a counter-offensive. "In this endeavor he counted on the support of the strongly Hellenized population of Babylonia and the sympathies of the Hellenistic ethnic groups in eastern Iran, Bactria, and India, who all looked upon this as the ideal moment to shake off the yoke of Parthia. Demetrius enjoyed successes in a series of several battles, and penetrated deep into Media (1 Mac 14, 2). But then he was defeated in a decisive battle by the general of Mithradates, and taken prisoner (140/39).[10] The commander brought him before Arsakes (1 Mac 14, 3), that is, Mithradates, since all the kings of the Parthians called themselves Arsakids after their family hereditary estate in Arsaka. In order to demonstrate the futility of any further resistance, Demetrius was locked up in a cage and put on public display throughout the conquered territories of his kingdom. Finally, the victor granted him a residence in Hyrcania, gave him his daughter in marriage, and thereafter treated him as an honored prisoner. After ten years'

---

9. E. Kornemann, *Weltgeschichte des Mittelmeerraumes*, I, 324.
10. *Ibid.*, 325.

captivity, Demetrius succeeded in regaining his freedom, and in fact he once again ascended to the tottering throne of the Seleucids in Antioch (129-125). It cannot be denied that there is a certain tragic grandeur about this figure; his adversary Tryphon, on the other hand, stands out as an unprincipled upstart who treads on corpses in his battle for power.

g. *Caught in the snare*: Jonathan had declared himself for Antiochus V, the child, in his struggle for the throne, since the least threat and the greatest advantage for his kingdom seemed to lie with this side of the conflict. With the help of his brother Simon he had asserted the claims of the new king in the territories of Coele-Syria which were subject to his control. Jerusalem was fortified stronger than ever before (1 Mac 12, 36). In order to eliminate any future threat from the citadel of Akra, Jonathan had a dividing wall raised between the Akra and the city.[11] Simon, meantime, was building a new fortification at Adida, not far from Lydda in the low country.[12] While Demetrius II was occupied in the east with the Parthian war, his adversary Tryphon, in Antioch, was planning to place the crown of Asia on his own head and do away with the child Antiochus (1 Mac 12, 39). Since he was not certain whether the powerful Jonathan would be willing to go along with this coup, he was determined to do away with him as well. With a considerable military force he marched into Palestine. Jonathan also prepared his army. The two forces met at Beth-shan (Scythopolis). Tryphon, defeated, was unwilling to risk a further confrontation; he persuaded Jonathan to dismiss the greater part of his troops and to return to Ptolemais with him, with only a small guard. Jonathan, the clever

---

11. The precise course of the walls is no longer discoverable, since the name of the site cannot be clearly interpreted. "He repaired the section called Chaphenatha" (1 Mac 12, 37) — obviously a destroyed quarter of the city was being restored. According to Dalman, *Grammatik des jüdisch-palästinischen Aramäisch*, (1960), 54, N. 6, Chaphenatha means "the doubled," hence the quarter that lay between the double walls; but which walls are meant can no longer be determined. Simons, *Jerusalem in the OT*, 155ff.

12. Simons, GTT §1189.

desert fox, walked unsuspectingly into the trap. Hardly had he passed through the city gate than the doors were closed behind him. He was a prisoner. Fear and apprehension seized upon the Jews. The rumor was spreading that Jonathan, their prince and liberator, had already been murdered. In the territories of mixed ethnic settlements, the hatred against the Jews once again broke out in a series of violent pogroms (1 Mac 12, 39-53).

In this hour of national crisis, Simon, the last of the surviving Maccabee brothers, undertook the leadership of his country's resistance forces. Tryphon exerted considerable pressure upon him. He had him informed that Jonathan was still alive, and he demanded money and hostages. Simon was willing to give him both, although he well knew that the unprincipled Tryphon would still refuse to set Jonathan free. Instead of liberation and peace, what actually occurred was a massive attack upon Judea. Tryphon made his way through Adora, 5 miles south of Hebron, and marched towards Jerusalem. His army was met by such a strong snowfall that further military operations in the mountain country were quite impossible. Tryphon sounded the retreat. In Bascama,[13] the ancient harbor of Haifa, he got rid of Jonathan before he boarded ship for Antioch. Jonathan's body was buried in the monument of his fathers at Modein (1 Mac 13, 1-30).

Upon his arrival in Antioch, Tryphon carried out his long-planned murder of the king. He quickly got rid of Antiochus V, the child, and put the "crown of Asia" on his own head (1 Mac 13, 32), and claimed for himself the title of autocrator, "ruler in his own right." This forceful seizure of power did not give the Seleucid Empire the peace it so desperately needed in order to ward off the Parthians in the east and the Romans in the west; it meant only a new struggle for power and new revolution. For Simon Maccabee, however, the time had finally come to reap the fruit of so many battles and so much suffering. From the crumbling Seleucid Empire, the Judaean state gradually broke loose into an autonomous and independent political entity.

---

13. An error for be-Saqma = in Sakma, that is, Sykaminos, near Haifa.

CHAPTER XIX

FREE FROM THE YOKE OF THE PAGANS

1) SIMON MACCABEE, "HIGH PRIEST, GENERAL, AND RULER"

AFTER Tryphon's seizure of power in Antioch, Simon turned to Demetrius II, who was still ruling in the east, and for whom the change of direction in Jerusalem politics came at a most opportune time. He was not sparing in his promises and concessions. He declared himself ready to grant perpetual peace and to renounce all taxes and gifts to the crown. Judea was thus freed of the administration of the Seleucid Empire and practically independent. The royal power insisted only on the recognition of a general suzerainty.

This decisive event was marked by a new era of chronology. The year 170, the year in which the yoke of the pagans was finally taken from the necks of the Jews, is also "the first year of Simon, the high priest, the general and commander" (ἀρχιερεὺς μεγάλος, στρατηγός, ἡγούμενος). Since this system of reckoning is also based on the Temple era, the first year of Jewish freedom would coincide with the time from spring 142 to spring 141 B.C.; Simon thus united the highest religious, military, and civil powers in his own person.

As strategos, he succeeded in removing the final remnants of Syrian military power from Jerusalem. The hither-to impregnable fortress of the Akra was finally occupied and transformed into the residence of the Maccabees. The day on which the citadel was occupied, the 23rd day of the 2nd month of the year 171 of the Temple era (June 3, 141), was long celebrated as a national holiday. Simon's next move was to secure the route to the harbor city of Joppe. He laid siege to the fortress of Gezer, expelled the pagan population, and settled Jews in their place. This extremely important strategical point along the highway leading from the mountain country to the coastal plain was thus definitely in his power. As commandant he set up his son John Hyrcanus (1 Mac 13, 41-53). The great era of peace had begun. "Each man sat under his vine and his fig tree, and there was none to make them afraid. No one was left in the land to fight them, and the kings were crushed in those days. He strengthened all the humble of his people; he sought out the law, and did away with every lawless and wicked man, he made the sanctuary glorious, and added to the vessels of the sanctuary" (1 Mac 14, 12-15).

In the Hellenistic cities it was customary to compose inscriptions in honor of important men and place them in public locations. By decree of the popular assembly of Elul 18, 172 of the Temple era (Sept. 13, 140), the 3rd year of Simon's rule, bronze tablets containing the mighty deeds of Simon were set up in the Temple precinct (1 Mac 14, 25-49). As high priest, general, and prince of his people, Simon held a combined power in his hands which needed only the royal title to be complete. What made the popular assembly's decree so different was the fact that Simon was granted the dignity of high priest, commander-in-chief, and ethnarch "forever," and the office was declared to be hereditary. A new high-priestly and princely dynasty was thus established, the Hasmoneans.[1] In order to provide some foreign political cover for his still tottering throne, Simon renewed the treaties with Rome and Sparta (1 Mac 14, 16-24).

---

1. Named after the family ancestor ḥašmon, Schürer, GJV I, 249.

2) WAR WITH ANTIOCHUS VII SIDETES

After Demetrius II had fallen into Parthian control as a prisoner, his wife Cleopatra Thea attempted to save what could still be saved. She appealed to her husband's brother, the young Antiochus VII Sidetes, who lived on the Isle of Rhodes. She offered him not only the crown, but also her hand, and this would have been the third marriage for "the divine one." From Rhodes, Sidetes organized a war against Tryphon. He too sought the favor of the Jewish prince and high priest Simon. He was not sparing in his promises. The former tax indemnities were all to be reconfirmed, and he held out, as further consideration, the right of striking his own coinage. Simon was thus determined to assist him in his battle against Tryphon.

In the year 174 of the Seleucid era (139/38) Antiochus Sidetes landed at the harbor city of Seleucia, where a part of the troops that had defected from Tryphon joined his banner. Tryphon could not maintain his position in the capital, but fled directly into the Palestinian harbor city of Dora. Antiochus pursued him and laid siege to Dora by both land and sea. The high priest Simon had sent an auxiliary corps of 2,000 men. But Antiochus felt himself already strong enough and brusquely rejected the Jewish support. He was apparently unwilling to recognize the peace treaty which had been granted by his brother Demetrius. The liberation of the Akra from the Syrian garrison, the siege of the fortresses of Joppe and Gezer he considered as a breach of peace. He thus sent Athenobios with an ultimatum to Jerusalem (1 Mac 15, 25-31). Simon gave what was the classic answer for the Zionism of his day: "We have neither taken foreign land nor seized foreign property, but only the inheritance of our fathers, which at one time had been unjustly taken by our enemies" (1 Mac 15, 33). Simon was, however, willing to pay 300 talents as indemnification for the three fortresses. Athenobios refused an answer, but stormed out of Jerusalem. Once again, the decision lay with military force.

Tryphon had meantime succeeded in breaking through the ring of besieging forces and making good his flight. Antiochus VII undertook his pursuit and entrusted the control of the Jewish problem to his general Cendebaeus. He assembled his forces against the fortified city of Cedron (Qatrah), 4 miles southwest of Jamnia. John Hyrcanus, the commander of the fortress of Gezer, turned to his father Simon in Jerusalem. Together they set out on the campaign. The army marched along the ancient route across Beth-horon into the coastal plain. The army camped at Modein. The next day, the forces were deployed near the fortress of Gezer, which is only 11 miles from Cedron. The battle which developed at the Wadi Qatrah, was a bitter struggle. By dint of supreme effort and valor, it was once again a typical Maccabean victory (1 Mac 15, 37 — 16, 10).

Simon had little opportunity to enjoy his success. For the first time we note the horrible spectre of murder within the family, an infection which was later to bring the Hasmonean dynasty to the verge of destruction. Simon's son-in-law, Ptolemy Ben-Abu, commandant of the territory of Jericho, invited his father-in-law to a banquet in the fortress city of Dok,[2] and had him murdered during the course of the dinner. The famous man thus met a most ignominious death. This happened in the 11th month of the year 177 of the Temple era (January/February, 134). Now the murderer courted the help of the Syrian king Antiochus VII Sidetes. He hoped in this way to seize the power for himself. In Jerusalem, however, Simon's son John Hyrcanus made a most energetic effort to recover his father's heritage. The battle for national independence had just been finished. But here the narrative of the Books of Maccabees breaks off, and we must turn to Flavius Josephus for the further course of profane history.

---

2. The name is derived from *dayek* = point of observation; apparently situated on the heights of Gebel Kuruntul. Simons, GTT §1201.

CHAPTER XX

THE ROMAN EAGLE IN THE ORIENT

THE Maccabees had turned with hope to the western skies, looking for help from the Roman eagle. The Seleucids, on the other hand, had collapsed when they felt the shadow of his wings. Rome is the mysterious power which stands in the background of the Books of the Maccabees. It could now be only a matter of time before the Seleucid empire would be liquidated and the new free state of the Jews, still tottering on its shaky foundations, would pass from Hasmonean control and be incorporated into the territories of the Roman Empire.

A) THE LIQUIDATION OF THE SELEUCID EMPIRE [1]

Antiochus VII Sidetes (139-129) was the last competent ruler from the Seleucid dynasty. He was the energetic adversary of the high priest Simon. It was his constant effort to reduce the liberties won in battle by the Maccabees, and to make Judah once again dependent upon the Syrian Empire. After the defeat of Cendebaeus, he set out against Judea with a considerable force; he cut Jerusalem off and began a formal siege. Famine was already beginning to claim the invested city. Then Antiochus VII declared

---

1. C. Bradford Welles, PropWG III, 511.

himself ready for a compromise. John Hyrcanus would have to make a considerable payment for the territories conquered by his father; he would have to surrender his weapons and deliver hostages.[2] The Maccabean dream of complete independence seemed once again to have been an idle hope.

Sidetes developed a very deliberate offensive policy against the Parthians in the east as well. He reorganized the military power of his kingdom and, in the year 129, after considerable preparation, began his far-reaching campaign against the east. He was, however, attacked by the Parthians in his winter quarters, where he was defeated and taken prisoner. The Parthians had freed their captive Demetrius, so that he, as counter-king, would force his brother to a contest for the rule. After the death of his brother, Demetrius II reigned for a few years on the Syrian throne (died 126). He was followed by the notorious Cleopatra Thea, who had coins struck in her own name. After she had poisoned her own son, she was poisoned in her turn by another son, who then became king as Antiochus VIII Grypos.

During the next few generations, the fates of the Seleucids are intimately bound up with those of the Ptolemies in Egypt. But there was no one hand strong enough to regroup the crumbling heritage of Alexander the Great. Rival claimants to the throne invited foreign powers to direct intervention. All these Syrian and Egyptian rulers found followers and adherents only in narrow local circles, and their constantly changing fates make the history of their struggle for power into an unpredictable seesaw. The Seleucid rule now extended only to Syria. The Parthians had advanced their control as far as the Euphrates. In Syria proper, one city after another asserted its independence. The eastern steppe country passed under the control of the Nabatean Arabs. The remaining Seleucids were too numerous, too weak, and too inclined towards internal strife to ever successfully oppose the rampant decay of the dynasty. Between 83 and 69, the Syrian throne was in the hands of Tigranes of Armenia, while the Seleucid princes ruled over a few individual cities or simply spent their

2. Flavius Josephus, Ant. XIII, 8, 2-3.

lives idly in exile. When Pompey marched into Syria in 64 he wisely refused to recognize Antiochus VIII as king; he felt that if he did so, the country would fall victim to the attacks of the Parthians, Jews, and Arabs. Although the rest of his efforts were directed towards a new distribution of the eastern boundaries, with several vassal kings, he felt that Syria could be made to serve a useful purpose only under the administration of a Roman governor. Roman Pompey had to come, to impose the Pax Romana upon a war-torn East.[3]

B) THE SPLENDOR AND DECAY OF THE HASMONEAN DYNASTY

After the death of Antiochus VII on the battlefields of Parthia, and the inner decay of the Ptolemaic and Seleucid ruling houses, Palestine enjoyed the classic possibility of an autonomous empire, just as it had under the glorious days of Solomon and David. So long as there were powerful rulers at the helm, along the Nile or between the two rivers, the middle of the Fertile Crescent could not be free to develop an autonomous rule. But when the giants along the rivers slumbered, the hour had come for Israel's freedom and her fullest development.

1) JOHN HYRCANUS I (134-104)

The Policy of Conquest

After the campaign against Parthia which had proved so disastrous for the Syrians, John Hyrcanus had a free hand in Palestine. He immediately did away with the payments to the crown demanded by Antiochus VII, and began a deliberate policy of strengthening his country from within and enlarging it by means of new conquests. His first campaign led him into Transjordania where, after six months of siege, he forced the city of Madaba. Particularly hard in its consequences was his battle against the Samaritans, which ended with the destruction of the

---

3. Welles, l. c. 512f.

temple on Mount Gerizim. The already existing rift between Judaean and Samaritan was only widened.[4] For the political development of the last centuries before Christ, the incorporation of Idumaea into the Jewish state is of far-reaching significance. After the conquest of the cities of Adora and Marisa, the Idumaeans were forced to adopt the rite of circumcision and the Jewish law. The most important scion of these forcibly Judaized Idumaeans was Herod the Great, who was destined to extirpate the Hasmonean dynasty.

The Maccabean revolt movement had begun under the auspices of religion. The Hyrcanian wars of conquest also exhibit some religious characteristics —annihilation of the schismatic Samaritans, forcible Judaization of the Idumaeans — but they were no longer waged in the fervor of the religiously inspired Hasideans.

The 30-year reign of Hyrcanus seems, judging from the sparse sources available, to have been extremely peaceful. He had coins struck with this inscription: "Johannan, the high priest, and the people of the Jews" or "Johannan, the high priest, the head of the Jewish community." This would appear to show that he thought of himself primarily as a high priest. The community that was thus beginning to assert its independence from the control of the Seleucid Empire was thus a priestly state. Religion and state were identical.

But this united front had several seams. The Hasideans, faithful to the covenant, had given their unqualified approval, support, and assistance to the Maccabean revolt and its attempt to recover religious freedom, while Hyrcanus' rule shows over and over again that these elements were not sympathetic with many of the measures advocated by the priestly princes. The priestly power had come more and more under the influence of secular considerations. Within the structure of the Hasideans, in this era, we find the thoroughly organized religious community of the

---

4. Cf. Jn 4, 9: The Jews and Samaritans do not associate with each other. The Samaritans' ancestors worshipped on Mt. Gerizim.

Pharisees.[5] The tension with the ruling house gradually became so strong that a rupture seemed inevitable. The real tragedy of the situation lies in the fact that the Maccabean John Hyrcanus gradually turned away from the circles who were faithful to the covenant, the men who had supported the revolt movement, and sought support more and more from the side of the ancient priestly circle and pro-Hellenistic circles. The extreme pro-Hellenes had gone so far, at the time of Epiphanes, that they were prepared to completely Hellenize the Temple and the Law. These elements had been completely done away with by the Maccabees. The moderate Hellenists, however, were continually agitating for a greater cultural contact with the world about them, although they agreed to hold to the basic framework of the Mosaic law. These counted primarily the leading priestly circles, especially the descendants of the high priestly family of Zadoc, from whom they derive their surname of Sadducees. The secular-ized Maccabees turned to these more open-minded circles for a more ready acceptance of their domestic and foreign policies than they could hope to achieve from the strictly orthodox Hasi-deans and Pharisees.[6]

The scrolls of Qumran on the Dead Sea add one important note to this picture. One branch of the "sons of Zadoc" cast their lot neither with the secularized policy of the Sadducean priestly nobility nor with the Maccabean princes; they withdrew into the wilderness in order to prepare the way of the Lord there, to renew the covenant and to create a new Israel. They threw in their lot with the community of the new, or better, the renewed covenant. The beginnings of the great community structure of Qumran go back into the days of Hyrcanus.[7]

Politically, Hyrcanus was successful. He has a place among those who increased the empire. East of the Dead Sea he acquired

---

5. On the Pharisees, cf. Schürer II, 447ff. — J. Jeremias, *Jerusalem zur Zeit Jesu*, II (1958), 115-140.
6. Schürer, GJV I, 256-273.
7. A whole literature has sprung up on the subject of Qumran. For a summary and bibliography, cf. my article: *Ausgrabungen und Höhlen-funde am Toten Meer*, WiWe (1957), 28-43.

the territory of Madaba; Samaria and Idumaea were also incorporated, access to the Western Sea was secured, and complete independence from Syria was won by warfare. "Hyrcanus thus created a Jewish state, on a scale that had not been realized since the collapse of the kingdom of the ten tribes, in fact, since the split of the kingdom after Solomon's death." [8]

2) ARISTOBULUS I, THE KING (103/4)

In the person of Aristobulus we note the first clear evidence of those tyrannical characteristics which caused the destruction of the Seleucids and the Ptolemies. In his battle for power there was no means from which he shrank. Hyrcanus had left five sons. The rule was to pass over to his widow, while Aristobulus was to function as high priest. But he was not content with this. He had his mother cast into prison and starved to death; he himself then undertook the sole rule. He had all his other brothers put aside. Antigonus, whose interests in the throne he had first preserved, he later ordered to be murdered by the guard.

This whole family tragedy casts the character of Aristobulus in a rather dark light. It is simply his interest in the rule which animates his whole activity. He was thus the first of the Hasmoneans to claim the royal title, a title which his successors all proudly bear until the advent of the Roman legions.

In his foreign policies, he continued the policy of conquest inaugurated by his father. After his successful battles against the Itureans on Lebanon, the most important accomplishment of his short reign was the conquest and Judaization of Galilee.[9] The acquisition of new territory for settlement set loose a large-scale migration from the traditional Jewish territories. In the course of this migration one branch of the family of David may well have made its way from Bethlehem to Nazareth in Galilee.

In the tradition of the Pharisees, the picture of Aristobulus I is cast in the dimmest possible light. The pagan authors [10] paint

---

8. Schürer, GJV I, 256-273.
9. Schürer, GJV II, 6ff.
10. Flavius Josephus, *Strabo*, Ant. XIII, 11, 3.

a more favorable picture. It may well be that political propaganda has disfigured the truth of the situation. But at all events, this state of confusion in the records only demonstrates how vigorously contested are the merits and accomplishments of this first king from the house of the Hasmoneans.

3) ALEXANDER JANNAEUS, THE "SACRILEGIOUS PRIEST"
(103-76)

After the death of Aristobulus, his wife Salome-Alexandra had the imprisoned brothers released from custody, and raised the eldest of them, Alexander Jannaeus, to the dignity of king and high priest. The 27 years of Jannaeus' rule were filled with a constant series of domestic and foreign wars, most of which resulted from deliberately picking a quarrel. Jannaeus at first attempted to incorporate the harbor city of Ptolemais into his empire. This led to an unsuccessful war with Egypt. It is owing to the rivalries of the Ptolemies among themselves that the Egyptians were forced to withdraw their troops and Jannaeus remained master in his country even after losing an important battle.[11] In his further military campaigns, he succeeded in conquering the entire sea coast, from the Egyptian frontier as far as Carmel, with the exception of Ascalon. Transjordania, from the Dead Sea as far as the Lake of Merom, in the north, he brought under his sway. He thus partially surpassed the territorial extension of the glorious kingdom of David and Solomon. The glory of the past seemed to have returned.

But this new kingdom, built by the power of the sword, had no interior cohesion. The resistance of the religious forces grew stronger and stronger. "It must have been the occasion of considerable anguish for the pious Jews to see how a wild man of war like Alexander Jannaeus saw to the services in the sanctuary. He certainly was not bothered by that painstaking ob-

---

11. Ch. C. Torrey, *Alexander Jannaeus and the Archangel Michael*, VT 4 (1954), 208-211. The rescue, seen as a miracle, was attributed to the Archangel Michael. Cf. Henoch 90, 13-16; and the vision of the "ram" in Henoch 85-90.

servance of all the provisions which the Pharisees regarded as divine. It was on the occasion of his priestly functioning that the first open rebellion is supposed to have taken place. On the Feast of the Huts, where the participants in the ritual observance each carried a palm branch (*lulab*) and a lemon (*'etrog*) as a festival bouquet, Alexander, standing at the altar to offer sacrifice, was actually pelted with lemons by the assembled populace." [12] Jannaeus attempted to break this resistance with a brutal show of violence. For six years he fought with foreign mercenaries against his own people. No less than 50,000 Jews are said to have met their death during this period of domestic war.

During this time of crisis, the Pharisees even turned to the hated Syrian kings for help. Demetrius made his way into Palestine at the head of an army. A part of those forces which had once borne the burden of the Maccabean revolt joined with him. The battle took place at Shechem. Jannaeus was defeated and forced to flee into the mountains. This opened many peoples' eyes. They preferred to live under a Maccabean prince than once again under a Seleucid king. 6,000 men went over to Jannaeus, so that Demetrius was forced to withdraw back to Syria. Jannaeus gave full vent to his revenge. 800 prisoners were crucified, while their children and wives were slaughtered before their eyes. His opponents in Jerusalem were seized by such a state of terror that they all — 8,000 of them — fled during the night.

The Seleucid empire was already in its final agony, but a new threat to the Jewish state was forming in the newly rising kingdom of the Nabateans. In the battle which flared up between the Syrians and the Nabateans, the Syrian Antiochus VIII wanted to march through the Palestinian coastal plain, in order to be in a position to attack the Nabateans in the south. Jannaeus did not agree with this policy. He threw up a ditch and earthworks between Joppe and Capharsaba, and further strengthened it with wooden towers. Antiochus VIII had them burnt to the ground and, forcing his way over the wall, continued his march to the south, where he met his death in battle with the Nabateans. The whole campaign was an utter failure.

---

12. Schürer, GJV I, 280f.

The warlike high priest met his death on the occasion of the siege of the fortress city of Ragaba in Transjordania. His body was transported back to Jerusalem and buried with full pomp. His great work of conquest had, unfortunately, been at the same time a great work of destruction. Not only had he destroyed the flourishing Hellenistic cities and forced them to adopt Jewish manners, but the bloody sword in the hand of the high priest had completely alienated the religious sensibilities of his own people. Despite his external successes, a kingdom built on sword and terror cannot survive for long.

4) ALEXANDRA'S WORK OF RECONCILIATION (76-67)

Jannaeus had arranged that after his death his wife Alexandra-Salome should follow him on the throne. She committed the high-priestly office to her eldest son Hyrcanus II. "Alexandra was in every respect the perfect opposite of her husband. Whereas he had hated the Pharisees and been hated by them in turn, she was friendly with them, and entrusted them with the reins of government. Whereas he was a despot in true oriental fashion, she was a god-fearing regent after the heart of the Pharisees." [13]

The establishment of peace with the Pharisees produced the long awaited domestic peace and tranquility. At this time the Pharisees seemed to have secured a constitutional basis for their influence. Formerly, the supreme administrative authority, the high council (Gerousia), had been composed of representatives from the nobility and the priesthood; now, however, the doors of the Jewish "senate" were open also to the Pharisees. Towards the end of Alexandra's reign, they succeeded in winning such a margin of power that a confrontation with the Sadduceans became absolutely unavoidable. Alexandra's own son Aristobulus II joined forces with the dissatisfied and dispossessed nobility and made an effort to secure the crown for himself. Alexandra died before this crisis was actually reached.

In her foreign policy, apart from a military campaign against Damascus, her reign was peaceful. That is why, in the Pharisaic

13. *Ibid.*, 287f.

tradition, the days of Alexandra are praised as a Golden Age, an age in which the very soil of the land itself — by way of re- warding the queen for her piety — bore a variety of miraculous fruit.

5) CIVIL WAR IN THE HOUSE OF HASMON

Hardly had the mother died when a civil war broke out between Aristobulus II (67-63) and Hyrcanus II. Hyrcanus would probably have been considered the legitimate successor to the throne, in that he had functioned in the office of high priest during the lifetime of his mother. He did, indeed, make a claim to the throne. Aristobulus, however, was unwilling to renounce the crown. He assembled a huge army. The confrontation oc- curred before Jericho. A great part of the soldiers of Hyrcanus went over to Aristobulus. Hyrcanus lost the battle and fled into the citadel of Jerusalem, where he was eventually forced to sur- render to his brother and renounce all his claims to the high priesthood and the crown alike. The victor claimed both powers for himself, but he generously allowed his defeated brother to enjoy the unchallenged income of his own properties. This would have settled the quarrel between the two brothers; Aristo- bulus, easily managed, would have prevailed. Left to his own resources, Hyrcanus, who is presented as peaceful and good- natured, would hardly have renewed the struggle against his brother. But now he becomes a chess piece in the hand of a newly rising power, Antipater the Idumaean.

As governor and strategos of the forcefully Judaized province of Idumaea, Antipater was interested in the growing weakness of the royal power in Jerusalem. Only after considerable negotiation did he win the indolent and indifferent Hyrcanus over to his plans for a coup. But when the king of the Nabateans, Aretas, promised his support, there was good hope for success. Hyrcanus then fled from Jerusalem and withdrew to the Nabatean capital of Petra. Here he pledged twelve cities in Transjordania to King Aretas. Escorted by a Nabatean-Idumaean military force, Hyr- canus began his march on Jerusalem, where he meant to seize the kingship for himself. His brother Aristobulus was defeated and was forced to retreat to the Temple precincts, with a few faithful followers. His fate would have been sealed, had not Rome chosen this moment to intervene.

C) PAX ROMANA

While these affairs were taking place in Palestine, Pompey had already begun his triumphal march through Asia Minor. In the year 66 he succeeded in subduing the obstinate enemy of Rome, Mithradates; Tigranes of Armenia thereupon freely submitted to the Roman yoke. While Pompey himself wanted to create a new system in the political affairs of Asia Minor, he had already, in the year 65, sent his general Scaurus ahead into Syria. Arrived in Damascus, Scaurus heard of the civil war in Judea and thought it wise to assert Roman interests in the affair. He immediately marched towards Jerusalem. The two claimants to the throne outdid each other in their attempt to court the favor of Rome. Scaurus decided for the energetic Aristobulus. He accordingly gave the king of the Nabateans, Aretas, the order to abandon the siege of Jerusalem. Furious, but still yielding to the power of Rome, Aretas withdrew into his tribal possessions.

After this initial success, Aristobulus also attempted to win the favor of Pompey, who had meantime marched to Damascus. He sent him a vine made of gold, valued at more than 500 talents. In Damascus, three delegations made a simultaneous appearance, the embassies of the two rivals, and representatives of the people. This last group wished to have nothing to do with either king. They were demanding the abrogation of the kingship and the restoration of the priestly constitution. Pompey held back with his decision until he had finished his war against the Nabateans.

Aristobulus took part in the campaign against the Nabateans, in the retinue of Pompey, but he left the campaign in Transjordania and made his way to the fortress of Alexandreion. Pompey was suspicious. He accordingly postponed his Nabatean campaign and marched into Judea. After the surrender of the fortress of Alexandreion, Aristobulus returned to Jerusalem. Pompey followed him across Jericho and pitched his camp in the neighborhood of the Jewish capital. Now Aristobulus lost his courage; he came to the Roman camp, gave Pompey even more rich gifts, and promised to surrender the city.

Pompey then sent his general Gabinius into Jerusalem. But the city closed its gates before him, and he was forced to withdraw to the Roman headquarters without accomplishing his mission. Pompey was so bitter at this turn of events that he had Aristobulus thrown into prison and prepared for an all-out attack upon the city. In Jerusalem there was a divided opinion. The party of Hyrcanus was for peace and surrender. Since they formed the majority, the city gates were once again opened. Pompey then sent his legate Piso into the city, and he made his triumphal entry without resistance. The war party of Aristobulus had, however, fortified themselves within the Temple citadel, determined upon a desperate resistance. Pompey ordered siege weapons from Tyre. After a siege of three months, a breach was finally made in the walls of the fortress. The Roman soldiers forced their way into the Temple precinct and launched a fearful massacre. No fewer than 12,000 Jews are supposed to have met their death in this wild slaughter. This happened in autumn of the year 63, under the consulship of Cicero.[14]

Pompey himself entered the Holy of Holies, but left the Temple treasures intact. He took every precaution to see that the Temple services were not interfered with. His judgment on the conquered city was strict. The fomentors of the war were executed, while the city and the surrounding country was placed under tribute. The great Jewish state built by the Hasmoneans was considerably reduced in size. All the coastal cities as well as the Hellenistic cities of Transjordania were broken off from the empire and made directly subject to the newly formed province of Syria. Hyrcanus II was installed as high priest over the remaining territories, but without the title of king.

After these great successes in the east, Pompey returned triumphant to Rome. When he celebrated his triumph at Rome

---

14. *Ibid.*, 298ff.

in the year 61, the Jewish priest-king Aristobulus was forced to march in front of the victor's chariot. In addition to Aristobulus and his family, Pompey also brought back a great number of Jewish prisoners who, once they were set free, formed the foundation of the Jewish community which was later to flourish at Rome.

With Pompey's new organization of power in Palestine, the national independence achieved by the Maccabean wars was definitively ended. What resulted was not an entirely new entity. Pompey did not interfere in the internal policies of Judea; he left the hierarchical system intact. The supreme head of the Jewish people, the high priest, was now the vassal of the Romans, just as he had earlier been the subject of the Persian or Hellenistic authorities. Religious freedom was still assured. Correspondingly, it would have been quite possible for this paltry religious remnant of Israel to develop in terms that corresponded to its divine mission precisely within this framework of the world-wide Roman Empire; but the Roman occupation could not guarantee the interior unity of the people, which had never really been achieved throughout the course of history. At all events, when the Romans first set foot on the soil of the Holy Land, there was already a clear development of those spiritual and political powers with which Jesus of Nazareth was destined to take issue in the fullness of time, in order to establish the kingdom of heaven, the new Israel of God, free from every political illusion.

CHAPTER XXI

THE HISTORIAN OF THE MACCABEAN ERA

PRECISE knowledge of the stormy course of the Maccabean revolt is owing to the two Books of Maccabees. According to the
Catholic interpretation, they belong to the canon of inspired
Scripture, while the Protestants regard them as pseudepigraphi-
cal. Both points of view, however, are forced to examine into the
strictly human credibility, the literary genre, and the date of
origin. Even a fleeting examination of the text shows that the
second Book of Maccabees is anything but the continuation of
the first. Both books are independent pieces of work, which have
developed independently of each other and pursue different political and religious objectives. The common name "Books of the
Maccabees" results simply from the fact that both books describe the Maccabean revolt, although there is no demonstrable
proof of literary dependence. Both books must, accordingly, be
briefly outlined and described.

A) THE FIRST BOOK OF MACCABEES

The first Book of Maccabees carries the history of the rebellion
as far as the death of Simon the high priest, which is explicitly
recorded; the book concludes with this formula: "The rest of

the acts of John and his wars and the brave deeds which he did and the building of the walls which he built, and his achievements, behold, they are written in the chronicles of the high priesthood, from the time that he became high priest after his father" (1 Mac 16, 23-24). Hence the conclusion that our historian composed his work during the reign of Hyrcanus (134-103) or shortly after his death, around 100. Works of history are not written without party interests and some subjectivity. The questionable reign of Jannaeus had given a bad name to the whole Maccabean rebellion. In an era in which the ancient ideals threatened to collapse, one man took up his pen and forcefully reminded his contemporaries of the heroic ideals of the early days. He described the national and religious crisis of Israel that had been averted by the bravery of the Maccabee brothers. Does that mean that this is only a typical example of court history?[1] This would make the first Book of Maccabees simply the glorification of a particular dynasty. While this aspect may be involved, it is certainly not the most characteristic. The fate of Israel still stands above the fate of the Maccabee family. It is not only archaic style that the ancient name of Israel is here used, by way of contrast to Judah; a new era demanded new words. That is why Israel refers not to the nation of the Jews, but rather to the people of God who have maintained fidelity to the covenant in the midst of general defection. The schismatic pro-Hellenistic, anti-covenant Jews no longer deserve to be referred to as Israel. The first Book of Maccabees does not describe a one-sided dynastic history; it portrays Israel's gradual rise to freedom, from crisis in faith and persecution.[2] The position taken with respect to covenant and law thus determines the entire course of history.

In this era of national and religious renaissance, our author wrote his history, neither in the popular Aramaic language, nor in Greek, the language of the civilized world; he wrote it in Hebrew, the sacred language of the Bible. He formed his style primarily on the basis of the older biblical works of history, espe-

---

1. M. A. Beek, *Geschichte Israels von Abraham bis Bar Kochba*, (1961), 123.
2. On the use and significance of "Israel," cf. Pfeiffer, HistNTT **493ff**.

cially the Books of Samuel and Kings. He succeeded in sketching some very imposing portraits: Judas the hero and leader of resistance, Jonathan the sly desert fox, Simon the zealot and high priest. Even persons who make only a very brief appearance, like the Syrian pretenders to the throne, are presented in considerable clarity of detail. The confusing course of history is presented in outline, while it is supported by appropriate sources at all its important junctures. The documents built into the text [3] which had formerly been the subject of considerable suspicion, have recently received more favorable verdicts. They are no longer regarded as the free invention of the writer himself, but rather as a faithful reproduction of ancient documents, not perfectly literal, but at least an accurate record of the intent.[4] This conclusion follows from the conscientious dating of the individual events.

Since the discovery of a cuneiform tablet [5] which contains the list and regnal dates of the Seleucid kings in Babylon from Alexander the Great to Demetrius II, it has been possible to supply a secure foundation for the formerly uncertain chronology of the Books of Maccabees. As a result there are two forms of dating. Events which are identified with reference to the history of the Syrian kings are, naturally enough, dated in terms of the Macedonian-Syrian Seleucid Era, in which the year begins in autumn. On the other hand, events which concern Israel and the Temple are dated in terms of the Temple Era, with years beginning in spring. In the same manner, the Babylonian Seleucid Era also begins the year with spring. Reducing the whole problem to a simple formula, we can speak of a system of reckoning time in terms of the profane year (beginning in autumn) and one beginning with the "church year" (beginning in spring).[6] The Macedonian-Syrian Seleucid Era began in autumn of 312, while

---

3. *Ibid.*, 494.
4. Robert-Feuillet, EinlAT 741.
5. E. Vogt, *Catalogus cuneiformis regum Seleucidarum*, Bibl 36 (1955), 261-262.
6. For the chronology of the Books of Maccabees, cf. J. Schaumberger, *Die neue Seleukiden-liste BM 35603 und die makkabäische Chronologie*, Bibl 36 (1955), 423-435.

the Babylonian Seleucid Era, which is identical with the Jewish "church year," begins only in spring of 311 B.C. There is thus a difference of half a year between the two systems of reckoning. If this fact is observed, the chronology of the Books of Maccabees no longer appears to be such an insoluble puzzle.[7]

Towards the turn of the first century B.C., the Jewish nation had long emerged from its Palestinian isolation. Important works for the history of culture were soon translated into Greek. The first Book of Maccabees, whose original Hebrew version has disappeared without leaving a trace, quickly found a translator. Jerome still managed to see the Hebrew text; Origen has handed down the original title of the work, which he claims was *Sarbet Sarbaniel,* words which cannot be clearly interpreted. According to Dalman,[8] the words are a defective version of the Aramaic *sefar beth hasmonaya,* "book of the house of the Hasmoneans." A thorough examination of the Greek text reveals the fact that the translator was better acquainted with Greek than Hebrew. It would seem that some errors had been made in the translation. Seen as a whole, however, his work is so absolutely precise that it is an easy matter to reconstruct the Hebrew original. His language is based on the style of the Septuagint. It is free from all Hellenistic pathos and contemporary rhetoric.

The first Book of Maccabees leads to the threshold of the first century before Christ. It is both a farewell to "Israel's" heroic age, and a record of tragedy. For the victorious Israel of the Maccabees that is here described already belongs to the past. The political victories certainly did not achieve the fulfillment of the "hope of Israel." Disillusion with politics was the result. The religious groups all withdrew from society. The Pharisees entrenched themselves behind the law, the Essenes went off into the desert to prepare the way of the Lord, the Sadducees attempted to find a middle road of compromise. But over all of them lies one unanswered question: "When will the true kingdom of heaven make its appearance?"

---

7. Robert-Feuillet, EinlAT 742 has simplified the problem. It is no longer sufficient to date simply in terms of the Seleucid Era.
8. Dalman, *Grammatik des jüdisch-palätinischen Aramäisch,* (1960), 7.

B) THE SECOND BOOK OF MACCABEES

The second Book of Maccabees breathes a quite different spirit than the first. In terms of content it describes a much shorter period of time, from Heliodorus' blasphemous encroachments upon the Temple to the victorious Day of Nicanor, events which are also described in the first Book of Maccabees (1 — 7); this is a span of only some 15 years (175-161). The interests of the historian are clearly visible at both termini. He is primarily concerned with the Temple, with its desecration and its eventual rededication. "Blessed is he who has kept his own place undefiled" (2 Mac 15, 34) — this can be considered the leit-motiv of the entire work. The actual history itself is preceded by two letters from the community at Jerusalem to the Jews in Egypt; the first is dated in the year 188 of the Temple era (124 B.C.), the 40th year after the rededication of the Temple. The Egyptian Jews are directed to celebrate the "feast of tabernacles in the month of the Kislev" (November-December) — this is the feast of the dedication of the Temple (*hanukkah*). The second letter describes the death of Antiochus Epiphanes the desecrator of the Temple, and the miracles attendant upon the building of the second Temple under Nehemiah. The largest part of the book is thus taken up with military events, very like the first Book of Maccabees, although there are some transpositions and some elaborations. It is obvious that the author was not a chronist, but rather an historian.

Whereas the historian stands completely in the background in the first Book of Maccabees, in the second book we suddenly hear the voice of a man who knows how to deal with words. Our author has been well educated in Greek rhetoric; he employs the pathos of Hellenistic historiography. In no other book of the Bible does the author judge his own work. Here we find commonplaces of historical rhetoric: "If it is well told and to the point, that is what I myself desire; if it is poorly done and mediocre, that was the best I could do. For just as it is harmful to drink wine alone, or, again, to drink water alone, while wine mixed with water is sweet and delicious and enhances one's enjoyment, so also the style of the story delights the ears of those who read the work" (2 Mac 15, 38ff.). Our author has betrayed the manner of his work. His history is an excerpt from the five Books of Jason the Cyrenian (2, 23). He feels that his task has not been an easy one. From the vast throng of dates and from the confusing manifold of narratives he claims to have chosen out only what is profitable and arresting. The basic outline is taken from Jason; he is the real architect of the work; our author has only adorned the edifice and spent considerable time and energy in his task, even to the point of "sweat and loss of sleep" (2, 26ff.).

The Greek historians of the Hellenistic era were fond of embellishing their histories with the addition of miracles and extraordinary events. Whereas in the first Book of Maccabees the name of God is replaced by the words "heaven," and there are absolutely no miraculous narratives, the second Book is full of miraculous stories and martyrs' legends. This fact clearly establishes the background against which our author sees the history of Israel: the true progress of that history takes place in heaven. In times of crisis it is always the hidden and heavenly mystery of Israel that comes to light. Then there are also documents worked into the narrative whose historical genuinity continues to win scholarly credence. Whereas the first Book of Maccabees can be called the solemn song of the nation of Israel, the second is the solemn song of the Temple and the high priesthood.

When and how did this sympathetic author live and write? Scholarship has argued that he must have lived shortly after the date of the letter addressed to the Jews in Egypt (mentioned in the introduction), and thus about the year 120 B.C. The history of Jason of Cyrene [9] which forms the basis for his history, was already current at this time. Jason is very close to the time of the events he describes. We might thus conclude that in the second Book of the Maccabees we have a fair contemporary

---

9. On the work of Jason and its use in 2 Mac, cf. Pfeiffer, HistNTT 506-518.

source which is even older than the first Book of Maccabees. It is composed after the manner of the pathetic Greek historiography and thus it must also be considered as an open statement directed to the Jews living in Hellenistic territory, biding them to hold true to the Temple at Jerusalem, with holy fear and reverence, from their dispersion throughout the far corners of the Roman Empire.

CHAPTER XXII

THE FULLNESS OF TIME

BY the term fullness of time, Christians always understand the Incarnation of the Son of God. This is, however, such a divine idea that no human mind could ever have conceived it. From the Old Testament point of view, one must put himself into the Mosaic era, into the era of the great kings and prophets, or into the days of the peaceful teachers of wisdom: from every side there was a clear presentiment of something great, something to come, something dawning like a great morning light. It was a fragmentary concept, something only hinted at. And thus it is only in terms of Christian retrospect that the faithful student of the Old Testament can observe a definite dynamism making its way through the centuries of Old Testament history, converging purposefully upon a single objective, the establishment of the kingship of God and his Messiah. Moses, on Sinai, had established God's covenant with the Twelve tribes of Israel. God's sovereignty was accomplished immediately, in thunder and lightning. There is only the least trace of eschatological expectation here; Israel, flesh and blood, is Yahweh's special property and his own royal domain. The messianic prophecies of even Isaiah himself are, despite their vision of the future, essentially bound up with the flesh and blood of a dynasty that has claim to earthly power. It was only the great historical catastrophes and reconstructions that led to the great *metanoia,* the great conversion. God's kingdom, which is destined to surely come, must be of quite another nature; it will eventually dawn as something perfectly new. "Behold something new will be made" (Jer 31, 22). In times of crisis, there was always the burning question as to when this dominion of God would finally dawn. The expatriates left the land of their captivity and returned to Zion, experiencing a new Exodus and a new migration through the wilderness into the promised land, where they hoped to experience an event of world-shaking significance. But what had arrived was only the era of the second Temple, the era of peace under the sovereignty of the Persians and the Ptolemies.

Only when the blasphemous horn rose up to speak against God, persecuting the holy ones of the Most High, erecting the abomination of desolation in the Temple itself, did the faithful remnant break into a cry of terrible crisis, stronger than it had ever been before: "How long shall our crisis last?", "When is the coming of the kingdom of God?" Scholars began to reexamine the history of salvation, and, pen in hand, to reexamine the past and re-plan the future. The results were alarming. The final week of the world is already in mid-course; the end of time is at the gates; the kingdom of God cannot tarry longer.

Some trace of this impatient activity is to be found in the Book of the prophet Daniel. In the collapse of the Persian Empire, Daniel became the herald of God's great kingdom to come. Hardly any other prophet was read in the Maccabean time of crisis with as much devotion as Daniel. What the book was made to supply was not the narrative of past history, but the answer for the crisis of the present time. In reading the ancient text, they introduced new interpretations. As a result, in the Book of Daniel as we know it today, ancient prophecy and new interpretation (*pešer*) are so intimately bound together that many critics, under the influence of the Maccabean reinterpretation, have completely forgotten the existence of the ancient prophet Daniel and declared his book to be a pseudepigraph. But this is not the case. As we have already demonstrated in the section dealing with the prophet Daniel, the two strata can be easily enough distinguished. Among the books of the prophets, Daniel, as the last of the books, has achieved the final stage. It leads directly into the New Testament, not only in terms of historical sequence, but also in terms of its content. It is the book of the end of days, of the fullness of time, of the dawning of God's dominion.

A) THE LAST WEEK OF YEARS

1) ONCE AGAIN DANIEL'S PROPHECY OF THE WEEKS OF YEARS

Daniel's prophecies on the 70 years of disaster (Dn 9, 24) were utilized by a man living in the Maccabean era and reexamining the history of the past.[1] He found himself in the same desperate situation as Daniel had once been. The Temple was desecrated and the people of God were subject to pagan power. The question as to how long this crisis should last was a burning issue in those days. The Maccabean scholar did not read the ancient prophecy as an historian; for him the words of the prophet were living words, words that had been addressed to his own age as well. As he meditated, he gained new insight.

The basis for his new interpretation was furnished by the two 70's (*šb'ym šb'ym*). Daniel had prophesied as follows: "The seventy, the seventy (years of disaster) are at an end" (9, 24). The Maccabean interpreter, however, read the same consonants first as *šabu'îm*, "weeks," and the second time as *šib'îm*, "seventy." Daniel's prophecy of 70 years thus becomes the prophecy of 70 weeks of years in the Maccabean era. The 70 weeks of years are now interpreted in terms of the basic outline provided in the inaugural vision: "Time, two times, time and a half," into three corresponding sections. The first 7 weeks of years encompass the time of the Exile; the time that elapsed from the day on which the "word" (Jer 25, 11; 29, 10) went out to the anointed prince (*mašîaḥ nagîd*). The reference is not to simply any messianic priest and king, but rather the king of Persia, Cyrus, the "anointed" (Is 45, 1). The long 62 weeks of years comprised the time from

1. Cf. above, p. 62.

the return, the restoration of the Temple, until the extirpation of an "anointed" (*mašiaḥ*). Once again the word messiah refers to a definite person: "The anointed" high priest Onias III, who was assassinated during the exile in Daphne near Antioch, in the year 171 B.C. (2 Mac 4, 1-6, 33-35). With this date, we are already at the eve of the Maccabean crisis. The last week of years is devoted entirely to this era. A prince who is to come, that is, Antiochus Epiphanes, will lay waste to city and sanctuary; he will effect "a covenant" with many, that is, he will form an "alliance" with the pro-Hellenistic apostate Jews. For half a week of years he will interrupt the sacrifices. In the Temple there will stand the "abomination of desolation." But this last week is already in mid-course. The end is close at hand; then the destroyer will himself be destroyed, and God's dominion will begin. This was the reinterpretation of the ancient prophecy of Daniel.[2] What is striking here is not the division of the course of history into individual periods; the truly remarkable element is the fact that the times are approaching their end, when sin and guilt is to be locked and barred and the Holy of Holies will once again be anointed. In the symbolism of numbers, we can catch a clear picture of the fullness of the messianic expectation in the coming of God's kingdom. Our interpreter was concerned, not with numbers, but with confirmation of his faith in the end-time.

2) BIBLICAL MATHEMATICS?

By failing to recognize the symbolic value of the number 70, scholars have attempted to establish a chronological system on the basis of numerical data. The 70 units of 70 would give 490 years. Various points of departure have been assumed: Jeremiah's "word" on the 70 years (605), the deportation into exile (586), an edict of Cyrus, Darius or Artaxerxes (538, 520, 458). But the hoped for results simply do not tally with the final

---

2. A third re-interpretation of the prophecy of Daniel occurs in the Gospel when Jesus is speaking of the destruction of Jerusalem and the end of the world (Mt 24, 1–25, 30). The *pešer* character of the text is indicated by his words, "Let him who reads pay close attention" (Mt 24, 15).

point which is being aimed at, in the post-Exilic, Maccabean, or Messianic era.[3] Borgorgini Duca [4] has gone so far, on the basis of the 401 words in ch. 9, to establish the most precise dates in the life of Jesus. But this is wasted effort. The Maccabean interpreter (*parsan*) had simply given a new and contemporary value to the symbolic number 70 already used by Jeremiah and Daniel. It is well known that the Old Testament contains two systems of reckoning time; one in terms of reliable historical numbers, and the other involving numbers symbolic for the history of salvation. Although generally the outline of a generation involving 12 times 40 years was predominant, our interpreter chose the sacred number 7 for his basis and developed it into a seven-times-seventy-years. It is an idle speculation to turn to mathematical calculation here; this was not the interpreter's aim at all. He was more concerned with demonstrating, on the basis of a convincing number symbolism, that the last week of years had already begun, and the fullness of time was very close.[5]

B) TIME, TWO TIMES, TIME AND A HALF

1) ONCE AGAIN THE INAUGURAL VISION OF DANIEL AND THE PROPHECY OF THE SON OF MAN

The mysterious system of counting, "time, two times, time and a half" is found in the inaugural vision (12, 7), as well as

3. Nötscher, EB III, 642. — Avigdor Orr, *The Seventy Years of Babylon*, VT 6 (1956), 304-306 reckons the 70 years from the Battle of Carchemisch, thus 605-539. — C. F. Whitley, *The Seventy Years of Desolation, a Rejoinder*, VT 7 (1957), 416-418, however, begins with the destruction of Jerusalem (586-516). Both of them misunderstand the symbolic nature of the number 70.
4. Cardinal Borgongini Duca, *Le LXX Settimane di Daniele e le date messianiche*, (Padua 1951). G. Lamparter, *Une exégése arithmétique de chapître IX de Daniel*, NouvRevTheol 74 (1952), 409-417.
5. The genealogies of Jesus (Mt 1, 1-17; Lk 3, 23-38) are also based on a similar end-time outline. According to Matthew, Jesus' public appearance initiates the seventh and last age, while in Luke it is the twelfth and last. The ancestors of Jesus are also grouped artificially, 6 x 7 in Matthew and 11 x 7 in Luke.

in the vision of the Son of Man (7, 25). The solution to the riddle lies in the fact that once again the sacred number seven, in its half form (1 + 2 + ½ = 3½) is taken as a symbolic value. By "week" we are to understand simply time as such, which, in terms of biblical thinking, is understood in terms of its beginning from God and its final end in God. Daniel's anguished question, "Oh, my Lord, what shall be the issue of these things?" is answered by the angel of revelation in words that are confirmed by an oath upon the eternal life of God: "Time, time and a half, half a time," that is, the "week" of the world is in mid-course, and the kingdom of God is drawing near. The great prince Michael is already prepared to do battle for the oppressed people of God. The days of final judgment are at hand. The departed will rise again to eternal life or to eternal shame.

Daniel receives the same answer to his question as to when the Son of Man is destined to come in his power and glory. The holy ones of the Most High are delivered to the blasphemous horn only for "a time, two times, and half a time" (7, 25). But then power, rule, and dominion will be given to the Son of Man. His kingdom is an eternal kingdom, and his rule is without end. Thus the signs of the Son of Man already stand out against the sky of the Old Testament. Belief in the coming kingdom of the Son of Man was the source of strength to which people in the Maccabean era of persecution liked to turn. Power had been given to the blasphemous horn only for a while, only for "half a week." Expressed without number symbolism this means that the Son of Man is coming soon, and that the time is drawing to its end.

2) THE MYSTERIOUS 2300 EVENINGS AND MORNINGS AND THE 1290 AND THE 1335 DAYS

After the death of the persecutor Antiochus Epiphanes, in their great joy at the recovery of religious and national freedom, it was possible to look back and establish more precise points of reckoning. In retrospect over the era of persecution which had just been survived, it was possible to elaborate the ancient scheme of weeks as foretold by Daniel.[6]

6. For more precise figures on these dates, cf. my article, *"Mystische*

a. 2300 Evenings and mornings: 1150 Days: This is the text from Daniel: "Then I heard a holy one speak; and another holy one said to the one that spoke, 'For how long is the vision concerning the continual burnt offering, the transgression that makes desolate, and the giving over of the sanctuary and host to be trampled underfoot?' and he said to him, 'For two thousand and three hundred evenings and mornings; then the sanctuary shall be restored to its rightful state' " (Dn 8, 13, 14) — The 2300 evenings and mornings make 1150 days. The point of departure for this reckoning is clearly expressed; it is the 15th day of Kislev in the year 145 of the Temple era (December 6, 167), the day of the desecration of the Temple by Antiochus Epiphanes. Counting the days from this point yields the final date of Šebat 15 in the year 148 of the Temple era (January 31, 163), a most important date for the Maccabean wars. Two months after the reconstruction of the Temple (December 4, 164), the citadel of Zion was newly fortified with towers and defenses, while the oppressing forces were driven from the sacred precinct and the prophecy thus fulfilled. The number can be derived from the basic numbers in the prophecy of Daniel:

Time (lunar year): 354 days; two times: 708 days; half a time (a quarter year): 88 days, for a total of 1150 days, which is 2300 evenings and mornings.

b. 1290 days: the text reads: "From the time the continual burnt offering is taken away . . . there shall be a thousand two hundred and ninety days" (Dn 2, 11). The point of departure for the reckoning is once again clearly expressed. But where do these 1290 days lead us? Once again to an important date from the Maccabean war of liberation, Sivan 6, in the year 145 of the Temple era (June 19, 163), the day on which the festival of weeks, or Pentecost, fell. We have already described how Judas Maccabee, after his successful conclusion of the campaign into Gilead, returned triumphant with his liberated brethren to Zion and celebrated the festival of Pentecost. — Reckoned in terms of

Arithmetik oder geschichtliche Zahlen," BZ 8 (1964), 101-105.

the numerical scheme in Daniel, the result is this: time (leap year): 384 days; two times: 708 days; half a time (half a leap year plus one week): 198 days; for a total once again of 1290 days.

c. 1355 days: the original text reads: "Blessed is he who waits and comes to the thousand three hundred and thirty-five days. But go your way till the end; and you shall rest, and shall stand in your allotted place at the end of the days" (Dn 12, 12-13). These words form the mysterious conclusion to the original Book of Daniel. Are these doubled figures a hint that an error had been made in calculating the day of the end of the world and, after the first terminus had failed, a second date was being proposed? This would be putting off the time of the *parousia*. But since the other numbers all have a very sober ring, we must attempt to interpret these data as a similar form of reckoning based on historical events. The point of departure for this calculation is not clearly expressed. But if we reckon the 1335 days backwards from the glorious Day of Nicanor which was instituted as an annual commemorative festival, we arrive at Ab 7, in the year 148 of the Temple era (July 31, 164), a truly surprising conclusion. For Ab 7 is not only a day of mourning for the destruction of Jerusalem, but also the day for the march upon Zion. After the battle at Beth-zur, Judas Maccabee marched up to Jerusalem, to the citadel of Zion. He found the sanctuary desolate, began to cleanse it, and, on Kislev 25, finally reconsecrated it. — In terms of number symbolism, we have the following: time (leap year): 384 days; two times: 708 days; rest of the time: 243 days; for a total of 1335 days. Shortly after the victorious Day of Nicanor, Judas Maccabee met his tragic end. The last verse of the Book of Daniel is not meant to be an exhortation to preparedness for the end-time; it is an epitaph spoken over Judas Maccabee, the hero of Israel.

The common focus of all these dates cannot be an accident. All three numbers are reinterpretations coming from the era of the Maccabees. In the events "of those days" the interpreter saw the fulfillment of the ancient prophecy of Daniel. The desecration of the Temple, Judas' march to Zion, the fortification of the Temple citadel, the return home to Zion, finally, the glorious Nicanor Day itself — all these events are reduced to a precise numeral formula for those who have sufficient insight. The numbers are not established on the basis of mysticism and speculation; the course of history has engraved them itself, with an iron stylus.

These precise calculations arouse the impression that the interpreter felt the fullness of time had arrived with the victory of the Maccabean forces. Time, two times, and half a time were accomplished in the course of the religious war for freedom. But time did not stand still, and the question of "when" was asked over and over again. Witness to this is the question asked by the Pharisees, and even the disciples of Christ. The question of the Pharisees sounds skeptical: "When does the kingdom of God come?" (Lk 17, 22), while the question of the disciples seems to imply faith, but no understanding, despite the fact of Christ's resurrection: "Lord, will you at this time restore the kingdom to Israel?" (Ac 1, 6). It has a further echo in the early Christian question into the second coming of Christ. As a result, we see that the plans of God cannot be determined by mathematical calculation, although they can be grasped in terms of symbolic numbers. The last week is already far advanced. Therefore "prepare the way of the Lord; for the kingdom of heaven is near at hand" (Mt 3, 2; Mk 1, 15; Lk 10, 9).

CONCLUSION

Hardly any other prophet has had such a strong influence on the New Testament as Daniel. Jesus preached the coming of the kingdom of heaven, that is, the accomplishment of the vision of Daniel. He particularly liked to refer to himself as Son of Man, in reference not so much to his human nature as rather to his divine origin. The tragedy of his life consists in the fact that, even in front of the High Council, he claimed the honorific title of Daniel, Son of Man, for himself; whereupon his judges rent their garments and condemned him to death as a blasphemer. Jesus' words about the end-time are a new re-interpretation of Daniel's prophecy of the end-time (Mt 24, 15; Mk 13, 14; Lk 16, 15). Stephen beheld Jesus sitting at the right hand of the glory of God, as the exalted Son of Man (Ac 7, 55). The Book of Revelations of St. John is, in its broader outlines, simply a Christian *pešer,* a re-actualization of Daniel. In the early-Christian preaching, the term Son of Man as a reference to Christ gradually disappears, yielding to the newer title of Kyrios.

Thus it is precisely the prophet Daniel who binds the two Testaments together. The ancient Christian commentator Aponius [7] makes use of the following picture in an allegorical setting: "The angel with the iron tongs took the glowing coals from the altar; the two claws of the tongs are the two testaments, which seize upon the glowing word of God." In Daniel we find this *verbum ignitum,* this glowing word; as he was praying, a word went forth" (9, 23). Theodotion translates: "The Logos came forth." Looking back from the New Testament, we can realize that the Logos, that is, the great Unnamed One of the inaugural vision, the Son of Man, was already at work even before he took human flesh and became man. The question of the pre-existence of the Messiah Jesus, but also the question of the angelic prince and the prince of devils, is taken up again in the Book of Daniel. There are powers at work, the forces of the high places and the deep places, fighting for or against God's glory and God's kingdom. On earth, the confrontation is in the offing, and it will decide the issue for the powers of heaven and the powers of the devil. In the introduction to his commentary on the Psalms, Jerome [8] discusses the interpretation of the title to the Psalms *lam.mᵉnassᵃh;* in Greek this would stand for εἰς τὸ τέλος, which should be translated in Latin as *in finem,* "for the end-time." But Jerome decides in favor of the translation *pro victoria,* "for victory," and applies this to the Book of Daniel. It is the book of the victory of the Son of Man and the kingdom of God, the book which binds both testaments indissolubly together; for God's word is one.

---

7. Migne, *Supplementum I* (1959), 810.
8. Migne, PL 28, 1130f.

INDEX

'Abar-nahara 106, 124
Abel 269
abomination of desolation 296ff
accession to throne 139
"actualization" 86, 114
Aetolian League 237
agent of the law of heaven 195
Aggaeus 119
Ahasuerus 135ff
Ahikar 168ff
Ahura-mazda 14ff
akinakes 113
Akra, citadel 299, 311, 329, 336f
Alexander Balas 326
Alexander the Great 231
Alexander Jannaeus 345
Alexandria 244, 276
Alcimus, highpriest 318
alliance: Egypt and Syria 233
amesa spenta 172
anabasis, Antiochus III 235
Anahita, mother goddess 15
Andronicos 296
angels 121, 171f
angel — *mal'ak* 181
angel of covenant 181
angel in Zarathustra 59ff
annals, Persian 136f
annihilation, angel of 218
Antioch, revolution 330
Antiochus III, Great 234
   anabasis 235
   IV Epiphanes 238f
   V the Child 333
   VII Sidetes 337f
   VIII Gripos 340f
anti-semitism 276
Apollo, marriage defender 166

Apollonius 291f, 306
Aponius, *Commentary* 370
apostates 303f
Araka-Nebuchadnezzar IV 63, 95
Aramaic, imperial 126ff
   popular tongue 264f
Aristobulus I 344
   II 349
Armenia 104
Arpakšad 101ff
Arphaxad 99
Arsakes Soter 332
Artabanos 187
Artaxerxes 135
Asmodaios 173
astrology 76
Astyages 11
'attîq yômîm 68
autocrator 334
auxiliary corps 330
Awil-Marduk 7

Ba'al haššamayim 241
Babylon, Greek city 239
Babylonian Job 225ff
Bacchides, inspection 317
basileia theou 282
basileion of Hades 284
Bectileth 106f
Behistun inscription 48ff, 62, 95
Belsazar 10, 75, 80
Bel, priests of 83
Bentresh, princess 167
Ben-Sirach, story of finding of
   text 248f
   personality 252
Berenice 233
Bet-Bessei, desert fortress 325

GEOGRAPHY OF
THE OLD TESTAMENT

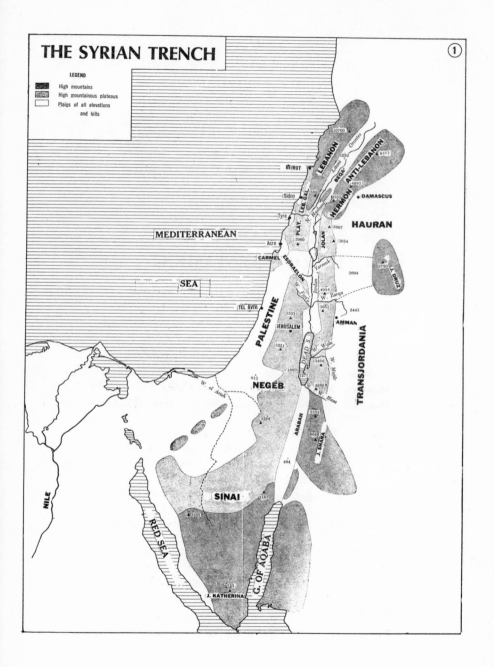

THE SYRIAN TRENCH

LEGEND

- High mountains
- High mountainous plateaus
- Plains of all elevations and hills

MEDITERRANEAN

SEA

BEIRUT

LEBANON

BEQA

ANTI-LEBANON

Litani

Orontes

10700

3250

8572

4093

Sidon

589

HERMON

DAMASCUS

Tyre

3392

W. Hasbani

PLAT.

LEB. GAL.

Acre

3960

HAURAN

3907

JOLAN

3024

CARMEL

ESDRAELON

Yarmuk

2604

J. DRUZ

3750

W. Farfa

Jordan

W. Zarqa

4054

TEL AVIV

3333

3651

2443

JERUSALEM

AMMAN

PALESTINE

3221

DEAD S.

W. Wala

TRANSJORDANIA

1660

3464

W. Mojib

913

NEGEB

4260

W. Hasa

W. el Arab

ARABAH

5353

3364

6045

494

J. SHARA

SINAI

3183

3705

RED SEA

G. OF AQABA

5733

J. KATHERINA

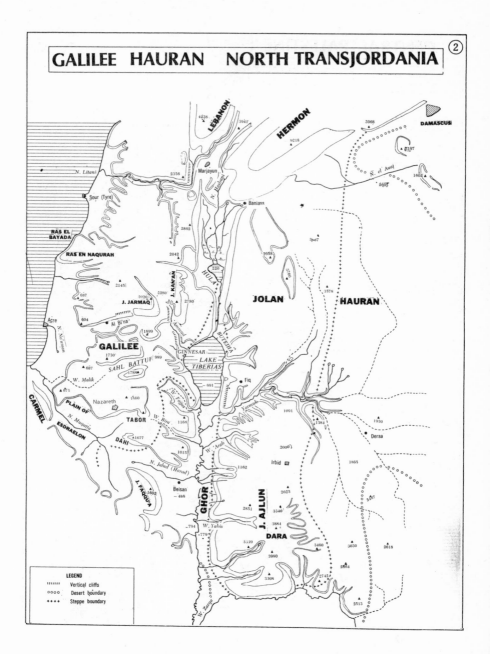

GALILEE HAURAN NORTH TRANSJORDANIA

②

LEGEND

′′′′′′′ Vertical cliffs
∘∘∘∘ Desert boundary
++++ Steppe boundary

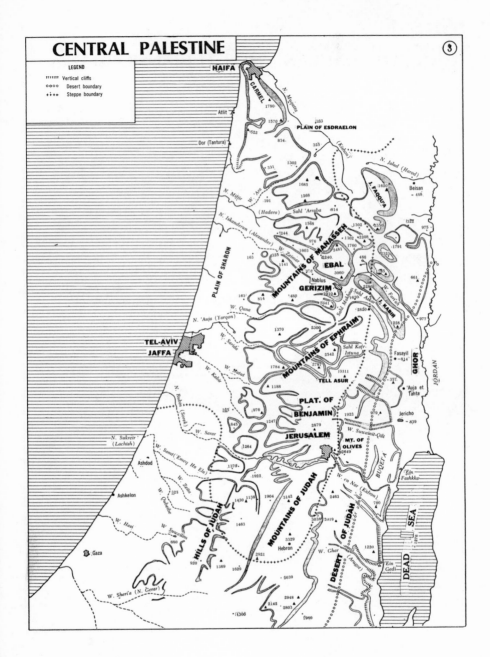

CENTRAL PALESTINE

LEGEND
- ᴧᴧᴧᴧᴧ Vertical cliffs
- ○○○○ Desert boundary
- ✛✛✛✛ Steppe boundary

③

HAIFA

CARMEL

N. Muqatta

1780

Atlit

1570

1522

1163

PLAIN OF ESDRAELON

Dor (Tantura)

834

325

N. Miffir

1302

W. 'Ara

331

Kishon

N. Jalud (Harod)

1685

1620

J. FAQUA

Beisan

- 488

1268

N. Miffir

391

Sahl 'Arraba

814

(Hadera)

N. Iskanderun (Alexander)

1568

1244

976

1302

1302 2208

975

.1791

W. Zeimar

1603

325

2481

1760

MOUNTAINS OF MANASSEH

PLAIN OF SHARON

1741

163

2240

488

2320

EBAL

3060

661

Nablus

GERIZIM

2010

163

814

480

2941

W. Fara

J. KABIR

1620

Sahl Mokhna

Sahl Askar

2820

977

N. 'Auja (Yarqon)

W. Qana

1370

2300

2820

1228

W. Sarida

TEL-AVIV

JAFFA

Sahl Kafr Istuna

2542

Fasayil

814

GHOR

W. Kabir

W. Nalut

1784

2787

MOUNTAINS OF EPHRAIM

3311

1188

TELL ASUR

'Auja et Tahta

327

JORDAN

N. Rubin (Sorek)

325

976

PLAT. OF

845

1247

1923

979

2879

Jericho

839

BENJAMIN

N. Sukreir (Lachish)

W. Sarar

1284

JERUSALEM

W. Suweinit-Qilt

Ashdod

W. Samt ('Emeq Ha Ela)

137d

1922

MT. OF OLIVES

2649

BUQE'A

'Ein Fashkha

Ashkelon

W. Zeita

325

W. en Nar (Kidron)

W. Osheite

1430

1138

1904

3143

2463

790

1276

SEA

N. Hasi

W. Suweilim

660

1463

3038 2619

MOUNTAINS OF JUDAH

HILLS OF JUDAH

Gaza

3329

Hebron

1220

W. Ghar

DEAD

920

1389

1629

2921

2639

(Aruga)

'Ein Gedi

DESERT   OF JUDAH

W. Sheri'a (N. Gerar)

2142

2948

2803

980

1300

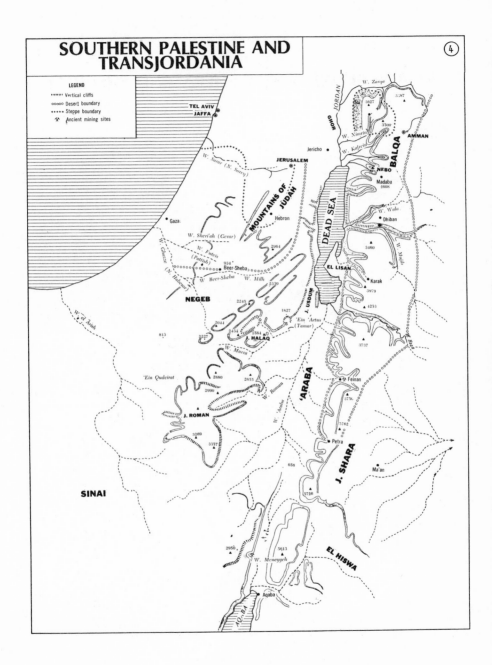

SOUTHERN PALESTINE AND TRANSJORDANIA

(4)

LEGEND
- ⁗⁗ Vertical cliffs
- ○○○○ Desert boundary
- ✦✦✦✦ Steppe boundary
- ⚒ Ancient mining sites

TEL AVIV
JAFFA

W. Zarqa

JORDAN

3627

3287

GHOR

W. Nimrin

3500

AMMAN

W. Kafrein

Jericho

JERUSALEM

BALQA

NEBO

W. Sarar (N. Sorey)

Madaba
2608

MOUNTAINS OF JUDAH

Hebron

DEAD SEA

W. Wala

Dhiban

Gaza

W. Sheri'ah (Gerar)

W. Faten
(Patish)

834

Beer-Sheba

W. Ghazze

(N. Habsor)

W. Beer-Sheba

W. Milh

2961

3460

W. Mujib

EL LISAN

Karak

3979

2330

NEGEB

2245

1827

J. UDUM

1253

2044

'Ein 'Artus
(Tamar)

W. el 'Arish

813

2227

2434

1584

J. HALAQ

3737

W. Mura

'Ein Qudeirat

2880

2655

'ARABA

Feinan

2990

W. Roman

3736

J. ROMAN

W. 'Araba

3762

3269

3357

Petra

J. SHARA

658

Ma'an

5726

SINAI

2950

3613

W. Meneyyeh

EL HISWA

Aqaba

G. OF 'AQABA

ROADS BETWEEN BEER SHEBA AND SHECHEM

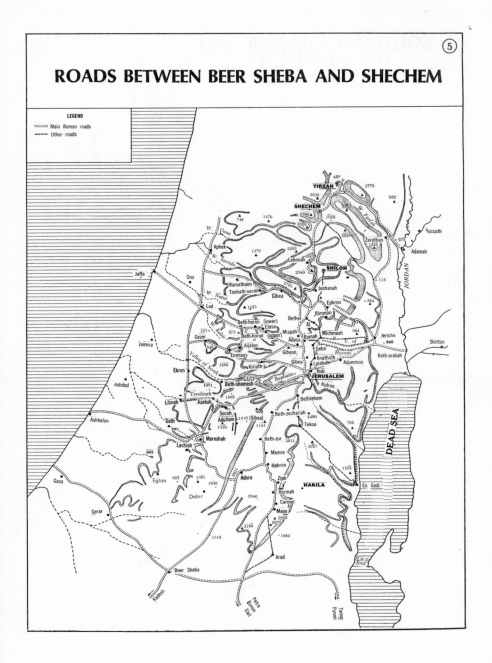

⑤

LEGEND
===== Main Roman roads
••••• Other roads

ROADS OF SAMARIA AND GALILEE

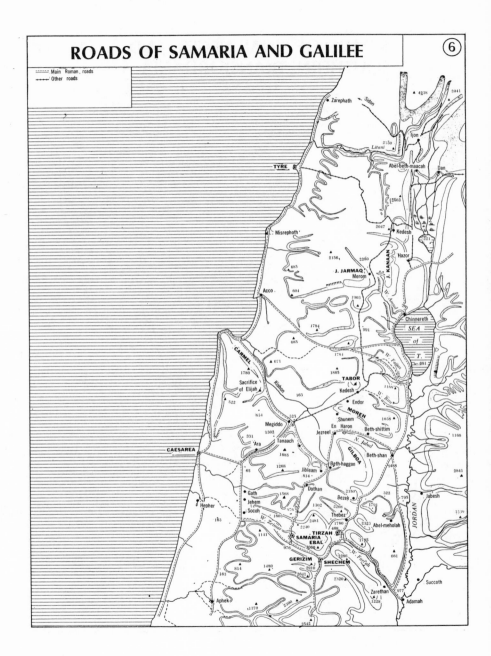

Main Roman roads
Other roads

Zarephath · Sidon

▲ 4238   3941

Ijon

2330
Litani

Abel-beth-maacah   Dan

TYRE

(3562)

Misrephoth ·

2047   Kedesh

2156 ▲   2280   Hazor

685   J. JARMAQ
Merom

Acco ·   604

1903 ▲

Chinnereth

1784   991   SEA

685   of

CARMEL   671 ▲   1784   T.

1780   1865   991

Sacrifice   TABOR
of Elijah   Kishon   163   Kedesh   1168

522   Endor

834   325   MOREH
Megiddo   Shunem   1038 ▲
En Haron
331   1302   Jezreel   Beth-shittim   1168

'Ara   Tanaach   N. Jalud

CAESAREA   1685   GILBOA   Beth-shan

1268   Jibleam   Beth-haggan   1488   2841
65   814 ·

Dothan   322
Gath   1568   Bezek   2350   795   Jabesh
Jehem   170
Hepher   Socoh   1603   1302   2208   1339
183   976   Thebez
2481   1780   2323   Abel-meholah
2240   488
1141   TIRZAH   1785
SAMARIA
EBAL   2286   661
976   3060
814   GERIZIM   2910   SHECHEM
163   1480   2643   2330
Aphek ·   1370   2300   Zarethan   977   Succoth
1228   Adamah
2542

JORDAN

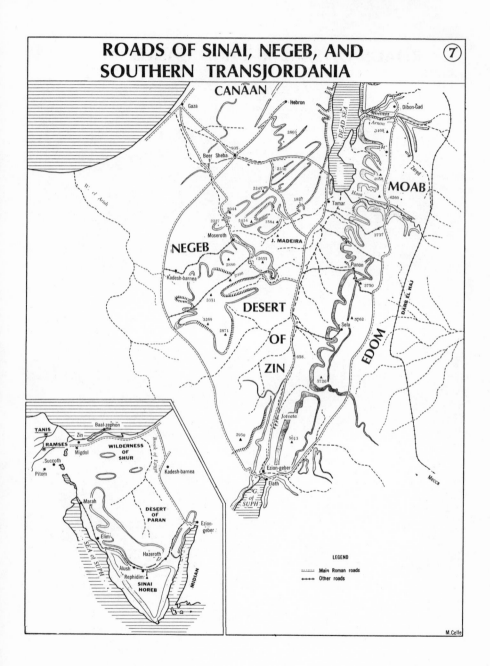

ROADS OF SINAI, NEGEB, AND SOUTHERN TRANSJORDANIA

⑦

CANAAN

Gaza
Hebron
Dibon-Gad

DEAD SEA
Arnon
3460

Beer Sheba
935
2801

2130

W. el Arab

2245
1827
Tamar
4058
Haua
4260
MOAB
Zered

2044
2237
3434
1584
Moseroth
3737

NEGEB
J. MADEIRA
2880
2635
Punon
2090
Kadesh-barnea
3750

3351
DARB EL HAJ

3269
2871
DESERT
OF
3762
Sela
ZIN
658
EDOM
3726

Jotvata
2950
5613
Ezion-geber
Elath
Mecca

Inset map (Sinai)

Baal-zephon
TANIS
Zin
RAMSES
Migdol
WILDERNESS
OF
SHUR
Brook of Egypt
Succoth
Pitom
Kadesh-barnea
G. of SUPH
Marah
DESERT
OF
PARAN
Ezion-geber
Elim
Hazeroth
SEA of SUPH
Alush
Rephidim
SINAI
HOREB
MIDIAN

LEGEND

----- Main Roman roads
++++ Other roads

M.Celle

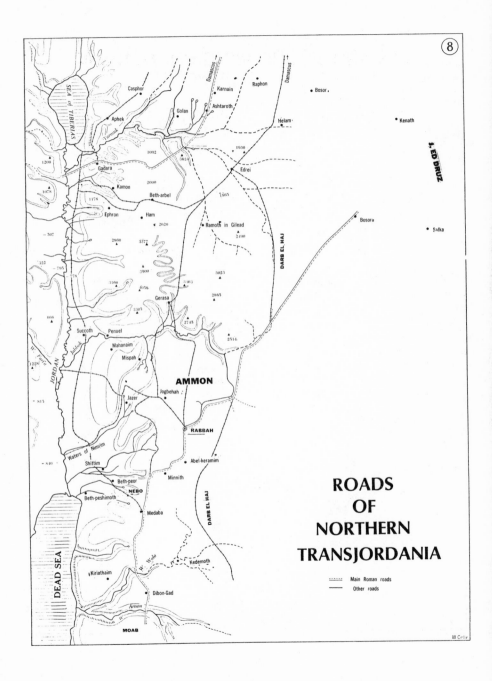

ROADS
OF
NORTHERN
TRANSJORDANIA

------- Main Roman roads
——— Other roads

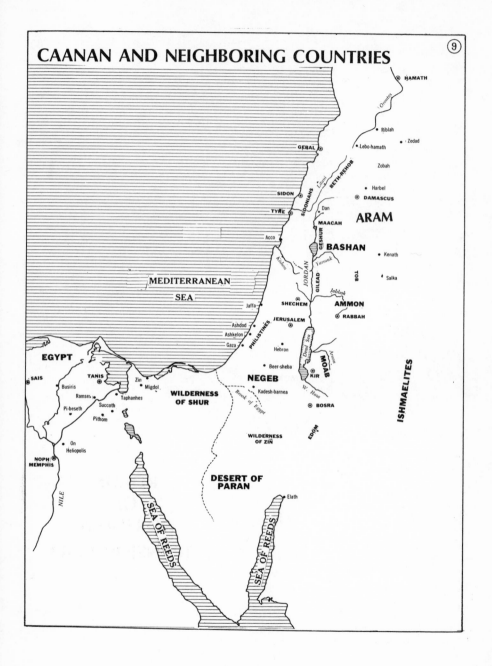

CAANAN AND NEIGHBORING COUNTRIES

⑨

HAMATH

Orontes

Riblah

GEBAL •Lebo-hamath • Zedad

Zobah

SIDON • Harbel

DAMASCUS

BETH-REHOB

TYRE Dan

SIDONIANS *Litani*

MAACAH

Acco GESHUR

ARAM

BASHAN

Kenath

Kishon *Yarmuk*

MEDITERRANEAN

SEA

JORDAN

GILEAD

TOB

Salka

Jabbok

Jaffa SHECHEM

AMMON

Ashdod JERUSALEM

Ashkelon RABBAH

Gaza PHILISTINES

Hebron *Dead Sea*

EGYPT

Beer-sheba MOAB

Arnon

SAIS NEGEB

TANIS Zin KIR

Busiris Migdol

Ramses Kadesh-barnea

Taphanhes WILDERNESS

Pi-beseth Succoth OF SHUR *Brook of Egypt*

BOSRA

Pithom

WILDERNESS

OF ZIN

On EDOM

Heliopolis

NOPH

MEMPHIS

ISHMAELITES

DESERT OF

PARAN

NILE Elath

SEA OF REEDS

SEA OF REEDS

TRIBES AND DISTRICTS UNDER SOLOMON, NEIGHBORING PEOPLES

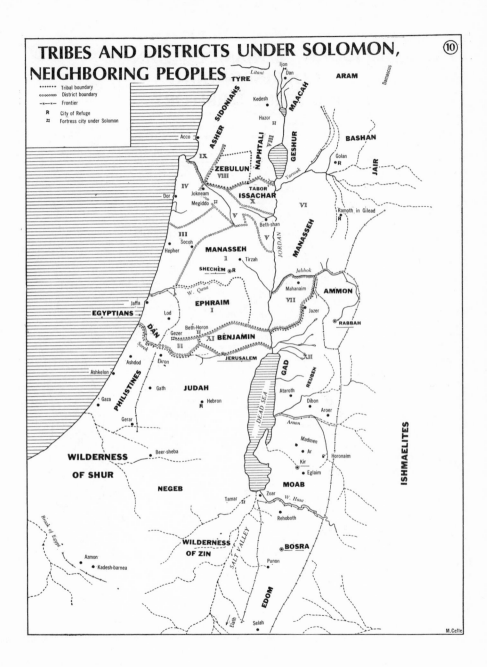

⑩

Litani
Ijon
Dan
ARAM
Damascus

TYRE
SIDONIANS
Kedesh
MAACAH
Hazor ⨯
Acco
ASHER
NAPHTALI VIII
GESHUR
BASHAN
IX
ZEBULUN VIII
Golan R
JAIR
Dor
Jokneam
Megiddo ⨯
IV
TABOR
ISSACHAR X
Yarmuk
VI
Ramoth in Gilead ⨯

······· Tribal boundary
∞∞∞∞∞ District boundary
–×–×– Frontier
R City of Refuge
⨯ Fortress city under Solomon

Socoh
III
Hepher
MANASSEH
II
Tirzah
SHECHÈM ●R
V
Beth-shan
V
MANASSEH
JORDAN
Jabbok
Mahanaim
AMMON

W. Qana
EPHRAIM I
VII
Jazer
RABBAH

Jaffa
EGYPTIANS
Lod
Beth-Horon
Gezer ⨯
III
XI BENJAMIN
Sorek
JERUSALEM
XII
GAD
REUBEN

Ashdod
Ekron
DAN
Ashkelon
PHILISTINES
Gath
JUDAH
Hebron R
Ataroth
Dibon
Aroer
Arnon
DEAD SEA

Gaza
Gerar
Beer-sheba
Madmen
Ar
Horonaim
Kir
Eglaim

WILDERNESS
OF SHUR
NEGEB
Tamar ⨯
Zoar
W. Hasa
MOAB
Rehoboth

Brook of Egypt
WILDERNESS
OF ZIN
SALT VALLEY
BOSRA
Punon

Azmon
Kadesh-barnea
EDOM
Elath
Selah

ISHMAELITES

M.Celle

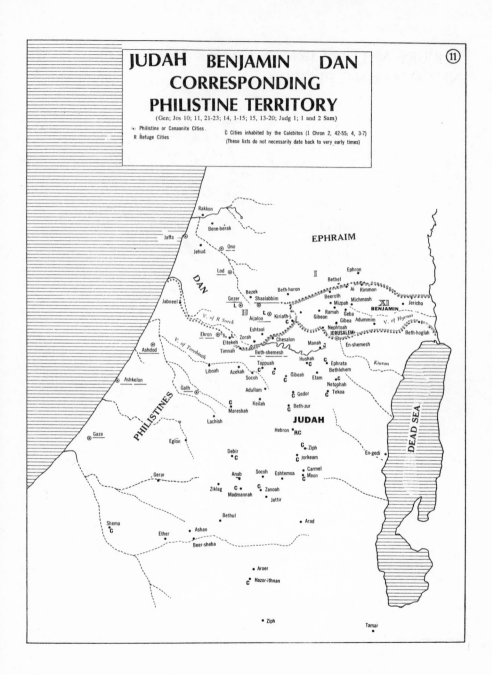

JUDAH BENJAMIN DAN
CORRESPONDING
PHILISTINE TERRITORY

(Gen; Jos 10; 11, 21-23; 14, 1-15; 15, 13-20; Judg 1; 1 and 2 Sam)

⊙ Philistine or Canaanite Cities
R Refuge Cities

C Cities inhabited by the Calebites (1 Chron 2, 42-55; 4, 3-7)
(These lists do not necessarily date back to very early times)

⑪

Rakkon

Bene-berak

Jaffa

Jehud

Ono

EPHRAIM

Lod

Ephron

II

Bethel

DAN

Bezek

Beth-horon

Ai   Rimmon

Gezer   Shaalabbim

Beeroth

Jabneel

III

Mizpah   Michmash

XII

Jericho

L

Ramah   Geba

BENJAMIN

V. of R Sorek

Aijalon   Kiriath-j.

Gibeon   Gibea   Adummim

V. of Hyenas

Eshtaol

Nephtoah

Ekron   Zorah

Chesalon

JERUSALEM

Beth-hoglah

Eltekeh

Manah

Ashdod

V. of Terebinth

Timnah

Beth-shemesh

En-shemesh

Tappuah   Hushah

Ephrata

Kiaron

Libnah   Azekah

Bethlehem

Ashkelon

Socoh

Gibeah   Etam

Gath

Adullam

Netophah

Gedor   Tekoa

Mareshah   Keilah

Beth-zur

Lachish

JUDAH

Gaza

PHILISTINES

Eglon

Hebron   RC

C   Ziph

Debir

C   Jorkeam

En-gedi

C

Gerar

Anab   Socoh   Eshtemoa

Carmel

Maon

Ziklag   C   C   Zanoah

Madmannah

Jattir

Bethul

Shema   C

Ashan

Arad

Ether

Beer-sheba

Aroer

C   Hazor-ithnan

DEAD SEA

Ziph

Tamar

NORTHERN AND CENTRAL TRIBES CORRESPONDING DISTRICTS

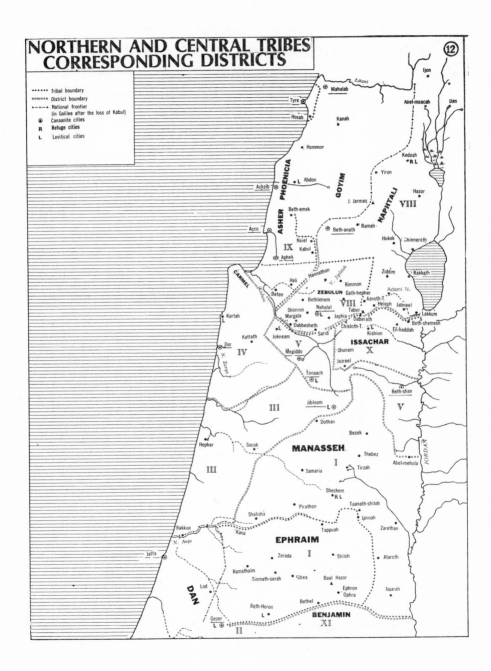

12

Tribal boundary
District boundary
National frontier
(in Galilee after the loss of Kabul)
® Canaanite cities
R Refuge cities
L Levitical cities

Ijon
Litani
Mahalab
Tyre
Abel-maacah
Dan
Hosah
Kanah
Hammon
Kedesh
R L
Yiron
Achzib
Abdon
Beth-emek
Hazor
J. Jarmaq
NAPHTALI
VIII
Acco
Beth-anath
Ramah
Neiel
Hukok
Chinnereth
Kabul
IX
Aphek
Ziddim
Rakkath
Hali
Hannathon
V. Jiphtah
Beten
Rimmon
Adami N.
ZEBULUN
Gath-hepher
Bethlehem
Aznoth-T.
Shimron
Nahalal
VIII
Tabor
Heleph
Jabneel
Margala
Japhia
Daberath
Lakkum
Kartah
Dabbesheth
Chisloth-T.
Beth-shemesh
Kattath
Jokneam
Sarid
En-haddah
Dor
V
Kishion
ISSACHAR
IV
Megiddo
Shunem
X
Jezreel
Tanaach
Beth-shan
III
Jibleam
L
V
Dothan
Bezek
Hepher
Socoh
MANASSEH
Thebez
Abel-mehola
III
Tirzah
Samaria
Shechem
R L
Taanath-shiloh
Pirathon
Janoah
Shalisha
Zarethan
Rakkon
Kana
Tappuah
N. Aujā
EPHRAIM
Jaffa
Zerada
I
Shiloh
Ataroth
Ramathaim
Lod
Timnath-serah
Gibea
Baal Hazor
DAN
Ephron
Naarah
Ophra
Beth-Horon
Bethel
Gezer
L
BENJAMIN
II
XI

PHOENICIA
ASHER
GOYIM
CARMEL
JORDAN

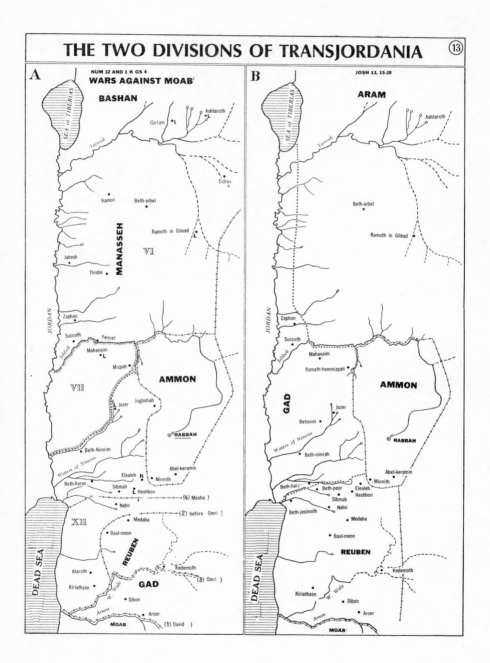

THE TWO DIVISIONS OF TRANSJORDANIA ⑬

A

NUM 32 AND 1 KGS 4
WARS AGAINST MOAB

SEA of TIBERIAS

BASHAN

Golan • L
Ashtaroth • L

Yarmuk

Edrei

Kamon • Beth-arbel •

MANASSEH VI

Ramoth in Gilead • L

Jabesh •
Thisbe •

JORDAN

Zaphon •

Succoth •
Penuel •
Mahanaim • L
Mizpah •

VII

Jazer L • Jogbehah •

AMMON

RABBAH ⊚

Beth-Nimrim •

Waters of Nimrim

Abel-keramin •

Elealeh R • Minnith •
Beth-haran • Sibmah • L Heshbon •

──── (4) Mesha }
Nebo •

──── (2) before Omri }

XII

Medaba •

Baal-meon •

REUBEN

DEAD SEA

Ataroth •
Kiriathaim •

Redemoth •

──── (3) Omri }

GAD

Dibon •

Arnon
Aroer •

MOAB ──── (1) David }

B

JOSH 13, 15-28

SEA of TIBERIAS

ARAM

Ashtaroth

Yarmuk

Beth-arbel •

Ramoth in Gilead •

JORDAN

Zaphon •

Succoth •
Jabbok

Mahanaim •

Ramath-hammizpah •

GAD

AMMON

Jazer •

Betonim •

RABBAH ⊚

Waters of Nimrim

Beth-nimrah •

Abel-keramin •

Beth-hara • Beth-peor • Elealeh • Minnith •
Sibmah • Heshbon •
Nebo •

Beth-jesimoth •

Medaba •

Baal-meon •

REUBEN

DEAD SEA

Kedemoth •

Kiriathaim •
W. Wala
Dibon •

Arnon
Aroer •

MOAB

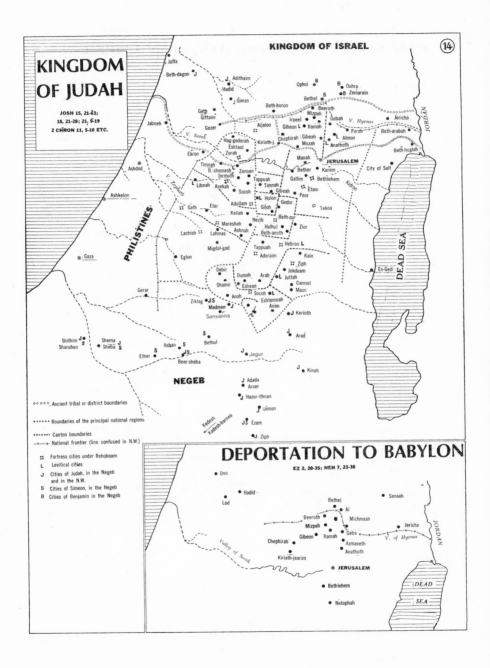

KINGDOM OF ISRAEL

(14)

KINGDOM OF JUDAH

JOSH 15, 21-63;
18, 21-28; 21, §-19
2 CHRON 11, 5-10 ETC.

Jaffa
Beth-dagon J
Hadid
J Gimzo
J Adithaim
Ophni B
B Ophra
B Zemarain
Bethel
Beeroth
Beth-horon
Mizpah
Gatb
Gittaim
Irpeel
Gebah
V. Hyenas
Jericho
Jabneh
Gezer
Aijalon
Gibeon L
Ramah
Parah
Beth-arabah
V. Sorek
Hag-gederah
Eshtaol
Kiriath-j.
Chephirah
Gibeah
Mozah
Almon
Anathoth
Ekron
Zorah
Manah
JERUSALEM
Beth-hoglah
Ashdod
Timnah
B.-shemesh
Jarmuth
Zanoah
Tappuah
Bether
Gallim
Karem
Bethlehem
City of Salt
Ashkelon
Libnah
Azekah
Socoh
Timnah
Gibeah
Peor
Etam
Kidron
Holon
Gedor
Gath
Eter
Adullam
Giloh
Beth-zur
Tekoa
Keilah
Nezib
Halhul
Mareshah
Ashnah
Beth-anoth
Zior
Lachish
Lahmas
Tappuah
Beth-anoth
Hebron L
Migdal-gad
Adoraim
Kain
Eglon
Ziph
Jokdeam
Debir
Arab
Dumah
Juttah
Shamir
Eshean
Socoh
Carmel
Anab
Eshtemoah
Maon
Ziklag JS
Madmen
Anim
J Kerioth
Sansanna
J Arad
Shilhim JS
Sharuhen
Shema J
Sheba S
Ashan S
Bethul
Ether S
Beer-sheba
JS
J Jagur
J Kinah

En-Gedi

DEAD SEA

JORDAN

NEGEB
J Adada
Aroer
J Hazor-ithnan
J Uimon
Kedesh
Kadesh-barnea
JS Ezem
J. Ziph

○○○○○○ Ancient tribal or district boundaries

++++++ Boundaries of the principal national regions

------- Canton boundaries

—x—x— National frontier (line confused in N.W.)

✠ Fortress cities under Rehoboam
L Levitical cities
J Cities of Judah, in the Negeb
   and in the N.W.
S Cities of Simeon, in the Negeb
B Cities of Benjamin in the Negeb

DEPORTATION TO BABYLON

EZ 2, 20-35; NEH 7, 23-38

Ono
Hadid
Lod
Senaah
Bethel
Ai
Beeroth
Michmash
Mizpah
Jericho
Chephirah
Gibeon
Ramah
Geba
V. of Hyenas
Azmaveth
Kiriath-jearim
Anathoth
JERUSALEM
Bethlehem
Netophah

JORDAN

DEAD SEA

PALESTINE UNDER THE ASSYRIAN EMPIRE

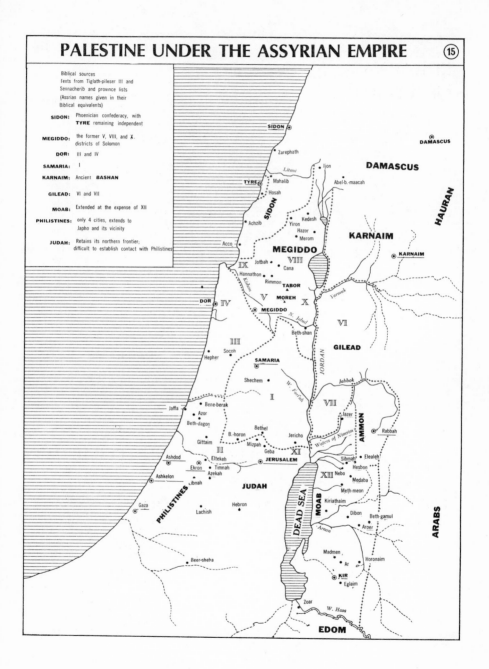

Biblical sources
Texts from Tiglath-pileser III and
Sennacherib and province lists
(Assrian names given in their
Biblical equivalents)

SIDON: Phoenician confederacy, with **TYRE** remaining independent

MEGIDDO: the former V, VIII, and X. districts of Solomon

DOR: III and IV

SAMARIA: I

KARNAIM: Ancient **BASHAN**

GILEAD: VI and VII

MOAB: Extended at the expense of XII

PHILISTINES: only 4 cities, extends to Japho and its vicinity

JUDAH: Retains its northern frontier; difficult to establish contact with Philistines

SIDON

DAMASCUS

Zarephath

Litani

DAMASCUS

Mahalib · Ijon

TYRE

Abel-b.-maacah

HAURAN

Hosah

Achzib

Kedesh
Yiron
Hazor · Merom

Acco

DOR IV

Kedesh

KARNAIM

Acco

MEGIDDO

KARNAIM

IX
Jotbah · VIII
Hannathon Cana
Rimmon TABOR
V MOREH
X

MEGIDDO

N. Jalud

Beth-shan

Yarmuk

VI

GILEAD

III
Socoh
Hepher

SAMARIA

Shechem · *W. Farah*

Jabbok

I

VII

Jaffa
Bene-berak
Azor
Beth-dagon

B.-horon Bethel
Mizpah Jericho

Jazer

Waters of Nimrim

AMMON

Rabbah

Gittaim

Geba
Ashdod Eltekeh XI
Ekron · Timnah JERUSALEM
Azekah
Ashkelon Libnah

Sibmah · Elealeh
Nebo Hesbon
XII

Medaba

JUDAH

Meth-meon

Gaza
Lachish

Hebron

MOAB

Kiriathaim

Dibon
Beth-gamul
Aroer

Arnon

ARABS

Beer-sheba

DEAD SEA

Madmen · Ar Horonaim

KIR
· Eglaim

Zoar *W. Hasa*

EDOM

PHILISTINES

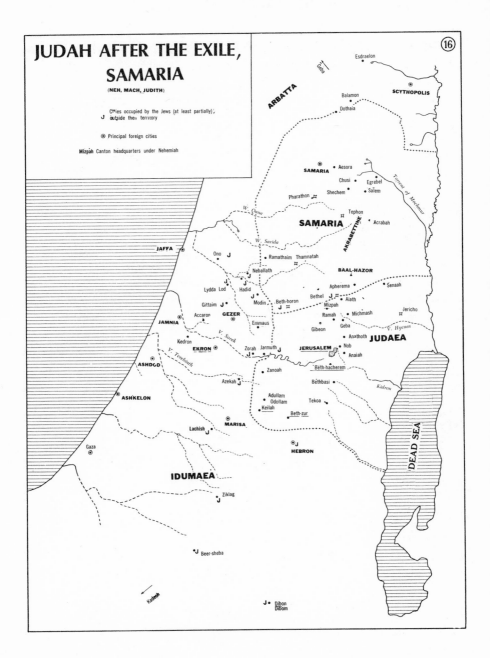

JUDAH AFTER THE EXILE, SAMARIA

(NEH, MACH, JUDITH)

J Cities occupied by the Jews (at least partially), outside their territory

⊙ Principal foreign cities

Mizpah Canton headquarters under Nehemiah

Esdraelon

ARBATTA

Geba

SCYTHOPOLIS

Balamon

Dothaia

⊙ SAMARIA

Aesora

Chusi

Egrebel

Shechem

Salem

Pharathon

Tephon

SAMARIA

Acrabah

Torrent of Mochmur

W. Qana

W. Sarida

AKRABBETTINE

JAFFA

Ono J

Ramathaim Thamnatah

Neballath

BAAL-HAZOR

Lydda Lod Hadid

Apherema

Senaah

Gittaim J

Modin Beth-horon

Bethel J

Aiath

Mizpah

Jericho

Accaron GEZER

Emmaus

Ramah

Michmash

JAMNIA

Gibeon

Geba

V. Hyenas

V. Sorek

Anathoth

JUDAEA

Kedron

Zorah Jarmuth J

JERUSALEM

Nob

EKRON ⊙

Anaiah

ASHDOD ⊙

V. Terebinth

Zanoah

Beth-hacherem

Azekah J

Bethbasi

Kidron

ASHKELON ⊙

Adullam
Odollam

Tekoa

Keilah

Beth-zur

Lachish J

MARISA ⊙

Gaza ⊙

⊙J

HEBRON

DEAD SEA

IDUMAEA

Ziklag
J

Kadesh

Beer-sheba
J

J⊙ Dibon
Dibom

KINGDOM OF HEROD   NEIGHBORING COUNTRIES

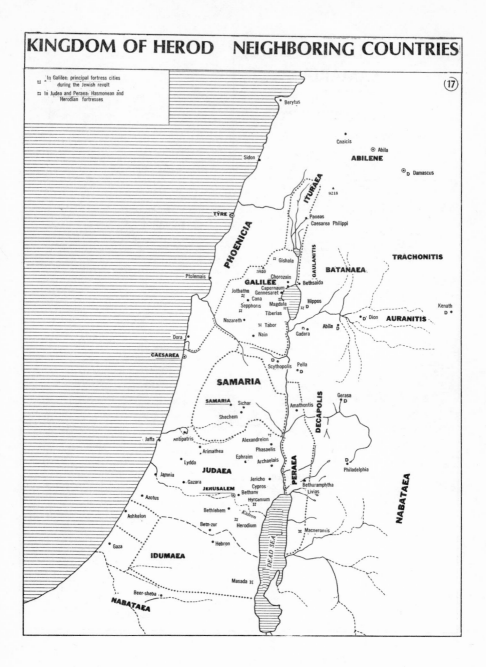

⊡ In Galilee: principal fortress cities
   during the Jewish revolt
⊡ In Judea and Peraea: Hasmonean and
   Herodian fortresses

(17)

Berytus

Cnaicis

⊙ Abila

ABILENE

⊙ᴅ Damascus

Sidon

ITURAEA

▲ 9218

TYRE ⊙

PHOENICIA

Paneas
Caesarea Philippi

⊡ Gishala

GAULANITIS

TRACHONITIS

BATANEA

Ptolemais

3920

Chorozain
GALILEE •
Jotbathe Capernaum
   Gennesaret
• Cana
Sepphoris Magdala
⊡   Tiberias
Nazareth •

Bethsaida

Hippos
⊡ᴅ

Kenath
ᴅ •

•ᴅ Dion **AURANITIS**

⊡ Tabor
• Nain

Abila ⊡
   ᴅ
Gadara

Dora •

CAESAREA ⊙

ᴅ •
Scythopolis Pella
      •ᴅ

SAMARIA

SAMARIA Sichar

Gerasa
   •ᴅ

Shechem

Amathontis

DECAPOLIS

Jaffa • Antipatris •

• Arimathea

Alexandreion •
      Phasaelis
Ephraim •
• Archaelais

Lydda •

Gerasa

Jamnia •

JUDAEA

• Gazara

Jericho •
Cypros
JERUSALEM ⊙ Bethany
      Hyrcanium
         ⊡

PERAEA

Betharamphtha
Livias

ᴅ •
Philadelphia

Azotus •

Ashkelon •

Bethlehem •

Betn-zur   Herodium
      • ⊡

Kidron

Macneronus •

Gaza •

IDUMAEA

• Hebron

DEAD SEA

NABATAEA

Masada ⊡

Beer-sheba •

NABATAEA

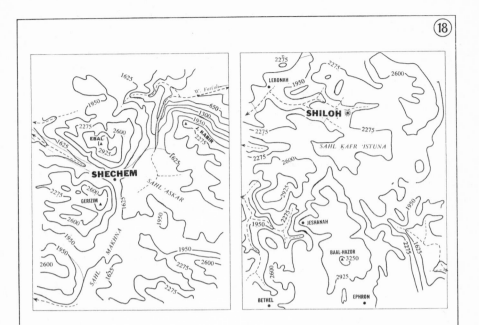

THE THREE CAPITALS

SHECHEM: Good soil, easy communications to North, East, and West; no natural defenses.

SHILOH: Good soil, difficult communications in all directions; natural defenses.

JERUSALEM: Mediocre soil, easy communications to North and South, difficult in other directions; natural defenses.

Geological Morphology

Hard Limestone: vicinity of **SHILOH** and West of **JERUSALEM**

Soft Limestone: East of **JERUSALEM**

Soft Limestone with overlying nummulite: West of **SHECHEM**

Plains or alluvial valleys.